FALLEN

"These essays provide a very thorough mapping of sin's ugly reality. Rarely do we meet such realism as we find here."

J. I. Packer, Board of Governors' Professor of Theology, Regent College

"In this fine little volume, Morgan and Peterson provide an excellent one-stop treatment of the doctrine of sin. As we have come to expect with all the volumes in this series, *Fallen* treats the doctrine of sin biblically, theologically, historically, and pastorally. This text should work very nicely for undergraduate or graduate students."

Bruce Ashford, Provost, Dean of Faculty, and Associate Professor of Theology and Culture, Southeastern Baptist Theological Seminary

"Sin is serious—that's the thrust of this timely collection of essays and, more importantly, the teaching of the Scriptures. But in our postmodern society where there are no absolutes, and in an effort not to offend anyone concerning the issue of sin, we sometimes use other language: 'done wrong,' 'erred,' or 'made a mistake.' Here is a bold book that encourages us not to be afraid to talk, preach, or teach concerning the Bible's understanding of sin and its effects both personally and societally. The Puritans were right—it is only when we have first grasped the depravity of the human heart that can we ever fully appreciate the greatness of the love of God in salvation."

Trevor J. Burke, Lecturer in New Testament and Greek, Oak Hill Theological College, London

"Sin is the great spoiler. It spoils our relation to God, each other, ourselves, and our environment. This important volume shows not only that sin is the great spoiler but also how to understand sin biblically and to face the temptation that comes with it. Without this dark backdrop, the coming and cross of Christ make little sense. A team of excellent scholars has served the church so well in this work. I commend it highly."

Graham Cole, Anglican Professor of Divinity, Beeson Divinity School

"Homiletical in arrangement, exegetical in essence, theological in content, and contemporary in expression, *Fallen* meets the need of the contemporary church to reflect on an often overlooked essential of the biblical story line and the gospel of Jesus Christ. Starting with a fresh note of application, the contributors skillfully and pastorally move through the topic, showing biblical foundations and offering fresh applications for the church today. *Fallen* helps believers rejoice in sin's defeat through the cross of Christ, discern sin's traces and impact on contemporary society, and warn us as believers, as Luther did, that we are at the same time just and sinner. A must-read for pastors, seminary students, and lay persons eager to learn more about the foundations of the faith."

John D. Massey, Associate Professor of Missions, Southwestern Baptist Theological Seminary

"The doctrine of sin has never been a popular teaching, but it is an irreducible essential for every generation to grasp, or else the gospel will be redefined or rejected. Counterfeit Christianity heralds a message about a god without wrath bringing people without sin into a kingdom without judgment. The removal of sin removes the very guts of what makes the gospel good news. The book you hold in your hands is the most far-reaching, well-rounded modern treatment of sin that I have ever read. I commend it highly."

Jason C. Meyer, Pastor for Preaching and Vision, Bethlehem Baptist Church, Minneapolis, Minnesota

"Sin is the inconvenient truth, the bad news that we are tempted to hurry past in our rush to get to the good news of the gospel. The authors of *Fallen* do not rush past this hard subject; they examine it carefully, patiently, and thoroughly in all its biblical, historical, systematic, and practical implications. Exceptionally well unified for a multi-author work, *Fallen* may be the most complete resource on the doctrine of sin in this generation and will certainly serve well as a comprehensive introduction to this neglected topic."

Fred Sanders, Associate Professor of Theology, Torrey Honors Institute, Biola University

Praise for the Theology in Community Series

"I do not know another series quite like this one. Each volume is grounded in both the Old and New Testaments and then goes on to wrestle with the way the chosen theme has been developed in history, shaped the lives of men and women, and fits in the scheme of confessionally strong Christian theology. The volumes are characterized by rigor and reverence, and, better yet, they remain accessible to all serious readers. If we are to pursue more than unintegrated biblical data, but what Paul calls 'the pattern of sound teaching,' this is an excellent place to begin."

D. A. Carson, Research Professor of New Testament, Trinity Evangelical Divinity School

"This distinguished series brings together some of the best theological work in the evangelical church on the greatest themes of the Christian faith. Each volume stretches the mind and anchors the soul. A treasury of devout scholarship not to be missed!"

Timothy George, Founding Dean, Beeson Divinity School; General Editor, Reformation Commentary on Scripture

"We live in a day of cloudy thinking about the most important matters of life. What is needed is meat, along with instructions about how to use a fork. In this series, Chris and Robert help us understand difficult doctrines by being both biblically faithful and culturally accessible. I highly recommend this series to all who want to know, love, and worship our great God."

Darrin Patrick, Pastor, The Journey, St. Louis, Missouri; author, *For the City* and *Church Planter*

"This series offers students, pastors, church leaders, and educators alike a marvelous resource characterized by theological fidelity, biblical faithfulness, and pastoral insight. Confessional, evangelical, and historically informed, each volume engages the best of Christian thinking through the centuries while addressing the important issues of our own day. Chris Morgan and Robert Peterson are to be commended for designing these most helpful volumes, which will serve the church well for years to come."

David S. Dockery, President, Union University

"Robert Peterson and Chris Morgan have put together an elegant and edifying series of books. This series tackles some big and juicy topics on theology, ranging from kingdom to suffering to sin to glory. They have recruited some of the best theological thinkers in the world to explain what it means to have a 'faith seeking understanding' in our contemporary age. The volumes are full of solid teaching in biblical, historical, systematic, and practical theologies and contain a wealth of immense learning. A valuable resource for any thinking Christian."

Michael F. Bird, Lecturer in Theology, Ridley Melbourne College of Mission and Ministry, Australia

FALLEN

A THEOLOGY OF SIN

Christopher W. Morgan and
Robert A. Peterson, editors

WHEATON, ILLINOIS

Fallen: A Theology of Sin

Copyright © 2013 by Christopher W. Morgan and Robert A. Peterson

Published by Crossway
   1300 Crescent Street
   Wheaton, Illinois 60187

Chapter 11, "Repentance That Sings," was first published in Bryan Chapell, *Holiness by Grace: Delighting in the Joy That Is Our Strength*, Crossway, 2002, 2012. Reprinted with permission.

Cover design: Erik Maldre

Cover image: The Bridgeman Art Library

First printing 2013

Printed in the United States of America

Unless otherwise indicated, Scripture quotations are from the ESV® Bible (*The Holy Bible, English Standard Version*®), copyright © 2001 by Crossway. 2011 Text Edition. Used by permission. All rights reserved.

Scripture quotations marked KJV are from the *King James Version* of the Bible.

Scripture quotations marked NASB are from *The New American Standard Bible*®. Copyright © The Lockman Foundation 1960, 1962, 1963, 1968, 1971, 1972, 1973, 1975, 1977, 1995. Used by permission.

Scripture references marked NIV are taken from The Holy Bible, New International Version®, NIV®. Copyright © 1973, 1978, 1984, 2011 by Biblica, Inc.™ Used by permission. All rights reserved worldwide.

Scripture references marked NKJV are from *The New King James Version*. Copyright © 1982, Thomas Nelson, Inc. Used by permission.

All emphases in Scripture quotations have been added by the authors.

Trade paperback ISBN: 978-1-4335-2212-3
PDF ISBN: 978-1-4335-2223-9
Mobipocket ISBN: 978-1-4335-2224-6
ePub ISBN: 978-1-4335-2225-3

Library of Congress Cataloging-in-Publication Data

Fallen : a theology of sin / Christopher W. Morgan and
Robert A. Peterson, editors.
  pages cm. — (Theology in community)
 Includes bibliographical references and index.
 ISBN 978-1-4335-2212-3
  1. Sin—Christianity. I. Morgan, Christopher W., 1971–
editor of compilation.
BT715.F35   2013
241'.3—dc23   2013008184

Crossway is a publishing ministry of Good News Publishers.

VP   23 22 21 20 19 18 17 16 15 14 13
15 14 13 12 11 10 9 8 7 6 5 4 3 2 1

To Shelley and Chelsey, gifts of God's grace to Chris.
To Mary Pat, Rob, Matt, Curtis, and David,
gifts of God's grace to Robert.

CONTENTS

LIST OF ABBREVIATIONS

AB	Anchor Bible
BDAG	Greek-English Lexicon of the New Testament and Other Early Christian Literature
BECNT	Baker Exegetical Commentary on the New Testament
BSac	*Bibliotheca sacra*
BBR	*Bulletin for Biblical Research*
Chm	*Churchman*
CTM	*Concordia Theological Monthly*
CTJ	*Calvin Theological Journal*
EvQ	*Evangelical Quarterly*
FC	Fathers of the Church
Int	*Interpretation*
IDBSup	*Interpreter's Dictionary of the Bible: Supplementary Volume.*
JBL	*Journal of Biblical Literature*
JETS	*Journal of the Evangelical Theological Society*
JPS	Torah Commentary
JSNT	*Journal for the Study of the New Testament*
JSNTSup	Journal for the Study of the New Testament: Supplement Series
JSOTSup	Journal for the Study of the Old Testament: Supplement Series
JTS	*Journal of Theological Studies*
NAC	New American Commentary
NIDNTT	*New International Dictionary of New Testament Theology*
NSBT	New Studies in Biblical Theology
NTS	*New Testament Studies*
NICNT	New International Commentary on the New Testament
NICOT	New International Commentary on the Old Testament
NIDOTTE	*New International Dictionary of Old Testament Theology and Exegesis.*
NIGTC	New International Greek Testament Commentary
NovTSup	Supplements to Novum Testamentum
OTL	Old Testament Library
Pillar	NT Commentary
PNTC	Pelican New Testament Commentaries

RevExp	*Review and Expositor*
SBET	*Scottish Bulletin of Evangelical Theology*
SBJT	*Southern Baptist Journal of Theology*
TDNT	*Theological Dictionary of the New Testament*
TLOT	*Theological Lexicon of the Old Testament*
TNTC	Tyndale New Testament Commentaries
TOTC	Tyndale Old Testament Commentaries
TynBul	*Tyndale Bulletin*
VT	*Vetus Testamentum*
WBC	Word Biblical Commentary

SERIES PREFACE

As the series name, *Theology in Community*, indicates, *theology* in community aims to promote clear thinking on and godly responses to historic and contemporary theological issues. The series examines issues central to the Christian faith, including traditional topics such as sin, the atonement, the church, and heaven, but also some which are more focused or contemporary, such as suffering and the goodness of God, the glory of God, the deity of Christ, and the kingdom of God. The series strives not only to follow a sound theological method but also to display it.

Chapters addressing the Old and New Testaments on the book's subject form the heart of each volume. Subsequent chapters synthesize the biblical teaching and link it to historical, philosophical, systematic, and pastoral concerns. Far from being mere collections of essays, the volumes are carefully crafted so that the voices of the various experts combine to proclaim a unified message.

Again, as the name suggests, theology *in community* also seeks to demonstrate that theology should be done in teams. The teachings of the Bible were forged in real-life situations by leaders in God's covenant communities. The biblical teachings addressed concerns of real people who needed the truth to guide their lives. Theology was formulated by the church and for the church. This series seeks to recapture that biblical reality. The volumes are written by scholars, from a variety of denominational backgrounds and life experiences with academic credentials and significant expertise across the spectrum of theological disciplines, who collaborate with each other. They write from a high view of Scripture with robust evangelical conviction and in a gracious manner. They are not detached academics but are personally involved in ministry, serving as teachers, pastors, and missionaries. The contributors to these volumes stand in continuity with the historic church, care about the global church, share life together with other believers in local churches, and aim to write for the good of the church to strengthen its leaders, particularly pastors, teachers, missionaries, lay leaders, students, and professors.

For the glory of God and the good of the church,
Christopher W. Morgan and Robert A. Peterson

ACKNOWLEDGMENTS

We have many people to thank for their help on this volume.

Allan Fisher, Justin Taylor, Jill Carter, and other friends at Crossway for their faithfulness and encouragement.

John Mahony for sparking Chris's interest in the doctrine of sin and for commenting on the manuscript.

John Massey and Tony Chute for reading the manuscript and making suggestions.

Elliott Pinegar, Robert's former teaching assistant and now pastor of First Presbyterian Church, Bad Axe, Michigan, for skillfully editing the entire manuscript.

Librarians James Pakala and Steve Jamieson of Covenant Seminary and Barry Parker of California Baptist University for valuable assistance.

CONTRIBUTORS

Gerald Bray (DLitt, University of Paris-Sorbonne), Research Professor of Divinity, History and Doctrine, Beeson Divinity School

David B. Calhoun (PhD, Princeton Theological Seminary), Emeritus Professor of Church History, Covenant Theological Seminary

D. A. Carson (PhD, University of Cambridge), Professor of New Testament, Trinity Evangelical Divinity School

Bryan Chapell (PhD, Southern Illinois University), President Emeritus and Adjunct Professor of Practical Theology, Covenant Theological Seminary

Paul R. House (PhD, The Southern Baptist Theological Seminary), Professor of Divinity, Old Testament, Beeson Divinity School

John W. Mahony (ThD, Mid-America Baptist Theological Seminary), Professor of Theological and Historical Studies, Mid-America Baptist Theological Seminary

Douglas J. Moo (PhD, University of St. Andrews), Professor of New Testament, Wheaton College Graduate School

Christopher W. Morgan (PhD, Mid-America Baptist Theological Seminary), Professor of Theology and Dean, School of Christian Ministries, California Baptist University

Sydney H. T. Page (PhD, University of Manchester), Emeritus Professor of New Testament, Taylor Seminary

Robert A. Peterson (PhD, Drew University), Professor of Systematic Theology, Covenant Theological Seminary

Robert W. Yarbrough (PhD, University of Aberdeen), Professor of New Testament, Covenant Theological Seminary

INTRODUCTION

CHRISTOPHER W. MORGAN
AND ROBERT A. PETERSON

Invest in sin? One online investment broker advertises a novel stock portfolio called the "Seven Deadly Sins," which organizes stocks around the vices of gluttony, sloth, vanity, greed, envy, lust, and wrath. This portfolio is built on the assumption that even in a sagging and unpredictable economy, there is one thing we can always count on—sin:

> Even in tough times, consumers continue to partake in things that may not be considered particularly virtuous. From cigarettes to sex, burgers to Botox®—consumer indulgences require products and services from a wide range of publicly traded companies. Some luxuries see reduced demand during tough times. But smokers could keep smoking, drinkers keep drinking, and the lustful keep . . . lusting. Bad habits are hard to break. And when times are rough, who wants to even try? Nobody can predict the markets, but consumers are only human. And economic conditions may not be able to defeat their appetites for sinful stuff. . . .

So the portfolio proposes:

> In the past, many investors who were interested in investing in sin, vice, and adult entertainment turned to individual stocks. Now with Motif Investing, you can invest in the Seven Deadly Sins motif, a carefully researched and balanced portfolio of stocks that may give investors diverse exposure to investing in sin, vice, and adult entertainment stocks.[1]

While we are disgusted by such warped conclusions, their assumption is telling: the inevitability of sin. In a postmodern world in constant change, at least one thing seems constant—sin. Moreover, we agree with Reinhold Niebuhr's famous remark: "The doctrine of original sin is the only empirically verifiable doctrine of the Christian faith."[2] Obviously, Niebuhr is speaking ironically, but the point stands. Sin unmistakably

---

[1] https://www.motifinvesting.com/motifs/seven-deadly-sins#/overview. Accessed October 13, 2012.
[2] Henri Blocher, *Original Sin: Illuminating the Riddle*, NSBT, ed. D. A. Carson (Grand Rapids, MI: Eerdmans, 1997), 84. Quoted in Ted Peters, *Radical Evil in Soul and Society* (Grand Rapids, MI: Eerdmans, 1994), 326, from Reinhold Niebuhr, *Man's Nature and His Communities* (New York: Scribner's, 1965), 24.

recurs—in person after person, generation after generation, and society after society around the globe.

But has the world always been characterized by sin? And will it always be? More basically, what is sin? Where did it come from? What effects does it bring? Additionally, how does it relate to God and his purposes? How does it relate to the goodness of creation? And how does it affect humans created in the image of God? What is temptation? How is Satan involved in all this? Most importantly, what does God do about sin? Is there a way to conquer our sins?

These questions are timely and perennial and deserve straightforward answers. The chapters that follow attempt to provide answers based on God's Word interpreted in the context of the biblical story, taking into consideration the history of the doctrine of sin and attempting to systematize that doctrine, all with a view to applying the doctrine of sin to contemporary life.

Don Carson breaks the ground for this volume with "Sin's Contemporary Significance."

The roots of sin run deep in the soil of the biblical story. Paul House uncovers sin in the Old Testament in two chapters: "Sin in the Law" and "Sin in the Former and Latter Prophets and the Writings." Robert Yarbrough and Douglas Moo dig deep in the New Testament in "Sin in the Gospels, Acts, and Hebrews to Revelation" and "Sin in Paul," respectively.

From the soil of Scripture springs the plant—the biblical, historical, and systematic theology of sin. Christopher Morgan presents a fresh biblical theology in "Sin in the Biblical Story." Gerald Bray helpfully surveys "Sin in Historical Theology." And systematic theologian John Mahony rounds out this section with "A Theology of Sin for Today."

Next bloom the plant's flowers, specialized topics and applications of the doctrine of sin. Sydney Page warns us of our Enemy in "Satan, Sin, and Evil." David Calhoun offers wise counsel and encouragement for struggling believers (all of us at times!) in "Sin and Temptation." And Bryan Chapell tells of believers' necessary response to sin in "Repentance That Sings."

We invite readers to join us in a difficult but important task—to look sin in the face so as to understand its ugliness and to appreciate better its beautiful remedy in Christ.

1

SIN'S CONTEMPORARY SIGNIFICANCE

D. A. CARSON

At first blush it may seem as if this volume has the ideal order rather badly reversed. Would it not be the part of wisdom to work through the biblical and theological material on sin before reflecting on its contemporary significance? Certainly a good case could be made for such a traditional ordering. So what defense can we offer for the fact that the editors in their wisdom have placed this essay first?

In fact, the editorial decision displays considerable insight—a kind of homiletical insight. A preacher may, of course, reserve the application of the message for the end of the sermon; alternatively, he may interweave application all through the sermon. On some occasions, however, that preacher is wise who sets the stage for the exegesis and biblical theology by displaying the relevance of the topic at the beginning of the address. Especially is this the case if for any reason the subject has become unpopular, or if it is often misconceived or induces cringe factors. In such cases, displaying the significance of the topic may constitute a compelling introduction to it.

It may be worthwhile to distinguish the topic's intrinsic and contemporary significance. These two cannot, of course, be kept absolutely separate. Nevertheless, under its intrinsic significance we ought to recall what place sin holds in the Bible, in the entire structure of Christian thought; under its contemporary significance, we shall probe in what ways the Bible's teaching on sin addresses some of the characteristics of our own age and historical location. The former is the more important heading, for it laps into the latter. Indeed, to outline ways in which sin is intrinsically important to a biblically faithful grasp of the gospel is to argue for its perennial significance and therefore *is also* to display its contemporary significance. Only then are we better positioned to reflect on ways in which a mature grasp of sin speaks prophetically and powerfully to our own cultural context.

Sin's Intrinsic Significance

There can be no agreement as to what salvation *is* unless there is agreement as to that from which salvation rescues us. The problem and the solution hang together: the one explicates the other. It is impossible to gain a deep grasp of what the cross achieves without plunging into a deep grasp of what sin is; conversely, to augment one's understanding of the cross is to augment one's understanding of sin.

To put the matter another way, sin establishes the plotline of the Bible. In this discussion, the word *sin* will normally be used as the generic term that includes iniquity, transgression, evil, idolatry, and the like, unless the context makes it clear that the word is being used in a more restricted sense. In the general sense, then, sin constitutes the problem that God resolves: the conflict carries us from the third chapter of Genesis to the closing chapter of Revelation. Before the fall, God's verdict is that everything he made is "very good." We are not told how the Serpent came to rebel, but the sin of the first human pair introduces us to many of the human dimensions of sin. We find rebellion against God, succumbing to the vicious temptation to become like God, an openness to the view that God will not impose the sentence of death on sinners (and thus the implicit charge that God's word cannot be trusted), defiance of a specific command (that is, transgression), the sacrifice of intimate fellowship with God, the introduction of shame and guilt, eager self-justification by blaming others, the introduction of pain and loss, and various dimensions of death. The fourth chapter of Genesis brings us the first murder, and the fifth chapter the refrain, "and then he died." The following four chapters bring us the judgment of the flood and its entailments, but humanity is not thereby improved, as the eleventh chapter makes clear.

It would be easy to keep running through the drama of the Scripture's story line, carefully observing the shape and depth of sin in the patriarchal period, in the years of the wilderness wanderings, in the time of the judges, in the decay of the Davidic monarchy, and in the malaise of the exile and the frequent sinful lapses among those who returned. Those whom Jesus confronts in his day are no better. The apostle Paul's massive indictment against all humanity (Rom. 1:18–3:20) sets the stage for one of the deepest statements about what the cross achieved (3:21–26). Indeed, so much of what the triune God discloses of himself is revealed in the context of showing how each member of the Godhead contributes to the salvation of God's elect—their salvation from sin. It is not for nothing that the very first chapter of the New Testament establishes that the child born of the Virgin Mary will be called "Jesus, because he will save his people from their sins" (Matt. 1:21).[1] Very little of the tabernacle/temple system of the old covenant makes sense unless one understands something of sin; certainly none of its antitype does, worked out with stunning care in the epistle to the Hebrews. Whether one considers the theme of God's wrath or the particular objects of his saving love, whether God thunders from Sinai or weeps over Jerusalem, whether we focus on individual believers or on the covenantal identity of the people of God, whether one stands aghast at the temporal judgments poured out on Jerusalem or stands in rapt anticipation of the glories of the new heaven and the new earth, the substratum that holds the entire account together is sin and how God, rich in mercy, deals with sins and sinners for his own glory and for his people's good.

Sin "offends God not only because it becomes an assault on God directly, as in impiety or blasphemy, but also because it assaults what God has made."[2] Sin is rebellion against God's very being, against his explicit word, against his wise and ordered reign. It results in the disorder of the creation and in the spiritual and physical death of God's image bearers. With perfect justice God could have condemned all sinners, and no one could have justly blamed him. In reality, the Bible's story line depicts God, out of sheer grace, saving a vast number of men and women from every tongue and tribe, bringing them safely and finally to a new heaven and a new earth where sin no longer has any sway and even its effects have been utterly banished.

In short, if we do not comprehend the massive role that sin plays in the Bible and therefore in biblically faithful Christianity, we shall misread the Bible. Positively, a sober and realistic grasp of sin is one of the things necessary to read the Bible in a percipient fashion; it is one of the required criteria for a responsible hermeneutic.

It may be helpful to lay out a handful of the theological structures that are shaped by what the Bible says about sin and that in turn shape our understanding of sin.

---

[1] Unless otherwise indicated, Scripture references in this chapter are taken from The Holy Bible, New International Version®, NIV®. Copyright © 1973, 1978, 1984, 2011 by Biblica, Inc.™ Used by permission. All rights reserved worldwide.

[2] Cornelius Plantinga Jr., *Not the Way It's Supposed to Be: A Breviary of Sin* (Grand Rapids, MI: Eerdmans, 1995), 16.

Sin Is Tied to Passages That Disclose Important Things about God

First, sin is deeply tied to any number of illuminating passages that disclose important things about God. Consider Exodus 34:6–7, where God intones certain words to Moses, who is hidden in a cleft of rock on Mount Sinai. Moses is neither permitted nor able to gaze directly on God; should he do so, he would die (33:20). He is permitted to see no more than the trailing edge of the afterglow of the glory of God. But he *is* permitted and able to *hear*: God discloses himself to Moses supremely in words, and those words are simultaneously moving and puzzling (the italicized words draw attention to what is puzzling): "The LORD, the LORD, the compassionate and gracious God, slow to anger, abounding in love and faithfulness, maintaining love to thousands, *and forgiving wickedness, rebellion and sin. Yet he does not leave the guilty unpunished; he punishes the children and their children for the sin of the parents to the third and fourth generation.*" Here is the God who forgives "wickedness, rebellion and sin," yet who "does not leave the guilty unpunished." Is this some sort of strange dialectic? Alternating procedures, perhaps? The tension is not finally resolved until Calvary. Certainly the focus of this strange tension is sin.

Or consider the words of David after his seduction of Bathsheba and his cold-blooded arrangements to murder her husband. Brought low in brokenness and repentance, he not only begs God for mercy (Ps. 51:1) but tells him, "Against you, you only, have I sinned and done what is evil in your sight" (v. 4). At one level, of course, this is blatantly untrue: David has sinned against Bathsheba, her husband, her child, his family, the military high command, and the nation as a whole, which he serves as chief magistrate. Yet there is something profound in David's words. What makes sin *sin*, in the deepest sense, is that it is *against God*. We let ourselves off the hook too easily when we think of sins along horizontal axes only—whether the horizontal sins of socially disapproved behavior or the horizontal sin of genocide. What makes sins really vile, intrinsically heinous—what makes them worthy of punishment by God himself—is that they are first, foremost, and most deeply sins against the living God, who has made us for himself and to whom we must one day give an account. In other words, this psalm of repentance from sin discloses important things about sin's relation to God.

Or we might remind ourselves of the fourth Servant Song, including the words:

> Surely he took up our pain
>   and bore our suffering,
> yet we considered him punished by God,
>   stricken by him, and afflicted.
> But he was pierced for our transgressions,
>   he was crushed for our iniquities;
> the punishment that brought us peace was on him,
>   and by his wounds we are healed. . . .
> Yet it was the LORD's will to crush him and cause him to suffer,
>   and though the LORD makes his life an offering for sin,
> he will see his offspring and prolong his days,
>   and the will of the LORD will prosper in his hand. (Isa. 53:4–5, 10)

Here is penal substitution by Yahweh's own design, taking our suffering, our transgressions, our iniquities, our punishment, and our sin.

Again, once we recall how in John's Gospel the word *world* commonly refers to the human moral order in deeply culpable rebellion against God (that is, the word *world* commonly means "this sinful world"), the words of John 3:16 shout matchless grace. God's love for the world is to be admired not because the world is so big but because the world is so bad. God so loved this sinful world that he gave his one and only Son—and the context shows that the locus of this gift is not in the incarnation only but in Jesus being "lifted up" in death (cf. "lifted up" in vv. 14–15, and the consistent use of ὑψόω in John). The plan of redemption for this sinful world is driven by God's undeserved love, most magnificently expressed in the gift of his Son, whose death alone is sufficient to lift the sentence of condemnation (vv. 17–18). To reject such love—that is, to continue in sin—is to remain under the wrath of God (v. 36). Even this handful of verses says much about God, his character, his redemptive purposes, his love, and his wrath—and the axis around which these themes revolve is sin.

One could easily draw attention to hundreds of passages where similar dynamics prevail between God and sin, but I shall restrict myself to one more. Toward the end of his famous chapter on the resurrection, Paul raises two rhetorical questions in words drawn from Hosea 13:14: "Where, O death, is your victory? Where, O death, is your sting?" (1 Cor. 15:55). Then he answers his own questions: "The sting of death is sin, and the power of sin is the law. But thanks be to God! He gives us the victory through our Lord Jesus Christ" (vv. 56–57). In other words, the death-dealing power of sin has been defeated by God's resurrection of his Son, our Lord Jesus Christ. Once again, then, the display of what God has done, supremely in the resurrection of his Son, is occasioned by sin and all its brutal power.

Sin is deeply tied to any number of illuminating passages that disclose important things about God, and if about God, then about the salvation that God has wrought in Jesus Christ.

Sin Is Tied to the Work of Satan

Second, sin is radically tied to the work of Satan and of demonic forces. Otherwise put, sin has a cosmic/demonic dimension. The first human descent into sin is stimulated by the Serpent (Genesis 3), later identified as Satan himself (Rev. 12:9). The text in Genesis does not tell us how it happened that *he* first sinned, but the opening lines of Genesis 3 make it clear that, since he was made by God, the Serpent has no independent status akin to God's but in darker hue. And since everything in the creation that God made was "very good" (1:31), one assumes that this was also true of the Serpent: when he was created, he was good. The obvious inference is that the Serpent had himself fallen at some point antecedent to the fall of Adam and Eve—an inference that Jude is prepared to draw (v. 6).

It follows, then, that sin has dimensions that stretch beyond the human race. I am not referring to the consequences of *human* sin that stretch beyond the human race—the corruption of the entire created order, the subjection of the created order to frustration, bondage, and decay (Rom. 8:20–21). Rather, I am referring to the sin of rebellious heavenly beings, of angels themselves. Although Scripture says relatively little about this wretched reality, the small windows it does provide into this antecedent fall are highly illuminating. Part of our own struggle is "against the powers of this dark world and against the spiritual forces of evil in the heavenly realms" (Eph. 6:12): there is a cosmic, indeed heavenly, dimension to the struggle, glimpsed again in the first two chapters of Job.

Three further characteristics of this angelic, nonhuman sin function in the Bible to provide something of a foil to the way human sin plays out: (1) the initial human sin infected the entire human race and brought down the wrath of God upon the entire human race; the initial angelic sin corrupted those who sinned, while the rest remained unaffected. Whether this fundamental difference in the way sin is structured in the two races turns on the nonorganic and nongenerating nature of angelic existence (according to Jesus, angels do not marry: Matt. 22:30) is nowhere made explicit. (2) In God's grace, there has arisen a redeemer for fallen human beings but none for angels: "For surely it is not angels he helps, but Abraham's descendants" (Heb. 2:16; cf. 2:5). The horde of demons lives utterly without hope: they know there is an "appointed time" for their endless, conscious torment (Matt. 8:29; cf. Rev. 20:10). None of them discovers that the words "Come to me, all you who are weary and burdened, and I will give you rest" (Matt. 11:28) are for them. At very least, the recognition of this truth ought to engender in redeemed men and women awestruck humility and gratitude at the sovereignty of grace. (3) No text depicts angels as having been made *imago Dei*, the way this claim is made of human beings (Gen. 1:26–27). Moreover, to sweep these three observations together, the culminating blessing for God's redeemed image bearers, once their sin has been entirely done away with, is the beatific vision: they will see his face (Rev. 22:4)—unlike the highest order of angelic beings, who in the presence of God constantly cover their faces with their wings (Isa. 6:2; cf. Rev. 4:8).

There is at least one way in which the outcome of the sin of Satan and his minions is akin to the outcome of the sin of unregenerate, unrepentant human beings: it ends in eternal conscious suffering (Rev. 20:10; cf. 14:11). Satan does not stop being Satan and become wonderfully pure and holy when he is finally and forever consigned to the lake of fire. Forever he will be evil and will be punished. Similarly there is no scrap of biblical evidence that hell will be filled with purified human beings. Its denizens will still pursue self-justification rather than God's justification, they will still love themselves while hating God, and they will continue to receive the punishment that is sin's just due.

Sin Is Depicted in Many Ways

Third, so far I have primarily used the generic word *sin*, but sin is depicted by many words, expressions, and narrative descriptions. Sin can be seen as transgression, which presupposes laws that are being transgressed. Sometimes sin is portrayed as a power that overcomes us. Frequently sin is tied ineluctably to idolatry. Sin can be envisaged as dirt, as missing the target, as folly, as tied to the "flesh" (a notoriously difficult concept to capture in one English word), as unbelief, as slavery, as spiritual adultery, as disobedience. Sin is the offense of individuals, but it is profoundly social and multi-generational: the sins of the fathers are visited on the children to the third and fourth generation, and sins committed in the days of Hezekiah carry their own inescapable entailment in the destruction of Jerusalem and its temple. The Bible frequently depicts sin in terms of the guilt of individuals; at other times it shows how the sins of some parties turn others into hopeless victims.

Some of the most powerful depictions of sin occur in narratives where the word is not used because it is not necessary to use it. One thinks, for example, of the description of the interchanges among Joseph's brothers as they debate whether to kill him or sell him, and again as they lie to their father. More potently, the final major narrative in Judges depicts such soul-destroying, God-dishonoring corruption and decay that even the ostensible "good guys" in the story are shockingly obscene. One simply cannot make sense of the Bible without a profound and growing sensitivity to the multifaceted and powerful ways the Bible portrays sin.

Sin Is Enmeshed in Theological Constructions

Fourth, just as sin is depicted by many words, expressions, and narrative descriptions (the point I have just made), so also is it enmeshed in powerful theological constructions. These constructions are so numerous and rich that to treat them in any detail would demand a very long book. Here I can merely list a few such constructions, in no particular order of importance.

1) *Anthropology.* The first two chapters of the Bible depict sinless human beings; the last two depict transformed, forgiven, sin-free human beings. All the chapters in between depict or presuppose sinful human beings, with the exception of those that describe the humanity of Jesus and insist he is utterly without sin. For the rest of us, we read descriptions of our sinfulness that set out sin's universality and sweep (e.g., Rom. 3:9–20) and its connection with Adam our federal head (e.g., Romans 5). Out of such evidence spring theological formulations that try to summarize what the Bible says in few words: we speak of original sin and total depravity, carefully explaining what we do and do not mean by such expressions. With the sole exception of Jesus the Messiah, we certainly mean not only that all human beings between Eden before the fall and resurrection existence in the new heaven and the new earth are not only sinful, but that sin is not an optional characteristic loosely tacked on to otherwise unblemished beings but a pervasive power and guilt and tragedy that define all human experience, crying out for grace.

2) The opening paragraphs of this essay point to some of the links between sin and *soteriology.* One might press on to *pneumatology*, especially the fundamental division of fallen humankind into those who are merely "natural" and those who have the Holy Spirit (1 Cor. 2:10b–15).[3] The ef-

---

[3] Cf. Abraham Kuyper, *Wisdom and Wonder: Common Grace in Science and Art* (Grand Rapids, MI: Christian's Library Press, 2011), 80: "It is clear that with its antithesis between a 'natural' man and a 'spiritual' man, Scripture is not merely referring to a person who does and another who does not take Holy Scripture into account.

fect of the Spirit's work is observable in all who have been born of God, even if the mechanisms are obscure (John 3:8). The Spirit produces the fruit of the Spirit (Gal. 5:22–23), which stands over against the acts of the flesh (vv. 19–21), which is another way of describing sin. At the moment I shall restrict myself to a few comments on just one element of God's saving plan, namely, *conversion*. In the sociology of religion, as in popular parlance, conversion signals the change of allegiance from one religion to another. A Buddhist becomes a Muslim, or the reverse; a Taoist becomes a Christian, a Christian becomes an atheist, an atheist becomes a Hindu— in every case, we commonly say that the person has converted. We may even use the language of conversion when a person changes denominational allegiance: we speak of a Baptist converting to Roman Catholicism, or the reverse. In confessional Christianity, however, conversion has a much more precise focus. Phenomenologically, when a person truly becomes a Christian, he or she has changed religious allegiance, and so we may still use the conversion word-group in a purely descriptive fashion, but underlying the outward phenomenon is supernatural transformation. In biblical terminology, a person has passed from darkness to light, from death to life. That person has been born again, born from above; once-blind eyes now see, the lost sheep has been found, "natural" has been overtaken by supernatural. Relationally and forensically, a sinner has been reconciled to God; eschatologically, that person already belongs to the kingdom that has been inaugurated and consequently lives in the sure and certain hope of the transforming resurrection and the consummation of all things. The final outcome will be perfection, for no sin or taint of evil will be permitted in the new heaven and the new earth. In such usage, of course, conversion cannot rightly be applied to people when they swap religious allegiances. It can be applied only to those who become Christians in the strongest NT sense of that word. In short, the transformation inherent in conversion in this theological sense is inescapably tied to God's plan and power to confront sin in an individual's life and ultimately destroy it utterly.

3) *Sanctification*. For present purposes we shall exclude such categories as positional or definitional sanctification. That leaves us with

---

Its pronouncement goes much deeper by positing the distinction between having and not having received the Spirit of God . . . (1 Cor. 2:12). This corresponds entirely with what Jesus himself said, that 'unless one is born of water and the Spirit, he *cannot enter the kingdom of God*' (John 3:5). If you agree that the kingdom of God is definitely not identical to the institutional church, but rules our entire world-and-life view, then Jesus' declaration means that only one who has received the inner illumination of the Holy Spirit is in a position to obtain such a perspective on the whole of things, one that corresponds to the truth and essence of things."

the theological concept of growing in holiness—a notion that can be expressed in many ways without using the term *sanctification*. For example, in Philippians 3 Paul does not hold that he has already attained full maturity in Christ; rather, he presses on "to take hold of that for which Christ Jesus took hold of me" (v. 12). What he strains toward, what lies ahead, is "the goal to win the prize for which God has called me heavenward in Christ Jesus" (v. 14)—resurrection existence (vv. 11, 21), which is opposed to the "enemies of the cross of Christ," whose "destiny is destruction" and whose "god is their stomach, and their glory is in their shame" (vv. 18–19). Those who are "mature" should adopt Paul's view, follow his example, and "live up to what we have already attained" (vv. 14–17). In other words, sanctification works now in Paul and in other believers the beginnings of what will finally be achieved in the ultimate glorification. That includes firm allegiance to the gospel that eschews all "confidence in the flesh" (v. 3) and is passionate for "the righteousness that comes from God on the basis of faith" (v. 9). In other words, sanctification is bound up with the "putting to death" of sin,[4] with conformity to Jesus, with moral and spiritual transformation now in anticipation of the climactic transformation to come.

4) *Sin and the law.* John tells us that "sin is lawlessness" (1 John 3:4). Although some have dismissed this pronouncement as a singularly shallow definition of sin, in fact it is painfully insightful once we remember whose law is in view. Conceptually this is not far removed from the dictum that whatever is not of faith is sin, once we recall who is to be the object of our faith; nor is it far removed from Jesus' insistence that the most important command is to love God with heart and soul and mind and strength, once we perceive that this is invariably the one command that is broken whenever we break any other command of God. Sin's odium lies in its defiance of God.

Yet the relationship between sin and the law is complex. It runs along several axes. The first we have just articulated: sin is breaking God's law and therefore defying God himself. This includes failing to do what God commands and doing what God prohibits. In the words of the General Confession, "We have left undone those things which we ought to have done; and we have done those things which we ought not to have done; and there is no health in us." Conceived along another axis, however, the

---

[4] The old word, of course, is "mortification," but that word has taken on such a different meaning that it is now almost unusable in the sense it had in the KJV.

law actually provokes sin, prompting it to lash out. In other words, sin is so rebellious of heart that commands and prohibitions, far from enabling sinners to overcome their sin, have the same effect as a rule does in the mind and heart of an immature teenager. Tweaked again, the law can be seen to operate not only on this psychological plane but along the axis of redemptive history: sin leading to death is abundantly present long before the giving of the law at Sinai (Rom. 5:13–14), such that when law is thought of as the revelation given through Moses, the law is relatively late on the scene. But another of its many functions is to establish complex structures of tabernacle/temple, priesthood, sacrificial system, and festivals such as Passover and Day of Atonement, all designed to establish trajectories taking us to Jesus, who is the ultimate temple, the ultimate priest, the ultimate sacrifice, the ultimate Passover, the ultimate bloody offering on the final Day of Atonement. Thus the law brings in Jesus, who destroys sin; it brings us to the gospel, which alone is the power of God that brings salvation.[5] The law has many roles in relation to sin, but it does not have the power to free the sinner from its enslaving power and its consequences.[6]

It would be easy to demonstrate sin's links with every important theological construction grounded in Scripture. As important as they are, the

---

[5] For a useful and thought-provoking analysis of the different ways in which the apostle Paul analyzes the law, see Brian Rosner, *Paul and the Law: Keeping the Commandments of God*, NSBT (Downers Grove, IL: InterVarsity, forthcoming).

[6] It is very easy to skew these matters away from the subtle nuances of Scripture. I cannot resist citing extensively from Archibald Alexander, a passage to which Fred Zaspel has drawn my attention: *Thoughts on Religious Experience* (repr. Charleston, SC: BiblioBazaar, 2009), 336–38:

> When persons are truly converted they always are sincerely desirous to make rapid progress in piety; and there are not wanting exceeding great and gracious promises of aid to encourage them to go forward with alacrity. Why then is so little advancement made? Are there not some practical mistakes very commonly entertained, which are the cause of this slowness of growth? I think there are, and will endeavour to specify some of them.
>
> And first, there is a defect in our belief of the freeness of divine grace. To exercise unshaken confidence in the doctrine of gratuitous pardon is one of the most difficult things in the world; and to preach this doctrine fully without verging towards Antinomianism is no easy task, and is therefore seldom done. But Christians cannot but be lean and feeble when deprived of their proper nutriment. It is by faith that the spiritual life is made to grow; and the doctrine of free grace, without any mixture of human merit, is the only true object of faith. Christians are too much inclined to depend on themselves, and not to derive their life entirely from Christ.
>
> There is a spurious legal religion, which may flourish without the practical belief in the absolute freeness of divine grace, but it possesses none of the characteristics of the Christian's life. It is found to exist in the rankest growth, in systems of religion which are utterly false. But even when the true doctrine is acknowledged in theory, often it is not practically felt and acted on. The new convert lives upon his frames rather than on Christ, while the older Christian is still found struggling in his own strength and, failing in his expectations of success, he becomes discouraged first, and then he sinks into a gloomy despondency, or becomes in a measure careless. At that point the spirit of the world comes in with resistless force. Here, I am persuaded, is the root of the evil; and until religious teachers inculcate clearly, fully, and practically, the grace of God as manifested in the Gospel, we shall have no vigorous growth of piety among professing Christians. We must be, as it were, identified with Christ—crucified with him, and living by him, and in him by faith, or rather, having Christ living in us. The covenant of grace must be more clearly and repeatedly expounded in all its rich plenitude of mercy and in all its absolute freeness.

four I have mentioned barely introduce the possibilities. In other words, it is impossible to engage in probing, biblically faithful theological reflection without thinking deeply about sin.

Reflection on Sin Is Necessary to Understand Suffering and Evil

Fifth, another way to demonstrate the ubiquity of sin in all serious theological discussion is to outline its place in theological analysis that is rather more synthetic and second-order than the kinds of theological constructions I have mentioned so far. I shall provide only one example. On three or four occasions during the last eight or ten years, I have given a rather lengthy lecture on theodicy. I never called it that; it was always titled something like "How Christians Should Think about Suffering and Evil" or something of that order. What I tried to do was to sink six major pillars into the ground. These six pillars, taken together, provided (I said) an adequate foundation to support a distinctively Christian way of reflecting on evil and suffering. The six had to be taken together. One pillar by itself was totally inadequate, and even four or five pillars were dangerously weak and left the structure poorly supported.

The interesting thing is that all of the pillars have to do with sin. The first pillar I label "Lessons from the Beginning of the Bible." This covers creation, in which God makes everything, institutes marriage, assigns human beings their responsibilities to reign under God, surrounds them with an idyllic setting and above all his own presence, and pronounces everything "good." The narrative proceeds to the fall, to the onset of idolatry, sin and its short- and long-term effects (including both death and alienation from God), and the curses pronounced on the various parties and what they mean. The brutal fact is that human beings have forfeited their right to expect their creator-God to love and care for them, so that if he does so, it is because he is infinitely kinder than they deserve. Theological reflection on the way these themes are teased out across the Scriptures reminds us that all the wars, hatred, lust, covetousness, and all the transgression, idolatry, sin, and its grim consequences, spring from human rebellion. Even what we call "natural disasters" are first and foremost an implicit call to repentance (Luke 13:1–5). Far from being something God created, sin is rebellion against the creator-God. The implications for theodicy are many, starting with the fact that God does not owe us blessing, prosperity, and health. What he owes us is justice, which in itself guarantees our ruin. My point for the purpose of this essay, however, is that this pillar, this "fix" in the biblical landscape, is tightly bound up with sin. One cannot think long about the complexities of theodicy in a biblically faithful way without wrestling with what the Bible says about sin.

And that is just the first pillar. The second is "Lessons from the End of the Bible," where we must think about hell, the new heavens and the new earth, resurrection existence, the New Jerusalem—a world where nothing impure will ever enter. One does not proceed very far before one recognizes that the discussion is again circling around the topic of sin. The third pillar is "The Mystery of Providence." Here one wrestles not only with many texts that talk about God's sovereignty but also with texts that talk about God's sovereignty *over a world highly charged with sin*. It would be easy to work through all six pillars and summarize their contribution toward the support of a well-formed and biblically faithful theodicy, but the point, in every case, is that these pillars make no sense if one tries to abstract them from profound reflections on sin. In short, sin is ubiquitous in all serious theological discussion that takes its cues from Scripture.

To summarize: if we are to think realistically about the relevance of the doctrine of sin to today's culture, we must begin with its intrinsic significance—the place sin holds within the matrix of biblically determined theological reflection.

Sin's Contemporary Significance

Under this heading I shall focus on some of the ways in which a biblically faithful doctrine of sin addresses some of the characteristics of our own age and of our own historical location. I shall briefly mention three.

We Live in a Time of Extraordinary Violence and Wickedness

First, only thirteen years have elapsed since we closed out the bloodiest century in human history. There was not just one holocaust: add to the Nazi slaughter of Jews the Stalinist starvation of twenty million Ukrainians, the Maoist slaughter of perhaps fifty million Chinese, the massacre of between a quarter and a third of the population of Cambodia, tribal slaughter of Tutsis and Hutus, and various ethnic cleansings. How shall we calculate the damage, material and psychological, of terrorism in all its forms, of unrestrained consumerism, of all the damage done by drug abuse of many kinds, including alcoholism? The digital revolution that ushers in spectacular improvements in research, data handling, and communication also brings us access to instant porn, with untold damage done to man/woman relationships in general and to marriages in particular.[7] Shall we add the cruelty of racism, the exploitation of the weak, and greed and laziness in all their forms?[8] And what of those massive and ubiquitous sins that are primarily the absence of particular virtues—*un*holiness, *im*piety, prayer*lessness*, *un*loving hearts, *in*gratitude?

Despite the massive evidence that surrounds us on every side, many in our generation have come to think of themselves as essentially good people. Pollyannaish outlooks abound. If there are bad things in the world, they are primarily what other people do—other religions, other races, other political parties, other generations, other economic sectors, other subcultures. Doubtless every generation thinks of itself as better than it actually is, but in the Western world *this* generation has multiplied such moral blindness to the highest degree. For example, one of the reasons the founding fathers of the United States constructed a Constitution with division of powers and a system of checks and balances was that they believed steps had to be taken to curtail pervasive sin, especially the lust for power. By contrast, many in our society are not even aware of the dangers that lurk everywhere when one block or another of government or society gains too much sway.

In short, the first and most obvious *contemporary* significance to preaching a robust doctrine of sin is that it confronts the almost universal absence of such teaching. In other words, the first *contemporary* significance of biblical teaching on sin is not that it meshes nicely with contemporary worldviews and therefore provides a pleasant way into thoughtful interaction but precisely that it confronts the painfully perverse absence of awareness of sin.

Across the stream of redemptive history, this was one of the primary functions of the law: to bring conviction of sin. Although many preachers in the Reformed tradition have treated Galatians 3 as if it mandates that the way to preach the gospel to individuals is to begin with the law, assured that the law is our "guardian" (παιδαγωγός, Gal. 3:24) to bring us to see our need of Christ and of grace, careful examination of the context shows that the focus of the chapter is not on the role of the law in the conversion of the individual but on the role of the law in the drama of salvation history. If Paul's understanding of the promise given to Abraham is correct (vv. 1–4), one may well ask why the law was given at all (v. 19). Why not run very quickly from promise to fulfillment? In various places Paul gives

---

[7] The essay by Robert Yarbrough in this volume makes many of the same points.
[8] Cf. especially Brian Rosner, *Greed as Idolatry: The Origin and Meaning of a Pauline Metaphor* (Grand Rapids, MI: Eerdmans, 2007).

several complementary answers to that question, but part of the answer is that the law in Scripture "locked up everything under the control of sin, so that what was promised, being given through faith in Jesus Christ, might be given to those who believe" (v. 22). Yet the fact that the law covenant should reign for almost a millennium and a half shows how important it was to God to get across the persistence, repetition, heinousness, enslaving power, and odium of human sin and the utter incapacity of human beings to break free from it. How else will human rebels cry to God for grace and accept by faith what was promised? Not dissimilarly, a generation that is singularly unaware of its sin while being awash in sin desperately needs a robust doctrine of sin to begin to understand redemption.

Postmodernism's Reluctance to Identify Evil

Second, today there are fewer books published defining and defending postmodernism than there were fifteen years ago. In Europe almost no one reads Michel Foucault anymore, let alone Jacques Derrida. Some American undergraduates are still prescribed toxic doses of postmodernism, but graduate students have increasingly turned away from the brew. As a sophisticated epistemological and cultural phenomenon, postmodernism in many parts of the Western world has passed its sell-by date. Yet nevertheless the detritus of postmodernism can be seen everywhere. Among the most noticeable pieces are those that are reluctant to identify evil, largely on the assumption that right and wrong, good and evil, are nothing more than social constructs. Such an environment may not appear to be the ideal cultural context for talking about sin. The related ill of moral relativism does not seem very conducive to virile reflection on what the Bible says about sin.

Once again, however, it is the need for it that makes biblical reflection on sin so desperately relevant. The deep cultural animus against the category of sin means that many preachers much prefer to talk about weaknesses, mistakes, tragedies, failures, inconsistencies, hurts, disappointment, blindness—anything but sin. The result is that biblical portrayal of God is distorted, as is his plan of redemption. Getting across what the Bible says about sin in this culture is, of course, extremely difficult. Looked at another way, that very difficulty is a measure of the need and therefore of the contemporary significance of robust treatments of sin.

The Supreme Virtue of the New Tolerance

Third, an array of issues has surfaced that cannot easily be addressed without a well-shaped biblical doctrine of sin. One of these is the current focus on tolerance—but a tolerance newly defined and newly positioned.[9] It is the new positioning that captures our attention at the moment. In the past, tolerance in any culture was discussed *relative to some broadly agreed or imposed value system, religious or otherwise.* Once the value system was in place in the culture, questions inevitably arose about how far one might vary from it before facing legal, judicial, or other coercive sanctions. Within limits, many cultures have concluded that some degree of dissent may actually be a good thing; only the most despotic of regimes allow almost no tolerance for those who disagree. But that means that the value system itself is the important thing; the virtue of tolerance is parasitic on the value system itself. And any society, no matter how tolerant, draws limits somewhere.[10] In much of the Western world at the moment, however, there is very little culture-wide consensus on right and wrong, good and evil, holiness and sin, while tolerance has been elevated to the highest spot in the moral echelon. It's not that we have self-consciously taken that step; rather, for reasons I've tried to outline elsewhere, tolerance has become more important than truth, morality, or any widely held value system. Tolerance becomes the supreme good, the supreme god in the culture's pantheon, in a sphere of existence that often argues by merest clichés[11] and that has very few other widely agreed desiderata. The complicating irony is that those who hold tenaciously to the supreme virtue of this new tolerance are by and large extremely intolerant of those who do not agree with them.

My purpose in indulging in this excursus is to point out that the overthrow of this new intolerant tolerance depends hugely on finding a value system that cherishes something more than this new tolerance. It is difficult to hold a mature and sustained debate on, say, the wisdom or otherwise of providing for homosexual marriage in law when one side, instead of wrestling with issues of substance, dismisses the other side as intolerant and is cheered on in the culture for doing so. Unchecked, this new tolerance will sooner or later put many people in chains. For it to be challenged, there must be a cultural value system deemed more precious, a higher good, than the new tolerance itself. And one of the necessary ingredients for achieving this end is the reconstitution of a robust view of sin, and therefore of good and evil, in the culture.

---

[9] Cf. D. A. Carson, *The Intolerance of Tolerance* (Grand Rapids, MI: Eerdmans, 2012).

[10] For example, Western culture is extremely open to diverse sexual activity, but all Western countries draw the line at the practice of pedophilia.

[11] Cf. especially Jonah Goldberg, *The Tyranny of Clichés* (New York: Sentinel, 2012).

＊ ＊ ＊ ＊ ＊ ＊ ＊

To sum up: the contemporary significance of biblical teaching on sin is best grasped, first, when the place of sin within the Bible itself is understood, and, second, when we perceive how desperately our culture needs to be shaped again by what the Bible says about sin.

2

SIN IN THE LAW

PAUL R. HOUSE

The Old Testament offers the Bible's oldest and most textured treatments of the doctrine of sin. Beginning with Adam and Eve, sin appears throughout the Hebrew Scriptures, acting as the main problem that God's redemptive work solves. Sin is humanity's chief impediment to glorifying God and enjoying him forever—the reason men and women were created, according to the Westminster Shorter Catechism. It is also their most shared transcultural characteristic. The Old Testament writers do not use a single comprehensive word to describe sin akin to the New Testament's *hamartia*. Rather, they depict the concept we normally deem "sin" in a variety of ways, using several concepts (see below). They relate sin's scope by noting the damage it does to young and old persons as well as to creatures and creation. Unfailingly honest, they include themselves among sin's practitioners. This comprehensive approach magnifies God's saving work through the Old Testament's promise of the Messiah and the New Testament's declaration of the fulfillment of that pledge in Jesus of Nazareth.

Definitions and Methodology

This chapter will seek to unfold a small measure of the Old Testament's treatment of this massive biblical concept. The compass of this theme means that some method of shaping the discussion must be chosen lest the chapter run aimlessly. Though many defensible approaches could be chosen, this essay will utilize three basic methods.

First, it will discuss Exodus 34:1–9, a seminal theological passage that provides a definition of God's character and gives three fundamental definitions of sin. Elmer Martens uses this approach in *God's Design*, where he

treats a comprehensive passage (Ex. 5:22–6:8) as a foundation for discussing major ideas in Old Testament theology.[1] Passages that deal with or use
basic words related to sin appear earlier in the biblical text, and this essay
will return to some of them after the analysis of Exodus 34, but examining
a paradigmatic passage before turning to other texts introduces key terms
in a representative context. This procedure has the potential to aid the
understanding of both previous and subsequent texts.

Second, it will examine the concepts found in Exodus 34:1–9 as they
appear in selected texts in the Law, the Prophets, and the Writings, the
three major parts of the Old Testament. It will introduce and analyze these
passages. In this way it follows the canonical method found in my *Old
Testament Theology* and in works such as Mark Boda's excellent monograph *A Severe Mercy: Sin and Its Remedy in the Old Testament.*[2] A variety
of canonical approaches has been utilized over the past thirty years. These
efforts have proved the flexibility and worthiness of this type of analysis.

Third, it will provide syntheses of key themes related to the doctrine
of sin as they unfold in the texts chosen. Providing synthetic observations
is in keeping with the methods utilized in well-known Old Testament
theologies such as those by Walther Eichrodt and John Goldingay.[3] The
synthesis sections will at times make use of New Testament texts, which
I believe have been breathed out by God (2 Tim. 3:14–17) just as the Old
Testament books have been (2 Pet. 1:19–21). New Testament authors
also represent the oldest Christian interpretative tradition. They would
be valuable for examining the Old Testament even if they were not God's
word written.

This chapter will use this proposed "multi-plex"[4] approach to argue
that the Old Testament defines sin as "faithless rebellion against God's
character and God's explicit word practiced by all human beings that
results in physical and spiritual death for them and damaged existence
for the created order." This definition agrees with Cornelius Plantinga's
assertion that sin "offends God not only because it bereaves or assaults
God directly, as in impiety or blasphemy, but also because it bereaves and

---

[1] Elmer Martens, *God's Design* (Grand Rapids, MI: Baker, 1981).

[2] Paul R. House, *Old Testament Theology* (Downers Grove, IL: InterVarsity, 1998); Mark Boda, *A Severe Mercy: Sin and Its Remedy in the Old Testament* (Winona Lake, IN: Eisenbrauns, 2009).

[3] Walther Eichrodt, *Theology of the Old Testament*, vol. 2, trans. J. A. Baker (Philadelphia: Westminster, 1967) 380–443; John Goldingay, *Old Testament Theology*, vol. 2: *Israel's Faith* (Downers Grove, IL: InterVarsity, 2006), 254–310.

[4] This term refers to using several types of traditional methods of Old Testament theology in newer writings on the subject and was coined by Gerhard Hasel in his *Old Testament Theology: Issues in the Current Debate*, 4th ed. (Grand Rapids, MI: Eerdmans, 1991), 207.

assaults what God has made."[5] As this chapter unfolds, I will attempt to keep faith with this definition by using the word *sin* as a comprehensive concept rather than as an individual category.

Sin is so serious and so pervasive in the world that God's redemptive work is the only antidote for it. Due to the assigned restrictions of this chapter and to this author's own limitations, this chapter will not deal with God's redemptive plans in detail. Nonetheless, in the spirit of full disclosure, I write as one who believes that sin's causes and effects have been and will be fully resolved by the incarnation, teaching, death, burial, resurrection, ascension, and second coming of Jesus, the Christ promised in the Old Testament. I strive not to minimize sin, in part because I honor God's sacrificial plan for removing it.

This chapter will dwell longer on the Law than on the Prophets and the Writings because of the Law's foundational nature. One could easily spend much more time on how the prophets denounce sin in detail. If one believes that the prophets are covenant preachers, however, then one can expect that they speak with the Torah in mind and with the context of the nation's history in full view.

Exodus 34:1–9: God's Character and the Definition of Sin

There are many Old Testament passages that reveal specific elements of God's character. None is more comprehensive and allusive than Exodus 34:1–9.[6] None is quoted as often in subsequent Old Testament passages. None is more thorough in its inclusion of God's personal characteristics and their implications for human beings. The value of this text for this chapter is that it defines God as gracious, compassionate, and just, while defining sin as missing the goal of human existence, trespassing the creator's boundaries, and twisting reality-defining truth for human beings. Later writers use this passage to deal with a variety of sin-laden situations.

Analysis

By this point in the Torah, Moses has taught readers about creation, the beginnings of sin, and Noah's flood (Genesis 1–11), and he has described the calling and blessing of Abraham and his clan (Genesis 12–50). He has reported God's magnificent deliverance of Israel from Egypt (Exo-

---

[5] Cornelius Plantinga Jr., *Not the Way It's Supposed to Be: A Breviary of Sin* (Grand Rapids, MI: Eerdmans, 1995), 16.

[6] I attempted to develop some of these ideas in my article "God's Character and the Wholeness of Scripture," *SBET* 23 (Spring 2005): 4–17.

dus 1–18) and has declared Israel's covenant identity as God's priests for the nations (Exodus 19). He has detailed the first relationship-based Sinai commands and case laws (Exodus 20–24) and given God's standards for Israel's own priests (Exodus 25–31). Sadly, Moses has also recounted the sordid tale of the golden calf incident, in which Israel breaks its commitments to Yahweh during the covenant's first weeks of existence (Exodus 32). After sustained intercession by Moses, Yahweh agrees to begin afresh with the people (Ex. 33:1–17). This act of divine grace leads Moses to desire to know more about Yahweh (vv. 18–23). Yahweh agrees to explain more of who he is to Moses, yet he does not grant Moses' wish to experience Yahweh's full presence or glory (vv. 18–23).

Thus, Yahweh's self-description in 34:1–9 comes in light of Moses' wondering why Yahweh does what he does. Apparently, Moses has several questions. These could understandably include such queries as: What sort of God keeps covenant, delivers, punishes, and begins afresh with a people? What sort of God responds to certain types of intercession? What sort of God do I serve?

The passage recounts Yahweh's encounter with Moses in four related parts. First, Yahweh instructs Moses in how he will receive the revelation (34:1–3). Second, Moses obeys Yahweh, appearing as ordered (vv. 4–5). Third, Yahweh states his character in relationship to human need and rebellion (vv. 6–7). Fourth, Moses bows before God and prays again for the errant Israelite people (vv. 8–9). Though every aspect of the passage carries significant theological weight, verses 6 and 7 are the most significant for understanding Yahweh's character and the issue of human sin.

Yahweh states his own character traits in several key phrases in 34:6–7a. He is "gracious and merciful" (v. 6).[7] These two conjoined terms[8] reflect Yahweh's parental kindness (see 1 Kings 3:26). They also demonstrate his tendency to show favor like that given by a kind king[9] or by a person who shows kindness to the poor,[10] respectively. Furthermore, he is "slow to anger and multiplies loyal covenant-type[11] love and faithfulness"

---

[7] The translations of Exodus 34:6–7 and the terms found there throughout the paper are the author's. All other scripture quotations are from the ESV.

[8] According to Mike Butterworth, the terms appear together eleven times in the Old Testament. Thus, they form a liturgical formula based on common understandings of the two words. See his "rhm," NIDOTTE, ed. Willem VanGemeren (Grand Rapids, MI: Zondervan, 1997), 3:1094.

[9] See H. J. Stoebe, "hnn," TLOT, trans. Mark E. Biddle, ed. Ernst Jenni and Claus Westermann (Peabody, MA: Hendrickson, 1997), 1:442–43.

[10] Robert C. Dentan, "The Literary Affinities of Exodus 34:6f.," VT 13 (1963): 42.

[11] Not every instance of this word occurs in a covenantal context, as Dentan ("Literary Affinities," 42) observes. However, the covenant context is a strong component of the word's usage, so it is likely that passages that are not specifically covenantal in context have something like "covenant-type" love or commitment in mind.

(Ex. 34:6). He is not quick to discipline his people, regardless of how it may seem to the Israelites. This slowness to anger amplifies his resolve to make covenants successful by always keeping his end of the relationship. Because of his determination to bring his will to fruition, he does not allow any covenant he makes to fail. His fidelity indicates that his integrity (loyal covenant-type love) and always-reliable[12] truthfulness (faithfulness) pervade all his actions. Indeed, he is always in the process of "keeping loyal covenant love for thousands" (v. 7), which Deuteronomy 7:9–10 indicates most likely refers to thousands of generations.[13]

In Exodus 34:7b, Yahweh relates why he displays this type of character: it allows him to be ever "forgiving [or, "bearing with"] iniquity and transgression and sin." This does not mean that he is unjust, for he "will by no means clear the guilty, visiting the iniquity of the fathers on the children and the children's children, to the third and fourth generation." Based on Exodus 20:4–5, the successive generations referenced here "hate" Yahweh, so this text does not present Yahweh as punishing persons who have not sinned. Rather, it describes him punishing sin as long as it occurs in a clan or nation.

To explain what he is constantly "forgiving," or "bearing with," Yahweh mentions three specific words that help define sin in the Old Testament.[14] This triad appears thirteen times in the Old Testament,[15] so placing them together is a fairly common way of expressing sin's totality. First, Yahweh forgives "iniquity" (*awon*). This word basically expresses the conscious twisting of a personality, idea, or thing.[16] Second, he forgives "transgression" (*pesa*), a word that describes rebelling against Yahweh that "breaks with him, takes away what is his, robs, embezzles, misappropriates it."[17] Third, Yahweh bears with "sin," a word that means "missing a goal" (*ht'*).[18] So, Yahweh's compassionate and merciful nature bears with and forgives people's twisting his words and will. It endures breaches of trust by persons with whom he has a relationship and suffers the missing of the goals he sets for his people.

In context, each of these three terms must be defined over against

---

[12] Nahum Sarna states that this word "encompasses reliability, durability, and faithfulness." See *Exodus*, JPS Torah Commentary (New York: Jewish Publication Society, 1991), 216.

[13] See Michael Fishbane, *Biblical Interpretation in Ancient Israel* (Oxford, UK: Clarendon, 1988), 343.

[14] For a discussion of these three terms as foundational to the problem of sin in the Old Testament, see T. V. Farris, *Mighty to Save: A Study in Old Testament Soteriology* (Nashville, TN: Broadman, 1993), 120–39; and Ludwig Kohler, *Old Testament Theology*, trans. A. S. Todd (Philadelphia: Westminster, 1957), 169–71.

[15] Alex Luc, "awon," *NIDOTTE*, 3:351.

[16] Rolf Knierim, "awon," *TLOT*, 2:863–64.

[17] Ibid., 1036.

[18] Rolf Knierim, "ht," *TLOT*, 1:406–11.

Yahweh's concern for and embodiment of covenant loyalty. By Exodus 34:1–9, it has become clear that he has been faithful to his covenant with Abraham, Isaac, and Jacob, even long after they have died (see 2:23–25). He has also kept his promises to the current generation of Israelites (3:13–18). In contrast, the golden calf incident indicates that they have twisted, rebelled against, and failed to reach the covenant standards they agreed to keep to reflect their relationship with him (24:3–8). They have twisted, broken faith with, and missed the goals set by the Ten Commandments and the other teachings they received in Exodus 20:1–17. To act in this twisted, treacherous, and wayward manner constitutes what we call "sin." They made the golden calf, declared this idol the god that brought them from Egypt, acted in a sensual manner, and generally treated Yahweh as a disposable deity (32:1–7). Yahweh has been unfailingly loyal, but the people have not. He has not chosen another people, though they have chosen to worship a god made with their own hands.

Synthesis

Exodus 34:1–9 helps make sense of what has come before it and aids an understanding of the rest of the Old Testament. Like Moses, readers of this text glean knowledge that has not been as clear previously. This knowledge includes several key elements about the nature of God and of human beings.

First, Yahweh's character is whole, good, and true. He is patient, kind, and yet just. Some commentators find these qualities contradictory, or at least in such tension that they cannot be reconciled satisfactorily.[19] Yet the multiple times that later Old Testament writers quote this passage indicate that these are the qualities of a personal deity ready for the whole range of human activity. These traits allow God the flexibility to plan and respond with grace, compassion, and justice appropriately in every circumstance.

Second, Israel has not shown this type of integrity. Their lack of reliability provides the basic definitions of sin that the Old Testament uses. This sin is fundamentally relational. Though not without redeeming qualities, Israel nonetheless demonstrates an astounding lack of personal loyalty to Yahweh, given all he has done for them. Thus, this sin is anti-covenantal. The people have not kept the standards they once agreed were

---

[19] See, for example, Walter Brueggemann, *Theology of the Old Testament: Testimony, Dispute, and Advocacy* (Minneapolis: Fortress, 1997), 227.

reasonable. Rather, they have twisted the truth about deity by calling an image a true god. They have broken their relationship with Yahweh by choosing another object of worship. They have rebelled against the limitations that Yahweh and Israel agreed upon in Exodus 20–24. In doing so, they have missed the goal of being a special people that Yahweh will use as priests to the rest of the world.

Third, though sin is far from innocuous, it cannot defeat Yahweh. He can overcome it through forgiveness (34:1–9) or through removal of those who sin (32:25–29). Yahweh's gracious character means that Israel has a chance for reconciliation and ongoing redemption. Sin is not the last word. Yahweh moves forward with Moses and the people. His grace is indefatigable, but so is his determination that the guilty not be cleared. These realities press readers to learn more about how God determines who is forgiven and who is punished.

The Law: Sin's Motives and Manners

In the Law, Moses depicts many prior instances of sin that fit the definition revealed in Exodus 34:1–9. These examples show sin's origins in human life. They explain how sin begins with faithlessness on humanity's part born of a lack of faith in God's character and God's Word. They also begin to demonstrate sin's massive infecting power in people's lives. Though many passages deserve explication, this portion of the chapter will examine briefly Genesis 3:1–21; Exodus 20:1–17; and Numbers 14:1–19 to discuss sin's motives, manners, and consequences. It is easy to see that the Law's standards reflect covenant faithfulness. Commentators have rightly examined these issues in detail throughout the history of interpretation. However, it is just as important to note how the Law reveals why people sin and what that sin looks like in daily culture.[20] These areas of the Law's teachings on sin probably deserve more attention.

Genesis 3:1–21 and the Origins of Human Sin

This foundational passage reveals the roots of sin and thus of humanity's broken relationship with Yahweh. It discloses that faithlessness begets every category of sin. Once released, sin produces many negative effects that no person avoids. This sad fact becomes increasingly apparent as the Bible proceeds.

---

[20] This is a theme in Mark Biddle's *Missing the Mark: Sin and Its Consequences in Biblical Theology* (Nashville, TN: Abingdon, 2005).

Analysis

This text follows the magnificent account of Yahweh's succinct, sweeping, and powerful creation of all that exists on earth and beyond in Genesis 1:1–2:3. It also comes after Yahweh's installation of Adam and Eve in the garden of Eden and his instructions that they not eat of one of the garden's trees (2:4–24). This prohibition seems to have no ill effect on the man and the woman or produce any immediate resentment in them. Rather, they live in perfect harmony with God and one another (v. 25). Elmer Martens observes that "there exists a relationship of mutual intimacy between them and God. There is no other God to whom they are tempted to give allegiance. Adam and Eve know God—he is not a stranger to them. He is described [in 3:8] as walking in the garden in the cool of the day: Creator and creature converse."[21]

This brilliantly positive situation does not endure. Without prior introduction, a third character in the garden, the Serpent, asks Eve what God has said about the trees (3:1). The woman answers rightly, noting that God has stated that they must not eat from one of the trees.[22] She also comments that God has warned that death is the penalty for breaking this command (vv. 2–3; see 2:17). Without hesitation, the Serpent denies that God has spoken truthfully, asserts that God does not want Eve to have the knowledge that God possesses, and promises fuller satisfaction for Eve if she will eat from the tree (3:4–5). In other words, he accuses God of lying to protect selfish interests. By doing so the Serpent attempts to break the close relationship that God, Adam, and Eve share.

Thinking it over (v. 6a), the woman chooses to believe the Serpent rather than God. She desires and then eats of the fruit. She next gives some to her husband, who follows her example. They gain new knowledge, but it does not make them feel more satisfied or wise. Indeed, it makes them ashamed of one another and fearful of God (vv. 6b–13). Their lack of faith in God's character and their ambition for what did not belong to them lead to their disobedience of God's word. John Calvin rightly asserts that they "never would have dared to resist God, unless they had first been incredulous of his word. And nothing allured them to covet the

---

[21] Martens, *God's Design*, 28.
[22] Contra J. A. Motyer, *Look to the Rock: An Old Testament Background to Our Understanding of Christ* (Leicester, UK: Inter-Varsity, 1996), 114. I have also heard several sermons through the years that assert that Eve's answer reveals incipient legalism, since she says she may not touch the tree when God has only said she must not eat the fruit. She could not eat the fruit without touching it, so I am not inclined to agree with this interpretation. If she "tampers with" God's word, as Motyer suggests, then I think this would be the first sin, not the root of the first sin.

fruit but mad ambition. So long as they, firmly believing in God's word, freely suffered themselves to be governed by Him, they had serene and duly regulated affections."[23] Until they ate the fruit, they knew that "to be loved by him is the consummation of a happy life."[24]

This lack of faith leads to a breach in relationship between God and the man and woman. When they express their fear at meeting with God due to their nakedness, God asks the question in verse 11 that summarizes all sins past and present: "Have you eaten of the tree of which I commanded you not to eat?" The answer is obvious, and no excuse suffices. Everything has changed, and death enters the picture.

Other results come in as well. God pronounces judgment on the Serpent, primarily by informing him that God will "put enmity between you and the woman, and between your offspring and her offspring; he shall bruise your head, and you shall bruise his heel" (v. 15). Nahum Sarna notes that the serpent was a symbol of many positive and negative traits in the ancient world, and that "it was often worshipped."[25] Thus, he thinks God's sentencing provides a "demythologizing" of the serpent.[26] He adds, "Of the three parties to the transgression, the serpent alone is summarily sentenced without prior interrogation—a token of God's withering disdain for it. Further, the voluble creature does not utter a word—a sure sign of its impotence in the presence of the Deity. In sum, the serpent is here reduced to an insignificant, demythologized stature."[27] Though one could disagree with Sarna's conclusion about the serpent's insignificance, he is correct about God's total control of the Serpent and the situation. God states the best news possible under the circumstances: evil will not triumph. The first human source of sin will play a key role in the Serpent's demise.

Nonetheless, the man and woman will experience pain with childbearing and presumably child rearing. They will endure pain with one another, and they will suffer pain as they attempt to grow food from the ground (vv. 16–19). Their walk with God, intimacy with one another, relationships with their children, and ability to make a living by acting as stewards of earth's resources (see 1:26–28) are all impaired. Were it not for the promise of eventual victory over the Serpent and his product, sin, there would be little reason for Adam and Eve to wish to live. Yet

---

[23] John Calvin, *Genesis*, trans. John King (1554; trans., 1847; repr. Grand Rapids, MI: Baker, 1996), 154.

[24] Ibid.

[25] Nahum Sarna, *Genesis*, JPS Torah Commentary (New York: Jewish Publication Society, 1989), 24.

[26] Ibid.

[27] Ibid.

they do live on, death delayed, though outside the delightful garden they have known. They can do so because God does not execute the penalty of death. Rather, he mercifully protects and aids them (3:19–21).

Synthesis

The motive and manners of sin take shape in this early passage. So do sin's far-reaching effects. This passage begins the Old Testament's development of sin's pervasive nature.[28] By doing so it introduces issues such as responsibility for sin, the intergenerational nature of sin, and the prevalence of sin in individual and corporate life.

This passage demonstrates that each individual is responsible for his or her actions. God made the man, the woman, and the Serpent. But he did not command the Serpent to tempt Adam and Eve. God made the fruit, but he warned the people not to eat it. Adam and Eve lacked the faith necessary to believe their Creator rather than another creature. When asked to keep a simple set of standards, the humans fail to do so. Their failure is their own. They were warned, and the Serpent hardly coerced them beyond what they could withstand.

The text also implies through the consequences outlined in 3:15–19 that sin will be an ongoing problem. Jewish and Christian scholars have argued for centuries that humans are born in sin after Adam and Eve eat the fruit. Many thinkers have also disagreed with this conclusion. Genesis 3:1–21 does not give an explicit answer to this matter, though Romans 5:12–21 strongly suggests that such is the case.[29] Clearly, no human being avoids sinning afterward. No person is sinless; the world is affected negatively. By birth, by choice, or by both, the result remains the same. Every person sins, and every human suffers for that sin spiritually, physically, emotionally, relationally, and vocationally.

The rest of the Old Testament deals with sin's prevalence and consequences in and for Israel. As will be referenced below, Moses mediates a covenant between Yahweh and Israel that defines sin and sets sacrifices for that sin. These standards reflect a proper covenant relationship with God, and the sacrifices reflect faith by penitent sinners. The Former Prophets[30] sketch how long-term, habitual sin, left unchecked, brings Israel down.

---

[28] This section follows closely my comments in *Old Testament Theology*, 67–68.

[29] For discussions of "original sin," see Alan Jacobs, *Original Sin: A Cultural History* (New York: HarperCollins, 2008); and Henri Blocher, *Original Sin* (Grand Rapids, MI: Eerdmans, 1999). For a good discussion of different approaches to this subject by Old Testament theologians, see Robin Routledge, *Old Testament Theology: A Thematic Approach* (Downers Grove, IL: InterVarsity, 2008) 147–58.

[30] Joshua; Judges; 1–2 Samuel; and 1–2 Kings.

The Latter Prophets and the Writings do the same.[31] Isaiah, Jeremiah, Ezekiel, and the Twelve provide a consistent testimony of Israel's need to believe God and walk with him. Lamentations, Ezra, Nehemiah, and 1–2 Chronicles describe the efforts of Israel's exiles to overcome the effects of national covenant breaking.

The Old Testament also details sin's presence outside of Israel. As was noted above, because Adam and Eve are the first humans, sin is a universal human problem. Before there was an Israel, the Ten Commandments, and the moral laws found in Exodus—Deuteronomy, there was a worldwide sin problem outlined in Genesis 1–11. Isaiah 13–27, Jeremiah 46–51, Ezekiel 25–32, Amos 1:2–2:3, and other passages testify to sin against the creator of all peoples in lands outside Israel. The psalmists state that there are no completely sinless persons (see Pss. 14:1–3; 53:1–3; 140:3). Job and Proverbs range well beyond Israel's borders to counsel wisdom in light of foolish sin.

In short, after Genesis 3 sin never skips a generation or an individual life. The Old Testament is not simply a long horror story of innumerable sins, but the teachings about sin are persistent and jarring. The standards warn successive generations of what can occur. No wonder, then, that in Romans 5:12–21 Paul cites this passage as a basis for arguing that one must choose between remaining "in Adam," and thus "in sin," or being "in Christ," the latter of which is God's means of forgiveness and reconciled relationship.

Exodus 20:1–21 and the Contours of Covenantal Sin

Exodus 20:1–21 contains one of the most famous of all biblical passages. It is hard to overestimate the role that the Ten Commandments have played in the history of Judaism and Christianity. As Patrick Miller asserts, "From their setting in Scripture to the contemporary debate [in the US] about their public display, the Commandments have seemed to embody God's will for human life as fully as any particular body of teaching or Scripture."[32] Miller goes on to note that the commandments have been used in Christian catechisms, thus marking them as a special portion of Christian Scripture.[33] He further notes that they have been considered a good summary of natural law, which has led to their use in a number of secular contexts.[34] This notoriety is certainly deserved. The command-

---

[31] Isaiah; Jeremiah; Ezekiel; and the Twelve (Minor Prophets).
[32] Patrick D. Miller, *The Ten Commandments* (Louisville: Westminster John Knox, 2009), 1.
[33] Ibid., 1–2.
[34] Ibid., 2–3.

ments cover a wide range of human behavior, and the rest of the Bible indicates that God ultimately holds all persons accountable for breaking these standards.

Because the Ten Commandments have been used in so many ways, it is important to treat this great text in the context of the whole of the Old Testament. Moses does not present these requirements to the nations; he gives them as the representative standards of Yahweh's covenant with Israel. It is then Israel's responsibility to state and demonstrate these principles to the world as they act as Yahweh's priests to the whole world (see Ex. 19:5–6). It is vital to emphasize the covenantal nature of the Ten Commandments before citing them as evidence of what Yahweh requires of all people. Seen this way, the commandments explain behavior that is or is not anchored in relationship with God.

Analysis

Much of the context of this passage was introduced in the comments on Exodus 34:1–9 above and will not be repeated here. Of that material it is most important to recall that Yahweh made a covenant with Abraham that includes the following blessings: his descendants will become a great nation; he will have a special relationship with God; his descendants will occupy Canaan; and his descendants will be a blessing to all nations (Gen. 12:1–9).[35] This covenant is the Creator's comprehensive response to the universal spread of sin in Genesis 1–11.[36] To fulfill these promises, Yahweh has protected Israel in Egypt (Genesis 37–50) and has redeemed them from Egyptian bondage in keeping with the pledges given Abraham and his descendants (Exodus 1–18; see esp. 2:23–25). Fully freed now, Israel stands ready to become a kingdom of priests for other nations (Ex. 19:5–6; see 1 Pet. 2:9–10). As Gary Schnittjer explains, "The Sinai covenant, then, was not designed to isolate Israel from the nations but to separate them to serve and represent the nations to their God."[37] What follows, therefore, occurs to help Israel become Yahweh's means of liberating the world from sin, a goal first stated in Genesis 3:15.

Exodus 20:1–21 may be divided several ways depending on how one handles the Ten Commandments. If one separates the commands into those that relate most directly to God and those that apply mainly to peo-

---

[35] For a list of the repetition of these promises in Genesis—Deuteronomy, consult David J. A. Clines, *The Theme of the Pentateuch*, JSOTSup 10 (Sheffield, UK: Sheffield Academic Press, 1978), 32–43.

[36] Ibid., 73.

[37] Gary Schnittjer, *The Torah Story: An Apprenticeship on the Pentateuch* (Grand Rapids, MI: Zondervan, 2006), 247.

ple, then the passage has four clear parts: verses 1–2; verses 3–11; verses 12–17; and verses 18–21.

Exodus 20:1–2 is critical to understanding the commandments' role in the Bible. Here Yahweh's relationship with Israel determines the nature of the commands. Everything Yahweh has done for Israel in Genesis 12—Exodus 19 stems from his promises to Abraham. All these crucial prefatory events stand behind this opening statement that Yahweh is their God, and he is the one who has brought them out of the land of Egypt. As in Genesis 2:4–25, relationship precedes requirements. Unlike Genesis 1–2, redemption does as well. Yahweh has already revealed and proven himself through unwavering faithfulness and overwhelmingly successful redeeming love. In short, his commandments and Israel's projected obedience to them *reflect* this existing relationship; it does not *create* the relationship. Breaking the commands shows faithlessness in action.

In Exodus 20:3–11, the first four commands set boundaries for Israel's faithfulness to God. Israel must have an exclusive commitment to Yahweh (v. 3). I argue throughout my *Old Testament Theology* that the Old Testament teaches monotheism, the belief in one God (see Deut. 4:35, 39; etc.).[38] Yet even if the Israelites did not believe that there is only one God, this verse binds them to acting as if such is the case. There is no room to flee to another deity. Furthermore, they are required to serve Yahweh without making any image of him, much less bowing down to any other image of a god (Ex. 20:4). Engaging in any sort of idolatry shows hatred, which basically means an unwillingness to choose Yahweh as he desires. Consequently, Yahweh will punish idolatry even though his first instinct is to show compassion and mercy (vv. 5–6; see 34:6–7).[39] What is more, the people must not swear falsely by, prophesy falsehood in, teach falsehood about, or claim access to Yahweh's blessings by false statements about Yahweh's "name,"[40] which encapsulates the character more fully outlined in 34:6–7. Doing so will bring guilt that Yahweh will address. Finally, Israel must follow Yahweh's example of resting one day in seven (20:8–11; see Gen. 2:1–3). Work and the pursuit of wealth must not consume them. Presumably worship will occur on this day since the other six days will be filled with work in an agriculturally based economy (Ex. 20:8). This command applies to the Israelites, resident aliens among

---

[38] Paul R. House, *Old Testament Theology* (Downers Grove, IL: Intervarsity, 1998).

[39] For a brief discussion of 20:6–7, see the comments on Ex. 34:6–7 above.

[40] For a description of the appropriateness of using a wide range of meanings for this commandment, see Brevard S. Childs, *The Book of Exodus: A Critical, Theological Commentary*, OTL (Philadelphia: Westminster, 1974), 409–12; and Miller, *The Ten Commandments*, 63–108.

them, and even their animals (vv. 9–10). Rest is God's comprehensive gift to all his creatures.

In verses 12–17, the last six commands set goals and boundaries for human relationships. These begin with respect for parents, a positive guideline that includes a promise of longevity in the land (v. 12) and presumably an unstated threat of the opposite if disobeyed. Then four very terse commands prohibit murder, adultery, stealing, and giving false witness (vv. 13–16). Each of these relates to temporarily or permanently taking something or someone that belongs to another person. The last command is perhaps the most comprehensive of all. In barring coveting (v. 17), Yahweh strikes at the heart of all sin. If one does not covet, or desire, what belongs to someone else, then one will not break the other commandments and thereby sin. Genesis 3:1–6 has demonstrated that sin begins with faith-killing desire. Concluding with coveting indicates the need to protect one's desires by directing them toward Yahweh and his Word.

Verses 18–21 present the people's reaction. They fear Yahweh's power and awesome presence (vv. 18–19), as well they should. But Moses comforts them. He assures them that Yahweh wants their reverence and respect ("fear") so that they "may not sin" (ESV), the third word in the triad in Exodus 34:6–7 (*ḥṭ'*), or, in other words, "miss God's goal" (20:20).[41] Yahweh wants them to have a relationship with him built on reverence and trust. As John Mackay explains, "The experience . . . of a direct encounter with God should have . . . led to ongoing faith and obedience on their part. It was such an overwhelming experience that thereafter they should always remember it and appreciate who their King was and what he required of them. In that way they would be inhibited from breaking his commands."[42] Exodus 20:20 summarizes succinctly the Bible's intention for every person's life on earth. Those who know and respect God are those who do not break faith with the one who made, redeems, and loves them.

Since verses 22–26 discuss sacrifices for sin, there is no way that verses 3–21 mean that Yahweh thinks Israel will keep the commandments flawlessly. Grace frames the commands, for verses 1–2 note how Yahweh redeemed Israel, and verses 22–26 show how Yahweh will forgive Israel. Grace also permeates the Ten Commandments, since as a whole they state how people prone to sin may walk with God and with one another.

---

[41] Author's translation.
[42] John Mackay, *Exodus*, Mentor Commentary Series (Fearn, Ross-shire, UK: Christian Focus, 2001), 356–57.

Synthesis

Like Genesis 3:1–21, this awe-inspiring passage unfolds against the backdrop of God's goodness and absolute trustworthiness. Also like Genesis 3:1–21, it sets forth sin's methods, manners, and consequences. Unlike the earlier text, this one also establishes a broader sense of what sin and its opposite look like in daily life. At least four conclusions are relevant at this point.

First, this text presents Yahweh as Israel's covenant God and great redeemer. What he has done for them has been due to the promises he made to their ancestors Abraham, Isaac, and Jacob (Ex. 2:23–25). It has also been due to his love for them as people living in their own generation (see 3:13–18). What he asks of them now will make them able to bless other nations by serving as a kingdom of priests (Gen. 12:1–9; Ex. 19:5–6). It will also help them fulfill God's original mandate to humanity to care for and rule over creation (see Gen. 1:28–30). This relationship with Israel provides Yahweh's means for restoring his relationship with others. To borrow one of Paul's metaphors for the church, Israel will be God's body on earth (see 1 Cor. 12:12–31; Eph. 2:11–22). Whatever one concludes about the role of the Ten Commandments in biblical theology, one must reckon with this context of a preexisting relationship.

Second, the commandments set standards to establish how Israel will reflect its relationship with Yahweh. Sin amounts to breaking faith with those covenant commands. As Edmund Jacob comments, "God is the one who enters into relationship and who makes the covenant; sin is a breaking of this relationship."[43] Though specific sin terminology does not appear until Exodus 20:20, the implication that breaking the commands amounts to sin is clearly intended. If Israel respects God (20:20), the one who delivered them from slavery (vv. 1–2), then Israel will obey God's Word (vv. 3–17). Alternatively, if Israel does not meet Yahweh's goals, in other words, if they sin (v. 20), then they may in good faith offer sacrifices that will restore fellowship with him (v. 24).

Third, the commandments hint strongly at consequences for disobedience. If Israel sins by bowing to idols, there will be severe consequences (vv. 5–6). If they do not show respect for parents, they will not live long in the land. As Exodus 34:6–7 warns, Yahweh will not clear the guilty. Adam and Eve discovered this fact in Genesis 3:14–26. Sadly, as the Bible unfolds, Israel learns the same in Exodus 32–33 and elsewhere.

---

[43] Edmond Jacob, *Theology of the Old Testament*, trans. Arthur W. Heathcote and Philip J. Allcock (New York: Harper & Row, 1958), 281.

Fourth, this passage implies the breadth of sin's results. As in Genesis 3:1–21, sin threatens to separate people from God. Those who serve other deities, set up idols of Yahweh or some other god, speak falsely about Yahweh, or fail to set aside the seventh day for rest and worship choose to stand apart from him. Such persons refuse to commune with him. They go their own way without the creator of the universe and the redeemer of Israel. Also as in Genesis 3:1–21, sin harms human relationships. People who dishonor parents, sexuality and marriage, life, property, justice, and right desire sow disruption in individual and community life. They tear apart homes, families, courts, and souls. Destruction follows them all the days of their lives. They embody distrust of God; they live by lesser laws. Happily, to the extent that people obey these basic covenantal words, the damage sin does may be minimized.

In these and other ways, God's Ten Commandments continue the Bible's description of sin. The definition remains faithlessness to God demonstrated by twisting, rebelling against, and missing the goals he has set. The motive for sin remains desiring something other than what God supplies through the riches of his grace sufficiently to keep from trusting some other person or pattern of life.[44] The manners of sin stand out more vividly here. One sins by acting contrary to ten very pervasive statements that entail several interconnected facets of life. Sin's consequences have not changed, though the punishments introduced in Genesis 3:16–19 become more identifiable. Through God's love for Israel, his redeemed people, he warns them of the dangers sin entails.

Leviticus 18–19 and Israel's Witness to Their Neighbors[45]

For most current Western readers, Leviticus is one of the Bible's strangest books. Its array of sacrifices, priestly activities, and laws related to agricultural community life is more recognizable to other current cultures.[46] As one studies Leviticus carefully, it becomes apparent that this is one of the most theologically oriented books in the Bible. More specifically to the point of this chapter, Leviticus addresses in detail how God, who is holy (see Lev. 11:44),[47] defines, forgives, and helps people avoid and over-

---

[44] On how future faith, hope, and love depend on understanding and trusting God due to his past acts of deliverance, see Scott J. Hafemann, *The God of Promise and the Life of Faith: Understanding the Heart of the Bible* (Wheaton, IL: Crossway, 2001).

[45] Much of this section is adapted from my *Old Testament Theology*, 126, 143–45; and my *Leviticus/Numbers*, Shepherd's Notes (Nashville: Broadman, 1999), 38–41.

[46] On this subject see Philip Jenkins, *The New Faces of Christianity: Believing the Bible in the Global South* (New York: Oxford University Press, 2008).

[47] Note the definition of this term below.

come sin. It states how God's people can display in their communities the standards declared in Exodus 20:1–17. This witness of faithfulness to God before their neighbors will mark them as a kingdom of priests for other nations, the goal for them that Yahweh sets in Exodus 19:5–6. Though all of Leviticus is relevant to understanding sin, Leviticus 18 and 19 particularly explain how God's standards affect Israel's daily life and through Israel potentially all humanity.

Analysis

Following the golden calf incident and subsequent relational renewal with Yahweh in Exodus 32–34, Israel rights its walk with God. The people and Moses build the tabernacle, and Yahweh blesses their efforts by being present in it (Exodus 35–40). Moses then receives standards for the sorts of sacrifices that will be made at the tabernacle (Leviticus 1–7). Sacrifices were introduced as early as Exodus 20:22–26 (see comments above), so these descriptions are hardly unexpected. Within this opening section, Leviticus 4:2, 13, 22, and 27 state that sacrifices must be made because Israelites will do what God's commands prohibit. Also in this section individuals offer sacrifices for their sins, as do families and the whole nation. Sacrifices are financially means tested, which indicates that all classes of people, rich and poor alike, sin, and also shows Yahweh's fairness in dealing with the sins of people of different economic conditions. Thus, in these opening chapters sin is personal, societal, and costly. All persons twist, rebel against, and miss the goal of God's standards. All may also be forgiven.

After Leviticus 8–10 depicts the setting apart of a priestly group to serve within Israel, chapters 11–15 offer a list of ways people or things may be deemed "unclean." This term basically means "currently or permanently unsuitable for use" (things) or "currently or permanently unsuitable for congregating" (people). The word *unclean* is not a synonym for *sin*. Rather, one's uncleanness may or may not be due to sin. To oversimplify terms, all who sin are unclean, but not all who are unclean have sinned. Leviticus 16 then presents the annual remedy to all sin and uncleanness: the Day of Atonement rituals and sacrifices. However one sins against God, those sins can be forgiven.

Leviticus 17–26 presents several standards for *holiness*, which basically means "persons or things set apart for particular purposes." Yahweh stated in 11:44 that he is holy and his people must be holy. This means that Israel must act as Yahweh's special people and thereby demonstrate his character to the world. In these chapters Moses makes it clear that this demonstration only occurs through reverence for God and his Word (Lev. 19:14, 32; 25:17, 36, 43).[48] As in Exodus 20:1–21, relationship with God remains the basis for obedience. Statements about where sacrifices may be made and why blood cannot be consumed in sacrificial rituals follow in Leviticus 17. Then, in chapters 18–19, Yahweh states some specific ways that Israel must act if they are to be his holy people. While doing so he mentions a standard that Jesus says summarizes all commands regarding human relationships: "Love your neighbor as yourself" (19:18; see Mark 12:28–32). At the end of this section, Leviticus 26:14–45 states the consequences that the people will face if they disobey God's covenant over long periods of time. The covenantal structure of Leviticus 17–26 makes the relational nature of sin ever plainer.

Leviticus 18 delves into the inner recesses of the Israelites' personal lives. Serving as Yahweh's kingdom of priests requires them to avoid sexual practices that happen in worship rituals and daily life in Egypt and Canaan (vv. 1–3). In short, Israel must follow God's laws, not those of the people around them (vv. 3–4).[49] His word remains paramount, just as it has since Genesis 1–3. Yahweh alerts them to the fact that they cannot serve lust, idols, and him at the same time. The chapter then proceeds to discuss sexuality, ethics, and worship.

Sexual ethics receive detailed treatment in Leviticus 18.[50] Yahweh prohibits four particular actions. Verse 6 introduces the exclusion of sexual relations with "close relatives," and verses 7–19 define this term. These commands against incest demonstrate Yahweh's opposition to sexual abuse, not just intermarriage in families. They also state God's disapproval of the misuse of authority for sexual purposes, and the use of any person, male or female, as merely an object of one's own pleasure.[51] These verses are the most detailed in the Bible on this subject, so they are vital for understanding how to protect victims today.

Verse 20 returns to the subject of adultery introduced in Exodus 20:14. Given the context of Leviticus, this passage asserts that adultery defiles its participants by violating a unique relationship in which they are set apart for a particular person. It blurs family lines, betrays trust, and

---

[48] See Boda, *A Severe Mercy*, 79.
[49] Paul makes a similar point in Rom. 12:1–2.
[50] For a detailed discussion of sexual ethics in the Old Testament, consult Hilary B. Lipka, *Sexual Transgression in the Hebrew Bible*, Hebrew Bible Monographs 7 (Sheffield, UK: Sheffield Phoenix Press, 2006); and Richard M. Davidson, *Flame of Yahweh: Sexuality in the Old Testament* (Peabody, MA: Hendrickson, 2007).
[51] See John E. Hartley, *Leviticus*, WBC 4 (Waco, TX: Word, 1992), 289–301.

harms familial relationships. Marital fidelity remains a significant building block in Yahweh's standards for a kingdom of priests.

Leviticus 18:22 prohibits homosexual acts. The context likely includes deeds committed in cultic[52] and noncultic[53] settings. Like the sins already mentioned, those who practice homosexuality set aside God's standards for couples and families set forth in Genesis 1–2. They do not set themselves apart for God's standards. Romans 1:18–32 and 1 Corinthians 6:9 list homosexual acts as one of many sinful activities in a fallen world. It must be remembered that Romans 3–8 and 1 Corinthians 6:11 teach that these acts can be forgiven, just as idolatry, coveting, adultery, and murder can be. Neither this sin nor any other overthrows God's capacity for grace. Yet it remains a sin, and it is a sin that can break the pattern for sexual activity the Creator has ordained.

Leviticus 18:23 bars bestiality. In this passage it is particularly a sin that debases women. As with homosexuality, there were ancient religions that included this activity. Gordon Wenham writes that it is mentioned in Egyptian, Canaanite, and Hittite sources. Specifically, he writes, "there was a cult in the Eastern delta that involved the cohabitation of women and goats. Indeed Ramses II, possibly the pharaoh of the exodus, claimed to be the offspring of the god Ptah, who took the form of a goat."[54] Whether the text refers to cultic or domestic activity, or both, bestiality in any culture is a sign that sexuality has gone very wrong.

Yahweh makes it clear that participating in these behaviors jeopardizes Israel's future. God reminds them that they are displacing the Canaanites in part because the current inhabitants of the Promised Land display corrupt theology and ethics (18:24–28; see Gen. 15:13–16). Israelites who act in these ways are to be excluded from the community, lest sin spread (Lev. 18:29–30). God's Word can save Israel from following other nations' self-destructive patterns. It can also show them how to display Yahweh's character to a world very much in need of protection, grace, and truth.

Leviticus 19 ranges well beyond sexual ethics. As in Exodus 20:1–17, respect for God and neighbor frames these laws (Lev. 19:2, 18), as does God's past relationship with Israel (vv. 3, 4, 10, 12, etc.). God's holiness is the basis for these rules (v. 2), and Israel's holiness as a people living as priests to the nations is their goal (v. 37). The chapter repeats or ex-

---

[52] Marvin Pope argues that homosexual acts were part of cultic activity in ancient times. See Marvin H. Pope, "Homosexuality," in *IDBSup*, ed. Keith R. Crim (Nashville: Abingdon, 1976), 415. See also Baruch A. Levine, *Leviticus*, JPS Torah Commentary (New York: Jewish Publication Society, 1989), 123.

[53] See Genesis 19 and Judges 19.

[54] Gordon J. Wenham, *The Book of Leviticus*, NICOT (Grand Rapids, MI: Eerdmans, 1979), 252.

plains several of the Ten Commandments. As in Exodus 20:1–11, idolatry is prohibited and proper worship required (Lev. 19:4–8, 30). Commands to spurn divination, sorcery, and mediums are also given (vv. 26, 31). All these reflect trust in other deities. Once again anything that replaces trust in Yahweh and his Word cannot be countenanced.

This chapter also contains very clear requirements for the treatment of one's neighbor. Israelites are not to avenge wrongs or bear grudges. Rather, they must love their neighbors as they love themselves (v. 18). This very positive statement includes persons of foreign descent who are not permanent in the land (vv. 33–34). Israel shows their love for God by showing love to one another and to strangers. Love is the heart of God's dealings with Israel, and it must be the basis for the kingdom of priests' dealings with others. Loving one another helps Israel to avoid stealing, bearing false witness, harming the poor, and perverting justice (vv. 9–16). It combats sin at its roots—in the heart (v. 17). It eliminates sins against foreigners, family, and business associates (vv. 20–36), even those who may be one's enemies. No person is outside the definition of "neighbor." Jesus was surely right, then, to expound the concept of "neighbor" through the parable of the good Samaritan (Luke 10:25–37). Paul was equally justified in telling the Romans to show love even for those who mistreated them (see Rom. 12:14–21).

Synthesis

Leviticus 18–19 provides further elaboration of the application of God's standards to daily life among his chosen kingdom of priests. First, sexual sins have the power to shred communities. They threaten what remains of the male-female intimacy in Genesis 2:25 and shake God's chosen foundation for human life as God's image (Gen. 1:26). Incest makes the pain between parents and children promised to Adam and Eve worse. Today we know that sexual abuse has particular power to harm people emotionally, spiritually, and physically. Adultery breaks faith so significantly that the Old Testament later uses adultery as a major metaphor to describe Israel's covenant faithlessness (see Hosea 1–3; Jer. 2:1–37; etc.). Bestiality turns women and animals into objects, treating them as if they were not creatures of the living God. Homosexuality violates God's purposes for sexuality. Again, all sins damage people. Sexual sins are not necessarily worse than other types of sin, but they do have horrific power to mar, ruin, and end relationships.

Second, sins against others begin with a lack of love for them. Sinning begins by placing self above the needs of others. It may take the form of loving only people like oneself. Yahweh does not give his people this option. The stranger deserves the same sort of love given oneself and one's own ethnic or geographical grouping.[55] Whatever the origins of the first-century AD belief that Jews should not mix at all with Gentiles, it is not in Leviticus. Israel cannot be the priests for other nations by shutting off their compassion for them. Racism in all its active and passive manifestations is a sin against one's neighbor and against God.

Third, sin is a very relational matter. It begins with not being holy, not being set apart for God. It starts with lack of love for neighbors. It occurs when one treats strangers and foreigners as less than one's neighbor. It affects one's sexuality; it harms one's nonfamilial relationships. As in earlier passages, it is not contained in one's mind; it cannot be localized in a person, clan, or race. It spills over into every arena of life. God's Word helps instruct those who trust God and follow his teaching, yet it also points out faithless behavior.

Jesus was, among other things, an excellent biblical theologian. He often crystallized massive portions of Scripture in a few words. One of those times was when he was asked to name the "great commandment in the Law" (Matt. 22:34). He responded, "You shall love the Lord your God with all your heart and with all your soul and with all your mind. This is the first and great commandment. And a second is like it: You shall love your neighbor as yourself. On these two commandments depend all the Law and the Prophets" (Matt. 22:37–40). In citing Deuteronomy 6:5 and Leviticus 19:18, he laid bare the essence of God's will. God desires a relationship with human beings based in love for him, demonstrated by acts of love for him and others. As was noted above, Jesus defined "neighbor" as Leviticus 19:18–37 does. In doing so, he linked God's mission for Israel to be a kingdom of priests with his plans for his followers to take his message to the world (see Matt. 28:16–20). Sinning by failing to show love or by hating enemies is simply unbiblical and inimical to God's will for his followers in any generation.

Numbers 13–14 and Sin's Origins and Destination

Among many other things, Genesis 12—Deuteronomy 34 is a travel document. Abraham, Isaac, Jacob, and their descendants are always heading

---

[55] For elaboration on love in action in Christian ethics, see Michael Hill, *The How and Why of Love: An Introduction to Evangelical Ethics* (Sydney: Matthias Media, 2002).

to one destination or another. Sin always seems to be on the move with them. As has been argued above, sin has its own points of origin and ultimate ends. In Numbers 13–14, Israel's movements toward fulfilling God's plans for them halt because sin moves among the people. This very sad convergence summarizes much of sin's march in the Torah.

Analysis

Yahweh continues his communications to Israel through Moses in Numbers (see 1:1). A year has passed since the exodus (1:1). It is time to move from Sinai to Canaan. God gives marching orders in Numbers 1–4 and then presents ways in which the people must prepare themselves to worship and make war in the Promised Land (5:1–10:10). The people, priests, and clan leaders commit themselves to doing God's will in all aspects of their lives. The nation enjoys their first Passover as free people (9:1–5). Following these preparations, they set out (10:11–36). They complain about their provisions in 11:1–15, and Aaron and Miriam complain about Moses and his new wife in 12:1–2. God deals very kindly with Moses' leadership burdens in 11:16–30 but very harshly with the complainers (11:31–35; 12:3–16). Overall, these chapters portray Israel's actions positively. Perhaps readers could be excused for thinking that after Exodus 34 the worst is past. Sadly, some terrible troubles lurk on the horizon.

Numbers 13–14 begins with hope-filled activity but soon describes confused debate about the future. The passage opens with a reconnaissance mission (13:1–24). Twelve spies traverse Canaan. In their initial report, ten spies admit that Canaan is a good land but do not think that Israel can conquer it. Two spies (Joshua and Caleb) disagree. Sorrow and dismay mount among the people. They despair. Then they talk of killing Moses and Aaron, replacing them, and going back to Egypt (14:1–4). Nothing Aaron, Moses, Joshua, and Caleb say dissuades them (vv. 5–10). Individual and corporate rebellion against God's stated promises and purposes runs rampant.

Everyone else seemingly heard, Yahweh clears away the disorder and its root causes (v. 10b). Addressing Moses, he wonders why the people despise him (v. 11a). Tellingly, he then asks, "And how long will they not believe in me, in spite of all the signs that I have done among them?" (v. 11b). The motive for sin remains unbelief. This unbelief is manifested as lack of faith in Yahweh. As was true of Adam and Eve, though God has given Israel all they need, they do not believe in him. They are not moved to faith for their future by the previous signs that he did in Egypt.

Those who do not trust Yahweh act accordingly. They rebel against Yahweh, his Word, and his chosen leaders. They set their own standards and follow their own course of life. Reasoning and pleading with them do not avail. Current trouble tends to cloud their vision. Without realizing it, they wreck their futures and mar their children's. As the Bible proceeds, they are remembered as prime examples of persons who twist the truth, rebel against God, and miss the goal he set for them (see Ezek. 20:13–16; Pss. 78:17–19, 40–55; 95:7–11; 1 Cor. 10:1–22; Heb. 3:7–19).

God and Moses next have a conversation reminiscent of Exodus 32–33. God tells Moses that he would just as soon start over with Moses and build a new people after destroying the wicked (Num. 14:12). In response, Moses prays Exodus 34:6–7. He affirms God's kind and forbearing character and Yahweh's redemption of Israel (Num. 14:13–18). Interestingly, he includes the fact that Yahweh does not clear the guilty. He knows that the people have sinned, yet he asks Yahweh to pardon them (v. 19).

Yahweh acts according to his character. He acts mercifully in that he does not destroy those who despise him and fail to trust him (v. 20). He also acts justly by not allowing those who rebel to enter Canaan (vv. 21–23). He acts graciously and with covenant loyalty by promising that Joshua, Caleb, and the next generation will receive the land promised to Abraham, Isaac, and Jacob (vv. 24–25).

The consequences of Israel's sins are tremendous. Their uprising costs the rebels everything they left Egypt to possess. The ten contentious spies lose their lives (vv. 36–38). When they see this, the people try to retrace their steps and invade after all (vv. 39–40). Moses responds by telling them they are once again "transgressing[56] the command of Yahweh" (v. 41), one of the hallmarks of sin. They should accept the situation and ready their children for Canaan. They refuse, and many die trying to invade the land, which is one more example of their stubborn refusal to obey Yahweh (vv. 44–45).

Synthesis

In Numbers 13–14, sin begins in the heart and ends with rebellion, just as before, yet this passage may help answer some questions readers might pose. For instance, one might ask, "What if people had more experience? Would they still sin?" This passage shows that long ages after Adam and Eve's unbelief led inevitably to a path of destructive action, the pattern

---

[56] This word is a form of *pesa*.

continues. Sin is not simply a bad habit that one overcomes. It is not a mistake corrected and contained. Of course people can learn to stop stupid and harmful behaviors, but sin still persists, threatening to start the madness all over again.

One might also ask, "What if God showed people more signs and wonders? What if he gave them more evidence of his existence and goodness? Would people still sin?" By Numbers 13–14, the people have seen amazing things. God has sent numerous startling plagues on Egypt. He has parted the Red Sea. He has fed and clothed them in a desert. One more miracle will hardly convince them. John's Gospel tells a similar tale. Some of the people who saw Jesus raise Lazarus from the dead believed in him (John 11:45), but not all who saw did. Some wanted Jesus stopped (vv. 46–53). None claimed that Lazarus was still in the grave instead of walking freely about in Bethany. No wonder Jesus once stated flatly that those who do not believe Moses and the prophets would not believe if one rose from the dead (Luke 16:31). Unbelief is tenacious.

Finally, one might ask, "What if God clarified his standards? With the fog of uncertainty lifted, would the people learn not to sin?" Leviticus, Numbers, and Deuteronomy explain God's ways as they relate to dozens of facets of personal, familial, and community life. These elaborations of the Ten Commandments certainly help those who humbly come to Yahweh for forgiveness, fellowship, and ongoing commitment to repentance. They help those who love God and teach his ways to their children (Deut. 6:4–9). At the same time, they reveal the multiple ways that people trust the wrong person or choose alternative paths to the ones that God has set. As helpful laws pour forth, so does the clarification of what constitutes sin. This knowledge and much more lies behind Paul's statements in Romans 7:7–25. He writes that God's laws are good and holy, yet the more one knows about them, the more one can see one's sins and need for grace.

Conclusion

More passages could be examined, especially in Deuteronomy, but the results will not change. Deuteronomy stands with the passages already examined in confirming certain core principles. Indeed, Deuteronomy reinforces them, for like Leviticus it is patterned as a covenant document[57]

---

[57] See Meredith G. Kline, *Treaty of the Great King: The Covenant Structure of Deuteronomy* (Grand Rapids, MI: Eerdmans, 1963); and Peter C. Craigie, *The Book of Deuteronomy*, NICOT (Grand Rapids, MI: Eerdmans, 1976).

that clearly reveals the consequences for rebellion (see Lev. 26:14–45; Deut. 28:15–68).

Sin's motives do not change. Humans inevitably eventually choose to believe someone other than God because they want something that God has not promised or because they simply do not believe what God has declared. The problem, then, is not with God. He provides for people, for he is kind, compassionate, and utterly committed to covenant relationship making. The problem lies in human beings' twisting, rebelling against, and missing the goals that God has set in his standards. Yet God stands ready to forgive. Adam, Eve, and Moses' Israelites all act against God and his word because of unbelief and its accompanying destructive desires and deeds.

Likewise, sin's manners do not alter, though the examples of sin multiply. Sin affects every aspect of human beings' existence. It corrupts their relationship with God, requiring his redemptive acts for them to be overcome. It mars their interactions with one another, making life in the home, in society, and in one's heart less than what God made it to be. It leads to decisions and deeds that scar the physical world around them. Without God's clear covenantal directions, the situation grows worse as people live in the darkness of their own ethical devices. Yet the more God teaches, the more sin becomes visible. Once again God's redemption is the only ultimate source of hope.

Finally, sin's consequences are not altered. Death comes to the ten rebellious spies in Numbers 13–14 just as it does to Adam and Eve. Failure at all levels of human life follows. These texts serve as warnings and as guides. Thus, they encourage readers to turn to Yahweh in faith and thereby to turn from sin. For those who refuse to heed these warnings, however, they become God's writ of condemnation. Warnings can cause hardening to those who ignore them, as was the case with Pharaoh in Exodus 5–15 and the tardy warriors in Numbers 13–14. God's standards can become ethical touchstones for people committed to Yahweh and to his means of restoring relationship after they sin (see Ex. 20:22–26). As always in the Bible, one's walk with God depends on one's faith in God, the creator, covenant maker, forgiver, and sender of his people to be a kingdom of priests that declare his glory to the world (1 Pet. 2:9–10). In all of life, that which "does not proceed from faith is sin" (Rom. 14:23). Faith leads to obedience to what God has said. Obedience to God because of who he is, what he has done, and what he commands remains the opposite of sin.

3

SIN IN THE FORMER AND LATTER PROPHETS AND THE WRITINGS

PAUL R. HOUSE

Though other peoples appear in the Torah, given his audience Moses understandably focuses on Israel after Genesis 1–11. Yet these introductory chapters place Yahweh's relationship with Israel in the context of the whole of creation. This indicates that the Bible's interests far exceed a single nation, even one as significant as Israel, Yahweh's kingdom of priests. The Former Prophets[1] continue to focus on Israel's story while noting the relationship of Israel to other peoples. The Latter Prophets[2] hardly neglect Israel's story, but they also include material on how God defines and judges sins among the nations. This chapter will survey particular contributions that each book of the Former Prophets makes to the Old Testament's unfolding delineation of sin in Israel's history, before offering syntheses and observations. It will then focus on some short passages in the Latter Prophets that demonstrate the universal scope of sin. Together the Former and Latter Prophets present comprehensive treatments of God's relationship to his creatures and his creation.

Sin's Stain on Israel's History: The Former Prophets

The Former Prophets resume the narrative that the Law begins. As Joshua opens, a new generation of Israelites stands poised to enter Canaan. This time they obey and succeed because of Yahweh's power. They do not rebel against Yahweh's Word nor fail to believe his promises about conquering the land. As this generation fades from the scene, however, in Judges the

---

[1] Joshua; Judges; 1–2 Samuel; and 1–2 Kings.
[2] Isaiah; Jeremiah; Ezekiel; and the Twelve (Minor Prophets).

people turn from God to the gods of the land. Thus begins a dark and gruesome era that eventually ebbs in 1–2 Samuel. New covenantal promises to David emerge. But once again the scene changes. In 1–2 Kings, the nation experiences the results of decades and centuries of faithlessness threatened in Leviticus 26:14–45 and Deuteronomy 28:15–68. It is not fair to act as if there were no godly persons in these books or as if the nation never did the right thing. Yet it is right to state that eventually the stain of sin so covered the nation that sin's consequences overtook Israel.

Sin's Threatening Presence: Joshua

Overall, Joshua is a very positive book, at least from the Israelites' perspective. It is not so positive for the nations they defeat. This generation of Israelites generally follows the faithful lead of Joshua, who hews closely to God's directions. At the outset of the book, Yahweh emphasizes that Joshua must follow the words that God gave to Moses (1:1–9). At the end of the book, the aging Joshua reminds the people of the same principle (23–24). Covenantal faithfulness to Yahweh remains the key to Israel's future.

One episode particularly demonstrates that sin's presence always lurks in the shadows,[3] looking for an opportunity to undercut obedience to Yahweh. Since Israel's venture into Canaan is partly God's judgment on the region's peoples (see Gen. 15:13–16; Lev. 18:1–3), God commands Israel not to hoard the treasures that they capture (Josh. 7:1). A man named Achan and his family break this crucial rule (vv. 16–21). When confronted, the guilty Achan confesses that he coveted the goods and took them (v. 21). He falls prey to the primary motive behind sin, just as Eve did. The whole nation suffers for his sin until it is uncovered and he and his family are executed (vv. 22–26). Even when Israel succeeds in its mission, the danger of sin perseveres.

Rejecting God's Ways for One's Own: Judges

In a way, one could write as much about sin in Judges as about sin in the entire Old Testament. Every one of the Ten Commandments is probably broken here, most of them evidently so. Greatly feared consequences develop. Many, many of the vilest deeds that humans perpetrate occur in these pages. Periodically the people realize their errors and cry out to

---

[3] For a good discussion of how the threat of sin is a part of Joshua, see Mark Boda, *A Severe Mercy: Sin and Its Remedy in the Old Testament* (Winona Lake, IN: Eisenbrauns, 2009), 126–37.

God. He hears them and sends deliverers (judges) who lead them out of their troubles for a time. Still, the acts and results of sin permeate the book, and it closes with its main theme: "There was no king in Israel. Everyone did what was right in his own eyes" (21:25; see 17:6). This concluding comment reflects the book's three major sins: faithlessness to Yahweh (see 1:1–3:6), self-destroying moral individualism (see 3:7–16:31), and society-killing murderous savagery (see 17:1–21:25).

Sin's Reality among God's Greatest Servants: 1–2 Samuel

Even God's greatest servants sin at times. The Old Testament has already revealed this fact. It honestly portrays Abraham as a man willing to put his wife in moral and physical danger to protect his own skin (see Gen. 12:10–20). It reveals Moses' murderous past (Ex. 2:11–15) and sometimes tragically self-serving leadership traits (see Num. 20:10–13). Like these earlier great covenant bearers, David, to whom God makes the covenant promise of an eternal kingdom (see 2 Sam. 7:1–29) from which the messianic promise derives, breaks faith with God. He commits adultery, he lies, and he murders (11:1–27). Samuel and Saul are likewise imperfect men prone to pique and pride (see 1 Sam. 12:1–5; 15:1–32). All these key figures in 1–2 Samuel have strengths, and they all serve God in distinct and helpful ways. But none rises above sin.

Sin's Nation-Killing Power: 1–2 Kings

The author of 1–2 Kings presents the next phase of Israel's history as a tragedy. The account begins with the heights of David and Solomon's reign (1 Kings 1–11) and concludes with the depths of defeat and exile (2 Kings 24–25). In between, the twelve tribes divide into two separate nations (1 Kings 12:16–24), Judah and Israel. Faithlessness to God too often typifies both nations. As Leviticus 26:14–45 and Deuteronomy 28:15–68 warned, the eventual result of this faithlessness was exile from the Promised Land.

This whole history, which spans 1010–560 BC, is summarized in 2 Kings 17:7–23, one of the Bible's greatest comprehensive passages. Israel's national tragedy occurred for many reasons, all of which relate to sin. The people feared other gods (v. 7). They acted like the nations around them (v. 8). They practiced idolatry (vv. 9–11) despite Yahweh's clear words to the contrary (v. 12) and despite the clear teaching of the prophets whom Yahweh sent (v. 13). This behavior happened because they did not listen to God or believe him (v. 14). Instead, like the Israelites in Numbers 13–14, they despised God and his covenant (v. 15). Both Israel and Judah acted in this manner, so both suffered the consequences of their actions (vv. 19–20).

In short, lack of belief in Yahweh led to despising God and his Word, which in turn led to breaking God's commandments, which over time led Yahweh to turn them out of the land. As verse 8 puts it so clearly, "They sinned."[4] They were not simply victims of overwhelmingly bad political odds. Left unattended, their sins stained centuries of the history of the kingdom of priests. It led to sorrows that the people could not have imagined. Interpreters of the whole Old Testament know that God's redemptive plan has not been derailed by these events, but they also discern how necessary God's redemption is by reading about them.

Synthesis

The Former Prophets reveal the motives, manners, and consequences of sin in historical context, or what is often referred to as "real life." If readers find the Torah overly theoretical or rhetorical, then they surely find the Former Prophets down to earth. Each portion supports what the others teach about sin, yet each has its own contribution to make to the concept.

First, Joshua proves that sin can intrude into generally faithful times. It always has the potential to break out in the lives of people, harming them and those around them. Second, Judges shows that sin can become the dominant feature of life when people set aside Yahweh's standards. When human beings chart their own path, it is simply a matter of time, opportunity, and circumstance before life becomes stained with some of humanity's most ugly deeds. Third, 1–2 Samuel demonstrates that not even the best of Yahweh's servants are free from sin. Sadly, sins by God's best can harm others in proportion to their prior personal greatness or level of responsibility. Fourth, 1–2 Kings reveals that a whole nation can display a long-term pattern of breaking faith with Yahweh and suffer the consequences that he determines.

All these books introduce readers to faithful persons, and some of these persons appear in Hebrews 11, a decidedly positive text. Nonetheless, any consideration of the doctrine of sin must include these sad facts of sin in human history. Sin lurks, degrades, damages, and defeats individuals and Israel as a whole. Unbelief and rebellion have their way in some measure in every era.

---

[4] The text uses a form of *ḥṭ'*.

Sin's Stain on International History: The Latter Prophets

The Latter Prophets include parts of Israel's and other nations' history from c. 760 to 425 BC. These books interpret and add perspective on the history that Genesis—2 Kings depicts. They begin with Isaiah using most of the terminology found in Exodus 34:6–7 and in the Law and Former Prophets to describe Israel and Judah's faithlessness to God (Isa. 1:1–31). They end with Malachi exhorting readers to follow God's Word given through Moses lest judgment come (Mal. 4:4–6). In between, the books offer extended treatments of Israel's breaking of the Ten Commandments (e.g., Jeremiah 7; 26; Hosea 4), Israel's faithlessness to God (Jeremiah 2–6; Ezekiel 16; 20; and 23; Hosea 1–3; etc.), and Israel's suffering of the consequences of their behavior (Jeremiah 39; 52; Zech. 1:1–6). They particularly demonstrate how Israel's sin takes the shape of cruelty to the poor through injustice and exploitation (Amos 2:4–15; 4:1–5; 6:1–7). In these and other ways they agree fully with the historians who wrote the Former Prophets.

They also declare explicitly that sin's stain extends beyond Israel and that Yahweh judges all nations. Addressing Babylon's future, Isaiah 13:1–22 introduces the subject of worldwide sin by using two of the three major terms found in Exodus 34:6–7. The prophet claims that Yahweh will send a great day of judgment "to destroy its sinners [those who miss the goal] from it" (Isa. 13:9), which includes sinners in Babylon. Yahweh furthermore pledges to "punish the world for its evil, and the wicked for their iniquity [twisting God's truth]" (v. 11). This "day of judgment" is the "day of the Lord" that several prophets highlight as the time (or times) in which people experience specific consequences for sin.[5] On his day, God reasserts his sovereignty over local and international affairs. Malachi 4:5–6 closes the Latter Prophets with the same judgment image, though Malachi aims his message at Jews. In between this introduction and conclusion, Isaiah 13–23, Jeremiah 46–51, Ezekiel 25–32, Joel 3:1–21, Amos 1:3–2:3, Obadiah 1–21, Jonah, Nahum, Habakkuk 2:6–20, and Zephaniah agree with Isaiah and Malachi. Many other passages deserve examination and will be cited as evidence, but this section will analyze briefly three short representative texts: Amos 1:3–2:3; Jonah 3:1–4:2; and Nahum 1:1–8. These last two passages echo Exodus 34:6–7, thereby connecting the Latter Prophets to the Law on these subjects.

---

[5] On the "day of Yahweh," see Paul R. House, "The Day of the Lord," in *Central Themes in Biblical Theology: Mapping Unity in Diversity*, ed. Scott J. Hafemann and Paul R. House (Grand Rapids, MI: Baker Academic, 2007), 179–224; and Paul R. House, "The Day of Yahweh as a Unifying Concept in Isaiah 1–12," *Trinity Journal for Theology and Ministry* 3/1 (Spring 2009): 89–110.

Transgression and the Nations: Amos 1:3–2:3

Amos may be the earliest of the canonical prophetic books. Set c. 760–750 BC during the reign of Jeroboam II of Israel, the book presents one of the Old Testament's strongest treatments of sin's nature, destructiveness, and consequences. Its opening salvo against "transgression" (*pesa*), or "rebellion," the second word of the sin-defining triad in Exodus 34:6–7, nets every one of Israel's neighbors.

Analysis

Having warned readers that Yahweh is roaring from Zion and that the result is mourning and withering below (1:2; see Joel 3:16), Amos exposes "transgressions" in several nations and declares the consequences. As in previous passages, this term refers to rebellion against God, who is these nations' overlord[6] because he is their Creator (see Amos 4:13; 5:8–9; 9:6). In swift succession he addresses the following places for the following rebellions: Damascus (1:3–5; treating people as objects);[7] Gaza (vv. 6–8; delivering exiles over to slavery); Tyre (vv. 9–10; selling allies into slavery);[8] Edom (vv. 11–12; implacable wrath against others); Ammon (vv. 13–15; war atrocities—ripping open pregnant women); and Moab (2:1–3; pursuing revenge even after death). Each transgression receives a severe penalty.

Synthesis

This telling text does not present a "Ten Commandments for Noncovenant Peoples." Nonetheless, it reflects what one would consider basic human decency. Yahweh rejects inhumanity to others, the breaking of one's word to others, the abuse of helpless ones simply to extend a border, and the enslaving of others. In short, Yahweh judges these nations based on the very simple principle that they do things to others that they do not want done to them. One could argue that these people have broken a lower standard than loving one's neighbor. It seems that they do not even keep from abusing their neighbor, which is several moral stages below Leviticus 19:18. These places cannot manage to check their wrath or to value life, the basic ideals stated in the covenant with Noah in Genesis 8:20–9:17. The creator of all the earth will bring them to account.

---

[6] Erling Hammerschaimb, *The Book of Amos: A Commentary*, trans. John Sturdy (Oxford, UK: Basil Blackwell, 1970), 22.

[7] J. A. Motyer, *The Day of the Lion: The Message of Amos*, The Bible Speaks Today (Downers Grove, IL: InterVarsity, 1974), 39–40. In other words, Damascus threshes Gilead as if the people there were wheat. This metaphor most likely reflects war atrocities.

[8] Peter C. Craigie, *Twelve Prophets*, vol. 1, Daily Study Bible (Philadelphia: Westminster, 1984), 131.

Repentance and the Nations: Jonah 3:1–4:2

Jonah has long provided fodder for all sorts of debates. It is not necessary to survey those battles here. What all readers should agree on is that Jonah represents an extraordinary mission[9] on Yahweh's part. Yahweh sends a prophet to Nineveh to proclaim judgment so that this Assyrian city will turn to him. Yahweh offers grace to these Assyrians on the same basis as he does to Israel in Exodus 34:6–7, Numbers 14:18–19, and Joel 2:12–17. Their repentance represents their acceptance of Yahweh's rule over them.

Analysis

When Jonah at long last reaches Nineveh, he preaches that judgment will occur in forty days (3:4). It is possible that this verse summarizes a much more detailed message, for the people believe (v. 5) and the whole city fasts to show that they know that they have sinned and are subject to punishment (vv. 5–8). The king expresses what they all hope, which is that Yahweh will relent of the disaster that he had threatened (v. 9). Their hopes are realized, for Yahweh indeed "relents" (v. 10), or "takes comfort" that he does not need to judge.[10] Yahweh shows the type of compassion and covenant-type love that he has shown Israel. His love does not apply only to the kingdom of priests.

Yahweh's kindness angers Jonah. Though the text does not state a specific reason for this anger, Jonah may accuse Yahweh of clearing the guilty. In a statement that includes a quotation of Exodus 34:6–7, Jonah registers his anger at Yahweh's character (4:2). Given Yahweh's graciousness and willingness to forgive, he did not wish to preach, for he likely thinks that Nineveh deserves punishment.[11] Though Jonah acts badly, Yahweh explains his desires to him. Yahweh has pity for Nineveh (vv. 10–11), just as he has pity for Israel. This pity begins with the announcement of sin, requires faith to accept, involves repentance for past sins, and reflects Yahweh's character.

Synthesis

It is tempting to focus on God's forgiveness in Jonah, since that is the book's major message. Still, for the purposes of this essay, it is necessary

---

[9] For a comprehensive discussion of how the Bible portrays God's redemptive mission in the world, see Christopher J. H. Wright, *The Mission of God: Unlocking the Bible's Grand Narrative* (Downers Grove, IL: InterVarsity, 2006).

[10] For an explanation of this reading of 3:10, see Paul R. House, "God's Character and the Wholeness of Scripture," *SBET* 23 (Spring 2005): 9–11.

[11] See Joyce Baldwin, "Jonah," in *The Minor Prophets, an Exegetical and Expository Commentary*, vol. 2, ed. Thomas E. McComiskey (Grand Rapids, MI: Baker, 1993), 584.

to observe that this forgiveness is needed because of Nineveh's admitted sin. Yahweh does not state Nineveh's specific sins, but he does say that the people there do not know their left hand from their right, presumably in the area of morality (4:10–11). As time passed, Assyria became known for all sorts of specific sins that Isaiah, Nahum, Zephaniah, and others expose. Nineveh's change of heart and action reflects their belief that they had transgressed as surely as the places in Amos 1:3–2:3 had.

Judgment and the Nations: Nahum 1:1–8

Yahweh's unwillingness to let guilty parties go free is highlighted in Nahum 1:1–8 but is balanced by the other characteristics that Exodus 34:6–7 mentions. The first verse announces that Nineveh is the subject of the book. Readers are thus alerted to passages ranging from the grace shown Nineveh in Jonah to the threats of judgment in other books noted above. By the second verse, readers grasp that Yahweh has no more patience with Nineveh, the seat of the great oppressing nation of Assyria. Yahweh will hold the world's most important capital accountable for its actions. This introductory section of Nahum has two parts, both of which carry the same fearsome message that sin in Nineveh has led to its downfall.

Analysis

In 1:1–5, the text includes various echoes of Exodus.[12] The prophet states that Yahweh is "a jealous and avenging God" (v. 2a), a concept from Exodus 20:5–6. Ralph Smith notes that to many current readers, this phraseology implies that Yahweh engages in "private retaliation."[13] He counters this notion by writing that in the ancient context, these terms most often referred to a person or group defending one of its own.[14] So Yahweh does not judge Nineveh to avenge some wrong done just to him, but wrongs done to Israel and the other nations in the Assyrian empire. Nahum continues, "Yahweh is avenging concerning his adversaries, but controls his anger[15] toward his adversaries. Yahweh is slow to anger and great in power, but Yahweh will by no means clear the guilty" (vv. 2b–3a). The phrase "slow to anger" appears in Exodus 34:6, and the phrase "will by no means clear the guilty" occurs in 34:7. Having stated Yahweh's kindness

---

[12] Donald E. Gowan, *Theology of the Prophetic Books: The Death and Resurrection of Israel* (Louisville: Westminster John Knox, 1998), 90.
[13] Ralph Smith, *Micah–Malachi*, WBC 32 (Waco, TX: Word, 1984), 73.
[14] Ibid.
[15] For this translation, see Ludwig Koehler and Walter Baumgartner, *The Hebrew and Aramaic Lexicon of the Old Testament*, vol. 1, rev. ed. (Leiden, UK: Brill, 2001), 695.

and justice, Nahum in 1:3b–5 proceeds to express God's power over creation in ominous terms that prepare readers for judgment imagery.

In verses 6 to 8, the prophet asserts that Yahweh is good (v. 7). He is good to those who take refuge in him (v. 7b) but pursues his enemies as long as necessary (v. 8). Those in relationship with Yahweh enjoy his protection, but those who are not face a very negative future. Clearly, Nineveh's deeds have placed it outside friendship with Yahweh. Trust in God is the key to this confession. Elizabeth Achtemeier writes, "In trouble and affliction and persecution, faith knows that God is good—that all his history with his people has been the working out of his goodness."[16] God's enemies cannot confess and experience what faith alone proves true.

As the book proceeds, Nahum explains that Nineveh shows itself Yahweh's enemy by plotting against him (v. 9). They plot against him by endlessly shedding blood (2:12; 3:1) and by breaking alliances (3:4). War, violence, oppression, and deceit had become normal for Nineveh. This significant city had come to embody all the sins of all the places that Amos 1:3–2:3 highlights. Though Yahweh is good, kind, compassionate, and slow to anger, he must judge lest the guilty escape.

Synthesis

Nahum asserts that Yahweh does not show favoritism when defining and punishing sin. He holds the greatest city of its day accountable, just as he does lesser cities like Gaza, Damascus, and Jerusalem (see Amos 1:3–2:16). Nineveh's sins are like those that Isaiah accuses Jerusalem of in Isaiah 1:1–31. Nineveh and Jerusalem have engaged in violence, oppression, mistreatment of the poor, and greed. The creator of the world does not show favoritism. Nahum's message is that sin will be punished wherever it is found. Yahweh does not mistreat Nineveh to Israel's advantage, nor does he treat the kingdom of priests more harshly than others. Sin remains breaking God's Word because one does not believe Yahweh's words. What the king of Nineveh confessed in Jonah was long neglected or forgotten there by Nahum's time.

Conclusion

The Former and Latter Prophets agree in their view of sin in human history. The Former Prophets assert that person after person and generation after generation of Israelites have broken the various commandments

---

[16] Elizabeth Achtemeier, *Nahum–Malachi*, Interpretation (Atlanta: John Knox, 1986), 9.

that the Law presents. Time and time again, the people in these narratives do not believe God's word to them. They turn to other gods or to alternative ways of worshiping Yahweh. Sadly, 2 Kings 17:7–23 bears out the seriousness of the warnings in Leviticus 26:14–45 and Deuteronomy 28:15–68. Idolatry, violence, injustice, mistreatment of one another—especially the poor and defenseless—sexual immorality, and perverting God's word all occur in these accounts. Not even those who walk closest to God live sinless lives.

The Latter Prophets present great messages about Judah's and Israel's sins. They interpret the Law for generations of hearers and readers in Israel. But they do not just address sin in Israel. They have a universal vision of sin that mirrors their universal vision of salvation (see Isa. 19:16–25). The ancient nations knew of Yahweh and Israel's claims about him. With some notable exceptions, though, the peoples of the nations simply did not believe those claims. Frankly, they did not live up to the ethical standards that their own cultures devised either. They abused the trust of other nations. They committed acts of violence that they would decry or avenge if the same were done to them. No nation keeps its own standards, much less Yahweh's. In short, the Former and Latter Prophets claim that there is no question that the nations, no less than Israel, stand as sinners in need of grace before Yahweh, the creator and redeemer of all persons.

The Writings: Sin's Personal and Corporate Depths

The books in the Writings are much more diverse than those in the Law and the Prophets. They range in genre from proverbs to narratives. They range in time from Moses to the postexilic era. Subjects covered include everything from advice for the young to comfort for the old. Intertwined into all these creative theological works one finds sin in all its various shapes and types. Psalms contains many confessions and descriptions of sin. Job begins with a deadly array of crimes against Job. Proverbs states how wisdom includes knowing what sin is and does. Ruth is the most "sin free" of the books in the Writings, followed by Song of Solomon, the most guilt free of the group. Ecclesiastes breaks this pleasant interlude by demonstrating how many ways that an intelligent person can neglect God's ways. Lamentations confesses the sins that brought Jerusalem to destruction, and Esther displays the many ways that exiles face the inhumanity of their captors. Daniel confesses the sins that he and his countrymen have committed that led to their exile, and Ezra and Nehemiah do the same. Though more positive than 1–2 Kings in many ways, 1–2 Chronicles provides a fitting end to the canon's comprehensive treatment of sin by noting one last time how repeated rebellion against God led to Israel's demise. To be sure, these books are not devoid of hope. They share the whole Bible's belief in redemption. Yet taken together they unearth the depths of human failure.

Given this wealth of material, it is once again hard to choose the best way to proceed. Several angles of vision could provide an accurate portrayal of this section's contribution to the biblical doctrine of sin. Yet perhaps confession, one of the segment's most comprehensive and heartfelt genres, connects the most vital contributions that the books make. Broadly speaking, "confessions" of many varieties exist in the Writings. Psalms contains numerous examples of individual and corporate confessions of sin and of laments over how a person has suffered for the sins of others. Job conveys confessions of sin by Job, not just complaints against God. Proverbs has fewer examples, but 30:1–9 includes the confession of a person who has failed to be wise. Ecclesiastes is one long confession of failed attempts to find wisdom outside of God's teachings. Lamentations presents five very connected laments that express sin, sorrow, and cries for deliverance. Ezra and Nehemiah include passages in which prayers concerning past and present sin and calls for help figure prominently. In many of these instances, the writer elaborates on sins committed, the motives and origins of those sins, and the consequences related to the sins depicted. As a way of collecting the Old Testament instruction on sin, this part of the chapter will focus on Psalm 51 and Nehemiah 9:1–38. The former is a detailed confession by an individual, and the latter is an extensive confession by the people of God. Both these texts utilize language found in Exodus 34:6–7, and both point to the need for redemption found throughout the Bible.

The Depths of Individual Sin: Psalm 51

Psalm 51 is probably the most outstanding example of confessed sin in the Psalter. Though any conclusion on its original usage is debatable, the constant first-person references indicate that it was penned as an individual prayer. Hermann Gunkel rightly labels Psalm 51 a "penitential psalm,"[17] for it portrays the inner struggle of a worshiper of Yahweh to confess his sin and find his way back to God. This psalm includes rich

---

[17] Hermann Gunkel, *What Remains of the Old Testament and Other Essays*, trans. A. K. Dallas (New York: Macmillan, 1928), 106.

metaphors related to the consequences of sin. The one praying mentions a broken spirit, crushed spiritual bones, and feeling the loss of God's presence. He confesses that his sins began the moment that he was conceived, have their roots in his sin-diseased heart, and are manifested as rebellion against a righteous creator and redeemer. At key places in the passage, the one praying uses language found in Exodus 34:6–7 to describe what he has done and what he needs from God.

Analysis

The psalm's superscription places it after David's sin with Bathsheba and the resulting murder of her husband, Uriah (see 2 Sam. 11:1–27). It is impossible to know if this was the exact setting, but the passage's sentiments fit that situation. It also fits other situations that involve multiple serious sins. The chapter has as many as six parts: a plea for mercy (Ps. 51:1–2); a confession of sin (vv. 3–6); a prayer for forgiveness (vv. 7–9); a request for inner renewal (vv. 10–12); a request for renewed joy and thanksgiving (vv. 13–17); and a prayer for Jerusalem (vv. 18–19). While the whole psalm matters for understanding sin and forgiveness, the first twelve verses contain the most relevant details about sin.

The psalmist lays the foundation for his prayer in verses 1 and 2. He addresses God, for "he realizes that he is wholly dependent on God in everything. This is why the forgiveness of sins is equivalent to the restoration of the broken relationship with God, which forms an essential part of his life."[18] He needs a restored relationship with God. In the initial verse he uses four terms related to God's character found in Exodus 34:6–7. He asks Yahweh to "be gracious" according to his "covenant-type mercy," and according to the multitude of his "compassion" to "blot out" his "rebellions" (or, "transgressions"). In the next verse he continues his elaboration of his sins, adding "my iniquity" (or, "the twisting of God's Word") and "my sin" (or, "missing of the goal that God set") to "my transgressions" from the previous verse. Only God's kind character can bail him out of the web of rebellion that he has woven. In short, he prays for himself in a similar manner that Moses prayed for the Israelites in Numbers 14:18–19. He admits that he has committed every category of negative behavior that Yahweh says he forgives in Exodus 34:6–7.

In Psalm 51:3–6, the writer makes his culpability for what he has done quite plain. As he does so, he continues to use the same three terms for

---

[18] Artur Weiser, *The Psalms*, OTL, trans. Herbert Hartwell (Philadelphia: Westminster, 1962), 402.

sin and even adds a fourth, "doing wrong" (or, "evil"). He begins by stating in verse 3 that his sin is always before him; it "looms up as an accusing presence."[19] He portrays his failures as a dangerous creature ready to stalk, threaten, and kill him. In verse 4 he once again expresses his realization that his sin is first and foremost an act against Yahweh. He is not so presumptuous as to claim that his sin did not wrong other people. Rather, he states that his sin is ultimately against the one who makes and regulates the behavior of human beings. Next, in verse 5 he notes that his sin goes back to his conception, which may mean that he recognizes sin's ongoing staining of human existence (original sin) or that he admits that he has sinned from the moment he existed, or both. Regardless, it is clear that he confesses that there is no time in his life that sin has not been part of what he did. As J. A. Motyer writes, "The purpose of the verse is to reveal that as far back as the personal entity, David, can be traced, he has been (lit.) 'in iniquity' (51:5a), 'in sin' (51:5b). Sin is undeniably a fact of life and experience, but it is also a fact of inheritance and of personality."[20] In verse 6 he recognizes that his sins begin in his "inward being," in his "heart." Thus, there is no part of him unaffected. Sin starts internally and works outward.

The psalmist reemphasizes sin's origins in the heart in his prayers for forgiveness in verses 7–12. He asks Yahweh the creator to "create in me a clean heart" (v. 10). He reckons that without Yahweh's presence to guide him, all is lost (v. 11). He knows that no joy or willingness to remain faithful can occur unless God re-creates him from the inside (v. 12). Greater loyalty and fidelity to God ("a right spirit") must come as a gift from God (v. 12). As before, sin is internal before it is external. People sin by rebelling against God. The only remedy is God's kind character showing itself through pardoning, purifying, and blotting out rebellion's effects. All ability to minister to others (vv. 13–19) must flow from Yahweh's cleansing and restoring work.

Synthesis

This passage shows the depths of sin in an individual's life. Sin is not simply on the surface of personal events. Sin comes from the heart, from the inner recesses of people's beings. This psalm agrees with earlier canonical texts. In particular it resonates with Jeremiah 17:5, 9–10: "Thus says the LORD,

---

[19] Derek Kidner, *Psalms 1–72*, TOTC (Downers Grove, IL: InterVarsity, 1978), 190.
[20] J. A. Motyer, *Look to the Rock: An Old Testament Background to Our Understanding of Christ* (Leicester, UK: Inter-Varsity, 1996), 133.

'Cursed is the man who trusts in man and makes flesh his strength, whose heart turns away from the LORD.' . . . The heart is deceitful above all things, and desperately sick; who can understand it? 'I the LORD search the heart and test the mind, to give every man according to his ways, according to the fruit of his deeds.'" It also affirms other passages in Psalms, such as 14:1–3 and 53:1–3, that claim that all people sin. If one looks for a human being whose heart has never strayed from God, one will look in vain.

In both texts, sin begins when one's trust strays from Yahweh. It takes root in the heart. Since God alone knows and can heal the heart, it is to God that worshipers must go when they sin. Left unchecked, sin can lead to "bloodguiltiness" (51:14) and to a "desperately sick" soul, which is the worst disease that humans can contract. Renewed trust in God through his life-giving pardon is the healing that must occur. Both texts also imply that individual sins do not often remain private. They spill over into other peoples' lives, and they cause great damage (v. 14). The sooner sin is recognized and dealt with, the better. A restored relationship with God is the gateway to loving one's neighbor again.

The Ravages of Corporate Sin: Nehemiah 9:1–38

Nehemiah comes near the end of the Hebrew canon, and its setting reflects some of the latest days that the Old Testament recounts. In the mid-fifth century BC, Nehemiah led efforts to restore Jerusalem's walls, population, priesthood, and corporate worship. In Nehemiah 8–9, the people gather to hear God's Word, confess sin, and renew their covenant vows. Priests lead a communal prayer that summarizes the sins that they and their fathers committed. Their prayer provides a fitting summary of the Old Testament's teachings on sin and its ravages on Israel.

Analysis

In 9:1–38, the people offer a corporate prayer that testifies to Yahweh's greatness, their ancestors' sins, and their own failings. This historical summary parallels 2 Kings 17, Psalm 78, Psalms 104–106, and Psalms 135–136. As for Yahweh, the people confess that he is the creator (Neh. 9:6), the one who made a covenant with Abraham (vv. 7–8), the one who delivered Israel from Egypt (vv. 9–11), the one who helped them survive in the desert (vv. 12–21), and the one who gave them the Promised Land.[21]

---

[21] This outline is suggested in M. A. Throntveit, *Ezra–Nehemiah*, Interpretation (Louisville: Westminster John Knox, 1992), 103.

He gave them "right rules and true laws, good statutes and command-ments" (v. 13). He can also help them face depressing life with restored hope in postexilic Jerusalem (vv. 32–37). The key to their future is cov-enant renewal now (v. 38).

As for their fathers' and their own deeds, their fathers "acted presump-tuously and stiffened their necks" in that they disobeyed God's commands (v. 16). They rebelled against God and Moses. Citing Exodus 34:6–7, the people confess that if Yahweh were not "a God ready to forgive, gracious and merciful, slow to anger and abounding in steadfast love" and unwill-ing to forsake them, they would have been lost (Neh. 9:17; see Ex. 34:6–7; Num. 14:18–19). They later add that if he were not "gracious and merci-ful" (Neh. 9:31), another echo of Exodus 34:6–7, he would have destroyed them. Once in the land, their ancestors rebelled. They rejected God's laws and killed God's prophets (Neh. 9:26). The current generation has likewise "acted wickedly" (v. 33), yet another way of describing sinful behavior. The people of Ezra and Nehemiah's days know that they suffer the punish-ments for what they have done (v. 37). They are not simply suffering for their ancestors' sins; they have contributed to their own dire situation.

Synthesis

Because it is a summary passage, Nehemiah 9:1–38 continues to stress many previous truths about sin. I will not recount all of those again now. But it is important to note at least one particular contribution that this passage makes. Nehemiah 9:1–38 and passages like Lamentations 5 in-dicate that Old Testament writers do not share contemporary Western views of time and responsibility that consider the past irrelevant to sin and its sorrows. Nehemiah argues that the sins committed long ago con-tinue to plague his generation. Actions taken decades ago affect persons unborn for good or ill. People long dead influence people alive now. Sin-ning can become a way of life in a nation's history. People's sins can per-vade the culture, making disobedience to God's Word a more natural course of action than it would have been under different conditions. Then people's sins become more obvious, more callous and brazen. People kill God's messengers, they mistreat one another, and they turn to false gods. Individual sins continue to matter in such settings, but corporate sins do as well. Both must be taken extremely seriously to avoid a lack of account-ability in either area.

Furthermore, wise people take stock of the history of sin. They exam-ine how long-term local and national practices have contributed to sinful behavior. They note the people who still provide a negative influence as well as look for positive examples of how to serve God. They observe how what once looked innocuous in the general scheme of things becomes something terrible over time. Israel's history of sin did not unfold in a day, or even in a decade. Their sins slowly became the source of the people's worst disasters. By Nehemiah's time, postexilic Israel could see all this. Their confession reflects careful thinking and hard-earned wisdom.

Conclusion

A. N. Wilson reports that C. S. Lewis claimed that writing *The Screwtape Letters* was tiring, "entailing as it did the ceaseless identification of himself with the malign and diabolic point of view."[22] Wilson proceeds to praise Lewis for expressing the demon's perspective *"without* succumbing to his terrible outlook."[23] Writing and reading about sin can be similarly tiring, for it forces readers and writers to face squarely our common human spiritual disease (see Jer. 17:9). It requires us to succumb to God's outlook on our serial faithlessness to him and its effects on us, on others, and on the world around us. Frankly, it is easier to look away from sin's wreckage to more positive topics, preferably to God's redemptive work in Christ. But taking God's perspective on sin requires perseverance. It is in that spirit that this section offers five summative statements about sin in the Old Testament.

First, sin is perversion. It is not part of God's good creation described in Genesis 1–2. It distorts the people whom God made and thus the world over which they exercise stewardship (1:26–28). Sin harms people's relationship with God, with one another, and with their environment (3:16–19). There is nothing fortunate about humanity's fall from sinless to sinful.

Second, sin is active. That is, people sin by thinking, planning, and doing the things that God has prohibited and by not doing the good things that God commands. Sin amounts to twisting the truth, rebelling against God, and purposefully missing God's goals (Ex. 34:6–7). It rejects God's grace, mercy, longsuffering, and justice (Ex. 34:6–7).[24] Thus, as Joyce Baldwin writes, "In the Old Testament the wrath of God is directed towards people, not to sin in the abstract, if there could be such a thing."[25] People sin deliberately. They are responsible for their actions.

---

[22] A. N. Wilson, *C. S. Lewis: A Biography* (London: HarperCollins: 1991), 178.
[23] Ibid.; emphasis added.
[24] John Goldingay, *Old Testament Theology*, vol. 2: *Israel's Faith* (Downers Grove, IL: InterVarsity, 2006), 254–55.
[25] Joyce Baldwin, *Haggai, Zechariah, Malachi*, TOTC (Downers Grove, IL: InterVarsity, 1972), 90.

God's punishment of sin always has redemption in mind, for it seeks to effect repentance. As Baldwin adds, Yahweh always saw "reason for hope in the present and future."[26]

Third, sin is relational. When one sins, it is because that person, due to a lack of trust in God, rejects love of God and/or love of neighbor as defined in the Bible. It is a violation of a covenant, comparable to adultery in marriage. Sins committed by people harm people; sins committed by nations harm other nations. Broken relationships lead to and are caused by idolatry, lies, adultery, and coveting.

Fourth, sin is pervasive. Sin scars every person and portion of life. The amount of instruction in the Bible is amazing. This breadth reflects God's grace in showing people who sin how to live in a world that they and their ancestors have harmed. Yet the scope of God's teaching indicates the multitude of ways one may sin. Because sin begins in the human heart and mind, the types and effects of sin are as varied and creative as the human mind can conceive, and they are as dangerous as human opportunity allows. Twisting, rebelling, and missing God's standards pertain to any and every human activity and are practiced at some level by every human being. These actions are so prevalent that they become a way of life, a sphere in which one walks (see Romans 7).

Fifth, sin is deadly. It harms what it touches, and it can kill wherever it goes. Left without remedy, it brings physical and eternal punishment. As Nahum 1:1–8 indicates, Yahweh is good and gracious to those who trust in him. But he pursues his enemies until they are subdued in darkness (see Isa. 66:18–24).

Because these principles are so sobering, they magnify God's redemptive work in Jesus Christ. Christians cannot really fathom all that it means to have forgiveness through the saving blood of Jesus. There is no way to fully comprehend how much each person sins and how those sins harm life. So there is no way to thank God fully for what he has provided. Once again, only by faith can one respond to God's promises, covenants, and teaching. Sheer divine grace alone prevails against sin.

---

[26] Ibid.

4

SIN IN THE GOSPELS, ACTS, AND HEBREWS TO REVELATION

ROBERT W. YARBROUGH

The focus of this chapter will be the New Testament apart from the Pauline epistles. Paul's writings will be treated in the next chapter. In each of the first three sections below we will consider (1) the Gospels, (2) Acts, and (3) the books of the New Testament from Hebrews to Revelation. Eight of the nine New Testament books from Hebrews to Revelation are letters. In this chapter when referring to them as a group we will call them the General Epistles.[1] A fourth and final section will sum up the findings of this chapter.

A preliminary word: even before we probe descriptions of sin as provided by various New Testament words[2] and passages, we can doubtless agree that sin in the broad sense of "wrongdoing" is not just a New Testament issue. It is as real as the front pages of daily newspapers. In early 2012, the North American world of professional sports was shaken by revelations that National Football League coaches in New Orleans had placed "bounties" on the star players of opposing teams. The defensive players of the New Orleans Saints were offered cash incentives to injure quarterbacks such as Brett Favre and Kurt Warner. Even supporters of "old school" or "smashmouth" football could agree this was ethically heinous. The recreational activity of spectator sports is too often corrupted by wrongdoing on massive scales and to shocking degrees.

Much more gravely, also in early 2012, the apparent massacre of

---

[1] For an excellent survey and in-depth study of these books see Karen Jobes, *Letters to the Church: A Survey of Hebrews and the General Epistles* (Grand Rapids, MI: Zondervan, 2011).
[2] For a summary of much of the relevant data see Colin Brown, ed., *NIDNTT* (Grand Rapids, MI: Zondervan, 1978), 3:573–87.

Afghan civilians by an American soldier sparked *New York Times* columnist David Brooks to reflect that such acts seem inexplicable for those who hold to today's prevalent view that "most people are naturally good, because nature is good. The monstrosities of the world are caused by the few people (like Hitler or Idi Amin) who are fundamentally warped and evil."[3] But Brooks goes on to note that "in centuries past most people would have been less shocked by the homicidal eruptions of formerly good men. That's because people in those centuries grew up with a worldview that put sinfulness at the center of the human personality." From this viewpoint, Brooks concludes, this United States soldier, if proven guilty,

> like all of us, is a mixture of virtue and depravity. His job is to struggle daily to strengthen the good and resist the evil, policing small transgressions to prevent larger ones. If he didn't do that, and if he was swept up in a whirlwind, then even a formerly good man is capable of monstrous acts that shock the soul and sear the brain.

The daily news at all levels is full of reminders that people in all places, cultures, and walks of life do things that are widely regarded as wrong. This is one reason why reflection on what the New Testament says about wrongdoing or sin is a timely and profitable exercise. The New Testament offers extensive input on what "wrongdoing" is, how God confronted it in his Son and in revelatory writings that Christians call Scripture, and how through faith in Jesus human wrongdoing can be forgiven. Moreover, wrongdoers can be transformed into people who replace their wrongdoing with good, no longer serving darkness but walking in increasing compliance with the God who is light and in whom there "is no darkness at all" (1 John 1:5).

If this is true, then problems plaguing the world today may find solutions in the New Testament's stories and teachings, for the more people who find this light and walk in it, the less that darkness will enjoy uncontested dominance in extending its devastating tentacles into lives, societies, and nations. That is the benefit in purely horizontal terms. Thinking vertically, the more that this happens, the more that the true and living God will receive the glory that he deserves.

---

[3] David Brooks, "When the Good Do Bad," *New York Times*, March 19, 2012. http://www.nytimes.com/2012/03/20/opinion/brooks-when-the-good-do-bad.html?r=3&hp. Accessed March 26, 2012. All quotations in this paragraph are from this article.

Indirect Evidence of Sin:
The Invitation to Repentance and Conversion

As will be shown below, the New Testament offers a rich collection of words that point directly to sin in its various types and forms. But before examining that evidence, we need to note the framework in which that evidence takes shape. The New Testament contains ubiquitous pointers to sin by its frequent and widespread calls for repentance and conversion.

The Gospels

When John the Baptist makes his appearance, his first recorded words are, "Repent, for the kingdom of heaven is at hand" (Matt. 3:2). This statement implies two things. First, there is a kingdom that people need to enter. Apparently they are presently outside it; they are in some sense lost or estranged. Second, to enter this kingdom repentance is necessary. A condition for repentance is acknowledgment of sin, as we see a few verses later: "And they were baptized by him in the river Jordan, confessing their sins" (v. 6). The fiery prophet John recognized sin in his listeners and called on them to confront it. This is true not only of the masses but even of the social and religious leaders: "When he saw many of the Pharisees and Sadducees coming to his baptism, he said to them, 'You brood of vipers! Who warned you to flee from the wrath to come?'" (v. 7). To avoid this wrath people must not only repent but "bear fruit in keeping with repentance" (v. 8). This implies abandoning certain wrong attitudes and actions and adopting others. It implies forsaking sin and replacing it with what is right.

Throughout Matthew's Gospel there is a stress on repentance, not only in John's preaching but even more so in that of Jesus. For Jesus as for John, sin is a major issue. Jesus preaches repentance as his ministry gets underway (4:17). He targets not only individuals but towns such as Chorazin and Bethsaida (11:21) with this message: "Then he began to denounce the cities where most of his mighty works had been done, because they did not repent" (v. 20). Jesus commends the repentance of Nineveh (see the Old Testament book of Jonah) and reproaches the hardness of his hearers (12:41), for as Isaiah prophesied, they refuse to "turn" (or repent) and be saved (13:15). Like John the Baptist, Jesus calls for a decisive shift or conversion to enter the kingdom he came to announce: "Truly, I say to you, unless you turn and become like children, you will never enter the kingdom of heaven" (18:3). Near the end of Jesus' earthly ministry he reproaches the religious leaders for not believing the Baptist's message. Even when they saw "the tax collectors and the prostitutes" responding to John's preaching, they "did not afterward change [their] minds and believe him" (21:32). This "change of mind" is repentance. It was a condition of rescue from sin that many of Jesus' (and John's) hearers were unwilling to perform.

Mark's Gospel echoes Matthew's in recording that first John the Baptist and then Jesus preached "repentance for the forgiveness of sins" (Mark 1:4; the words are from the Baptist) and "repent and believe in the gospel" (Jesus in v. 15). Also like Matthew, Mark reports that Jesus applied Isaiah's insight that among his listeners would be many who would refuse to "turn and be forgiven" (Mark 4:12). This lament is based on the conviction that the generation and the individuals to whom Jesus came were mired in sin. Mark goes beyond Matthew in stating that when Jesus commissioned the Twelve and sent them out to preach (6:7–13), "they went out and proclaimed that people should repent" (v. 12). The twelve imitated Jesus in their conviction that all persons need to acknowledge sin, repent, and believe in the good news that Jesus announced and embodied.

It should be noted in all of this that the Gospels record preaching primarily by Jews (i.e., John the Baptist, Jesus, Jesus' disciples) to other Jews. From the Bible's perspective, the Jews had for centuries possessed "the oracles of God" (see Rom. 3:2). In that respect, they had more knowledge from and about God than other peoples on the earth. If anyone should have been "better" and less susceptible to sin, it was these people. Yet it is precisely to these people that so many calls to "repent!" are addressed. If the Jews of Jesus' day were so sinful in God's sight, how much more dire was the predicament of all other peoples, who from Scripture's perspective were "having no hope and without God in the world" (Eph. 2:12)?

Early in Luke's Gospel the theme of "turning" or conversion is broached. The angel announces to Zechariah that the offspring of Elizabeth and him "will turn many of the children of Israel to the Lord their God" (1:16). He will "turn the hearts of the fathers to the children, and the disobedient to the wisdom of the just, to make ready for the Lord a people prepared" (v. 17). It is accordingly no surprise that their son John proclaims "a baptism of repentance for the forgiveness of sins" (3:3) and calls for "fruits in keeping with repentance" (v. 8).

In Luke's Gospel Jesus explicitly connects his ministry to repentance due to sin: "I have not come to call the righteous but sinners to repentance" (5:32). The stakes in this call are gravely lofty: "Unless you repent, you will all likewise perish" (13:3, 5). When there is repentance, there is heavenly joy that sin's condemnation has been lifted: "There will be . . . joy in heaven over one sinner who repents. . . . Just so, I tell you, there is joy before the angels of God over one sinner who repents" (15:7, 10). In Jesus' understanding of life among his followers, what we call the church, repentance and sin are critical issues: "Pay attention to yourselves! If your brother sins, rebuke him, and if he repents, forgive him" (17:3).

Luke's equivalent to Matthew's Great Commission (Matt. 28:18–20) connects the gospel message, repentance, and sin: Jesus "said to them, 'Thus it is written, that the Christ should suffer and on the third day rise from the dead, and that repentance and forgiveness of sins should be proclaimed in his name to all nations, beginning from Jerusalem'" (Luke 24:46–47).

John's Gospel contrasts with the previous three by not using the "repent/repentance" word group. Yet John echoes Jesus' lament drawn from Isaiah that the people would not "turn" or convert (12:40). And John's Gospel is informed by Jesus' conviction that people languish in darkness and need to come to his light:

> Jesus said to them, "The light is among you for a little while longer. Walk while you have the light, lest darkness overtake you. The one who walks in the darkness does not know where he is going. While you have the light, believe in the light, that you may become sons of light." (vv. 35–36)

This is conversion, without use of the word. It is the call for life-changing "believing" in Jesus, the Fourth Gospel's signature stress, as forms of the verb "believe" occur about one hundred times. As the quote above shows, there can be no "believing" in John's sense without turning from darkness to light. This is the essence of repentance. Therefore, while John does not use the word, his conviction and Jesus' teaching that the world is in darkness (1:5; 8:12) are eloquent testimony to the prevalence of sin ("people loved the darkness rather than the light because their works were evil"; 3:19) and their need to turn (repent) and by believing find the light: "I have come into the world as light, so that whoever believes in me may not remain in darkness" (12:46).

The Gospels are united in calling for repentance and thereby highlighting the universal implication that people—even the Jews (John 1:11)—languish in darkness and rejection of God. All four Gospels agree in their outlook on the reality and problem of human sin.

Acts

Acts preserves a rich echo of the gospel witness regarding repentance and conversion. "While repentance and conversion are central foci in all the

Gospels, Luke, especially in Acts, seems to highlight these themes just a little more, too."[4] Regarding the latter, Luke uses the word *epistrephō* (I turn, turn around, convert) nearly a dozen times. From the start it is clear that this "turning" comes in conjunction with repenting of sins, as Peter's Acts 3 sermon makes clear: "Repent therefore, and turn back, that your sins may be blotted out" (v. 19). The divine role in sinners' turning or conversion is underscored in the final recorded words of that same sermon: "God, having raised up his servant, sent him to you first, to bless you by turning[5] every one of you from your wickedness" (v. 26).

Sin and condemnation are a factor when Luke employs the related word *strephō* (I turn) in recording Stephen's speech. Stephen charges that his and his hearers' forefathers in Egypt would not obey God "but thrust him aside, and in their hearts . . . turned to Egypt" (7:39). The baleful consequence was a corresponding "turn" on God's part: "God turned away and gave them over to worship the host of heaven" (v. 42). In both of these instances, the "turning" has unpleasant consequences.

Acts's stress, however, is on "turning" or conversion (cf. *epistrephō*) that moves in God's direction and results in his present and eternal blessing. As a result of Peter's healing of Aeneas at Lydda, "all the residents of Lydda and Sharon . . . turned to the Lord" (9:35). Christian presence at Syrian Antioch was established when men from Cyprus and Cyrene preached there, "and the hand of the Lord was with them, and a great number who believed turned to the Lord" (11:21). At Lystra, Paul and Barnabas brought "good news" that their hearers "should turn from" their polytheism "to a living God, who made the heaven and the earth and the sea and all that is in them" (14:15). Luke's summary of the first missionary journey (chaps. 13–14) pictures Paul and Barnabas "describing in detail the conversion of the Gentiles" (15:3).

Since the very nature of the gospel is decided on in Acts 15, it is significant that "turning" or conversion is part of James's concluding endorsement of the apostolic gospel as proclaimed to the Gentiles by Paul: "Therefore my judgment is that we should not trouble those of the Gentiles who turn to God" (v. 19). This corresponds to Paul's defense of his ministry before Agrippa II: he was sent to the Gentiles "to open their eyes, so that they may turn from darkness to light and from the power of Satan to God, that they may receive forgiveness of sin" (26:18).

---

[4] Craig Blomberg, *Jesus and the Gospels* (Grand Rapids, MI: Baker Academic, 2009), 170.
[5] Here Luke uses the cognate word *apostrephō*.

Paul very nearly quotes John the Baptist on the same occasion as he describes how after his own conversion he preached at Damascus, in Jerusalem, throughout Judea, and finally "also to the Gentiles, that they should repent and turn to God, performing deeds in keeping with their repentance" (26:20; cf. 13:24). Acts ends with Paul's grim announcement, drawing on Isaiah, that many of his Jewish listeners are dull of hearing and blind of heart; they cannot (because they will not) "turn" so that God "would heal them" (28:27).

If Acts's stress on turning or conversion implies the inherent sinful status and direction of persons apart from the gospel good news, its frequent mention of repentance is an even more direct indictment of humans in their sin. We have already seen verses above that speak of both turning and repenting of sin (3:19; 26:20). Other key passages confirm the connection between sin and repentance. Before the Sanhedrin Peter says of Christ, "God exalted him at his right hand as Leader and Savior, to give repentance to Israel and forgiveness of sins" (5:31). In Samaria Peter tells Simon the sorcerer, "Repent, therefore, of this wickedness of yours, and pray to the Lord that, if possible, the intent of your heart may be forgiven you" (8:22). In the wake of Cornelius's acceptance of the gospel message, incredulous Jewish believers exclaim, "Then to the Gentiles also God has granted repentance that leads to life" (11:18). At Athens Paul states, "The times of ignorance God overlooked, but now he commands all people everywhere to repent" (17:30). At Ephesus he recalls that "John baptized with the baptism of repentance, telling the people to believe in the one who was to come after him, that is, Jesus" (19:4). Paul summarizes his lengthy ministry at Ephesus as "teaching you in public and from house to house, testifying both to Jews and to Greeks of repentance toward God and of faith in our Lord Jesus Christ" (20:20–21).

We see, then, that in Acts, quite apart from explicit reference to sin (to be treated below), we learn much about the human condition and the remedy for it by frequent mention of conversion and its often stated precondition, repentance. To a lesser but still significant degree, this will be true of the Hebrews to Revelation corpus as well.

Hebrews to Revelation

The Gospels and Acts tell the story of gospel good news going out into settings where people had not heard it and were invited to respond. In such situations, "repentance" and "turning" to God understandably receive frequent mention. The situation shifts with the New Testament letters. They are written primarily to people who have already received the message. We would not expect to find so much talk of repentance and conversion. These are already facts of life for the first readers of these writings.

This is certainly true of the notion of turning to God. The term favored in Luke and Acts, *epistrephō* (I turn, turn back, convert), appears only three times in the General Epistles (James 5:19, 20; 1 Pet. 2:25) and not at all in Revelation. There is a connection with sin in the James and Peter passages, so the implicit affirmation of human sinfulness is present. But it is not pronounced like it was in the Gospels and Acts.

References to repentance are nominally more numerous, though frequent only in Revelation. In the General Epistles, Hebrews groups "repentance from dead works" with "faith toward God" as part of "the elementary doctrine of Christ" (6:1). A few verses later there is mention of the impossibility for those who "have fallen away" to be restored "again to repentance" (v. 6). These fleeting references at least show that the writer shared the conviction of other New Testament authors that humans share in a sinful condition requiring repentance to remedy. Such repentance can be elusive, as Esau discovered when "he found no place for repentance, although he sought it with tears" (12:17, author's translation).

The only other mention of repentance in the General Epistles comes from Peter's observation that "the Lord is not slow to fulfill his promise as some count slowness, but is patient toward you, not wishing that any should perish, but that all should reach repentance" (2 Pet. 3:9). All people, not just some, need to repent. God is patient toward that end. Those who fail to heed this call will perish.

The last book of the New Testament mentions repentance a total of ten times in seven connections. These can be surveyed effectively in tabular form:

References to Repentance in Revelation

Those Called to Repentance	Text/s	Sins Requiring Repentance
Church at Ephesus	2:5	Loss of first love; neglect of works done at first
Church at Pergamum	2:16	Embrace of the false teaching of Balaam and the Nicolaitans
Jezebel and her collaborators in the church at Thyatira	2:21–22	False teaching, sexual immorality, idolatry

Those Called to Repentance	Text/s	Sins Requiring Repentance
Church at Sardis	3:3	Appearance but not reality of spiritual life; dead works not complete in the sight of God
Church at Laodicea	3:19	Pride, complacency, spiritual tepidity
Survivors of the plagues of the sixth trumpet	9:20–21	Evil works, worship of demons and idols; murder, sorcery, sexual immorality, theft
Victims of the fourth and fifth bowls of God's wrath	16:9, 11	Reception of the mark of the beast and worship of its image

The table above shows two things. First, repentance is an issue and often a need in Christ's churches. It is not just an act for those who have not received the gospel. Five of the seven churches of Asia Minor are called to repentance. The two that are not, Smyrna and Philadelphia, are spared this only by persecution (Smyrna) and "patient endurance" (3:10) under indignity and adversity. Second, repentance is needed not just for the general reason that people have sinned, or that sin is in the world, although both of those needs are true and real. Rather, repentance in Revelation is also connected to particular sins. This brings us squarely back to the subject of this chapter, "Sin in the New Testament." We have been arguing that relevant to that subject is the indirect evidence of the New Testament's calls for turning (or conversion) and repentance. These calls are implicit recognition of sin. In Revelation this implicit recognition becomes explicit, as the right-hand column in the table above shows. This is not a comprehensive list of sins for which God judges churches and the world and calls them to repent, of course. But it gives a fairly broad and graphic sketch of ways in which people do wrong in God's sight, sometimes in congregations right under his nose. Revelation affords one final lurid glimpse of what the New Testament describes and condemns as sin.

Words for Sin: the *Hamartia* Group

We now turn to several word-groups that refer to sin, sins, or sinning. Words carry their meaning in sentences, paragraphs, and documents, so it is not words in isolation that will concern us but words as they actually appear and function in the non-Pauline portions of the New Testament. The most prominent word-group is related to the noun *hamartia* (sin). Other words in this group are the verb *hamartanō* (I sin), the noun *hamartēma* (sin, transgression), and the adjective *hamartōlos* (sinful), which is often made into a noun and then means "sinner."

These words occur a total of 176 times in the New Testament outside of Paul's writings. (Paul uses these words a total of ninety-one times.) We can set forth the number of occurrences of these words in each New Testament book as follows:

Matthew	15
Mark	14
Luke	33
John	25
Acts	9
Hebrews	29
James	9
1 Peter	8
2 Peter	3
1 John	27
2–3 John	0[6]
Jude	1
Revelation	3

In this section we will not look at every single occurrence. We will rather characterize how these words are used in each book and what this tells us about our overall subject.

Gospels

In Matthew's opening chapter, an angel reveals that Jesus' very name directly addresses our topic: his earthly father Joseph is told to "call his name Jesus, for he will save his people from their sins" (Matt. 1:21). This mission is confirmed decades later at a meal where "many tax collectors and sinners came and were reclining with Jesus and his disciples" (9:10). Jesus is rebuffed by the Pharisees for this unholy mingling with transgressors. But Jesus defends his action, observing that it is the ailing, not the healthy, who need a doctor. Accordingly, he tells his detractors, "Go and learn what this means, 'I desire mercy, and not sacrifice.' For I came not to call the righteous, but sinners" (v. 13). The New Testament does not minimize or whitewash sin. But neither does it present sin as an insoluble

---

[6] The word for "evil" (*ponēros*) occurs once in 2 John and once in 3 John.

problem, for Jesus came for the sake of sinners. He remained true to this mission despite those who maligned him for it, saying, "Look at him! A glutton and a drunkard, a friend of tax collectors and sinners!" (11:19). In response, Jesus calmly replied in that same verse, "Yet wisdom is justified by her deeds."

Also in Matthew, Jesus shows that he has authority to forgive sins (9:6). "Since *hamartia* [sins] . . . is used in the plural, 'sinful acts' are clearly in mind, rather than sin in the abstract."[7] He counsels his disciples regarding how to deal with sins when they threaten fellowship between brothers: "If your brother sins against you, go and tell him his fault, between you and him alone. If he listens to you, you have gained your brother" (18:15). Since Jesus' willingness to forgive sins is so vast, his followers are empowered to profound depths of forgiveness, not just the seven times that Peter feared (v. 21) but even to seventy-seven times (v. 22).

Jesus' earthly life was ended as the result of being "betrayed into the hands of sinners" (26:45). An example would be Judas, who confesses too late, "I have sinned by betraying innocent blood" (27:4). Nevertheless, there would be hope for those who turned against him and fled like Peter and the others, for Jesus' "blood of the covenant" was "poured out for many for the forgiveness of sins" (26:28).

Mark's Gospel is much shorter than Matthew's but contains almost as many references to the *hamartia* word-group. In general, these references echo insights found in Matthew. Jesus as the Son of Man has authority to forgive sins (2:5–11). He dined with "sinners," was criticized for it, and responded, "I came not to call the righteous, but sinners" (v. 17). Yet despite reaching out to sinners, falling into their hands would be his undoing: at the end of his Gethsemane prayer, he tells his slumbering inner circle, "The Son of Man is betrayed into the hands of sinners" (14:41). While all sins can be forgiven except for blasphemy against the Holy Spirit (3:38–29), in Mark Jesus speaks of "this adulterous and sinful generation" to be judged when the Son of Man returns (8:38).

A note here is in order about "blasphemy against the Holy Spirit," often called "the unpardonable sin." What is this terrible misdeed? Based on those to whom Jesus seemed to attribute it, it appears to have been a state of hardness of heart in which the Holy Spirit's gracious conviction is resisted so long and adamantly that the sinner becomes impervious to God's softening, beckoning love. Sinners' hostility toward God's redemp-

---

[7] Donald Guthrie, *New Testament Theology* (Downers Grove, IL: InterVarsity, 1981), 188.

tive working seats human self-righteousness on the throne of lordship over their souls. No forgiveness is possible because sinners' will to oppose God's gracious Spirit has walled off their lives from God's means of grace. As in the case of Esau (Heb. 13:17) or of some of Jesus' most brazen and entrenched adversaries, the sinner's hard commitment to autonomy proves stronger than his wistful but weaker will to repent.

In both Matthew and Mark, sin is a prominent motif that explains the need for Jesus' coming and defines the predicament of those he came to rescue. Luke's Gospel sounds these same notes. But it contains more than twice as many references to the *hamartia* word-group than either Matthew or Mark. Some of these references are Luke's versions of accounts found in the other two (Luke 3:3; 5:20–21, 23–24, 30, 32; 7:34; 17:3–4). But at twelve points Luke gives fresh information utilizing *hamartia* expressions:

1) Only Luke records Zechariah's Spirit-led prophecy (1:67) that his son John would "give knowledge of salvation to his people in the forgiveness of their sins" (v. 77). John's ministry like Jesus' was bound up in addressing the problem of human sin.

2) Only Luke records Peter's sense of abject sinfulness at the call of the first disciples when a large catch of fish was taken: "But when Simon Peter saw it, he fell down at Jesus' knees, saying, 'Depart from me, for I am a sinful man, O Lord'" (5:8). Peter is often depicted as mercurial, but his deep sense of guilt and unworthiness from early in his relationship with Jesus deserves more attention as a contributing factor to his at-times fanatical zeal. His seeming volatility and instability may have been driven by a desperate, wise, and in fact deeply insightful sense of his sinfulness.

3) Only Luke is explicit about "sinners" (6:32–34) in his version of the Sermon on the Mount. (Matthew's version speaks instead of "tax collectors" and "Gentiles.")

4) Only Luke records Jesus' anointing by a woman at the home of Simon the Pharisee, a woman who was "a sinner" (7:37). A sinner's touching Jesus was scandalous for Simon and discredited Jesus in his eyes (v. 39). But her example of loving contrition despite her many sins (v. 47) testified to the forgiveness of sins that Jesus pronounced: "And he said to her, 'Your sins are forgiven'" (v. 48). This prompted everyone else at the dinner "to say among themselves, 'Who is this, who even forgives sins?'" (v. 49).

5) Only Luke speaks of "sins" in the Lord's Prayer (11:4). (Matthew's version uses "debts.")

6) Only Luke details Jesus' comments when he was told about Pilate's slaughtering some Galileans as they worshiped. Jesus warned his

listeners not to think that those Galileans were "worse sinners" (or "offenders") than all other people (13:2–5).

7) Only Luke records that when Jesus told the parable of the lost sheep, "tax collectors and sinners were all drawing near to hear him" (15:1), so that "the Pharisees and the scribes grumbled, saying, 'This man receives sinners and eats with them'" (v. 2). Disgruntled observers of Jesus aside, there is "joy in heaven" (v. 7) and "before the angels of God over one sinner who repents" (v. 10).

8) Only Luke tells of the Prodigal Son and the redemptive effect of his realization of his sin: "Father, I have sinned against heaven and before you" (15:18, 21). This is the revelation and, on the son's part, contrite humility that made a happy ending to the story possible.

9) Only Luke tells of the Pharisee and the tax collector, the latter of whom was justified when he "would not even lift up his eyes to heaven, but beat his breast, saying, 'God, be merciful to me, a sinner!'" (18:13). Jesus here forcefully and memorably commends a sense of personal sinfulness as fundamental to reconciliation with God.

10) Only Luke tells of Zacchaeus and the consternation of some over Jesus' fraternizing with him as onlookers "grumbled, 'He has gone in to be the guest of a man who is a sinner'" (19:7). Zacchaeus would own up to his sorry track record and take steps to make amends that Jesus would approve (v. 9). Jesus would conclude that Zacchaeus was one of "the lost" whom "the Son of Man came to seek and to save" (v. 10). "Sinner" and "lost" are seen to be synonymous.

11) Only Luke records that the women at the tomb were steadied by "two men . . . in dazzling apparel (24:4) who reminded and reassured them that the Son of Man had to "be delivered into the hands of sinful men" (v. 7).

12) Only Luke makes explicit the role that "forgiveness of sins" plays in the gospel proclamation that Jesus commissions to be taken "in his name to all nations" (24:47).

Like Luke, the Gospel of John contains more references to the *hamartia* word-group than Matthew or Mark. Most of these references are not found in the other three Gospels. For example, John alone records the Baptist's identification of Jesus as "the Lamb of God, who takes away the sin of the world!" (1:29). Only in John do we read of a healed man whom Jesus admonished, "See, you are well! Sin no more, that nothing worse may happen to you" (5:14). He speaks similarly to the woman taken in adultery (8:11). Sin is clearly a matter to which Jesus is not indifferent in the lives of those to whom he ministers.

Sin is a central issue in a sharp conflict between Jesus and religious leaders whom Jesus eventually calls sons of the Devil (8:44) and liars

(v. 55). He tells them they will die in their sin (v. 21) and their sins (v. 24) unless they believe in him. How serious is the human sin problem? "Truly, truly, I say to you, everyone who practices sin is a slave to sin" (v. 34). In Jesus' outlook this applies to all who do not trust in him, as well as to those whose trust is only superficial (see 2:23–25).

Jesus' insight into sin can be trusted since he is free from sin (8:46), though some accuse him of being a sinner (9:16, 24). He draws heavily and authoritatively on his insight in the interchange with the man who was born blind because of someone's sin, according to his disciples (v. 2). Jesus denies the direct tie between blindness and someone's moral failure in this particular case (v. 3). Sin abides in those who think that they can see without the light that only Jesus can provide; their "guilt remains" (v. 41). Sin is not an innocent shortfall but a toxic and damning condition of guilt before God.

Remaining references to sin in the Fourth Gospel are found in the Upper Room Discourse (chaps. 13–17), at Jesus' trial, and after he arose. In the upper room, he states that his opponents are "guilty of sin" because he has "come and spoken to them," and "now they have no excuse for their sin" (15:22). They are guilty not only for rejecting what Jesus said but also for rejecting the implications of the works "done among them . . . that no one else did"; by seeing yet hating both Jesus and the Father, they are "guilty of sin" (v. 24). Jesus promises to send "the Helper," who "will convict the world concerning sin and righteousness and judgment" (16:8).

At Jesus' trial Jesus implies that Pilate is doing wrong in his dealings with Jesus but that the one who handed him over to Pilate "has the greater sin" (19:11). Not all sins are of the same significance and gravity, apparently. At the Johannine "Little Pentecost," where the risen Jesus shows his hands and side and says, "Receive the Holy Spirit" (20:22), Jesus tells the Eleven, "If you forgive the sins of any, they are forgiven them; if you withhold forgiveness from any, it is withheld" (v. 23). Jesus' ministry of helping people deal with their sins is in some sense extended through his apostolic followers. Pronouncements of absolution in (especially liturgical) churches today can be traced back to Jesus' words on this occasion.

Acts

Acts's use of the *hamartia* word-group has already been glimpsed above in passages that speak of both repentance and sin, sins, or sinning (2:38; 3:19; 5:31), or in one case of both turning (converting) and forgiveness of sins (26:18). But there are other explicit references to sin in Acts, too.

Among dying Stephen's last concerns was the guilt of his accusers: "'Lord, do not hold this sin against them.' And when he had said this, he fell asleep" (7:60). The Holy Spirit descended on Cornelius and his relatives and friends (10:24) immediately after Peter said, "To [Jesus of Nazareth] all the prophets bear witness that everyone who believes in him receives forgiveness of sins through his name" (v. 43). A similar pronouncement occurs at the climax of Paul's synagogue sermon at Pisidian Antioch: "Let it be known to you therefore, brothers, that through this man forgiveness of sins is proclaimed to you, and by him everyone who believes is freed from everything from which you could not be freed by the law of Moses" (13:38–39). This passage reminds us of the close relation between sin and the law in terms of guilt and also faith as the means of Jesus' death working its liberating effect.

Acts also recalls how an appointed spiritual guide named Ananias addressed the sin problem of Saul of Tarsus after his Damascus road encounter: "And now why do you wait? Rise and be baptized and wash away your sins, calling on his name" (22:16). At his arraignment before Festus at Caesarea, Paul protests that he has not "sinned" (*hēmarton*) "against the law of the Jews, nor against the temple, nor against Caesar" (25:8). Therefore he is innocent of the trumped-up charges being brought against him. Here "sin" is used in a civil rather than moral or theological sense; hence the ESV translates "committed . . . offense." All human wrongdoing, not just religious infractions, counts as sin.

Hebrews to Revelation

The *hamartia* word-group is prominent in Hebrews, occurring twenty-nine times (see table above). A *hamartia*-based word is found in every chapter of Hebrews except chapter 6. The references can be grouped as follows:

1) *Christ, the ultimate sacrifice for sin.* The Son of God won his exaltation by "making purification for sins," after which he took his honorific seat at God's right hand (1:3; cf. 10:12). His full humanity enabled him to "become a merciful and faithful high priest in the service of God, to make propitiation for the sins of the people" (2:17). In this he resembles the earthly high priest as established in the law of Moses (5:1). But there is a major difference: the earthly high priest "is obligated to offer sacrifice for his own sins just as he does for those of the people" (v. 3). Christ, by contrast, is "holy, innocent, unstained, separated from sinners, and exalted above the heavens" (7:26). Unlike earthly high priests,

he does not need to offer daily sacrifices for himself and the people, "since he did this once for all when he offered up himself" (v. 27; cf. 9:26; 10:11–12).

2) *Warnings about sin.* Israel's example of unbelief and judgment is applied to the readers of Hebrews. They are told to "exhort one another every day, as long as it is called 'today', that none of you may be hardened by the deceitfulness of sin" (3:13). Failure to heed this will prove disastrous: "And with whom was he provoked for forty years? Was it not with those who sinned, whose bodies fell in the wilderness?" (v. 17). The writer puts a still finer point on this later on: "For if we go on sinning deliberately after receiving the knowledge of the truth, there no longer remains a sacrifice for sins" (10:26). Many Old Testament saints realized this and followed a course like that of Moses, who wisely chose "rather to be mistreated with the people of God than to enjoy the fleeting pleasures of sin" (11:25).

3) *Promise and imperative in forsaking sin.* God has promised: "For I will be merciful toward their iniquities, and I will remember their sins no more" (8:12; cf. 10:17). Christ has done what the Old Testament sacrifices only anticipated (10:4). There is no further need of "any offering for sin" (v. 18). But, since "we do not have a high priest who is unable to sympathize with our weaknesses, but one who in every respect has been tempted as we are, yet without sin" (4:15), Christ's work is not merely to be admired. There is need to "lay aside every weight, and sin which clings so closely, and [to] run with endurance the race that is set before us" (12:1). The readers of Hebrews are told, "Consider him who endured from sinners such hostility against himself, so that you may not grow weary or fainthearted" (v. 3). Christ's self-sacrifice for the Father and for God's people sets a high bar for his followers, who are virtually taunted that "in [their] struggle against sin [they] have not yet resisted to the point of shedding [their] blood" (v. 4). Just as according to Old Testament ordinance "the bodies of those animals whose blood is brought into the holy places by the high priest as a sacrifice for sin are burned outside the camp" (13:11), and just as Jesus "suffered outside the gate" (v. 12), believers in Christ are exhorted to "go to him outside the camp and bear the reproach he endured" (v. 13).

There is purpose and hope in this for two reasons. The first reason is who Christ is for those who call on him as their mediator before God: "We do not have a high priest who is unable to sympathize with our weaknesses, but one who in every respect has been tempted as we are, yet without sin" (4:15). The second reason is what Christ will do in the future: "Christ, having been offered once to bear the sins of many, will appear a second time, not to deal with sin but to save those who are eagerly waiting for him" (9:28).

The book of Hebrews keeps the sin problem constantly before the reader's eye. Of significant words found in Hebrews, only three other words are used more times than the word "sin" (twenty-five times).[8] Hebrews is equally persistent in commending Jesus as God's eternal and only solution.

In James sin is given a clear definition: "Whoever knows the right thing to do and fails to do it, for him it is sin" (4:17). Sin is also acts condemned by God's law: "If you show partiality, you are committing sin and are convicted by the law as transgressors" (2:9). Sin is associated with being "double-minded" (*dipsychos*): "Cleanse your hands, you sinners, and purify your hearts, you double-minded" (4:8). Being "double-minded" connotes instability (1:8), among other things. James explains how illicit desire morphs into sin and brings on death: "Desire when it has conceived gives birth to sin, and sin when it is fully grown brings forth death" (v. 15).

Yet sin can be forgiven through prayer and confession (5:15–16). A priority in congregational life should be bringing back sinners from their wanderings, for this saves souls from death and "will cover a multitude of sins" (v. 20). A *hamartia* word ("sins") is, tellingly and memorably, the last word to appear in James's epistle.

In 1 Peter, readers are reminded that Christ "committed no sin" (2:22), he bore believers' sins so they "might die to sin and live to righteousness" (v. 24), and he "suffered once [decisively] for sins . . . to bring us to God" (3:18). Christians should do good and suffer, if necessary, rather than sin and endure the punishment that it brings (2:20). Christ's suffering furnishes his followers with a template for their own lives; a decisive identification with Christ in this respect is tantamount to a decisive break with sin (4:1). The highest priority in congregational life is persistence in love that will overshadow and overwhelm the sins that proliferate in human lives: "Above all, keep loving one another earnestly, since love covers a multitude of sins" (v. 8). First Peter's final mention of sin quotes Proverbs 11:31 to underscore sin's gravity: "If the righteous is scarcely saved, what will become of the ungodly and the sinner?"

Second Peter reminds of the punishment for sin (including hell) that rebellious angels incurred (2:4). It warns against false prophets and teachers who arise in the church. Their description is a colorful mini-guide for describing sin: "They have eyes full of adultery, insatiable for sin. They entice unsteady souls. They have hearts trained in greed. Accursed children!" (v. 14). It is important that believers keep before them their

---

[8] *Theos* (God) appears sixty-eight times, *legō* (I say, speak) forty-four times, *pistis* (faith) thirty-two times.

cleansing from former sins (1:9) and vigorously pursue the divinely bestowed characteristics that make for godliness (vv. 3–8). Knowledge of
sin is not an end in itself, much less a free-standing virtue; it is rather an
entrée to divine cleansing and provocation to pursue all the graces that
constitute righteousness.

First John contains numerous references to the *hamartia* word-group.
Several of these highlight Christ's role in dealing with sin:

- "But if we walk in the light, as he is in the light, we have fellowship with
  one another, and the blood of Jesus his Son cleanses us from all sin" (1:7).
- "If anyone does sin, we have an advocate with the Father, Jesus Christ the
  righteous. He is the propitiation for our sins, and not for ours only but also
  for the sins of the whole world" (2:1b–2).
- "Your sins are forgiven for his name's sake" (v. 12b).
- "You know that he appeared in order to take away sins, and in him there
  is no sin" (3:5).
- "The reason the Son of God appeared was to destroy the works of the
  devil" (v. 8b).
- "God . . . loved us and sent his Son to be the propitiation for our sins" (4:10b).
- "We know that everyone who has been born of God does not keep on sinning, but he who was born of God protects him, and the evil one does not
  touch him" (5:18).

Other passages wrestle with how the believer needs to regard and
deal with sin. Denial is not the solution (1:8, 10); confession is, so that
God may forgive and cleanse (v. 9) by "the blood of Jesus his Son" (v. 7).
Sin can be trivialized, but there is nothing trivial about sin, which is a
manifestation of lawlessness (*anomia*; 3:4). This word can denote not just
falling short of God's moral law (like "sin" often does) but a positive and
extreme rejection of that law. It occurs only fifteen times in the New Testament[9] and sometimes connotes acts or attitudes that attract maximum
divine disapproval and opposition. For example, Paul speaks of "the man
of lawlessness" and "the mystery of lawlessness" (2 Thess. 2:3, 7). Envi-
sioning the day of judgment, Jesus pictures himself banishing pretend-
ers who call him "Lord" but whom he views as "workers of lawlessness"
(Matt. 7:23). In the end times, "because lawlessness will be increased, the
love of many will grow cold" (24:12).

John's equating of "sin" and "lawlessness" in 1 John 3:4 may explain

---

[9] Matt. 7:23; 13:41; 23:38; 24:12; Rom. 4:7; 6:19 (twice); 2 Cor. 6:14; 2 Thess. 2:3, 7, 14; Heb. 1:9; 10:17; 1 John
3:4 (twice).

his statements that make it sound as though believers do not sin (3:6, 9; 5:18; in 2:1 he makes clear that believers may sin). John may be saying that when sin escalates to the point of *anomia* (lawlessness), it is incompatible with the very identity of those who have "been born of God" (3:9). Since 1 John warns against such sins as denial of Jesus as the Christ (2:22) and hatred of fellow believers (vv. 14–15), both of which are surely *anomia*-class transgressions, he may be saying that truly reborn believers who would commit such actions are a contradiction in terms and ultimately not God's children, whatever their claims to Christian belief.

One other challenging reference to *hamartia* (sin) in 1 John relates to the so-called sin unto death. John states, "All wrongdoing is sin, but there is sin that does not lead to death" (5:17). Believers should pray for one another so that "God will give . . . life" to erring brethren (v. 16) in those areas where all humans, including Christians, struggle and fall short of God's glory. This sin is serious but forgivable. Yet there is also "sin that leads to death," sin so lethal that even to intercede for it is risky: "I do not say one should pray for that" (v. 16). In the overall context of 1 John it would make sense if this were sin of the *anomia* variety mentioned above. John may be saying that when professing believers abide in anti-Christian convictions (such as denying that Jesus is the Christ or that he came in the flesh) or practices such as hatred of one another (racism is a familiar example), they have made their own bed and must now lie down in it— they cannot expect, and God does not require, heartfelt intercession for such hardened transgressors. Yet John also does not forbid intercession for them, though caution is advised lest compassion for wrongdoers lead to entrapment in their ways (see Jude 23).

Admittedly, 1 John's teaching on sin is complicated. Any solutions require careful thought and wording, along with ongoing openness to clearer understanding of just how all of John's *hamartia* expressions interrelate, both with each other and with his teaching on other subjects.

In Jude there is one reference to "sinners" (v. 15), identifying them with the "ungodly" people and their "ungodly" actions about which Jude has much to say (see also vv. 4, 18). Second Peter likewise warns against these individuals and their ways (2:5–6; 3:7). Their sin includes perversion of God's grace so that they condone immorality along with denial of Christ (Jude 4). Central to Jude's message is the warning that God will "execute judgment on all and to convict all the ungodly of all their deeds of ungodliness that they have committed in such an ungodly way, and of all the harsh things that ungodly sinners have spoken against him" (v. 15).

The final mentions of *hamartia* are found in Revelation. This book begins by extolling "Jesus Christ the faithful witness, the firstborn of the dead, and the ruler of kings on earth, . . . who loves us and has freed us from our sins by his blood" (1:5). Jesus' role as sin sacrifice frames Revelation from start to finish (22:1, 3: "the throne of God and of the Lamb"). Late in the book God's people are warned to abandon and abhor Babylon, a symbol "of earth's abominations" (17:5), a place and power "drunk with the blood of the saints, the blood of the martyrs of Jesus" (v. 6). God's people are told: "Come out of her, my people, lest you take part in her sins, lest you share in her plagues; for her sins are heaped high as heaven, and God has remembered her iniquities" (18:4–5).

Here "sins" are equated with "iniquities," a word that points to another cluster of terms in the New Testament that shed light on its view of sin.

Words for Sin: the *Adikia* Group

The next prominent New Testament word-group that often speaks of "sin" or near equivalents is related to the noun *adikia* (injustice, wrong, wickedness, unrighteousness). Other words in this group are the verb *adikeō* (I do wrong, harm), the noun *adikēma* (misdeed), the adjective *adikos* (unjust, unrighteous), and the adverb *adikōs* (unjustly). These words occur a total of forty-eight times in the New Testament outside of Paul's writings. (Paul uses these words a total of twenty-four times.) The non-Pauline occurrences are as follows:

Matthew	2
Mark	0
Luke	12
John	1
Acts	10
Hebrews	2
James	1
1 Peter	2
2 Peter	4
1 John	2
2–3 John	0
Jude	0
Revelation	12

The range of words used in the ESV to translate *adikia* word-group occurrences is as follows: unjust, do wrong, hurt, evil, shrewdness, unrighteous, dishonest, falsehood, wickedness, being wronged, iniquity/-ies, wrongdo-ing, wrongdoer, unrighteousness, suffering wrong, harm, evildoer, and do evil. This impressively diverse range of meanings shows how contextually varied and rich the *adikia* word-group is.

Gospels

All the Gospel occurrences of the *adikia* word-group appear in sayings of Jesus. He uses *adikia* in the Sermon on the Mount statement, "For he makes his sun rise on the evil and on the good, and sends rain on the just and on the unjust [*adikous*]" (Matt. 5:45). Here "unjust" occurs in parallel with "evil" (*ponēros*), a word found sixty-five times in the non-Pauline New Testament writings, forty-four of those times in the Gospels. Not only sin (*hamartia*) and injustice (*adikia*) but also evil are topics frequently on Jesus' lips. Space does not permit in-depth investigation of Jesus' view of evil, but this would be part of any more in-depth look at sin in the New Testament.

Jesus uses an *adikia* form in speaking about the master of the house who must tell bogus devotees, "I do not know where you come from. Depart from me, all you workers of evil!" (Luke 13:27). He uses the same word four times to describe "unrighteous" mammon or earthly wealth in the parable of the dishonest manager (16:1–13; see *adikia* uses in vv. 8, 9, 10, 11). The hard-hearted judge whom a persistent widow wears down is called *adikia* (10:6). "Unjust" appears in parallel with extortionists, adulterers, and tax collectors in 18:11. The same word occurs as an antonym to "true" in John 7:18, where the ESV translates *adikia* as "falsehood."

We can summarize Gospel use of *adikia* as showing Jesus to have what we might call a realist moral vision in how he characterized humans and society. While his love and compassion are prominent in the Gospels, these were not ideals that blinded him to a dark side found in people and their circumstances. He diagnosed the human condition as subtly but strongly tainted with elements of injustice, unrighteousness, and wrong.

Acts

Acts uses *adikia* words to spotlight people and actions very much like those described in the Gospels using the same word-group. Judas is said to have "acquired a field with the reward of his wickedness [*adikias*]" (1:18). Deeds of wrongdoing observed by Moses are denoted by the verbal form *adikeō* ("I do wrong, harm") in 7:24, 26–27. Greedy Simon is said to be "in the bond of iniquity" (8:23). Gallio declines to name gospel witness at Corinth "a matter of wrongdoing [*adikēma*] or vicious crime" (18:14).

In Paul's defense before Felix at Caesarea he speaks of "a resurrection of both the just and the unjust [*adikos*]" (24:15), and he challenges his accusers to name the "wrongdoing" (*adikēma*) of which they wish to convict him (v. 20). In his subsequent defense before Porcius Festus, Paul denies any culpable behavior (note forms of *adikeō* ["I do wrong"] in 25:10–11).

From start to finish in Acts there is testimony to injustice and wrongdoing, or lack of the same, by use of *adikia*-related words.

Hebrews to Revelation

Nearly half of non-Pauline occurrences of *adikia* words are found in this portion of the New Testament. About half of these are found in Revelation, where "harm" is mentioned frequently due to various forces or events (2:11; 6:6; 7:2–3; 9:4, 10, 19; 11:5; in some of these cases "harm" is suppressed by God). As Revelation draws to a close, "iniquities" (*adikēmata*) are paired with "sins": "For her sins are heaped high as heaven, and God has remembered her iniquities" (18:5). In Revelation's final chapter "wrongdoers" and the "filthy" are contrasted with the just: "Let the evildoer still do evil [cf. *adikeō*], and the filthy still be filthy, and the righteous still do right, and the holy still be holy" (22:11). *Adikia* words in Revelation remind the reader that we inhabit a moral universe, and the complexion of the end of all things is to be determined along lines characterized by their good or evil in relation to God, who resources and rewards the former but punishes and banishes the latter.

In the General Epistles as elsewhere in Scripture, God is emphatically "not unjust" *(ou ... adikia*; Heb. 6:10). He will be "merciful toward" his people's "iniquities" just as he "will remember their sins no more" (8:12). James calls the tongue "a fire, a world of unrighteousness [*adikia*]" (3:6). Peter speaks of suffering "unjustly" (*adikōs*; 1 Pet. 2:19). He also notes that Christ, who was righteous, suffered for "the unrighteous" (*adikos*; 3:18). Using the same word-group, 2 Peter speaks of "the unrighteous" who are kept "under punishment until the day of judgment" (2:9), of those who suffer "wrong [cf. *adikeō*] as the wage for their wrongdoing [*adikia*]" (v. 13), and of Balaam, "who loved gain from wrongdoing" (v. 15). The well-known verse 1 John 1:9 promises "[cleansing] from all unrighteousness [*adikia*]" through confession of sin and faith in Christ's saving work.

New Testament writings from Hebrews to Revelation are united in their testimony to a God who is above wrongdoing, empowers his followers to shun unrighteous deeds, and is graphically explicit about what he disapproves and will punish, if not always immediately in this age then surely and irreversibly in the age to come. This helps explain the frequency and pungency of many uses of the *adikia* word-group in this portion of the New Testament.

Conclusion

Space does not permit in-depth consideration of other sin-related words groups.[10] Matthew, for example, speaks of "trespasses" (6:14–15; 11:25). Hebrews speaks of drifting away (2:1) and falling away (6:6). Jesus speaks of transgressing God's commandments (Matt. 15:3), and James of being "convicted by the law as transgressors" (2:9; see also v. 11). And then there is a host of non-Pauline New Testament words denoting acts such as adultery (twenty references), stealing or theft (ten), and immorality (twenty-one). There are lists of sinful acts such as those found in 1 Peter 4:3 ("sensuality, passions, drunkenness, orgies, drinking parties, and lawless idolatry") or in the Gospels regarding what "defiles" a person (see Matt. 15:20; Mark 7:15, 18; cf. Jude 8). A memorable list of deeds condemned by Jesus appears in the Markan passage just cited:

> What comes out of a person is what defiles him. For from within, out of the heart of man, come evil thoughts, sexual immorality, theft, murder, adultery, coveting, wickedness, deceit, sensuality, envy, slander, pride, foolishness. All these evil things come from within, and they defile a person. (Mark 7:20–23)

It might not be correct to say that this chapter has merely scratched the surface of what non-Pauline portions of the New Testament say about sin. But we have certainly not been comprehensive in scope. And space has afforded little in the way of achieving depth of treatment in the broad areas of word-groups surveyed through interaction with contemporary New Testament scholarship. Brief reference to a slice of that scholarship may therefore be fitting in conclusion.

The late Donald Guthrie authored a voluminous New Testament theology[11] in which he helpfully summed up New Testament views on sin in the various divisions of the New Testament writings treated in this chapter, e.g., Acts,[12] Hebrews,[13] and "the rest of the New Testament."[14] Guthrie

---

[10] See, e.g., Colin Brown, ed., *NIDNTT*, 3:383–587.
[11] See n8.
[12] Ibid., 199–200.
[13] Ibid., 213–15.
[14] Ibid., 215–17.

is particularly clear in his "Summary of Jesus' Estimate of Man's Sin in the Synoptic Gospels," where he notes that sin is "universal," "internal," "enslavement," "rebellion," and deserving of "condemnation."[15] In the Fourth Gospel, Guthrie finds sin characterized as "alienation from God," "unbelief," "mortal" (i.e., bringing about death), "universal," and "lawlessness."[16] Guthrie's findings in general echo and emphasize much of what has emerged in the discussion above.

Other New Testament theologies have helpfully traversed the same ground. Thomas Schreiner comments on the Fourth Gospel's stress on "lawlessness" by observing, "Sin, then, is lawlessness, for it represents the refusal to believe in Jesus as the Christ; it is a fierce rebellion that refuses to submit to Jesus as Lord."[17] Some New Testament theologies are not so helpful. In Georg Strecker's magnum opus, for example, "sin" does not even appear in the subject index, which is over eight pages long.[18] It seems that just as people struggled to come to grips with sin in Jesus' time, scholars vacillate in their treatment of it today.

What should not be forgotten, however, are the ways in which New Testament depictions of sin "contribute to the different interpretations of the work of Christ."[19] The non-Pauline portions of the New Testament do not dwell on sin as an academic question for ethicists or metaphysicians. Nor do they expound on sin for the sake of fueling some Christian moralism. They rather regard sin as a human plight that God has sworn to address. And they do this by steadily bringing the sin problem into proximity with Jesus. As Guthrie puts it, "If sin is enslavement, Christ brings deliverance. If it is falsehood, Christ presents truth. If disobedience, Christ shows the way of obedience. If deviation from the will of God, Christ sets the perfect example of righteousness."[20] Christ does all of this, and more, by virtue of his death and resurrection, which break forever the tyranny of sin and death. But that is where the writings of Paul come powerfully into play, as the next chapter will show.

---

[15] Ibid., 191–92.
[16] Ibid., 193–97.
[17] Thomas Schreiner, *New Testament Theology: Magnifying God in Christ* (Grand Rapids, MI: Baker Academic, 2008), 519.
[18] Georg Strecker, *Theology of the New Testament*, ed. Friedrich Wilhelm Horn, trans. M. Eugene Boring (Louisville: Westminster John Knox, 2000), 740–48.
[19] Guthrie, *New Testament Theology*, 217.
[20] Ibid., 217–18.

5

SIN IN PAUL

DOUGLAS J. MOO

> As for you, you were dead in your transgressions and sins,
> in which you used to live when you followed the ways of this
> world and of the ruler of the kingdom of the air, the spirit
> who is now at work in those who are disobedient. All of us
> also lived among them at one time, gratifying the cravings of
> our flesh and following its desires and thoughts. Like the rest,
> we were by nature deserving of wrath. —Ephesians 2:1–3[1]

This passage from Paul's letter to the Ephesians (2:1–3) touches on many of the most important aspects of sin that Paul wants to communicate to us. Sin, Paul notes, is endemic to life on this earth: people "live in" it. Sin involves, fundamentally, an obsessive concern with one's own interests and pleasures: humans are engaged in "gratifying the cravings of our flesh." Human sin is part of a bigger picture, enmeshed in a nexus of evil: people who sin follow "the ways of this world" and are under the influence of "the ruler of the kingdom of the air." And sin has consequences: people who sin are "dead" and "deserving of wrath." Finally, as the temporal focus of these verses suggests—"you *were* dead"; "you *used* to live"; "at one time"; "we *were* by nature deserving of wrath"—this life under the dominion of sin is past for the believer. Paul goes on to say, "But because of his great love for us, God, who is rich in mercy, made us alive with Christ" (vv. 4–5a). The terrible reality of sin is the setting that explains what God has

---

done for us in Christ. Indeed, there is a close reciprocating relationship between sin and salvation: salvation takes the form it does precisely because of the nature of the sin problem; and the sin problem is rightly understood only in light of the form that God's salvation has taken.

In his groundbreaking 1977 monograph *Paul and Palestinian Judaism*, E. P. Sanders famously argued that Paul's theological reasoning moved "from solution to plight." In contrast to many popular perceptions, Sanders maintained, the pre-Christian Paul did not struggle with sin, seeking a solution to his plight that he discovered in Christ. Rather, he was confronted, suddenly and surprisingly, with the reality of the resurrected Christ, a reality from which all his theological reasoning proceeds. Convinced that the "solution" was the good news of God's intervention on behalf of humanity in Christ, Paul was then forced to reflect on the kind of "plight" that might have led to this solution. Having come to the conviction that a crucified Messiah was the means through whom God acted to provide salvation for both Israel and the world, Paul would have engaged in a thorough reassessment of his own Jewish experience and, eventually, the nature of humanity's problem. Sanders's "solution to plight" analysis of Paul's theology has been widely accepted. Du Toit, for instance, claims that "Paul's personal experience of grace led him to a new hamartiology."[2] However, the "solution-to-plight" reading of Paul's theology has not gone unchallenged.[3] Among other points, it is certainly likely that the pre-Christian Paul, like virtually any self-reflective religious person, would occasionally have reflected on his failure to live up to the standards of his faith. Nevertheless, passages such as Philippians 3:2–11 do indeed suggest that Paul was a pretty self-satisfied Jew, confident in his standing with God provided by "the righteousness of the law." For him personally, "solution" probably did precede "plight."

However, the direction of Paul's experience need not be the direction of his theological argument. Of course Paul's letters, being the occasional documents that they are, do not usually furnish us with clear evidence of the sequence of his theological argument. The clues they do contain suggest variety in the sequence of Paul's theological reasoning. Whatever the sequence, however, it is clear that Paul engages in significant, if not always systematic, reflection on the nature of the human predicament.

---

[2] André du Toit, "The Centrality of Grace in the Theology of Paul," in *Focusing on Paul: Persuasion and Theological Design in Romans and Galatians*, ed. Cliffers Breytenbach and David S. du Toit (New York: de Gruyter, 2007), 89.

[3] See especially Frank Thielman, *From Plight to Solution: A Jewish Framework to Understanding Paul's View of the Law in Galatians and Romans*, NovTSup 41 (Leiden, UK: Brill, 1989).

In this chapter, I survey the main lines of Paul's teaching about this predicament, what we usually call simply "sin." I begin with a brief discussion of the key terminology before analyzing more generally the nature of sin and the various forms that it takes. As I have noted with reference to the text from Ephesians above, Paul sets sin in a wider "environment" of evil, a matter that I discuss in the next section of the chapter. Sin, Paul makes clear, has consequences; and those consequences are the focus of the next part of this chapter. I conclude with a brief overview of the Christian's relationship to sin. I will be focusing especially on the letter to the Romans, because by far the most extensive Pauline commentary on sin comes in this, his most significant theological contribution.

The Vocabulary of Sin

Paul signals the importance of sin for his theology by the number of different words that he deploys for the concept. Most of these words denote specific sins—e.g., "greed" or "covetousness" (*pleonexia*), "murder" (*phonos*), "drunkenness" (*methē*). While these words for specific forms of sin help us to understand the nature and many facets of sin in Paul, our focus here is on the twenty or so words that Paul uses to denote sin in general. Four words, or word-groups, deserve special mention.

"Sin"/"commit sin"/"sinful"/"sinner" (*hamartia* and *harmatēma, hamartanō, hamartōlos*). This word-group occurs ninety times in Paul's letters, with fully two-thirds of the occurrences (sixty) found in Romans. The relevant Greek words regularly translate words from the most significant word for sin in the Hebrew Old Testament, the verb *ḥṭ'* and its corresponding noun, *ḥṭ'h*.[4] The word-group in Greek has the basic sense of "missing a target" (a point often heard in preaching about sin!).[5] In fact, however, it is doubtful if the word's etymology plays any role in Paul's conception of sin. Paul rarely uses the noun *hamartia* in the plural, preferring the singular. We will consider below the importance of this pattern for Paul's teaching about sin. A representative text is Romans 3:9: "What then? Do we have any advantage? Not at all! For we have already made the charge that Jews and Gentiles alike are all under sin [*hyph' hamartian*]" (my translation).

"Trespass" (*paraptōma*). Paul uses this word fifteen times, nine of them in Romans (other New Testament writers use it four times total). The

---

[4] The Greek noun *hamartia* translates the Hebrew *ḥṭ'h* over 230 times, while the verb *hamartanō* renders the Hebrew *ḥṭ'* over 160 times. See G. Quell, *TDNT*, ed. G. Kittel and G. Friedrich, trans. G. W. Bromiley. 10 vols (Grand Rapids, MI: Eerdmans, 1964), 1:268.

[5] See, e.g., ibid., 294.

root idea of the word is "falling by the way," although (again) it is doubtful that its etymology holds significance for Paul's usage. Paul uses the word to refer to sin in general. See, for example, Ephesians 1:7: "In him we have redemption through his blood, the forgiveness of sins [*paraptōmatōn*], in accordance with the riches of God's grace."

"Desire"/"passion" (*epithymia*). This word can have a neutral meaning in Paul (Phil. 1:23) but usually denotes some kind of illicit desire or the "passions" that characterize human beings outside of Christ (nineteen times in Paul). (We might mention here also two related words that are often connected with *epithymia*, both usually translated "passion" or "passions": *pathos* and *pathēmos*—used together five times with reference to sin in Paul.) See 2 Timothy 2:22: "Flee the evil desires [*epithymiais*] of youth and pursue righteousness, faith, love and peace, along with those who call on the Lord out of a pure heart."

"Transgression" (*parabasis*) and "transgressor" (*parabatēs*), while not used that often by Paul (five and three occurrences, respectively), are significant pointers to an important aspect of sin in Paul: disobedience to the commands of God. Every occurrence of these words in Paul has this nuance, a nuance that bears significantly on the meaning of the texts in which they occur. See, for example, Romans 4:15b: "And where there is no law there is no transgression."

The many other words that Paul uses to describe sin are important indicators of his understanding of sin. Several of these stress the negative, being formed by a base word with the prefix *a*- added. This Greek alpha functions much like our prefixes "un-" or "dis-" in English. Thus sin can be characterized as "unrighteousness" (*adikia* [twelve times]; see also *adikos*, "unrighteous" [two times]), "disobedience" (*apetheia* and the corresponding verb *apetheiō* [nine times]; see also *parakoē* [two times]), "uncleanness" (*akatharsia* [nine times]), "lawless" (*anomos* [six times]), "godlessness" (*asebeia* [four times]; cf. *asebēs*, "ungodly" [three times]), "unbelief"/"unfaithfulness" (*apistia* [five times]; cf. *apisteuō*, "disbelieve"/"to be unfaithful" [two times]), "ignorance" (*agnoia* [one time]). Other words denoting sin in general in Paul are "error" (*planē* [four times]), "vanity"/"futility" (*mataiotēs* [two times]; cf. *mataioomai*, "become futile" [one time]), "lie" (*pseusma* [one time]; cf. *pseustēs*, "liar" [one time]), "to stumble" (*proskoptō* [two times]), and "to cause to stumble" (*skandalizō* [two times]). In addition, of course, Paul uses a number of phrases to express the idea of sin, such as "[doing] what is evil"

(Rom. 13:4 NASB), "deeds of darkness" (Rom. 13:12), and "do not obey the gospel" (2 Thess. 1:8).

Two observations about this survey are worth mentioning. First, Paul's use of so many different words to refer to sin in its basic sense suggests how important the topic was for him and how many dimensions sin has. Second, the concentration of words describing sin in Romans is quite remarkable. No other letter of Paul even comes close to the level of focus on sin and its consequences that Romans does.

The Nature of Sin

Sin as Power

The many words that Paul uses to describe sin suggest the manifold forms that sin takes in human experience. Humans have discovered an astonishing number of ways to manifest their estrangement from their creator. But Paul's focus is often more on the fundamental fact of sin and its implications for humans than on its variety. This focus is reflected especially in Romans, where forty-eight of the sixty-four Pauline occurrences of *hamartia* occur. Of these forty-eight, forty-five are in the singular (and two of the three plurals come in OT quotes: 4:7 [= Ps. 31:1]; 11:27 [= Isa. 27:9]; see also 7:5). (By way of contrast, only seven of the sixteen occurrences of *hamartia* in the other Pauline letters are in the singular.) Moreover, Paul attributes quasi-personal powers to "sin": it "reigns" (5:20; cf. 6:13, 14), can be "obeyed" (6:16–17), pays wages (6:23), seizes opportunity (7:8, 11), "deceives," and "kills" (7:11, 13). Some interpreters think that this language suggests that Paul views sin as an evil spiritual power, a kind of demon.[6] But this would be to mistake personification for personalization. Paul attributes personal qualities to sin in order vividly to picture the power and devastating effects of human sin in the lives of human beings. He shows that individual acts of sin constitute a principle, or network, of sin that is so pervasive and dominant that the person's destiny is determined by those actions. In doing so, he follows Old Testament precedent, which also pictures sin as a power: it is "crouching at your door; it desires to have you" (Gen. 4:7).

Paul's point in appropriating this language is to make clear just what the human predicament really is. In a key summary statement, Paul claims that "Jews and Gentiles alike are all under the power of sin." Paul does not say that all people "commit sins," as if doing things contrary to God's will

---

[6] E.g., W. Grundmann, *TDNT* 1:310–11.

was just an occasional problem. Nor does he even say that all people are "sinners"—suggesting that sin is a pervasive problem. Rather, he says that all people are "under the power of sin." Paul uses this kind of language to speak of a situation of domination, even slavery. See, for instance, Galatians 3:22: "But Scripture has locked up everything under the control of sin [literally, "held prisoner *under* sin"], so that what was promised, being given through faith in Jesus Christ, might be given to those who believe" (and see also Rom. 6:14, 15; 7:14; 1 Cor. 9:20; Gal. 3:23, 25; 4:2–5, 9, 21; Eph. 1:22). The NIV's "under the power of sin" in Romans 3:9 therefore appropriately brings out the force of the Greek *hyph' hamartian*. For Paul, the human plight is not that people commit sins, or even that they are in the habit of committing sins. The problem is that people are helpless prisoners of sin.

The power that sin holds over humans is vital in understanding Paul's view of sin and has direct bearing on his view of the solution that God has provided in Christ. Paul, in line with Scripture generally, views humans as addicted to sin. They are imprisoned under it, unable to free themselves by anything they can do. Knowing this, God has sent to us not a teacher or a politician but a liberator—one who has the power to set us free from our sins (this idea is suggested by the language of "redemption" in Rom. 3:24). When we really see the people all around us—at work, in our neighborhoods, at the store—as helpless captives of sin, we will be better motivated to help them find the liberator who alone can rescue them from their captivity. Only Jesus Christ, proclaimed in the gospel, can break through the walls of sin that imprison human beings.

Sin and the Law

Another important facet of Paul's presentation of sin is its relationship to God's law. Much of Paul's theology, especially in Romans, where Paul says so much about sin, revolves around the meaning and significance of the law. We are not surprised, then, to find that Paul focuses quite a bit on the way that sin and the law interact. He makes three basic points.

First, Paul makes clear that sin's power means that the law cannot liberate humans from the power and consequences of sin. "No one will be declared righteous in God's sight by the works of the law," affirms Paul (Rom. 3:20). This is not the place to enter into the contentious matter of the meaning of "works of the law." Suffice to say here that the phrase probably refers generally to obedience to the Mosaic law and, as the Reformers recognized, by extension to anything that humans beings do: their "works" in general.[7] Obedience to law in any form cannot put a human being in right relationship with God. Nor can obedience to law enable humans to conquer sin's power in their lives. However we identify the person whose experience Paul relates in Romans 7:7–25, this much is clear: the law, because it was given to humans already locked up under sin's power, cannot liberate human beings from the lifestyle of sin (see Rom. 8:3: "what the law was powerless to do because it was weakened by the flesh").

Second, in keeping with the Old Testament, sin can be defined as disobedience to the law. As we have noted, *parabasis* (see also the cognate *parabatēs*) is a technical word denoting "transgression" of a commandment or of the law. Paul's description of sinners as "lawless" evokes the same idea (see esp. 1 Tim. 1:9). Several occurrences of the language of "disobedience" also have the law of God in view. This particular aspect of sin typifies the initial human sin, Paul suggests: Adam sinned "by breaking a command" (Rom. 5:14, as the NIV translates the noun *parabasis* here; the same point is made with respect to Eve in 1 Tim. 2:14: she "became a transgressor" [my translation]). The law of Moses that God gave to Israel parallels in a certain basic sense the commandment that God gave to Adam and Eve in the garden (see esp. Rom. 5:13–14). We might expect, then, that Paul would also define sin as violation of the law of Moses. He speaks in these terms especially in Romans 2:17–29, where he argues that the genuine privileges that God gave to Israel have not been of ultimate benefit to the Jews because of their repeated failure to do the law. But Paul goes beyond this fairly obvious point to make another, more controversial one.

The law not only defines sin, Paul argues—it also exacerbates it. Sin's co-opting of God's law for its own purposes, says Paul, has enabled sin to be seen as "utterly sinful" (Rom. 7:13). While debated, it is this "catalytic" effect of the law that Paul probably also has in view when he claims that through the law is knowledge of sin (3:20) and that the law enabled Paul to know what sin was (Rom. 7:7; see also 1 Cor. 15:56).[8] This perspective on the effect of the law in salvation history also explains Romans 4:15: ". . . the law brings wrath. And where there is no law there is no transgression." The key to understanding this text is the technical sense of "transgression" (*parabasis*) that we have noted above. The last sentence in this verse reflects this basic meaning of the word for Paul: only where some

---

[7] For this viewpoint see Douglas J. Moo, *The Epistle to the Romans*, NICNT (Grand Rapids, MI: Eerdmans, 1996), 206–10.

[8] I pick up this language of "the catalytic effect of the law" from the important monograph by Chris Vlachos, *The Law and the Knowledge of Good and Evil: The Edenic Background of the Catalytic Operation of the Law in Paul* (Eugene, OR: Wipf & Stock, 2009).

kind of law is present can one speak of "transgression." All transgression is sin, but not all sin is transgression. One can sin apart from an express command or prohibition from God. What Paul is saying in this context in Romans 4, then, is that the coming of the law into the history of salvation did not rescue Israel from her plight. Indeed, quite the opposite: by spelling out in detail the demands of God to his people, God raised their level of accountability, rendering their inevitable disobedience even worse than in the absence of that law. While it is debated, it is probably just this point that Paul is making in Romans 7:7–25. And the same idea is arguably found in two other texts, Romans 5:20 and Galatians 3:19. In the former, Paul acknowledges that the law came into the situation of sin and death that Adam's original sin had created. The law did not, however, ameliorate the situation; rather, Paul affirms that "the law was brought in that the trespass might increase." Just how the law "increased" the trespass is debated; but it is likely that Paul is thinking here again of the way that the law, in its specificity, served to increase the seriousness of the trespass. Galatians 3:19 is likewise debated: the law "was added because of transgressions." The Greek word translated "because of" (*charin*) could mean "*because of* the need to deal with transgressions" or "*in order to* stimulate transgressions." The latter is slightly to be preferred because Paul uses here again the word for sin as "disobedience to a law" (*parabasis*). The law was given by God in order to make manifest the true nature and utter seriousness of sin, pointing all the more clearly to the need for a radical solution to deal with the problem of sin.

The Essence of Sin

When discussing the relationship of sin and the law, then, Paul takes the standard Old Testament and Jewish view that the law can serve to define sin and that sin can often be seen specifically as violation of God's commandments. But he is particularly concerned to go beyond these views to show how the law of God is itself incapable of solving the sin problem. In making this point, Paul is saying nothing that the Old Testament itself does not say. But he needs to insist on this point again and again in response to a tendency among Jews in his day to view the giving of God's law to Israel as itself the solution to their problem. Implicit in Paul's argument on this point is his understanding of the extent of sin's power over human beings. Showing people what is right—teaching them the law of God—while an obvious good in itself, will not liberate people from the power of sin.

While the Jewish context in which Paul was setting forth his theology

demanded that he spend quite a lot of time talking about the relationship of sin and the law, it would be a mistake to give the law too much
importance in Paul's theology of sin. Following the Old Testament,[9] Paul
ultimately defines sin not in relationship to the law but in relationship to
God. The justly famous summary claim of Romans 3:23 makes this point:
". . . all have sinned and fall short of the glory of God." The second verb
elaborates the first: sin consists in the failure to live in accordance with
the nature of God, stated as so often in Scripture in terms of his "glory."
Similar in emphasis is the quotation from Psalm 36:1 that climaxes the
series of Old Testament quotations through which Paul grounds his claim
that all are under sin (Rom. 3:10b–18; cf. v. 9): "There is no fear of God
before their eyes." Romans 1:18–32 makes the same point. Paul focuses in
this passage on the state of human beings in general as they confront the
evidence of God's person and nature in the world that he has made (vv.
19–20).[10] At the end of the passage, Paul enumerates, in the longest "vice
list" in the New Testament, the many ways in which sin is manifested
among humans (vv. 29–31). Following Jewish precedent (see esp. Wisdom
14–15), Paul also notes how humans in general have fallen into serious
sexual sin (Rom. 1:25–27). But giving rise to all these sins is the decision
of humans to turn away from God and to embrace idols of their own making (v. 23)—just as the Israelites did when they fashioned a golden calf
to worship (1 Cor. 10:7; cf. Exodus 32). Their basic sin is personal: they
refuse to glorify God or to give thanks to him (Rom. 1:21). In Paul's day
idolatry often took the very specific form of making images that people
would worship in place of the God of the Bible. But the essence of idolatry,
of course, is putting anything or anyone in the place of primary allegiance
that only God deserves to have.[11] Idolatry is manifested in an infinite variety of ways in our day: pursuing money or power or sex—or yes, even
photography, one of my own interests!—in place of God.

Sin and Sins

Paul's focus on sin as a power that rules over humans apart from Christ
does not mean that he ignores the many ways in which sin manifests itself.
It is not possible, or necessary, to enumerate here all the specific sins that

---

[9] See House, 39–63.

[10] Many interpreters think that the passage addresses Gentiles, and this is not far from the mark. But Paul's
failure to identify the people he refers to as Gentiles and the transition from chapter 1 to chapter 2 in 2:1 suggest that his focus is on a certain kind of revelation. And all people, Jews as well as Gentiles, are confronted
with the evidence of natural revelation.

[11] James D. G. Dunn likewise emphasizes "misdirected religion" as a key aspect of Paul's view of sin in *The
Theology of Paul the Apostle* (Grand Rapids, MI: Eerdmans, 1998), 114–17.

Paul identifies in the course of his letters. Nowhere does Paul attempt any kind of systematic listing or categorization of sins. But he regularly castigates three general sins: greed or self-indulgence, inappropriate sexual relations, and harmful or negligent speech.

Paul mentions greed, or covetousness, several times (Eph. 4:19; 5:3, 5; Col. 3:5; 1 Tim. 3:3, 8; 6:5–10, 17; 2 Tim 3:2; Titus 1:7, 11). Particularly striking is Colossians 3:5 (with a partial parallel in Eph. 5:5), where Paul concludes a list of sins with "greed" (*pleonexia*) and then claims that greed "is idolatry." The identification of greed with idolatry has its roots in the Old Testament and has parallels in Judaism and in the New Testament. The Old Testament frequently sets wealth in competition with God as a source of security (e.g., Ps. 52:7; Prov. 10:15; Jer. 48:7). The Jewish philosopher/theologian Philo, a rough contemporary of Paul, claimed that the first commandment prohibits "money-lovers" (*Spec. Laws* 1.23). And the New Testament frequently highlights the love of material possessions as offering a particularly enticing and entrapping alternative to the love of God (e.g., Matt. 6:25–34; 1 Tim. 6:17; Heb. 13:5).[12] Because greed is the inappropriate desire to accumulate more and more, it is a fundamental attitude that underlies and gives greater impetus to other sins (see Eph. 4:19).

Sex was in Paul's day, as in ours, a form of behavior in which biblical standards clashed especially harshly with contemporary mores. We are not surprised then that he says so much about the matter to his Gentile converts (see esp. Rom. 1:24–27; 1 Cor. 5–6; Eph. 4:19; 5:3; 1 Thess. 4:3–6; 1 Tim. 1:10). As we have already noted, Paul follows Jewish precedent in identifying inappropriate sexual conduct as an especially clear indication of the way in which humans have turned from the worship of God (Rom. 1:24–27). In one of his first letters he reminds Gentile converts that their sanctification consists, especially and first of all, in their avoidance of "sexual immorality" (*porneia*; 1 Thess. 4:3). Paul provides no enumeration of specific sexual sins, although homosexual relationships are clearly included (Rom. 1:26–27; 1 Cor. 6:9; 1 Tim. 1:10).[13]

Mentioned even more often than either greed or sex, however, are sins of speech (Eph. 4:25, 29; 5:4; Col. 3:8–9; 1 Tim. 1:6; 3:11; 5:13; 6:4; 2 Tim. 2:14, 16, 23; Titus 1:10; 2:3; 3:2, 9). One reason for the prominence

---

[12] See on this topic especially Brian S. Rosner, *Greed as Idolatry: The Origin and Meaning of a Pauline Metaphor* (Grand Rapids, MI: Eerdmans, 2007).

[13] On the issue of homosexuality in the teaching of Paul (and the NT generally), see especially Richard Hays, *The Moral Vision of the New Testament* (San Francisco: Harper, 1996), 379–406; Robert Gagnon, *The Bible and Homosexual Practice: Texts and Hermeneutics* (Nashville: Abingdon, 2002).

of this form of sin was the situation that Paul was addressing: the Pastoral Epistles focus on this matter because the false teachers were occupying themselves with unfruitful and divisive speech. But Paul may also be following the same path that James takes, who famously draws attention to the way in which sin is especially manifested in speech (James 3:1–12).

It is also important to note that sin involves not just our actions; it is rooted in our very pattern of thinking. As we have seen, the sinful actions that humans commit (or the things that they sinfully fail to do) are the manifestation of a more fundamental condition—being "under sin." And this condition, as we would expect, affects the mind. When people turned away from the knowledge of God, God "gave them over to a depraved mind" (Rom. 1:28). Their minds are hardened (2 Cor. 3:14); they are "darkened in their understanding and separated from the life of God because of the ignorance that is in them" (Eph. 4:18). They have a pattern of thinking, a mind-set, that is "set on earthly things" (Phil. 3:19; see Rom. 8:5–7). We should not be surprised, then, when non-Christians have trouble understanding things that seem very logical to us believers, such as that taking the life of a child in the womb is wrong or that labeling a homosexual union "marriage" is a fundamental category error. Non-Christians are incapable of thinking rightly about many such issues. A critical part of God's new-covenant work, therefore, is the "renewing" of the mind (Rom. 12:2; Eph. 4:23).

Since sin is basically the failure to honor God as God, it can also be described in terms of a failure to live up to the fundamental response that people are to make to God: faith. As we noted above, then, Paul can describe sin in terms of a failure to believe. Not believing is the root of other sins and of estrangement from God (Rom. 3:3; 4:20; 11:20, 23). Especially interesting is the claim that Paul makes in warning the strong in faith not to compel the weak in faith to act against their consciences: "everything that does not come from faith is sin" (14:23). Paul suggests here that sin can be relative to the believer's own strength of conscience. Eating meat (14:3, 6) or drinking wine (v. 21) would not be sinful, Paul makes clear, for those whose faith is strong, for those who are convinced in Christ that it is not wrong to eat meat or to drink wine (v. 14). But these acts would be sinful for the Christian who has not yet been convinced that they are free in Christ to do them. The sin in this case would appear to be a disconnect between mind and act. Indirectly, then, Romans 14:23 testifies to the importance of the mind in Paul's conception of sin.

The Larger Environment of Sin

In order fully to understand Paul's teaching about sin, we must set it in the context of what we might call its "environment." While an inescapably personal decision, sin is an act that flows from a nexus of relationships and from a specific context. Paul repeatedly focuses on three critical aspects to this environment of sin: the flesh, Adam, and the "powers."

Flesh[14]

Sin is an inevitable aspect of the "the present evil age" from which Christ redeemed his people (Gal. 1:4). One of the words that Paul most often associates with this old realm, and therefore with sin as well, is "flesh" (*sarx*). This is one of the most difficult words in Paul's theological vocabulary. The complexity of Paul's use of this word is reflected in the NIV, where twenty-eight different words or phrases are used to translate *sarx* (and the NIV is no outlier here; every other modern English Bible displays a similar pattern). As Anthony Thiselton has pointed out, *sarx* in Paul is a "polymorphous concept," and its meaning is very much context dependent.[15] The large number of different renderings of *sarx* in the NIV simply reflects this fact. Many scholars and lexicographers have attempted to categorize Paul's uses of *sarx*. For the sake of the argument of this chapter, five basic senses can be distinguished. The most basic meaning of *sarx*, and the most common in secular Greek, is (1) "the material that covers the bones of a human or animal body."[16] Paul occasionally uses the word with this sense. The clearest is 1 Corinthians 15:39: "Not all flesh is the same: People have one kind of flesh, animals have another, birds another and fish another" (see also Eph. 2:11; Col. 2:13; cf. Gal. 6:13). Following precedents in secular Greek, Paul also (2) applies *sarx* to the human body as whole: e.g., 2 Corinthians 7:1: "Since we have these promises, dear friends, let us purify ourselves from everything that contaminates body [*sarx*] and spirit, perfecting holiness out of reverence for God" (see also 1 Cor. 5:5[?]; 6:16; 2 Cor. 12:7; Gal. 4:13; Eph. 5:31). But more often, Paul (3) uses *sarx* to refer not to the human body narrowly but to the human being generally. First Corinthians 1:28–29 illustrates this use of the word:

---

[14] Material in this section is taken from my article "'Flesh' in Romans: A Problem for the Translator," in *The Challenge of Bible Translation: Communicating God's Word to the World: Essays in Honor of Ronald F. Youngblood*, ed. Glen S. Scorgie, Mark L. Strauss, and Steven M. Voth (Grand Rapids, MI: Zondervan, 2003), 365–79.
[15] Anthony Thiselton, *The Two Horizons: New Testament Hermeneutics and Philosophical Description with Special Reference to Bultmann, Heidegger, Gadamer, and Wittgenstein* (Grand Rapids, MI: Eerdmans, 1979), 408–11.
[16] W. Bauer, F. W. Danker, W. F. Arndt, and F. W. Gingrich, eds., BDAG, 3rd ed. (Chicago: University of Chicago Press, 1999), 743.

"God chose the lowly things of this world and the despised things—and the things that are not—to nullify the things that are, so that no one [*sarx*] may boast before him" (see also 1 Cor. 1:29; Gal. 1:16; 2:16). This sense of the word merges almost imperceptibly into a bit broader concept: (4) the human state or condition. While debated, 1 Corinthians 10:18, where Paul refers to Israel *kata sarka* ("according to the flesh"), probably falls into this category. Finally, in a usage that is distinctively (though not uniquely) Pauline, *sarx* can (5) designate the human condition in its fallenness. As Timo Laato has neatly put it, the difference between meanings (4) and (5) is the difference between the human being in *distinction* from God and the human being in *contrast* to God.[17] The latter is often called the "ethical" use of *sarx*, in contrast to the "neutral" use of its meaning (4).[18] A clear example of the "ethical" use is Gal. 5:16–17: "So I say, walk by the Spirit, and you will not gratify the desires of the flesh [*sarx*]. For the flesh [*sarx*] desires what is contrary to the Spirit, and the Spirit what is contrary to the flesh [*sarx*]. They are in conflict with each other, so that you are not to do whatever you want." This sense of *sarx* is quite common in Paul (anywhere from twenty-five to thirty occurrences, depending on how one interprets several notoriously difficult texts).

In what we have said about Paul's use of *sarx* thus far, we have followed the traditional distinction between Paul's "neutral" and "ethical" uses of the term. James D. G. Dunn, however, has called into question this distinction. He argues that the meanings of *sarx* in Paul do not fall into separate, watertight categories but occupy a spectrum of meaning. In contrast to scholars who suggest that Paul may have derived his more neutral sense of *sarx* from the Old Testament and Jewish world and the more negative sense from the Greek world, Dunn, along with many others before him, traces the spectrum of Paul's usage to the Hebrew *bsr*, with its sense of "human mortality."[19] One implication of this conclusion is that a certain negative nuance often clings to *sarx* even when Paul uses it in apparently neutral senses. Dunn has a point, as several texts make clear (Rom. 1:3–4; 4:1; 9:5, 8; Gal. 4:23, 29).

The tendency to use "flesh" in this negative way, it must be emphasized, distances this word from Paul's use of "body." To be sure, Paul can

---

[17] Timo Laato, *Paulus und das Judentum: Anthropologische Erwägungen* (Åbo: Åbo Academy, 1991), 95.
[18] See, e.g., W. D. Davies, *Paul and Rabbinic Judaism*, 4th ed. (Philadelphia: Fortress, 1981), 19; D. E. H. Whitely, *The Theology of St. Paul* (Oxford, UK: Blackwell, 1964), 39.
[19] Dunn, *The Theology of Paul the Apostle*, 62–70; cf. also Dunn's "Jesus—Flesh and Spirit: An Exposition of Romans I.3–4," *JTS* 24 (1973): 44–51; W. D. Stacey, *The Pauline View of Man: In Relation to its Judaic and Hellenistic Background* (London: Macmillan, 1956), 154–73.

sometimes suggest that sin is rooted in our bodily existence (see esp. Rom. 6:6; 8:13, 23). But he says this simply to remind us that our bodies in this life, unredeemed as they are, can become the platform for sin. In a point that follows biblical precedent and that differs fundamentally from the typical Greco-Roman viewpoint (and the tendency toward dualism in many forms of thinking since Paul's day), the body, Paul affirms, is destined for resurrection. We will live forever in bodies. Sin in Paul is not, then, tied inescapably to life in the body. He therefore makes clear that ascetic practices—the "denial" of the body and its natural functions—in themselves have no power to conquer our sinful tendencies (Col. 2:23).

For our purposes, what is especially important is to trace the connection between "flesh" and human sin. The natural human condition is to be "in the flesh," to be fundamentally determined by the perspective of this world, in contrast to the world to come. And sin is the inevitable result of this condition. We are people who, by virtue of our belonging to this world, are governed by the flesh, "gratifying" its cravings and "following its desires and thoughts" (Eph. 2:3). The natural person therefore cannot please God (Rom. 8:8); he or she sins and dies (7:5), thinking and acting as a person who takes no account of the divine realm (8:4–7). Christians, because they are still in this world, must strive to avoid falling into such patterns of thought and activity (8:12–13; 13:14).

Adam[20]

In Romans 1:18–32, Paul strongly implies that all people have participated in the fatal turn from God to idols that he chronicles in these verses. The universality of sin becomes explicit in chapter 3: "Jews and Gentiles alike are under the power of sin" (v. 9); "all have sinned and fall short of the glory of God" (v. 23). But Paul reserves his explanation for the universality of sin (and death, which follows on sin) until chapter 5, in his famous comparison between Adam and Christ (vv. 12–21). These verses highlight Christ's power as the "second Adam" who more than reverses the dire consequences of the first Adam's sin to ensure that those in him will have eternal life (vv. 20–21). The basic building block of the paragraph is a "just as ... so also" comparison. Paul introduces this comparison in verse 12 but never completes it (most English versions, like the NIV, signal the break with a dash at the end of the verse). But he resumes the comparison and finally completes it in verses 18–19.

---

[20] This section depends on and, indeed, quotes from my treatment of the passage in *Romans*, NICNT, 319–29.

The fact that Paul attributes to Adam this sin is significant since he certainly knows from Genesis that the woman, Eve, sinned first (cf. 2 Cor. 11:3; 1 Tim. 2:14). Already we see that Adam is being given a status in salvation history that is not tied only to temporal priority.

Paul's claim that "sin entered the world through one man" would have been nothing new to anyone who knew his or her Old Testament or Jewish tradition. Nor would his second assertion in this verse: ". . . and death through sin [came into the world]." The unbreakable connection between sin and death, made clear in Genesis 2–3, was a staple of Jewish theology. But what does Paul mean by death here? He may refer to physical death only, since "death" in verse 14 seems to have this meaning. But the passage goes on to contrast death with eternal life (v. 21). Moreover, in verses 16 and 18 Paul uses "condemnation" in the same way that he uses "death" here. These points suggest that Paul is referring to "spiritual" death: the estrangement from God that is a result of sin and that, if not healed through Christ, will lead to "eternal" death. In fact, however, we are not forced to make a choice between these options. Paul frequently uses "death" and related words to designate a "physio-spiritual entity" of "total death," the penalty incurred for sin. Here, then, Paul may focus on physical death as the evidence, the outward manifestation of this total death; or, better, he may simply have in mind this death in both its physical and spiritual aspects.

As verse 12b depicts the *entrance* of death as the consequence of sin, verse 12c makes explicit that this death has *spread* to every single person. Paul connects this assertion to the first part of verse 12 with "in this way" (*houtōs*). He is drawing a comparison between the manner in which death came into the world through sin and the manner in which death spread to everyone also through sin. Verse 12 then is a neatly balanced chiasm:

A   sin (12a) produces
   B   death (12b);
   B'   all die (12c)
A'   because all sin (12d).

If this reading of the structure of the verse is right, then verse 12d has the purpose of showing that death is universal because sin is universal: "all sinned." This means, in turn, that we are giving the opening words of this last clause (*eph' hō*) a causal meaning. This is the meaning adopted by most commentators and by almost all English translations. But it is not the only possible rendering. Perhaps the most famous alternative is the translation "in whom," adopted by Augustine and by a few others. In that case, assuming that "the one man" is the antecedent of the pronoun, we have an explicit statement of "original sin": "in Adam all sinned." But this interpretation, and others that rest on a similar grammatical basis, is un-likely. The two words in the Greek phrase probably function together as a conjunction. The phrase may then mean "from which it follows," "with the result that," "inasmuch as," or "because." The last suggestion is by far the most popular among modern scholars, although the evidence in its favor is not nearly as strong as some suggest. Nevertheless, this is the meaning the phrase almost certainly has in 2 Corinthians 5:4 and probably also in Philippians 3:12 (it almost certainly does not in Phil. 4:10), and it is the meaning that fits best in the context here.

Paul, then, has shown that the entrance of death into the world through the sin of Adam has led to death for all people; all people die, Paul asserts, because all people "sinned." In a sense, then, Paul's focus in this verse, and throughout the passage, is not with "original sin," but with "original death." Paul says nothing explicitly about *how* the sin of one man, Adam, has resulted in death for everyone; nor has he made clear the connection if any between Adam's sin (v. 12a) and the sin of all people (v. 12d). What he *has* made clear is that the causal nexus between sin and death, exhibited in the case of Adam, has repeated itself in the case of every human being. No one, Paul makes clear, escapes the reign of death, because no one escapes the power of sin.

But we cannot stop here. For the fact that Paul in this verse asserts the universality of sin (v. 12d) after mentioning the responsibility of Adam in unleashing sin in the world forces us to ask the question: What is the relationship between Adam's sin and ours? Or, to put it another way, why do all people without exception sin? This question is made even more insistent by Paul's focus on the sin of Adam as the reason for universal condemnation in verses 18–19. How is it that the sin of Adam led to the condemnation of all people? These questions force us to look more care-fully at just what Paul means in verse 12d when he asserts that "all sinned."

At first sight, this question would appear easy to answer. Paul cer-tainly uses the verb "sin" regularly to denote voluntary sinful acts com-mitted by individuals; and this is what most commentators think that this same word, in the same tense as is used here (aorist), designates in 3:23: that all people, "in their own persons," commit sins. Probably a majority of contemporary scholars interpret 5:12d, then, to assert that the death of each person (v. 12c) is directly caused by that person's own individual sinning. The question is then how this "individual" explanation of death is to be squared with the "corporate" explanation of the universality of death in verse 12a–b and, with even greater emphasis, in verses 15–19. In other words, how can we logically relate the assertions "each person dies because *each person* sins [in the course of history]" and "*one [man's]* trespass resulted in condemnation for all people" (v. 18a)?

First, we could posit an unresolved tension between the individual and the corporate emphases.[21] Paul in verse 12 asserts that all people die because they sin on their own account; and in verses 18–19 he claims that they die because of Adam's sin. Paul does not resolve these two perspectives; and we do wrong to try to force a resolution that Paul himself never made. Now it is certainly the case that we can err by insisting that a text give us answers to all our questions about a topic or (still worse) by foisting on a biblical author theological categories that do not fit that author's teaching. But we can also fail to do our job by failing to pursue reasonable harmonizations that the author may assume or intend. So we think it is legitimate to ask whether Paul suggests any resolution of the tension between individual and Adamic responsibility for sin in this text.

One popular explanation holds that Paul assumes a "middle term" in the connection between Adam's sin and the condemnation of all human beings: a corrupted human nature.[22] Verse 12d refers, indeed, to sins committed by individuals in the course of history but as the necessary result of a corrupt nature inherited from Adam. Death, then, is due immediately to the sinning of each individual but ultimately to the sin of Adam; for it was Adam's sin that corrupted human nature and made individual sinning inevitable.[23] This view has much in its favor: it retains the "normal" meaning of "sin" in verse 12 while explaining at the same time how Paul could assert that Adam's sin brings condemnation upon all (vv. 18–19). It also explains why all people act contrary to the will of God: there is a fatal,

---

[21] Cf. particularly A. J. M. Wedderburn, "The Theological Structure of Romans v. 12," *NTS* 19 (1973): 339–54. Advocates of this approach find confirmation for this view in the fact that contemporary Judaism evidenced a similar tension between individual and Adamic responsibility for sin and death. Note, for example, how the Syriac *Apocalypse of Baruch* can assert, on the one hand, "When Adam sinned a death was decreed against those who were to be born" (23:4), and "What did you [Adam] do to all who were born after you?" (48:42); and, on the other hand, "Adam is, therefore, not the cause, except only for himself, but each of us has become our own Adam" (54:19). Similarly, note 54:15: "although Adam sinned first and has brought death upon all who were not in his own time, yet each of them who has been born from him has prepared for himself the coming torments."

[22] Indeed, some scholars (e.g., Luther and Calvin) think that "all sinned" in verse 12 means just that: all people exist "in a state of sin."

[23] Representative is the succinct summary of the early seventeenth-century theologian Johannes Wollebius: "As person has infected nature, so in turn the nature has infected persons." Quoted in Heinrich Heppe, *Reformed Dogmatics* (repr. Eugene, OR: Wipf & Stock, 2007), 314.

God-resisting bent in all people, inherited from Adam (Adam as fallen, not as created). For this reason alone most theologians have assumed the necessity of some such view of the effects of Adam's sin. Nevertheless, we may question whether this is what Paul means in verse 12d. The most serious objection is that this interpretation requires us to supply the crucial "middle term" in the argument: Adam's having and passing on a corrupt nature. For in each case where Adam's sin and the death of all are related, the relationship is stated directly: "many died by the trespass of the one man" (v. 15a); "the judgment followed one sin and brought condemnation" (v. 16b); "by the trespass of the one man, death reigned" (v. 17a); "one trespass resulted in condemnation for all people" (v. 18a). In the view we are examining, these statements must be expanded to mean "one man's trespass *resulted in the corruption of human nature, which caused all people to sin, and so* brought condemnation on all people." While it is possible that Paul would want us to assume these additions, he has given us little basis for doing so.

If, then, we are to read verse 12d in light of verses 18–19, "all sinned" must be given some kind of "corporate" meaning: "sinning" not as voluntary acts of sin in "one's own person," but sinning "in and with" Adam. This is not to adopt the translation "in Adam" rejected above. The point is rather that the sin attributed to the "all" is to be understood, in the light of verses 12a–c and 15–19, as a sin that in some manner is identical to the sin committed by Adam. Paul can therefore say both "all die because all sin" and "all die because Adam sinned" with no hint of conflict, because the sin of Adam *is* the sin of all. All people, therefore, stand condemned "in Adam," guilty by reason of the sin all committed "in him." This interpretation is defended by a great number of exegetes and theologians. It maintains the close connection between Adam's sin and the condemnation of all that is required by verse 15–19, a connection suggested also by 1 Corinthians 15:22: "in Adam all die." And a sin committed before individual consciousness also explains how Paul could consider all people as "by nature deserving of wrath" (Eph. 2:3). The major problem with this view is, of course, whether it is the most natural way to read verse 12d. While Paul does not make explicit a connection with Adam's sin in this clause, the parallel created by Paul ("and in this way") between the entrance into the world of sin and death (v. 12a–b) and the spread of death to all people (v. 12c) makes it possible to argue that the causes of these phenomena—the sin of the "one man" and the sin of "all"—are also closely related.

We must admit that the case for interpreting "all sinned" in verse 12d as meaning "all people sinned in and with Adam" rests almost entirely on the juxtaposition of verse 12 with verses 18–19. And maybe we should not force this combination when Paul himself did not explicitly do so. But one further point inclines us to think that Paul may, indeed, have been think- ing along these lines: the popularity of conceptions of corporate solidarity in the Jewish world of Paul's day. This notion, rooted in the Old Testa- ment, held that actions of certain individuals could have a representative character, being regarded as, in some sense, the actions of many other individuals at the same time. I think that there is good reason to suppose that Paul adopted such a concept as a fruitful way of explaining the signifi- cance in salvation history of both Adam and Christ. For Paul, Adam, like Christ, was a corporate figure whose sin could be regarded at the same time as the sin of all his descendants.

Of course, this interpretation of Romans 5 raises a serious question: the question of fairness. The German theologian Wolfhart Pannenberg puts it bluntly: "It is impossible for me to be held jointly responsible as though I were a joint cause for an act that another did many generations ago and in a situation radically different from mine."[24] Various theological and philosophical constructs can offer more or less help in answering this question, but no explanation ultimately removes the problem. "Original sin" remains an "offense to reason."[25] On the other hand, some such doc- trine is necessary to explain the fact of universal sin and evil. Pascal in a famous passage put it like this:

> Original sin is foolishness to men, but it is admitted to be such. You must not then reproach me for the want of reason in this doctrine, since I admit it to be without reason. But this foolishness is wiser than all the wisdom of men. For without this, what can we say that man is? His whole state depends on this imperceptible point. And how should it be perceived by his reason, since it is a thing against reason, and since reason, far from finding it out by her own ways, is averse to it when it is presented to her?[26]

The folly, degradation, and hatred that are the chief characteristics of human history demand an explanation. Why do people so consistently

---

[24] *Anthropology in Theological Perspective* (Louisville: Westminster John Knox, 1985), 124; cf. C. W. Carter, "Harmartiology: Evil, the Marrer of God's Creative Purpose and Work," in *A Contemporary Wesleyan Theology*, ed. C. W. Carter, 2 vols (Grand Rapids, MI: Zondervan, 1983), 1:267: "Guilt stems from a culpable act traceable to the unethical conduct of a morally responsible person."
[25] *Offense to Reason* is the title of Bernard Ramm's study of the doctrine (San Francisco: Harper & Row, 1985).
[26] *Pensées*, 445.

turn from good to evil of all kinds? Paul affirms in this passage that human solidarity in the sin of Adam is the explanation. Whether we explain this solidarity in terms of sinning in and with Adam or because of a corrupt nature inherited from him does not matter at this point. In any case, this biblical explanation for universal human sinfulness appears to explain the data of history and experience as well as, or better than, any rival theory.

Sin in Paul, then, while a matter of individual choice—a choice for which humans are justly held accountable (see Rom. 1:21)—is also a matter of necessity rooted in one's solidarity with Adam.

The Powers

A third important part of the human environment related to sin is the presence and influence of the "powers," evil spiritual beings. Paul uses a variety of terms to refer to these beings: "angels" (*angeloi*; see Rom. 8:38); "authorities" (*exousiai*; see 1 Cor. 15:24; Eph. 1:21; 2:2; 3:10; 6:12; Col. 1:16; 2:10, 15); "ruler/s" (1 Cor. 15:24; Eph. 3:10; 6:12; Col. 1:18; 2:10, 15); "powers" (*dynameis*; see Rom. 8:38; 1 Cor. 15:24; Eph. 1:21; also *kyriotētes*; see Eph 1:21; Col 1:16); "thrones" (*thrōnai*; see Col. 1:16).[27] Following the Old Testament, Paul also refers to a spiritual being who is particularly involved in tempting humans to abandon God and follow the way of sin: the "devil" (*diabolos*; see Eph. 4:27; 6:11; 1 Tim. 3:6, 7; 2 Tim. 2:26) or "Satan" (*Satanas*; see Rom. 16:20; 1 Cor. 5:5; 7:5; 2 Cor. 2:11; 11:14; 12:7; 1 Thess. 2:18; 2 Thess. 2:9; 1 Tim. 1:20; 5:15). Paul makes clear just how great is the influence of Satan over this world and the humans who belong to it. He is "the god of this age" (2 Cor. 4:4) and "the ruler of the kingdom of the air, the spirit who is now at work in those who are disobedient" (Eph. 2:2). The existence of spiritual beings of various sorts and their critical impact on the affairs of human beings were fundamental components of the ancient worldview. Translation of this emphasis into our culture is contested. On the one hand, the ancient worldview about the significance of spiritual beings for the affairs of this world is, in a fundamental sense at least, the biblical worldview as well. Spiritual powers, while defeated in Christ (Col. 2:15), are still active and powerful. Human sin, Paul makes clear, can often be traced to the influence of these beings. More contested is whether we are justified in finding reference in a text such as this one to the various

---

[27] The references in Col. 1:16 may, however, be to spiritual beings in general, whether good or evil; see Douglas J. Moo, *The Letters to the Colossians and to Philemon*, PNTC (Grand Rapids, MI: Eerdmans, 2008), 122–23. "The elements of the world" (*ta stoicheiai tou kosmou*; cf. Gal. 4:3, 9; Col. 2:8, 20) is often taken as a reference to spiritual beings also, but this identification is unlikely; the reference is probably to the material "elements" of the universe, with possible derivative significance for spiritual powers. See Moo, *Colossians*, 187–93.

structures, persons, and institutions through whom evil "powers" might be working today. On this view, the language of these texts can be applied to "unseen forces working in the world through pagan religion, astrology, or magic, or through the oppressive systems that enslaved or tyrannized human beings."[28]

The Consequences of Sin

Sin, Paul teaches, affects the entire created world.

> For the creation waits in eager expectation for the children of God to be revealed. For the creation was subjected to frustration, not by its own choice, but by the will of the one who subjected it, in hope that the creation itself will be liberated from its bondage to decay and brought into the freedom and glory of the children of God. We know that the whole creation has been groaning as in the pains of childbirth right up to the present time. (Rom. 8:19–22)

This passage makes no direct reference to human sin. But Paul clearly has the story of Genesis 3 in view here; "the one who subjected [creation]" is clearly God, and his subjection must be the curse that he pronounces on "the ground" (Gen. 3:17). The "creation" that Paul has in view here, as most interpreters recognize, is the "subhuman" creation. Following the lead of psalmists and prophets (e.g., Ps. 65:12–13; Isa. 24:4; Jer. 4:28; 12:4), Paul personifies the world of nature in order to portray its "fall" and anticipated glory. Human sin, Paul is affirming, has led to some kind of change in the nature of the cosmos itself. It has been subject, Paul says, to "frustration" or "vanity"; the Greek word suggests that creation has been unable to attain the purpose for which it was created. The natural world itself has been affected in some way by the human fall into sin and is therefore no longer in its pristine created state. Human sin has affected the state of nature itself—and will continue to do so until the end of this age. But if creation has suffered the consequences of human sin, it will also enjoy the fruits of human deliverance. When believers are glorified, creation's "bondage to decay" will be ended and it will participate in the "freedom and glory" for which Christians are destined. Nature, Paul affirms, has a

---

[28] N. T. Wright, *The Epistles of Paul to the Colossians and to Philemon*, TNTC (Grand Rapids, MI: Eerdmans, 1986), 72. See, for this general way of thinking about the "powers" in the NT, the three-volume project of Walter Wink: *Naming the Powers; Unmasking the Powers: The Invisible Forces that Determine Human Existence; Engaging the Powers: Discernment and Resistance in a World of Domination* (Philadelphia: Fortress, 1984, 1986, 1992). Clinton Arnold is reluctant to make this hermeneutical move; cf. *Powers of Darkness: Principalities and Powers in Paul's Letters* (Downers Grove, IL: InterVarsity, 1992).

future within the plan of God. It is destined not simply for destruction but for transformation.[29]

More often, however, Paul refers to the effects of sin on those humans who are held captive under its power. In one text Paul implies clearly that sin can result in physical problems. In rebuking the Corinthians for their selfishness in the way that they are failing to share food when they gather to celebrate the Lord's Supper, Paul warns them they may "eat and drink judgment on themselves" and goes on to say: "That is why many among you are weak and sick, and a number of you have fallen asleep" (1 Cor. 11:30).

Paul typically focuses on the broad spiritual consequences that arise from the state of being under sin's power. He expresses this state in a wide number of ways: "die/death" (*apothanō, thanatos*); "condemn/condemnation" (*katakrinō, katakrima*); "wrath" (*orgē*, once *thymos*); "trouble and distress" (*thlipsis kai stenochōria*); "curse" (*katara*, cf. *anathema*); "punish/punishment" (*ekdikos, ekdikēsis, dikē*); "perish," "destroy/destruction" (usually *apollymi, apōleia*, three times *olethros*, once *phthora*). The most important of these terms is "death." Death, Paul teaches, echoing Genesis 2:17, is the immediate and inevitable consequence of sin (Rom. 5:12). As I noted above, the exact meaning of this "death" is not easy to pin down but probably includes both physical and spiritual elements. In the Genesis account, as in Paul's appropriation of it, physical death and spiritual death are intertwined in ways that make it difficult neatly to separate them. Paul, with other New Testament authors, teaches that all people, including believers, must still experience physical death (e.g., Rom. 8:10), the "last enemy" (1 Cor. 15:26). But believers have been rescued from spiritual death through their union with Christ (note the past tense in Eph. 2:1: "You were dead in your transgressions and sins"); and, while having to pass through the experience of death, they are assured that they will escape the "eternal death" that unbelievers will suffer. It is vitally important for Christians to allow this biblical teaching about the desperate status of non-Christians to mold their thinking. Only when we truly perceive the nature of the "plight" will we be adequately motivated to proclaim the "solution" provided by God in Christ.

The consequences of sin are therefore both present and future: as there is in Paul an inaugurated eschatology of life—believers enjoy life now as the first stage of life eternal—so there is also an inaugurated es-

---

[29] This paragraph relies on my article "Nature in the New Creation," *JETS* 49 (2006): 459–63.

chatology of death—human beings suffer condemnation and wrath now as the first stage of eternal death.[30]

Sin and the Christian

The inaugurated nature of God's work in salvation is the indispensable backdrop for understanding Paul's teaching about the believer's relationship to sin. On the one hand, as Paul's many warnings and exhortations to Christians make clear, sin remains a real possibility, a danger to which the believer must always be alert. Indeed, while Paul never expresses the point in such straightforward language, he would surely agree with John: "If we claim that we have not sinned, we make him out to be a liar and his word is not in us" (1 John 1:10). The reason why sin will continue to threaten the believer is the "not yet" side of God's eschatological work. While justified, reconciled, and adopted into God's family, Christians are not yet glorified. We are still in our earthbound bodies, constantly affected by the passions of those bodies and by the unredeemed world in which we live (see esp. Rom. 5:2–19; 8:18–30).

But Paul's special focus is on the other, "already," side of our status. He emphasizes this status in terms of our relationship to sin in Romans 6. The main point of this paragraph is that God has decisively changed the believer's relationship to sin. Paul uses the imagery of slavery, mastery, and freedom to make his point. We should no longer serve sin (v. 6) because we have been "set free" from sin and have become "slaves" to God/righteousness (vv. 17–22); sin is no longer our "master" (v. 14a). Specifically, Paul says, "we died to sin" (v. 2). What does Paul mean by this? Clearly he does not mean that Christians are not tempted by sin or that we are incapable of sinning—as both his commands in verses 11–14 and the "not yet" side of our salvation that we noted above make clear. He apparently uses this imagery of "death" for two reasons. First, it creates an obvious point of contact with the death of Christ, an important step in Paul's argument here (vv. 3–4). Second, it is a powerful image of a decisive shift in state. When someone becomes a Christian, Paul implies, their change of state in relationship to sin is as dramatic as the change from life to death. Paul spells out the implication of this change in a rhetorical question: "How can we live in it any longer?" (v. 2). This question might be turned into a statement: we who are Christians no longer live

---

[30] Douglas J. Moo, "Paul on Hell," in *Hell under Fire*, ed. Christopher W. Morgan and Robert A. Peterson (Grand Rapids, MI: Zondervan, 2004), 91–109.

under the domination of sin. We cannot, therefore, just go on living in sin the way we used to.

Yet this "indicative" emphasis is matched in this text by a corresponding "imperative" focus, a hallmark of Paul's balanced teaching about the believer's relationship to sin. Believers, Paul insists, must actively and continually regard themselves as people who have been placed in this new relationship to sin (v. 11). And they must then act on this recognition. Paul demands: "Do not let sin reign" (v. 12). Yet at the same time as he issues this imperative, Paul again circles back to the indicative, claiming in verse 14 that "sin shall no longer be your master." The victory over sin that God has won for us in Christ is a victory that must be appropriated. Putting away those sins that plague us will be no automatic process, something that will happen without our cooperation. No, Paul insists, a determination of our own will is called for to turn what has happened in principle into actuality. Verse 13 makes the same point in a different way. With the words "members" and "weapons" Paul brings before us a picture of all our varied capacities and abilities. All of them we are to withdraw from the use of our master sin and place at the disposal of our new master, God. It is "righteousness," that standard of right behavior that God reveals to us, that we are now to serve.

As we dedicate ourselves to this life of righteousness and renunciation of sin in all its forms, we do so with the joyful assurance that our work will not be in vain.

> When the perishable has been clothed with the imperishable, and the mortal with immortality, then the saying that is written will come true: "Death has been swallowed up in victory."
>
> "Where, O death, is your victory?
> Where, O death, is your sting?"
>
> The sting of death is sin, and the power of sin is the law. But thanks be to God! He gives us the victory through our Lord Jesus Christ. Therefore, my dear brothers and sisters, stand firm. Let nothing move you. Always give yourselves fully to the work of the Lord, because you know that your labor in the Lord is not in vain. (1 Cor. 15:54–58)

6

SIN IN THE BIBLICAL STORY

CHRISTOPHER W. MORGAN

A troubling YouTube video pictures a sixty-eight-year-old bus monitor named Karen being bullied by several teenagers who repeatedly hurl insults at her. At least four students from Greece, New York, curse this widow and grandmother for ten straight minutes, threatening to hurt her, deriding her, and calling her old, poor, fat, an elephant, and a troll. One teen heartlessly mocks that she does not have a family because they killed themselves, not wanting to be near her.[1] The video went viral (two million people viewed it in two days), and outrage erupted. Parents, school officials, police, and reporters alike asked: How could these teens do such a thing? What is wrong with *them*?

And in one of the worst scandals in sports history, retired Penn State University assistant football coach Jerry Sandusky was recently convicted of sexually abusing ten boys whom he met through his Second Mile charity, a group foster home devoted to helping troubled boys. Penn State University then fired its president, as well as longtime coach Joe Paterno.[2] The NCAA gave Penn State serious sanctions, as NCAA President Mark Emmert commented:

> This case involves tragic and tragically unnecessary circumstances. One of the grave damages stemming from our love of sports is that the sports themselves can become too big to fail, indeed too big to even challenge. The result can be an erosion of academic values that are replaced by the

---

[1] Niamh Scallan, "Video of Bus Monitor Bullied by Students Goes Viral," *Toronto Star*, June 22, 2012. http://www.thestar.com/news/world/article/1214780—video-of-bus-monitor-bullied-by-students-goes-viral. Accessed September 16, 2012.

[2] Bill Chappell, "Penn State Abuse Scandal: A Guide and Timeline," National Public Radio, July 28, 2012. http://www.npr.org/2011/11/08/142111804/penn-state-abuse-scandal-a-guide-and-timeline. Accessed September 16, 2012.

value of hero worship and winning at all costs. . . . In the Penn State case, the results were perverse and unconscionable. . . . No price the NCAA can levy will repair the grievous damage inflicted by Jerry Sandusky on his victims. However, we can make clear that the culture, actions and inactions that allowed them to be victimized will not be tolerated in collegiate athletics.[3]

Though a few continue to defend coach Joe Paterno, most are rightly asking not only, "What is wrong with Sandusky?" but also, "What is wrong with universities that so value football that obvious evil is tolerated?" Thankfully, some trustees of the university and some influencers inside college sports are starting to ask, "What is wrong with *us* that we have built a system in which this could have happened?"

Something is wrong with the world. With minimal reflection we read the news and ask: What is wrong with *them*? Terrorism, ethnic cleansing, child abuse, robbery, and sex trafficking together cry out that this world is not the way it is supposed to be.[4]

With honest self-examination we may also be able to ask: What is wrong with *us*? Blind loyalty to some, disloyalty to others, slander, gossip, neglect of the poor, and disunity exclaim that we too are not the way we are supposed to be. Governments, businesses, universities, athletic teams, families, and churches each testify that something is wrong with us. *We* are not the way we are supposed to be.

Seldom do we forthrightly vocalize: What is wrong with *me*? But we may wonder: Why do I do what I should not? Why do I fail to do what I should? Why do I think what I should not, and why do I feel what I should not? Why do I want what I should not, and not want what I should? And when I do what I should, why do I often do so with mixed motives? And when I do want what I should, why do I not want it with the level of intensity that I should? Why does God's glory often not capture my heart? Why do I often show so little interest in the needs of others? Pride, greed, lust, selfishness, discontent, and apathy should not characterize me. But too often they do. Why am *I* not the way I am supposed to be? The human phenomenon bears witness that something is wrong—with the world, with us, and with me. And yet the human phenomenon also testifies that something is right.

---

[3] Edith Honan, "NCAA sanctions Penn State for Sandusky scandal," *Reuters*, July 24, 2012. http://www.reuters.com/article/2012/07/24/us-usa-pennstate-idUSBRE86L07F20120724. Accessed September 16, 2012.
[4] Cornelius Plantinga Jr., *Not the Way It's Supposed to Be: A Breviary of Sin* (Grand Rapids, MI: Eerdmans, 1995).

In our first example, parents, school officials, and people from around the world were indignant at the school monitor's being so scorned. Some of the students apologized, parents were horrified, the school took action, and a stranger organized a collection for Karen. Hundreds of thousands of dollars poured in.

Penn State officials also took action, firing many who failed to speak out. And the NCAA forcefully addressed the atrocity and the school's early inaction, giving the university and its football team heavy sanctions.

Further, that we realize that there are things wrong with the world reveals that there is still something right in it. Despite the intrinsic tensions, contemporary postmodernists and pluralists even live with an "oughtness," criticizing people for misunderstanding their assertions, rightly condemning violence against homosexuals, and denouncing colonialism, racism, and sexism.

Even more, what is right in the world is often entangled with what is wrong. What is wrong can flow in people and systems apparently committed to the good. Henri Blocher wisely asks:

> If humans are capable of so much evil, how is it that they also reach heights of heroism, performing admirable deeds of selfless service and devotion to the truth? ... We have to acknowledge the complexity of the human phenomenon. ... Actually the complexity is worse that many imagine; one may discover worthy motives in outrageous actions, and ugly roots under the flowering of virtue. How can we make sense of the entanglement of these things?[5]

Blocher's question merits attention: How do we make sense of such things?

The testimony of Scripture acknowledges this human phenomenon, even clarifying portions of it for us. Scripture bears witness that something is very wrong in the world. And it indicates that creation is good, humans are created in God's image, and that many aspects of life are good (even if often corrupted).

So *what* is wrong? How does this wrong relate to this sense of rightness? And what is the *root* of what is wrong? Previous chapters have examined particular biblical passages and their teachings related to such questions. Here it is hoped that asking these questions in light of the

---

[5] Henri Blocher, *Original Sin: Illuminating the Riddle*, NSBT, ed. D. A. Carson (Grand Rapids, MI: Eerdmans, 1997), 11–12.

broader flow of the plotline of Scripture will shed some light on what is wrong and the roots of it. The major epochs in salvation history are commonly summarized as creation, fall, redemption, and consummation. They will instruct us in the theology of sin—directly and indirectly—indicating how things were, how they are supposed to be, how things are, and how things will be. The biblical story will shed light on what went wrong and what God does to address the human predicament.

Creation and Sin

The story of the Bible starts suddenly: "In the beginning God created the heavens and the earth" (Gen. 1:1). Already in existence prior to matter, space, or time, the eternal, self-existent God creates the universe and all that exists. Bruce Waltke introduces Genesis 1:1–2:3: "The creation account is a highly sophisticated presentation, designed to emphasize the sublimity (power, majesty, and wisdom) of the Creator God and to lay the foundation for the worldview of the covenant community."[6] As the chief character, God "creates, says, sees, separates, names, makes, appoints, blesses, finishes, makes holy, and rests."[7] God transforms the initially unformed, empty, dark, and watery cosmos into something good—carefully crafted, filled, and blessed with light and land. God creates out of nothing, tames the chaos, forms it according to his purposes, and fills it with plants and animals. God is not like other gods in the ancient Near East. Gordon Wenham observes: "God is without peer and competitor. He does not have to establish his power in struggle with other members of a polytheistic pantheon. The sun and moon are his handiwork, not his rivals."[8] The true God is not the sky, sun, moon, water, trees, animals, or anything else created; God created them, and they are subject to him. The creation is neither God nor a part of God; he is absolute and has independent existence, and creation has derived existence from him and continually depends on him as its sustainer (see Acts 17:25–28).

The transcendent creator is sovereign, with amazing authority and power. Like a king, he can effect his will by his very word, even bringing things into being out of nothing (Gen. 1:3; cf. Heb. 11:3). He further displays his authority over all creation by his calling and naming the elements (Gen. 1:5).

---

[6] Bruce K. Waltke, *Genesis: A Commentary* (Grand Rapids, MI: Zondervan, 2001), 56.
[7] C. John Collins, *Genesis 1–4: A Linguistic, Literary, and Theological Commentary* (Phillipsburg, NJ: P&R, 2006), 71.
[8] Gordon J. Wenham, *Genesis 1–15*, WBC (Waco, TX: Word, 1987), 37–38.

The transcendent, sovereign creator is also personal. On each day God is personally involved in every detail of the creation, crafting it in a way that pleases him and benefits his creatures. In dramatic fashion, on the sixth day he personally creates man in his own image, breathing life into him. The personal God has made humans personal as well, with the ability to relate to him, live in community with one other, and have dominion over creation. As D. A. Carson reminds, "We are accorded with an astonishing dignity" and have "implanted within us a profound capacity for knowing God intimately."[9] By creating us in his image, God distinguishes us from the rest of creation and establishes that he is distinct from us—we are not gods but creatures made in his image.

Genesis 1 also stresses God's goodness, which is reflected in the goodness of his creation and reinforced in the steady refrain, "And God saw that it was good" (1:10, 12, 18, 21, 25; see also 1:4). On the sixth day creation is even described as "very good" (v. 31). The inherent goodness of creation leaves no room for a fundamental dualism between spirit and matter such that spirit is good and matter is bad. Indeed, material creation reflects God's goodness, which is also evident in his generous provisions of light, land, vegetation, animals, and even "creeping" things. These are blessings given for humanity's benefit, as are the ability to relate to God, fertility to procreate, and authority to use the abundant provisions for their good. Although creation reaches its summit in God creating man in his image, Genesis 1:1–2:3 culminates in the resting of God. By the seventh day God finishes his creative work, rests, and blesses and sanctifies the day as holy, as a Sabbath to be kept. In doing so, God displays his joy and satisfaction in his creation, and his celebration of completion, and he commemorates this special event.[10]

Whereas Genesis 1:1–2:3 centers on God's creation and rest, Genesis 2:4–25 focuses on God's formation of man and woman and his provision of the garden of Eden as a place for them to live and work.[11] Or, as Allen Ross summarizes, "God has prepared human beings, male and female, with the spiritual capacity and communal assistance to serve him and to keep his commands so that they might live and enjoy the bounty of his creation."[12] This section starts with Genesis's typical structural introduc-

---

[9] D. A. Carson, *The Gagging of God: Christianity Confronts Pluralism* (Grand Rapids, MI: Zondervan, 1996), 205.
[10] Allen P. Ross, *Creation and Blessing: A Guide to the Study and Exposition of Genesis* (Grand Rapids, MI: Baker, 1996), 114.
[11] Collins, *Genesis 1–4*, 39, 101.
[12] Ross, *Creation and Blessing*, 127.

tion—"These are the generations of" (2:4)—but atypically refers to God as "the Lord God." Wenham notes:

> Usually one or the other name is used, but here the two are combined, suggesting no doubt that this story reveals both God's character as sovereign creator of the universe (God) and his intimate covenant-like relationship with mankind (the Lord).
>
> Both traits are prominent in the first scene (2:5–17), which shows the Lord God creating man and a perfect environment for him. It discloses God's sovereignty over man his creature and his loving concern for his well-being.[13]

In Genesis 2:4–19, "The Lord God" is "the sole actor, as he forms the man, plants the garden, transports man there, sets up the terms of a relationship with man, and searches for a helper fit for the man, which culminates in the woman."[14] Man is formed from the dust of the ground but is more than dust—his life comes directly from the very breath of God (2:7). In planting the garden and moving man there, the Creator and covenant Lord provides a delightful and sacred space in which humans are able to enjoy a harmonious relationship with him, each other, the animals, and the land. Waltke observes, "The Garden of Eden is a temple-garden, represented later in the tabernacle."[15] As such the garden highlights God's presence with man.

God establishes the terms for living in his presence and graciously puts forward only one prohibition: man shall not eat from the Tree of the Knowledge of Good and Evil. Contrary to what might be expected, man is allowed to eat of the Tree of Life (which confers immortality) but not the Tree of the Knowledge of Good and Evil (which gives access to wisdom), "for that leads to human autonomy and an independence of the creator incompatible with the trustful relationship between man and his maker which the story presupposes."[16] Because God's generosity to man is so abundant, his prohibition would not seem difficult to accept.

God's generosity to Adam is further depicted as God notices that "it is not good that man should be alone" and meets man's need by creating woman as a complementary and intimate companion united with him for life together. Chapter 2 of Genesis ends positively, and given the be-

---

[13] Wenham, *Genesis 1–15*, 87.
[14] Collins, *Genesis 1–4*, 132.
[15] Waltke, *Genesis*, 85.
[16] Wenham, *Genesis 1–15*, 87.

liefs of ancient Israel, surprisingly—"and the man and his wife were both naked and not ashamed" (v. 25). In the garden, nakedness is not reason for shame but points to their innocence and the pristine delight they have in each other.[17]

At first glance, one might conclude that this first epoch of the biblical story has little to contribute to our understanding of sin. After all, sin is not even mentioned. Ah, but that silence speaks volumes! In particular, Genesis's teaching about God's creation clarifies two critical principles related to sin.

First, *sin is not something created or authored by God. Rather, God created a good universe and good human beings.* As we have seen, Genesis 1–2 shows the Creator to be transcendent, sovereign, personal, immanent, and *good*. God's goodness is displayed in his turning the chaos into something good—the heavens and the earth. His goodness is even more clearly reflected in the goodness of his creation, evidenced by the steady refrain, "And God saw that it was good," a goodness accentuated on the sixth day: "Behold, it was very good." God's generous provisions of light, land, vegetation, and animals are blessings given for man's benefit, as are the abilities to know God, work, marry, and procreate. God blesses man with the Sabbath, places him in the delightful garden of Eden, gives him a helper, and establishes only one prohibition, given not to stifle man but to promote his welfare.

The good God created a good world for the good of his creatures. Humans too were created good and blessed beyond measure, being made in God's image, with an unhindered relationship with God and with freedom. As a result, casting blame for sin on the good and generous God is unbiblical and unfounded. Michael Williams observes: "By beginning with the story of creation rather than the fall, Scripture proclaims categorically that sin is an intruder. It is not the product of God's creativity. It does not belong."[18] Indeed, in the beginning, God created a good cosmos with good humans who had good relationships with God, themselves, one another, and with creation itself.

Second, *sin is not original. It has not always existed.* From a theological standpoint, God's creation of the universe out of nothing shows that he alone is independent, absolute, and eternal. Everything else has been created. Further, the inherent goodness of creation leaves no room for a

---

[17] Ibid., 88; Collins, *Genesis 1–4*, 139.
[18] Michael D. Williams, *Far as the Curse Is Found: The Covenant Story of Redemption* (Phillipsburg, NJ: P&R, 2005), 64.

fundamental dualism between spirit and matter. Contrary to some philosophical and religious traditions, the Bible teaches that matter is a part of God's creation and is good. Sin is ethical, not physical or tied to the cosmos itself.

From a historical standpoint, the story of creation recounts that there was a time when there was no sin. Sin is not original. Indeed, the very fact that our world now includes sin testifies that it is not now the way it was, and therefore, as Cornelius Plantinga helpfully states, "it is not the way it is supposed to be."[19]

The Fall and Sin

We know from the biblical account of creation that sin is not created by God and that there was a time when there was no sin. We also know from experience, however, that evil exists. The world is now not the way it was, and it is no longer the way it is supposed to be.

What went wrong? Carson notes:

> The Bible begins with God creating the heavens and the earth (Gen. 1–2). Repeatedly, God's verdict is that all of his handiwork is "very good." There is no sin and no suffering. The garden of Eden brings forth food without the sweat of toil being mixed into the earth. But the first human rebellion (Gen. 3) marks the onset of suffering, toil, pain, and death. A mere two chapters later, we read the endlessly repeated and hauntingly pitiful refrain, "then he died . . . then he died . . . then he died . . . then he died."[20]

We saw from Genesis 1–2 that God creates Adam and Eve in his image as good and with wonderful privileges and significant responsibilities in the garden of Eden. They experience an unhindered relationship with God, intimate enjoyment of each other, and delegated authority over creation. They are given only one prohibition: they must not eat of the Tree of the Knowledge of Good and Evil.

Sadly, Genesis 3 informs us that they do not obey God's command but "fall." The account begins with a tempter who calls into question God's truthfulness, sovereignty, and goodness. The Tempter is "crafty" and deflects the woman's attention from the covenantal relationship that God has established.[21] In verses 6–8 the central scene in the story of the fall

---

[19] Plantinga, *Not the Way It's Supposed to Be*, 2.

[20] D. A. Carson, *How Long, O Lord? Reflections on Suffering and Evil* (Grand Rapids, MI: Baker, 1990), 41.

[21] "It is interesting to note that, though the deity throughout Genesis 2:4–3:24 is 'the LORD God,' the Serpent only calls him 'God,' and he and the woman use only that title in their conversation (3:1b–5). Now, as many have observed, the name God designates the deity in his role of cosmic creator and ruler (its use in 1:1–2:3),

reaches its climax. The fatal sequence is described rapidly in 3:6: "she saw," "she took," "she ate," and "she gave," and it culminates in "he ate." Wenham observes that the midpoint of 3:6–8, "and he ate," employs the key verb of the narrative—"eat"—and is placed between the woman's inflated expectations in eating ("good to eat," "delight to the eyes," and "giving insight") and the actual effects: "eyes opened," "knowing they were nude," and "hiding in the trees."[22] The contrast is striking: the forbidden fruit did not deliver what the Tempter promised but brought new dark realities warned of by the good and truthful covenant Lord.

This initial act of human rebellion brings divine justice: "They sinned by eating, and so would suffer to eat; she led her husband to sin, and so would be mastered by him; they brought pain into the world by their disobedience, and so would have painful toil in their respective lives."[23] Collins adds:

> There are small ironic wordplays. . . . For example, in Genesis 3:5 the serpent promises that the humans' eyes will be *opened* and they will *know* something, while in verse 7 it is fulfilled: their eyes were *opened* and they *knew* something—but it was just that they were naked! . . . Similarly, there is a play between the use of the root *r-b-h* in 3:16 ("I will surely *multiply* your pain in childbearing") and its use in the commission of 1:28 ("Be fruitful and *multiply*"). Whereas procreation had previously been the sphere of blessing, now it is to be the area of pain and danger.[24]

The consequences of their sin are fitting and devastating. The couple immediately feels shame, realizing they are naked (3:7). They sense their estrangement from God, even foolishly trying to hide from him (vv. 8–10). They are afraid of God and how he might respond (vv. 9–10). Their alienation from each other also emerges as the woman blames the Serpent, while the man blames the woman and by intimation even God (vv. 10–13). Pain and sorrow also ensue. The woman experiences pain in childbirth, the man toils in trying to grow food in a land with pests and weeds, and both discover dissonance in their relationship (vv. 15–19). Even worse, the couple is banished from Eden and God's glorious presence (vv. 22–24).

---

while 'the LORD' ('Yahweh') is particularly his name as he enters into covenantal relationship with human beings. By dropping the covenant name, then, the Serpent is probably advancing his program of temptation by diverting the woman's attention from the relationship the Lord has established. The woman's use of it shows that she is trapped, and we begin to have a clue as to how she could be led into disobedience by forgetting the covenant." Collins, *Genesis 1–4*, 171.

[22] Wenham, *Genesis 1–15*, 75.

[23] Ross, *Creation and Blessing*, 148.

[24] Collins, *Genesis 1–4*, 169; emphasis original.

How they wish they had listened to God's warning: If you eat of the Tree of the Knowledge of Good and Evil, "you shall surely die!" (2:17). Upon eating the forbidden fruit they do not immediately fall over and die from something like cardiac arrest. But die they do. They die spiritually, and their bodies also begin to experience the gradual decay that ultimately leads to their physical deaths (as God's judgment states: "To dust you shall return"; 3:19).

Most devastating of all is that these consequences do not only befall Adam and Eve but extend to their descendants as well. Robert Pyne describes the dismal scene:

> Standing together east of Eden [Adam and Eve] each felt alone—betrayed by the other, alienated from God, and confused about how it had all come apart so quickly. . . .
>
> The children were all born outside of Eden. . . . None of them ever saw the tree of life or had a chance to taste or reject the forbidden fruit. At the same time, none of them enjoyed marriage relationships without some degree of rivalry or resentment, and they inevitably ate bread produced by the sweat of their brow. Born in a fallen world, they knew only the curse, never Eden. Still they knew that this was not the way life was supposed to be. . . .
>
> Adam and Even sinned alone, but they were not the only ones locked out of the Garden. Cut off from the tree of life, they and their descendants were all destined to die.[25]

So in the beginning, God created a good cosmos with good humans who had good relationships with him, themselves, one another, and with creation itself. But now, sin has entered the picture and has brought disruption and alienation in each human relationship—with God, oneself, one another, and creation.

The immediate context and story line of Genesis 4–11 confirm this gloomy new reality of human fallenness. In Genesis 4:7, God warns Cain that sin is "crouching at the door" and "its desire is for you, but you must rule over it." Sadly, Cain refuses to heed the advice and kills his brother, Abel. He is consequently cursed by God, alienated from the earth, and banished from God's presence (vv. 10–16).

Genesis 5 reminds that God created humans in his image and blessed them, offers hope through mention of Enoch and Noah, but soberly underlines the domain of death with the refrain, "and he died" (vv. 5, 8, 11,

---

[25] Robert A. Pyne, *Humanity and Sin* (Dallas: Word, 1999), 162.

14, 17, 20, 27, 31). Genesis 6 clarifies the extension and intensification of sin, which is portrayed as considerable, pervasive, perpetual, and characteristic: "The LORD saw that the wickedness of man was great upon the earth, and that every intention of the thoughts of his heart was only evil continually" (v. 5); "the earth was corrupt in God's sight, and the earth was filled with violence" (v. 11). God graciously establishes a covenant with Noah and appropriately judges humanity with the flood (Genesis 6–9). Yet just after God reemphasizes the creational blessing and mandate (9:1–7) and offers a covenant promise (vv. 8–17), Noah and his family are still marked by sin (vv. 18–29). Further sobriety about the human phenomenon emerges from the story of the tower of Babel, in which God judges proud, self-seeking humans who try to make a name for themselves and to multiply their influence rather than serve as God's image bearers and advance his name (11:1–9).

Genesis 4–11 unveils the new human phenomenon. Humans are still in the image of God, blessed by God, commanded to be fruitful and multiply, and recipients of God's presence, promise, and grace. Yet society is marked by sin, and all human relationships to God, self, others, and creation are marred by sin.

Paul's well-known observations in Romans 5:12–21 also shed light on the fall.[26] It is worth noting that the thesis of Romans 5:12–21 centers on Christ's obedience and how that brings about our justification. In this sense, the passage is not primarily about original sin. But Romans 5:12–21 is quite instructive about sin as it sets Christ's work and our salvation against the backdrop of Adam's sin and our condemnation.[27] In Adam, sin enters, death is spread and reigns, and condemnation is sentenced. In contrast, through Christ's obedience/act of righteousness, the grace of God and the free gift of righteousness abound, justification is brought, many will be made righteous, recipients of grace reign in life, and grace abounds and reigns through righteousness leading to eternal life through Jesus our Lord.

---

[26] Since the exegetical details of this passage have already been ably addressed in Douglas Moo's chapter, the focus here will be only on Paul's theological argument as it sheds light on the doctrine of sin. See Moo, "Sin in Paul," 120–26.

[27] In Romans Paul has already concluded that all are sinners and guilty before God (3:9–20, 23). He has stressed that only Christ can bring about our righteousness. Nothing else can—not human sincerity, religious privilege, the law, or works. All human beings are under God's wrath; Paul shows this by including pagans, moralists, and Jews in his argument. Pagans have resisted God, though he has communicated himself through creation. Moralists have resisted God, though he has given a law written on their hearts. Jews have resisted God, though God has given them the law, his very oracles. Indeed, that humans are in a pitiable state of sin is manifest from Paul's emphasis that Christ died for us while we were still "ungodly" (5:6), "sinners" (v. 8), and "enemies" of God (v. 10).

Though this passage is filled with interpretive challenges, the following assertions about sin are set forth:

- Sin came into the world through one man, Adam (v. 12).
- Death came into the world through sin (v. 12).[28]
- Death spread to all because all sinned (v. 12).
- As the example of death shows, sin was present in the world before the law was given (vv. 12–14).
- Many died through Adam's trespass/sin (v. 15).
- God's judgment following one trespass brought condemnation (v. 16).
- Because of Adam's trespass, death reigned (v. 17).
- One trespass led to condemnation for all men (v. 18).
- By Adam's disobedience, the many were made sinners (v. 19).
- The law came in to increase the trespass (v. 20).
- Where sin increased, grace abounded all the more (v. 20).
- As sin reigned in death, grace will also reign through righteousness leading to eternal life through Christ (v. 21).

From these accounts of the fall, several insights into sin and the human phenomenon emerge.

Sin Is Fundamentally against God

Most fundamentally, sin must be defined as against God. The accounts depicting the fall suggest that sin is rebellion against God, breaking his covenant, and failing to live as his image bearers by serving as kings and priests according to his will and on his mission.[29] As such, sin is exchanging the glory of the incorruptible God for something less, like idols (Rom. 1:23; cf. Ps. 106:20; Jer. 2:11–12). Sin is falling short of the glory of God (Rom. 3:23) and brings disrepute on the name of God (2:24). And all this relates to the image of God, as Richard Gaffin cogently explains:

> Sin enters in the creation through Adam (Rom. 5:12–19). Consequently, "although they knew God," human beings "neither glorified him as God nor gave thanks" (Rom. 1:21); that is, they have withheld worship and adoration, their due response to the divine glory reflected in the creation around them and in themselves as God's image bearers. Instead, with futile minds and foolish, darkened hearts (cf. 1 Cor. 1:18–25), they have idolatrously exchanged God's glory for creaturely images, human

---

[28] As Moo suggests ("Sin in Paul," 121), this death is likely physical and spiritual. The context includes physical death but also seems to contrast it with spiritual life (as in 6:23). It also portrays death as a domain.

[29] There is no need to rehearse the definitions and nature of sin here since that is given careful treatment in the chapter by John W. Mahony, "Toward a Theology of Sin," 194–206.

and otherwise (Rom. 1:21–23). Having so drastically defaced the divine image, they have, without exception, forfeited the privilege of reflecting his glory (Rom. 3:23). This *doxa*-less condition, resulting in unrelieved futility, corruption and death, permeates the entire created order (Rom. 8:20–22).[30]

Sin Enters the Human Experience in Adam's Sin

That sin is an intruder,[31] entering the human experience in Adam's sin, is clear historically from Genesis (the goodness of creation, the pristine state of Adam, the unhindered relationships, the presence of God in Eden, etc.). That sin enters human history in Adam's sin is also clear theologically in Romans 5. Verse 12 is striking: "Sin came into the world through one man."[32] But much about the intrusion of sin is not clear, as Hoekema suggests:

> The fact that we can discern these stages in the temptation and fall of our first parents, however, does not mean that we have in the Genesis narrative an explanation for the entrance of sin into the human world. What we have here is the biblical narrative of the origin of sin, but not an explanation for that origin. One of the most important things we must remember about sin . . . is that it is inexplicable. The origin of evil is . . . one of the greatest riddles of life.[33]

The riddle centers on the question, Why would Adam and Eve sin? Augustine taught that Adam was able not to sin and able to sin, so that there was an inherent possibility to sin in him. This is helpful, but as Hoekema advises: "But how this possibility became actuality is a mystery that we shall never be able to fathom. We shall never know how doubt first arose in Eve's mind. We shall never understand how a person who had been created in a state of rectitude, in a state of sinlessness, could begin to sin."[34]

Adam and Eve were created good and did not initially have a corrupt heart to lead them astray. They had a close relationship with the Lord, enjoyed intimacy with each other, and retained authority over creation.

---

[30] Richard B. Gaffin Jr., "Glory, Glorification," in *Dictionary of Paul and His Letters*, ed. Gerald F. Hawthorne and Ralph P. Martin (Downers Grove, IL: InterVarsity, 1993), 348. See also Richard B. Gaffin, "The Glory of God in Paul's Epistles," and Christopher W. Morgan, "Toward a Theology of the Glory of God," in *The Glory of God*, Theology in Community 2, ed. Christopher W. Morgan and Robert A. Peterson (Wheaton, IL: Crossway, 2010).
[31] Obviously, the fall is not outside God's eternal design for history.
[32] Since we discover a tempter already in the otherwise pristine garden, sin was evidently present in the angelic world before the human world. See Anthony A. Hoekema, *Created in God's Image* (Grand Rapids, MI: Eerdmans, 1986), 121–32. See also the chapter by Sydney H. T. Page, "Sin, Satan, and Evil," 219–42.
[33] Hoekema, *Created in God's Image*, 130–31.
[34] Ibid., 131.

It would seem that they had everything in Eden; they lived, after all, in paradise! Collins notes:

> In 3:6, as [the woman] regards the tree and sees that it is "good for food, a delight to the eyes, and desirable for giving insight," the irony of the parallel with 2:9 (there was already "every tree desirable to the sight and good for food" in the garden) should not escape us. She already had everything she could possibly want, and she even had the resources to get everything she thought the tree had to offer.[35]

The first couple had everything they could ever want, and yet history records that, in unfaithfulness to God and disobedience to his one prohibition, they absurdly threw it all away. As Augustine noted, trying to determine reasons for such foolishness is like trying to see darkness or hear silence. Or as Plantinga describes, sin is like sawing off a branch that supports us—it cuts us off from our only help.[36] We cannot make sense of such folly or find clear-cut explanations for the irrationality of this original sin.[37]

Adam's Sin Results in the Fall[38]

Although clarity on the reason(s) for Adam's sin remains out of reach, Scripture does indicate that Adam's sin not only results in his own punishment but also has dire consequences for all humanity. Adam sinned not merely as the first bad example but as the representative of all humanity.[39] Recall Romans 5:12–21 and the contrast between Adam's representation of us and Christ's representation of us. In Adam, there is sin, death, and condemnation. In Christ, there is righteousness, life, and justification. In Adam, there is the old era, the dominion of sin and death. In Christ, there is a new reign, marked by grace and life (cf. 1 Cor. 15:20–57). Note the outcomes of Adam's representative trespass:[40]

---

[35] Collins, *Genesis 1–4*, 172.

[36] Plantinga, *Not the Way It's Supposed to Be*, 123.

[37] Paul's words "now I know in part" (1 Cor. 13:9, 12) show that for some matters even apostolic revelation is partial. See Carl F. H. Henry, *God, Revelation, and Authority* (Waco, TX: Word, 1976–83; repr. Wheaton, IL: Crossway, 1999), 6:302. Blocher also reminds that not everything about sin is mysterious, and some theologians too quickly appeal to mystery (*Original Sin*, 107–9).

[38] For more on the historicity of Adam's sin and its theological importance, see John W. Mahony, "Why an Historical Adam Matters for a Biblical Doctrine of Sin," *SBJT* 15 (Spring 2011): 60–79; C. John Collins, *Did Adam and Eve Really Exist? Who They Were and Why You Should Care* (Wheaton, IL: Crossway, 2012); Hoekema, *Created in God's Image*, 112; Blocher, *Original Sin*, 42–59.

[39] Thus, the Council of Carthage in 418 and the Synod of Orange in 529 condemned teachings of Pelagius. For a clear historical overview of Pelagius and Augustine's response, see Gregg R. Allison, *Historical Theology: An Introduction to Christian Doctrine* (Grand Rapids, MI: Zondervan, 2011), 342–52.

[40] Thomas R. Schreiner, *Romans*, BECNT (Grand Rapids, MI: Baker, 1998), 268.

- "many died" because of his sin (v. 15);
- his sin brought "condemnation" to all (v. 16);
- "death reigned" over all human beings (v. 17);
- all people were condemned because of his one trespass (v. 18);
- by virtue of his sin "many were made sinners" (v. 19).

Note also the greater outcomes of Christ's representative work:

- his grace and gift abounded for many (v. 15);
- his grace brought "justification" where Adam introduced "condemnation" (v. 16);
- instead of death reigning, believers now "reign in life" by virtue of the grace of Jesus Christ (v. 17);
- the righteous act of Jesus Christ brought "justification and life" for all (v. 18);
- through Christ's obedience the many are now "made righteous" (v. 19).

And note four particular effects that result from Adam's sin and representation:

1) Many/all were constituted sinners (v. 19).[41]
2) Many/all died (v. 15).
3) Condemnation is upon all (vv. 16, 18).
4) Death reigned over all humans (v. 17).

Thus, and as we will see, in Adam, all are sinners; all die; all are under the domain of death; and all are condemned.

The Fall Results in Universal Human Sinfulness

That the fall of Adam results in universal human sinfulness is suggested by Genesis 3–11 and emphasized by Romans 5:12–21. In particular, verse 19 clarifies, "For as by the one man's disobedience the many were made sinners, so by the one man's obedience the many will be made righteous."

That all are sinners is of no surprise to Christians. The universality of sin is well-known and famously expressed in Romans 3:23: "For all have sinned and fall short of the glory of God," which crystallizes Paul's more developed case in 1:18–3:20. Note also the universal scope of sin reiterated by Paul as he concludes his argument in 3:9–20:

---

[41] Paul does not set "many" in comparison against "all," or vice versa. Rather, he contrasts Adam's one act with the widespread effects of that sin upon humanity, "many." Likewise, Paul contrasts Christ's act with its incalculable effects on "many." Paul uses "all" similarly here. For example, many die and all die.

What then? Are we Jews any better off? No, not at all. For we have already charged that *all, both Jews and Greeks, are under sin*, as it is written:

> "*None* is righteous, no, *not one*;
>   *no one* understands;
>   *no one* seeks for God.

> *All* have turned aside; *together* they have become worthless;
>   *no one* does good,
>   *not even one.*"

> "Their throat is an open grave;
>   they use their tongues to deceive."
> "The venom of asps is under their lips."

> "Their mouth is full of curses and bitterness."
> "Their feet are swift to shed blood;
>   in their paths are ruin and misery,
> and the way of peace they have not known."
>   "There is no fear of God before their eyes."

Now we know that whatever the law says it speaks to those who are under the law, so that *every mouth* may be stopped, and the *whole world* may be held accountable to God. For by works of the law *no human being* will be justified in his sight, since through the law comes knowledge of sin.

How all are constituted sinners in Adam is harder to understand.[42] Even so, some sort of forensic nature of Adam's representation is most plausible, due to the comparison with Christ as the other unique representative, whose work for us is not merely moral but also vicarious, substitutionary, representative. In an essay on Romans 5:12–21, Lewis Johnson puts forward several arguments for this perspective. Three stand out. First, he maintains: "So, just as the act of the Last Adam is a representative act, becoming the judicial ground of the justification of believers,

---

[42] Several perspectives have been set forth, including Pelagianism, mediate imputation, realism, and immediate imputation. In very broad strokes, *Pelagianism* envisions Adam as merely setting a bad example for his descendants; it denies that humans are sinful, corrupt, or guilty in Adam. Those holding to *mediate imputation* suggest that humans derive sinful corruption from Adam through their parents, and that Adam's guilt is mediated through the condition in which we have been born. *Realism* is the view that all humans are guilty of Adam's sin because everyone is a part of the generic human nature of Adam. *Immediate imputation* is the view that Adam is both the physical progenitor and the representative of all humans; when Adam sinned, he did so as the representative of all, and therefore his condemnation is applied to all. See Hoekema, *Created in God's Image*, 154–67.

it follows that the act of the first Adam is a representative act, becoming the judicial ground of the condemnation of those united in him."[43] Second, Johnson argues:

> In v. 12, the apostle makes the point that all die because all sinned. In the following verses, vv. 13–19 (including both the parenthesis of vv. 13–17 and the apodosis of vv. 18–19), he makes the point that all die because one sinned. Can the apostle be dealing with two different things? Hardly. The one fact may be expressed in terms of both plurality and singularity. The sin of all is the sin of one. There must be some kind of solidarity. It is that of federal representation.[44]

Third, Johnson suggests that immediate imputation "enables us to see why only the first sin of Adam and not his subsequent sins, nor the sin of Eve, is imputed to men."[45]

The salvation historical nature of Adam's representation of humanity is also significant. Herman Ridderbos comments on Paul's argument in Romans 5:12–21 and "the reckoning of many as sinners on the grounds of Adam's sin and their share in it":

> This is apparent not only from parallel expression in verse 19b: "will be constituted righteous," which likewise has a forensic and not a moral significance, but also from the preceding pronouncements, which describe the share of all in Adam's sin again and again as a sentence extending to all. . . .
>
> By the entrance of sin into the world the situation has been profoundly changed. Sin has begun its calamitous regime. To be constituted sinners also means to have been placed under the power of sin and death (cf. v. 21).[46]

The Fall Results in Universal Human Guilt and Condemnation

Romans 5:12–21 displays this, particularly in verses 16 and 18: "The judgment following one trespass brought condemnation" (v. 16); ". . . as one trespass led to condemnation for all men" (v. 18). Paul's teaching in Ephesians 2:1–3 speaks similarly: we were all "by nature children of wrath" (v. 3). Blocher puts it well: "Sinfulness has become our quasi-nature while

---

[43] S. Lewis Johnson Jr., "Romans 5:12—An Exercise in Exegesis and Theology," in *New Dimensions in New Testament Study*, ed. Richard N. Longenecker and Merrill C. Tenney (Grand Rapids, MI: Zondervan, 1974), 312.
[44] Ibid., 313.
[45] Ibid.
[46] Herman Ridderbos, *Paul: An Outline of His Theology*, trans. John Richard de Witt (Grand Rapids, MI: Eerdmans, 1997), 98–99.

remaining truly our anti-nature."[47] Humans are universally guilty, in that state by nature (by birth, see Gal. 2:15), and thereby stand condemned under the wrath of God.

The biblical material addressing the relationship of sin and guilt is complex. Take, for example, sin and guilt in Romans. In Romans 1:18–32, Paul highlights that everyone is guilty because everyone suppresses and rejects God, who has communicated himself universally and persistently through creation. In Romans 2, Paul reiterates the universality of guilt, pointing to human guilt's emergence from failure to follow the law written in the hearts of people. In Romans 3, Paul underlines the guilt of the Jews for failure to follow God and his ways, even though they are blessed with God's clear revelation—his very oracles. Paul further concludes that everyone is judged guilty, and the law plays a central role in this (3:19–20). And here in Romans 5 he points to the entrance of sin, death, and condemnation—all three of which are interrelated and enter through Adam, as we have seen. So humans are universally guilty—through rejection of God's general revelation in creation, failure to embrace God's general revelation in this internal law of conscience, and failure to live according to God's special revelation in the Torah; and they are guilty in Adam.

Passages such as John 3 also illustrate the complexities of the biblical portrait of human guilt. Take John 3:18, for example: "Whoever believes in him is not condemned, but whoever does not believe is condemned already, because he has not believed in the name of the only Son of God." John 3:19–20 underlines that condemnation comes because people love the darkness. John 3:36 points to the present wrath of God upon the current state of unbelievers. So according to John's Gospel, everyone who does not believe in Jesus is already spiritually dead (3:3–5) and presently condemned; they are now under God's wrath. Further, they do not believe because they love the darkness, and they are judged because they love the darkness.

The complexity of sin and guilt can also be seen in passages that relate guilt to factors of knowledge (Matt. 10:15; Luke 9:13–14; 12:47–48; John 19:11; 1 Tim. 1:13)[48] or intention (Lev. 4:22; Num. 15:27–30), and those

---

[47] Blocher, *Original Sin*, 30.

[48] See Hoekema, *Created in God's Image*, 177–86. For discussions on the state of infants and the mentally challenged, see Ronald H. Nash, *When a Baby Dies: Answers to Comfort Grieving Parents* (Grand Rapids, MI: Zondervan 1999); Robert A. Peterson, *Hell on Trial: The Case for Eternal Punishment* (Phillipsburg, NJ: P&R, 1995), 235–36. For a discussion on the state of those who have not heard the gospel, see Christopher W. Morgan and Robert A. Peterson, eds., *Faith Comes by Hearing: A Response to Inclusivism* (Downers Grove, IL: InterVarsity, 2008).

that occasionally focus God's judgment upon the individual's sin (Deut. 24:16; Ezek. 18:20; Jer. 31:30). But while guilt may be adduced in various ways and in varied degrees (cf. Rom. 2:5), all humans are guilty in Adam.

The Fall Results in Universal Human Death

This is evident from Genesis, including God's warning in 2:17, "Of the tree of the knowledge of good and evil you shall not eat, for in the day that you eat of it, you shall surely die." It is evident from God's judgment upon Adam, "By the sweat of your face you shall eat bread, till you return to the ground, for out of it you were taken; for you are dust, and to dust you shall return" (3:19). The new entrance of death is also clear from the banishment of Adam and Eve from Eden and from participation in the Tree of Life (vv. 22–24). Death first becomes a physical reality in Cain's murder of Abel, then soon after in Lamech, "an arrogant bully who openly boasted of his murderous exploits" (4:23–24).[49] Death is even underscored in the newborn boy's bizarre name, "Enosh." This term connotes humanity in the sense of frailty and mortality (cf. Pss. 9:20; 103:15; Job 25:4). Death, originally abnormal to humanity, becomes so commonplace that it seems ordinary.[50] Genesis 5 testifies to the regularity of death through the refrain, "and he died" (vv. 5, 8, 11, 14, 17, 20, 27, 31).

That Adam's sin results in the universality of human death is also manifest in Romans 5:12–21. Death enters human history through Adam's sin (v. 12) and spreads to all (v. 12). Indeed, the universality of death clarifies that sin was in the world before the law was given (vv. 13–14). Paul puts it starkly: "Many died through one man's trespass" (v. 15); "sin reigned in death" (v. 21); and later, "For the wages of sin is death, but the free gift of God is eternal life through Jesus Christ our Lord" (6:23). And because death as a whole is viewed in these biblical accounts as a penalty or judgment, it is related to and results from humans' being sinful in Adam and being guilty in Adam.

Though death in these accounts includes physical death, obviously, what is too often forgotten is *the domain of sin and death* that results from the fall. Ridderbos captured the idea:

> So sin has entered in, here represented as a personified power (cf., e.g., v. 21); through and with sin death has come in as the inseparable follower and companion of sin. . . .

---

[49] T. V. Farris, *Mighty to Save: A Study in Old Testament Soteriology* (Nashville: Broadman, 1993), 40.
[50] Ibid., 52–53.

That the share of all men in the sin of Adam is indicated, however, and as its consequence they have been brought under the dominion and power of sin and death. The presupposition of the whole chain of reasoning lies in the inclusion in the supraindividual situation of sin and death represented by Adam. Here again the basic structures of Pauline theology are not individualizing, but redemptive-historical and corporate. It is a matter of two different modes of existence, that of the old and that of the new man, which are determined by two different aeons, and concerning which an all-embracing decision has been made in Adam and Christ. . . .

Death is thereby not only a punishment that puts an end to life, but a condition in which the destiny of life outside of Christ is turned into its opposite. . . .

In addition to the future, however, sin brings forth death already in this life. . . . Thus death works itself out in the sinful life of man.[51]

Such a salvation-historical reading makes sense of the overall comparison of Adam and Christ as our representatives,[52] the importance of the law in the argument here, the emphasis on reigning, and the overall cosmic thrust.

The domain of sin and death is also apparent in Ephesians 2:1–3:

And you were dead in the trespasses and sins in which you once walked, following the course of this world, following the prince of the power of the air, the spirit that is now at work in the sons of disobedience—among whom we all once lived in the passions of our flesh, carrying out the desires of the body and the mind, and were by nature children of wrath, like the rest of mankind.

This passage is replete with teachings related to sin.[53] But especially notice how the domain of sin and death is central: the state of spiritual death; the lifestyle that flows from it; the environmental influence of the world, Satan, and the flesh on human behavior; the designation of sinners as those characterized by sin ("sons of disobedience" and "children of wrath"); and the universal guilt of all by nature.[54]

---

[51] Ridderbos, *Paul*, 96, 99, 112–13. See also J. Julius Scott Jr., "Life and Death," in *Dictionary of Paul and His Letters*, ed. Gerald F. Hawthorne and Ralph P. Martin (Downers Grove, IL: InterVarsity, 1993), 553–55.

[52] Note how 1 Cor. 15:20–58 also puts forward a cosmic, salvation-historical comparison of Adam and Christ.

[53] For an outstanding analysis of this passage and its teachings related to sin, see Peter T. O'Brien, *The Letter to the Ephesians*, Pillar New Testament Commentary (Grand Rapids, MI: Eerdmans, 1999), 153–64.

[54] This domain of sin and death emerges often, particularly in Rom. 3:9 ("all are under sin"); 2 Cor. 4:4 ("god of this world"); Gal. 1:4 ("present evil age"); and Col. 1:13 ("domain of darkness").

The Fall Results in Universal Human Corruption

This is directly related to the domain of sin and death just mentioned. Indeed, Romans 5:12–21 conjoins Adam's sin, humans constituted as sinners, universal guilt, universal death, and the domain of death. The domain of sin and death is the macro-environmental condition in which life occurs; the particular human corruption is a part of the personal and individual aspects of the domain of sin and death.

As we noted above, Ephesians 2:1–3 relates these. Spiritual death is a condition "in which you once walked" (v. 1). There is a following after the way of the world, the present evil age, and Satan (vv. 1–2). There is a spirit that is at work in sinners (v. 2). There is a living after the passions of the flesh, a carrying out of improper mental and physical desires (v. 3).

Scripture explains this corruption in various ways. It uses various metaphors to indicate our corruption: spiritual death, darkness, hardness, bondage, blindness, flesh, and more.[55]

- *Death*: "And you were dead in the trespasses and sins in which you once walked" (Eph. 2:1)
- *Darkness*: "Now this I say and testify in the Lord, that you must no longer walk as the Gentiles do, in the futility of their minds" (Eph. 4:17).
- *Hardness*: "They are darkened in their understanding, alienated from the life of God because of the ignorance that is in them, due to their hardness of heart. They have become callous and have given themselves up to sensuality, greedy to practice every kind of impurity" (Eph. 4:18–19).
- *Bondage*: "We know that our old self was crucified with him in order that the body of sin might be brought to nothing, so that we would no longer be enslaved to sin" (Rom. 6:6).
- *Blindness*: "And even if our gospel is veiled, it is veiled to those who are perishing. In their case the god of this world has blinded the minds of the unbelievers, to keep them from seeing the light of the gospel of the glory of Christ, who is the image of God" (2 Cor. 4:3–4).
- *Flesh*: "For if you live according to the flesh you will die, but if by the Spirit you put to death the deeds of the body, you will live" (Rom. 8:13).

Scripture also links the corruption to a wide range of human faculties and behaviors: mind, will, actions, words, ways, attitudes, and inaction. In Romans 3:9–20, for example, the overall condition of sinners is bleak: all are "under sin" (v. 9); "none is righteous, no, not one" (v. 10);

---

[55] Several of these terms are used more broadly than this, too. For the example of flesh, see Moo, "Paul on Sin, 118–20.

every mouth will be stopped (v. 19); the whole world will be judged guilty before God (v. 19); no human being will be justified by the works of the law (v. 20). But also notice the wide range in how this fallenness is depicted:

- *Mind*: "no one understands" (v. 11).
- *Will*: "no one seeks for God" (v. 11).
- *Actions*: "All have turned aside. . . . No one does good, not even one" (v. 12).[56]
- *Words*: "Their throat is an open grave; they use their tongues to deceive. The venom of asps is under their lips. Their mouth is full of curses and bitterness" (vv. 13–14).
- *Ways*: "Their feet are swift to shed blood; in their paths are ruin and misery, and the way of peace they have not known" (vv. 15–17).
- *Attitude*: "There is no fear of God before their eyes" (v. 18).

Paul stresses that the corruption is pervasive, from head to toe as it were, and includes the mind, will, throat, tongue, mouth, and feet. Jonathan Edwards perceptively observed: "Their heads and their hearts are totally depraved; all the members of their bodies are only instruments of sin, and all their senses (seeing, hearing, tasting) are only inlets and outlets of sin, channels of corruption. . . . There are breaches of every command in thought, word, and deed."[57]

Scripture does not just locate this universal corruption environmentally in the domain of sin and death but as directly as is conceivable, even from within the person. Jesus maintained:

What comes out of a person is what defiles him. For from within, out of the heart of man, come evil thoughts, sexual immorality, theft, murder, adultery, coveting, wickedness, deceit, sensuality, envy, slander, pride, foolishness. All these evil things come from within, and they defile a person. (Mark 7:20–23; cf. Matt. 15:10–20)

If you then, who are evil, know how to give good gifts to your children, how much more will the heavenly Father give the Holy Spirit to those who ask him! (Luke 11:13; cf. Matt. 7:11)

In Mark 7:20–23, Jesus teaches that evil thoughts, actions, desires, attitudes, and ways of life are all rooted in the corrupt human heart. And as

---

[56] See Gal. 5:16–25.
[57] Jonathan Edwards, "The Eternity of Hell Torments," in *The Wrath of Almighty God: Jonathan Edwards on God's Judgment against Sinners*, ed. Don Kistler (Morgan, PA: Soli Deo Gloria, 1996), 91–92.

Jesus teaches his disciples about prayer in Luke 11:13, one of his examples compares the generosity of the good God with the giving of humans, who are designated quite starkly as "evil."[58]

James's teaching about temptation also demonstrates that this corruption is rooted in the very core of all people: "Let no one say when he is tempted, 'I am being tempted by God,' for God cannot be tempted with evil, and he himself tempts no one. But each person is tempted when he is lured and enticed by his own desire. Then desire when it has conceived gives birth to sin, and sin when it is fully grown brings forth death" (James 1:13–15). Those tempted need not look to God or others for the source; they need look no further than their own warped hearts, as their "own desire" is the root.[59] The person's own heart (the internal desire) is the core problem. It gives birth to sin, and when sin grows up into adulthood, the outcome is death.[60]

That this corruption is not only pervasive but internally driven suggests its radical power. Sinners who sin according to their very sinful core have minds, wills, desires, actions, and attitudes shaped by such sin. They cannot disentangle themselves from sin's grip but need something or someone from the outside to rescue them and change their hearts. All humans are sinful, guilty, under the domain of death, fundamentally corrupt, and therefore in desperate need for grace, as Philip Hughes observes:

> Original sin, however mysterious its nature may be, tells us that the reality of sin is something far deeper than the mere outward commission of sinful deeds.... It tells us there is an inner root of sinfulness which corrupts man's true nature and from which his sinful deeds spring. Like a deadly poison, sin has penetrated to and infected the very center of man's being: hence his need for the total experience of rebirth by which, through the grace of God in Christ Jesus, the restoration of his true manhood is effected.[61]

---

[58] Addressing the same topic from a different text (Ps. 51:5, "Behold, I was brought forth in iniquity, and in sin did my mother conceive me"), Blocher comments: "Far from attempting to downplay his own guilt, David refers to his birth and conception in the clear realization that his very being is shot through and through with the tendencies that produced the fruits of adultery and murder. As far back as he can go, he sees his life as sinful." *Original Sin*, 28–29.

[59] See Christopher W. Morgan, *A Theology of James: Wisdom for God's People*, Explorations in Biblical Theology, ed. Robert A. Peterson (Phillipsburg, NJ: P&R, 2010), 156–59.

[60] For a helpful introduction to the related doctrines of total depravity and inability, see Hoekema, *Created in God's Image*, 147–54. For a comparison of the Arminian and Reformed views of human inability, and for clear exposition of related passages, see Robert A. Peterson and Michael D. Williams, *Why I Am Not an Arminian* (Downers Grove, IL: InterVarsity, 2004), 162–72.

[61] Philip E. Hughes, "Another Dogma Falls," *Christianity Today* (May 23, 1969), 13. Cited in Hoekema, *Created in God's Image*, 154.

The Fall Results in Human Suffering

As sin enters through Adam, so do its consequences, suffering included. And just as God is not the author of sin, so he is not the author of suffering. Suffering is not a part of God's originally good creation but rather a by-product of sin, as Carson explains:

> Between the beginning and the end of the Bible, there is evil and there is suffering. But the point to be observed is that from the perspective of the Bible's large-scale story line, the two are profoundly related: evil is the primal cause of suffering, rebellion is the root of pain, sin is the source of death.[62]

On a cosmic scale, therefore, all suffering is an effect of the fall.[63] Indeed, because we live in this fallen world, we will suffer and "reap sin's consequences in the home, the workplace, and the cemetery."[64]

Thus, sin is not the only intruder, but its evil children—suffering and death—have intruded as well. We intuitively know this but often do not consider its significance. When we encounter suffering, something inside us often cries out: "This is wrong. The world should not be like this. Children should not be abused; senior adults should not get Alzheimer's; missionaries should not be tortured!" Or on a more personal level we might protest: "Why me? What did I do to deserve this?" Such instincts are valid because they recognize that this world is not the way it is supposed to be. We know this when we consider sin; we know to hate rape, murder, bigotry, and child abuse. We oppose sin and refuse to be at ease with it. In the same way, we are not to be comfortable with the reality of suffering (although we are to be at peace with God in the midst of it) and should do our best to alleviate it. Like sin, suffering is an intruder and cannot be welcomed as natural. The horror of suffering's intrusion points to the horror of sin, its fundamental source.[65]

The Fall Results in a Matrix of Shattered Relationships

As we previously noted, in the beginning God created a good cosmos with good humans who had good relationships with God, themselves,

---

[62] Carson, *How Long, O Lord?*, 42.
[63] This is not to suggest that particular instances of suffering can be or should be traced back to particular sins. In some cases, that is possible, but in other instances it is unfounded. The point is that all suffering results from Adam's sin.
[64] Pyne, *Humanity and Sin*, 160.
[65] For more on suffering, see Christopher W. Morgan and Robert A. Peterson, eds., *Suffering and the Goodness of God*, Theology in Community 1 (Wheaton, IL: Crossway, 2008).

one another, and creation itself. But now, sin has entered the picture and has brought disruption and alienation in each human relationship—with God, oneself, one another, and creation.[66]

The account in Genesis shows the couple's wrecked relationship with God. Once, Adam and Eve enjoyed the intimacy of God's presence, but after they eat the forbidden fruit they hide from him (3:8). They realize they are naked (vv. 7–11), lie to God (vv. 12–13), are judged by God (vv. 16–19), face death (v. 19), and are banished from God's temple-garden (22–24).[67] Even more, they fail to live out their identity and mission as humans created in the image of God. They do not display his goodness or serve his purposes.

Genesis also depicts how sin even hurts the perpetrators. In addition to being subject to death, they find themselves naked and ashamed. Being fruitful and multiplying would now require pain in childbirth, and having dominion over the creation would now require toil in work. Further, there is a failure to live out the image of God, to be what they were always intended to be, to do what they were created to do, and even to want and will rightly. Marguerite Shuster observes:

> These paradoxes reveal something corrupt at the root of our acts and impulses: our "natural" desires for pleasure and for a goodness of our own are deeply self-centered and so twisted that they cannot reach their own proper ends but tend to destroy self and others. Even the effort to rid oneself of excessive self-concern may intensify it. Thus, at the superficial level, the paradox is simply the observation that we cannot reach certain goals by aiming at them; at a deeper level, the paradox points to our profound moral inability to do that which we ought to do, to love what we ought to love, or to will as we ought to will.[68]

Sin also disorders human interpersonal relationships. Adam blames Eve for the sin, and in an episode of telling stupidity and self-justification, he even insinuates that God is somehow at fault. Their previous intimate relationship is replaced by enmity, evasion of responsibility, and blame of the other. Cain kills Abel (Genesis 4), societal evil becomes rampant (chap. 6), and social sin marches on as mistreatment often leads to further mistreatment and as victims often become perpetrators.

---

[66] For helpful material on the effects of sin on the sinner's relationship to God, himself, and others, see T. V. Farris, *Mighty to Save*, 28–43; Millard Erickson, *Christian Theology*, vol. 1 (Grand Rapids, MI: Baker, 1984), 601–19; and Hoekema, *Created in God's Image*, 133–40.

[67] For more on the garden of Eden as a temple, see Gregory K. Beale, *A New Testament Biblical Theology: The Unfolding of the Old Testament in the New* (Grand Rapids, MI: Baker, 2011), 614–48.

[68] Marguerite Shuster, *The Fall and Sin: What We Have Become as Sinners* (Grand Rapids, MI: Eerdmans, 2004), 166. See also her perceptive comments on pp. 163–65; 190–207.

The fallout is also seen in human relations with the creation and cosmos. As previously mentioned, there is new pain in being fruitful and multiplying, new toil and pain in working the ground, as Farris depicts: "History's first family now faced a fallen and perverted order that featured hostile death-dealing conditions, a violent world of chaos and destruction."[69] Indeed, God judges, "Cursed is the ground because of you" (Gen. 3:17).[70] Paul clarifies:

> For the creation waits with eager longing for the revealing of the sons of God. For the creation was subjected to futility, not willingly, but because of him who subjected it, in hope that the creation itself will be set free from its bondage to corruption and obtain the freedom of the glory of the children of God. For we know that the whole creation has been groaning together in the pains of childbirth until now. And not only the creation, but we ourselves, who have the firstfruits of the Spirit, groan inwardly as we wait eagerly for adoption as sons, the redemption of our bodies. (Rom. 8:19–23)

Even creation has been affected by the fall, being "subjected to futility," "in bondage to corruption," and longing for full freedom and groaning for the final redemption (cf. Rev. 22:3).

Redemption and Sin

The irony of sin in the biblical story is striking: as humans we all refused to acknowledge God's glory, accept our own identity as being created in the image of God, and serve our image-bearing mission as expressions of his mission. We sought our own glory and defined ourselves autonomously, and in so doing we forfeited the glory that God intended for us as his image bearers. Thankfully, God does not completely eradicate humanity for such cosmic treason but graciously begins a restoration project. He begins the process of redeeming humanity and the cosmos, particularly restoring humans as full image bearers so that we can participate in and reflect the glory, identity, and mission that we longed for the whole time. Establishing a covenant with a people (Israel) whom he chooses and calls, God promises to bless those people so that they can in turn bless the nations, and then the nations in turn will worship and glorify him.

---

[69] Farris, *Mighty to Save*, 40.
[70] Shuster reminds: "We ought not, of course, identify the whole pre-Fall creation with Eden. It is easy to forget that the image of the "garden" of Eden distinguishes this spot from the rest of the world, as does the image of Adam and Eve being driven from it after the Fall." *The Fall and Sin*, 77.

Every step of the way, sin is evident—the sin of the hostile nations, the sin of Israel, and even the sin of the very best leaders of Israel. But every step of the way, God's grace is also evident—establishing a covenant with his people, displaying covenant faithfulness even when his people do not reciprocate. God resiliently links his name to his people and guides them with his presence. Along the way, he displays his holiness through the giving of the Law, his greatness through prescriptions for appropriate worship, and his glory through awe-inspiring theophanies, the tabernacle, the ark of the covenant, the temple, and the kingdom. He sends prophets at key points to redirect the sinful people away from empty and worthless idols and back to himself. These prophets also point to a time when Israel will no longer be characterized by sin but become what it was intended to be—glorious (see Isaiah 60–66)—a time linked to the Messiah's arrival (see Luke 2:29–32).

The Messiah Jesus addresses sin, but not in the way most Jews expected. They hoped for a political, military, and spiritual leader to restore Israel to its former glory as a kingdom; and they hoped for a judgment on the sins of the nations. But Jesus's redemption was of a different sort and his mission not so nationalistic. Jesus' response to sin is beyond what anyone anticipated, because he is the Holy One, the Lord of glory (1 Cor. 2:8; James 2:1), Yahweh himself (cf. John 12:41; Isa. 6:1; Dan. 7:13–14).[71] Jesus the Messiah is the eternal Son, born of a virgin, who humbles himself to become incarnate (John 1:1–18; Phil. 2:5–11). He is the new Adam and the new Israel, successfully resisting Satan's schemes in the wilderness. Jesus' entire life is marked by complete faithfulness to God, obedience to his law, and freedom from sin. His preaching calls for repentance from sin, not just for the notoriously wicked but also for religious devotees. His miracles/signs witness that the presence of God and his kingdom have arrived. The kingdom of sin and death is in for a battle as Jesus powerfully and systematically displays his reign—through taming the chaotic sea, healing the sick and unclean, casting out demons, and even raising the dead (Luke 8; cf. John 11:38–44).

Even more, Jesus, the Messiah, the Son of Man, is also the Suffering Servant (Isaiah 52–53) who asserts: "The Son of Man must suffer many things and be rejected by the elders and chief priests and scribes, and be killed, and on the third day be raised" (Luke 9:22). Jesus' sense of the

---

[71] For more on Jesus' deity, see Christopher W. Morgan and Robert A. Peterson, eds., *The Deity of Christ,* Theology in Community 3 (Wheaton, IL: Crossway, 2012).

necessity of his mission is striking, as when he declares, "For even the Son of Man came not to be served but to serve, and to give his life as a ransom for many" (Mark 10:45; see also Matt. 20:28; Luke 4:16–21; John 12:23–28). Jesus came to serve; he came to save. And while the entire life of Jesus displays this, Robert Peterson helpfully highlights Christ's nine major "saving events":

1) Incarnation (Luke 2:11; Gal. 4:4–5; Heb. 2:14–15).
2) Sinless life (2 Cor. 5:21; Heb. 5:8–10; 1 Pet. 3:18).
3) Death (Gal. 3:13; Heb. 10:14).
4) Resurrection (Rom. 4:25; 1 Cor. 15:21–22; 1 Pet. 1:3).
5) Ascension (John 14:2–3; Acts 5:31; Heb. 9:24).
6) Session (Col. 3:1–3; Heb. 1:3; 10:11–12).
7) Pentecost (John 20:22–23; Acts 1:5).
8) Intercession (Rom. 8:34; Heb. 7:25).
9) Second coming (Matt. 25:46; 1 Thess. 1:9–10; 1 Pet. 1:13).[72]

Peterson also suggests that the Bible includes six major pictures of Christ's saving work. Note his chart below:[73]

Biblical Pictures of Christ's Saving Work

Sphere	Need	Christ	His Work	Result	Passages
Relations	Alienation	Peacemaker	Reconciles	Peace	Rom. 5:10; 2 Cor. 5:18–20; Eph. 2:12–17; Col. 1:20–23
Slavery	Bondage	Redeemer	Delivers	Freedom	1 Cor. 6:20; Heb. 9:15; 1 Pet. 1:19
Law	Guilt	Substitute	Pays penalty	Justification	Rom. 3:25–26; Gal. 3:13; Col. 2:14
Warfare	Enemies	Champion	Defeats foes	Victory	Col. 2:15; Heb. 2:14–15; Rev. 5:5
Creation	Disorder	Second Adam	Obeys	Restoration	Rom. 5:18–19; 1 Cor. 15:22; Col. 1:18
Worship	Defilement	Priest	Makes sacrifice	Purification	Eph 5:2, 25–26; Heb 9:12, 14; 10:14

---

[72] Robert A. Peterson, *Salvation Accomplished by the Son: The Work of Christ* (Wheaton, IL: Crossway, 2011), 553.
[73] Ibid., 555. Used with permission.

For our purposes, notice how Christ's saving work sheds light on the doctrine of sin, especially through "saving events" such as his sinless life, substitutionary death, life-giving resurrection, and triumphant coming. And Christ's saving work sheds light on the doctrine of sin through the biblical pictures, as Peterson shows:

> The multiplicity of images of salvation corresponds to the multiplicity of the images of sin. The many ways of speaking about our plight correspond to the many ways God in his grace comes to our aid. Sin is so odious to God that he depicts it in a variety of ways, as the discussion of the need for each picture in the preceding shows.
>
> Each need, each way of describing sin, corresponds to God's way of overturning sin in Christ's work. So, God overturns sin as alienation with Christ's reconciliation. He overcomes bondage with Christ's redemption. He overturns guilt with Christ's propitiation. He overcomes our mighty enemies with a mightier champion's victory. He overturns Adam's disobedience with the second Adam's obedience. He overcomes our spiritual defilement with Christ's purifying blood. But the key point here is that these are multiple ways of communicating the same truth— Christ's death and resurrection save sinners![74]

Similarly, the Bible's portraits of salvation also teach much about sin. Examples include: regeneration addresses our state of spiritual death; justification, our guilt; adoption, our condition as slaves and outside God's family; sanctification, our unholy lives as well as the lingering reality of indwelling sin even in believers who continually need mortification, renewal, and repentance (Eph. 4:20–24).

Further, the nature of the church as the people of God's salvation is also instructive for our understanding of sin.[75] The church is God's temple, the people characterized by God's presence and holiness (Eph. 2:11–22). The church is likewise the new humanity in which believing Jews and Gentiles are no longer the standard illustration for ethnic division but the model of the one new society that depicts what the human community was always intended to be (Eph. 2:15; 3:9–12; 4:11–16). The church is God's contrast community, characterized by holiness, unity, truth, and love (Eph. 2:11–22; 4:1–6, 11–16) in a society marked by sin, discord, dis-

---

[74] Ibid., 556.
[75] For more on this and related ideas, see Christopher W. Morgan, "Toward a Theology of the Unity of the Church," in *Why We Belong: Stories of Evangelical Unity amidst Diversity*, ed. Anthony L. Chute, Christopher W. Morgan, and Robert A. Peterson (Wheaton, IL: Crossway, forthcoming). See also Christopher W. Morgan and Kendell H. Easley, eds., *The Community of Jesus: A Theology of the Church* (Nashville: Broadman, 2013).

tortion, and self-seeking (4:17–5:21). And as the community of the kingdom, the church lives in the already and not yet of the kingdom, which
indicates that the world is not what it should be. The current already and
not yet of the kingdom also indicates that this world is not what it will be,
that there is a fuller "already" with no "not yet" kingdom to come.

The Consummation and Sin

Indeed, there is a time coming when the kingdom of God will not only
be in-breaking into our world but will fundamentally define it. There is
a time coming when the fullness of salvation will be received. There is a
time coming when justice will prevail, sin will be finally overthrown, and
God's glory will be fully displayed in the new heaven and the new earth
as his temple. This time is often called the "consummation" and includes
major events and states such as the second coming of Christ, the final
judgment, and the final states of hell and heaven.

The consummation is instructive about sin in several ways, as we
will see below: *sin will be defeated*; *sin will be judged*; *unbelievers will be
punished eternally in hell*; and *believers will be free from sin and revel in
perfect goodness in heaven*. John Piper is helpful: "The evil and suffering
in this world are greater than any of us can comprehend. But evil and suffering are not ultimate. God is. Satan, the great lover of evil and suffering,
is not sovereign. God is."[76]

The classic passage depicting the consummation and these related
truths is Revelation 20–22. Just as Genesis 1–2 reveals that the biblical
story begins with God's creation of the heavens and the earth, Revelation
20–22 shows that it ends with God's creation of a new heavens and a new
earth. The story begins with the goodness of creation, and it ends with the
goodness of the new creation. The story begins with God dwelling with
his people in a garden-temple, and it ends with God dwelling with his
covenant people in heaven, a new earth-city-garden-temple.

Once and for all God's victory is consummated. God's judgment is
final, sin has been vanquished, justice prevails, holiness predominates,
God's glory is unobstructed, and the kingdom is realized. God's eternal
plan of cosmic reconciliation in Christ is actualized, and Christ is "all in all."

As a part of his victory, God casts the Devil and his demons into the
lake of fire, where they are not consumed but "tormented day and night

---

[76] John Piper, "Suffering and the Sovereignty of God: Ten Aspects of God's Sovereignty in Suffering and Satan's
Hand in It," in *Suffering and the Sovereignty of God*, ed. John Piper and Justin Taylor (Wheaton, IL: Crossway,
2006), 29.

forever and ever" (20:10). Satan and the demons are not restored but go to hell to receive their due punishment; and they remain there to suffer forever.

Then God judges everyone—those whom the world deems important, those whom the world never notices, and everyone in between. "If anyone's name was not found written in the book of life, he was thrown into the lake of fire" (v. 15). God does not only send the ruthless Roman emperors to hell (which we might expect), but he consigns to hell all who are not the people of Jesus (cf. Dan. 12:1; Rev. 13:8; 21:8, 27). Three pictures of hell emerge here in Revelation 20–22: hell as punishment (20:10–15), destruction/death (20:14–15; 21:8), and banishment (22:15).[77] And each picture of hell sheds light on the doctrine of sin: hell as punishment clarifies that sin is a crime; hell as destruction shows sin as spiritual death; hell as banishment views sin as alienation from God. Indeed, the pictures of hell can be viewed as culminations, extensions, intensifications, and logical continuations of the unbeliever's current state of sin.[78]

Magnificently, the new heavens and new earth arrive and God dwells with his covenant people (note the covenant formulas of 21:3, 7), brings comfort to his people (no more pain, death, etc., in v. 4), makes all things new (v. 5), and proclaims, "It is done!" (v. 6).

Heaven is then depicted as a perfect temple, glorious, multi-national, and holy (vv. 9–27). The people of God will rightly bear God's image— serving him, reigning with him, encountering him directly, and worshiping him (22:1–5). God receives the worship he is due, and humans are blessed beyond description, finally living to the fullest the realities of being created in his image.[79]

As we have seen, the biblical story sheds much light on sin. But,

---

[77] For how Jesus and Paul use these three pictures of hell, see Matt. 24–25; 2 Thess. 1:6–11. See also Christopher W. Morgan, "Biblical Theology: Three Pictures of Hell," in *Hell under Fire: Modern Scholarship Reinvents Eternal Punishment*, ed. Christopher W. Morgan and Robert A. Peterson (Grand Rapids, MI: Zondervan, 2004), 135–51.

[78] "Various pictures of hell also extend the here-and-now judgment of God on sin. God's wrath is on sinners, and hell is the culmination of that wrath. Sinners are condemned already, but they await the ultimate condemnation in hell. Sinners are now dead spiritually but await the second death. Unbelievers are alienated from God now but will be finally excluded from his presence. Sinners' hearts are dark now but will eternally be in 'outer darkness' and 'blackest darkness.' The evidence is compelling: The pictures of hell can be viewed as culminations, extensions, intensifications, and logical continuations of the unbeliever's current state of sin. It is also significant that the pictures of punishment, destruction, and banishment have Old Testament roots. They can be found as early as the fall recorded in Genesis 3, when God punished Adam and Eve with a curse, warned of sin's consequence of death, and banished the first humans from the Garden of Eden." Christopher W. Morgan, "Three Pictures of Hell," in *Is Hell for Real or Does Everyone Go to Heaven?*, ed. Christopher W. Morgan and Robert A. Peterson (Grand Rapids, MI: Zondervan, 2011), 46–47.

[79] Note that during this scene, sinners still exist—outside of heaven, outside the kingdom, outside the temple (Rev. 22:14–15). And they still exist on the outside *after* being cast into the lake of fire (20:14–15; 21:8).

clearly, sin is only the backdrop, never the point. It emerges in God's good creation as a temporary intruder, causes much havoc, and holds many in its clutches. But it is no match for the work of God in Christ. Through his sinless life, sin-bearing death, sin-defeating resurrection, and sin-crushing second coming, sin and its offspring of suffering and death are given the death blow. Sin abounded, but grace super-abounds! In the biblical story, God has the first word. And, thankfully, God also has the last word, as the apostle Paul so marvelously proclaims:

> I tell you this, brothers: flesh and blood cannot inherit the kingdom of God, nor does the perishable inherit the imperishable. Behold! I tell you a mystery. We shall not all sleep, but we shall all be changed, in a moment, in the twinkling of an eye, at the last trumpet. For the trumpet will sound, and the dead will be raised imperishable, and we shall be changed. For this perishable body must put on the imperishable, and this mortal body must put on immortality. When the perishable puts on the imperishable, and the mortal puts on immortality, then shall come to pass the saying that is written:
>
> > "Death is swallowed up in victory."
> > "O death, where is your victory?
> >   O death, where is your sting?"
>
> The sting of death is sin, and the power of sin is the law. But thanks be to God, who gives us the victory through our Lord Jesus Christ. (1 Cor. 15:50–57)

7

SIN IN HISTORICAL THEOLOGY

GERALD BRAY

There is no subject of greater importance to Christian theology than its understanding of the concept of sin and its effects. That may seem like an odd statement to make, but if we think about what the Christian gospel is, we shall quickly see why this is so. The gospel is a message of salvation from sin, achieved for us by Jesus Christ. To do that, he became sin for us, although he was himself sinless, and gave us his Holy Spirit so that we might be able to overcome sin and its effects in our own lives. Had there been no sin to begin with, there would have been no gospel and no Christianity because they would not have been necessary. Paradoxical as it sounds, sin and its consequences are the immediate cause of the coming of Christ into the world and of the work that he has done on our behalf. For that reason, we need to know what sin is in order to understand what that work accomplished. Just as a disease cannot be cured unless it is properly diagnosed, so salvation has no meaning unless we understand what it is that we have been saved from and why salvation is necessary in the first place. Knowing the nature and effects of sin is the essential preliminary to understanding what Christ did to defeat it. If we get that wrong, our appreciation of salvation will be distorted and the gospel will be lost. Understanding sin is not enough in itself to save us, but it can be said with complete certainty that failure to understand it will ensure that we shall never come to the knowledge of Christ and his salvation that God wants us to have.

Jewish and Gentile Concepts of Sin

From the beginning, the Christian church had an understanding of sin that it had inherited from Judaism. A Jew in the time of Jesus would normally have thought of sin primarily as disobedience to the law of Moses contained in the Old Testament. This law had many ramifications, but for most people it was essentially a matter of maintaining ritual purity. To eat nonkosher foods or to socialize with non-Jewish people was sinful because such things challenged the boundary markers that set Jews apart from others and maintained their identity as the people of God. Thoughtful Jews understood that there was much more to the law than that, but there was a strong tendency to objectify the commandments and find ways of keeping them according to the letter, if not always according to the spirit, in which they were originally given. That much is clear from the teaching of Jesus, which is echoed in the letters of the apostle Paul. Modern attempts to recover an appreciation of the spiritual nature of first-century Judaism do not negate this perspective, because both Jesus and Paul recognized the law's spiritual character. They were not criticizing their fellow Jews for honoring the law as the answer to sin but for tailoring it to what they could accomplish and ignoring its deeper implications.

The message of Jesus was that the principles of the law must be internalized in the heart and mind of the believer. It was not enough to refrain from murdering other people; it was also necessary to expunge every thought that might tend toward malice and hatred of others (Matt. 5:21–22). As the apostle Paul later put it: "The letter kills, but the Spirit gives life" (2 Cor. 3:6). Because of this, the early Christians were taught that the Mosaic law, which was intended to bring blessing to God's people, had become instead a curse, because every time the law put its finger on human sinfulness, the urge to rebel sprang up and took over the minds of those who were subjected to it (Rom. 7:7–9). Sinfulness was latent in every human being from the fall of Adam onward, but the law gave it a focus and so made it more dangerous. Furthermore, although the law could do a brilliant job of pointing out what sin was, it had no power to overcome it. As a result, it was a message of condemnation rather than of salvation, and those Jews who thought they could keep it were only fooling themselves. A Jew who became a Christian had to stop thinking of the law as a way of salvation and see that, by its very holiness, it was a way of condemnation instead.

How hard it was for many Jewish Christians to abandon that way of thinking can be seen from the struggles between them and the Gentiles in the early church. Non-Jewish converts had no sense of obligation toward a Jewish law that many of them found bizarre and distressingly unspiritual in its focus on such things as circumcision and food laws. In dealing with this conflict, Paul had to tread a careful pathway between two ex-tremes. On the one hand, he could not accept the Jewish argument that the law could and should be kept in every detail, but neither could he simply abandon it, as the Gentiles apparently wished. He compromised by coming up with the notion of the "weaker brother," which in its original use meant primarily a Jewish Christian who was unable to abandon the law and the ingrained prejudices that it nurtured. Paul advised the Gen-tiles to treat such people gently and with great consideration, but on the principle of the matter he clearly sided with the Gentiles and agreed with their understanding of the true nature of sin.

What was that understanding? The Gentile converts we meet in the New Testament had inherited a number of different conceptions of sin, none of which had any direct connection with the law of Moses. Many of them came to Christ with notions of ritual purity derived from their na-tive pagan cults, and some of their ideas became influential in the Chris-tian church, especially if they could be harmonized with authentic biblical teaching. The more intellectual Gentiles had also inherited philosophical concepts of good and evil that were rather different from Jewish teach-ings about these things, and these often had to be modified in order to fit the Christian gospel. As the church became more Gentile and less Jew-ish in composition, the influence of such Gentile beliefs became more prominent, and it would not be too much to say that the doctrine of sin developed by the fathers of the church was in essence an attempt to bring Graeco-Roman ideas about sin into line with the teaching of the Bible.

Gentiles whose concept of sin was closely tied to ritual purity often thought of this in ways unknown to Judaism. The classic example of this was the attitude toward virginity and celibacy that was characteristic of ancient Rome. There, virginity was highly prized in the pagan cult of Vesta, the goddess of the hearth, and to defile one of her priestesses was a terrible sin. It was easy for Romans who came from that background to think that celibacy was a sign of purity and that sexual intercourse was in itself a sin, something that was quite foreign to Judaism. This idea crept into the Christian church in spite of its pagan origins because although Judaism promoted marriage and procreation, there was undoubtedly a certain preference given to celibacy in the New Testament (1 Corinthians 7; see also Rev. 14:4). Of course, the reasons for this had nothing to do with ritual purity, and the apostle Paul was careful to insist that those who married did not sin in doing so, but his caution in this matter could easily be overlooked by people who were already inclined to favor celibacy for other reasons. They could use the apostle's stated preference for it as a justification for allowing their paganism to intrude on Christian practice, and they did so, even to the point where it became the preferred norm, although the church never went to the extreme of condemning sexual intercourse within the bond of marriage.

Gentiles were also more inclined than Jews to think of sin in connection with material existence. Many of them believed that human beings were immortal souls that had been trapped in material bodies and become corrupted because of it. To their minds, sinfulness was the inevitable consequence of human finitude, and the only way to escape it was to be reintegrated into the spiritual reality from which the immortal souls of men had separated. These Gentiles did not distinguish clearly between creation and the fall, a confusion of concepts that is completely contrary to the teaching of Genesis. In the Bible, creation is good because it has been made by God, and sin is an unnatural corruption of that. Getting this message across to Gentiles was one of the most difficult tasks the early church faced, but it was a necessary preliminary to preaching the gospel. If finitude had been sinful in itself, the incarnation of the Son of God would have been impossible, and the resurrection of the body would have been a contradiction in terms. The Christian doctrine of sin had to be cast evangelistically in order to address a Gentile audience that needed to understand the biblical worldview before it could accept the gospel message of salvation.

Sin and the Created Order

It should therefore come as no surprise to discover that the biblical passage most frequently commented on in the early church was Genesis 1–3, which is the account of the creation, sin, and fall of mankind. Virtually every church father wrote at length on this foundational text, and some did so more than once. Augustine of Hippo, who did not write many commentaries on the Bible, nevertheless penned no fewer than four treatises on this subject, which gives us a good indication of how important it was to him.[1] Despite their many apparent differences, the general drift of these treatises is the same. Augustine says that creation is good, that sin is a corruption or distortion of that original goodness, and that once sin has occurred there is no way to get rid of it other than by divine interven-

---

[1] This includes the two books he wrote against the Manichees (written in 389), an unfinished commentary on the literal sense of Genesis (written in 393), the final books of his *Confessions* (written about 400), and the twelve books of a literal commentary on Genesis (written between 401 and 415).

tion. However sorry we may be for it, however hard we may try to put it right, however much we may desire to be sinless, none of this is possible without the grace of God freely given to us in the person of his Son Jesus Christ. Only by dying spiritually to the forces of this world and by being born again in Christ can a human being overcome the power of sin in his life and hope to inherit the kingdom of God.

As it was understood by the church fathers, sin is a condition we have inherited from our first parents, Adam and Eve, who disobeyed God in the garden of Eden and were expelled from it for that reason. But if their sin was their own fault, it was not their own idea. Above and beyond the sin of the first human beings was a power of evil that had lured them into it by temptation. This power was personified in Satan and his angels, who had rebelled against God at some point before the creation of the world. Why God did not immediately destroy them, and why Satan was allowed to tempt mankind into following him in his rebellion, were mysteries that no one could solve, although it was clear that they corresponded to human experience. To be cleansed from sin was therefore to enter into spiritual warfare with Satan, the prince of evil, who continues to do everything in his power to tempt us back into his kingdom. In the end, Satan will be destroyed, but until he is, evil will be a reality with which we shall have to contend and against which we shall need to be protected. This does not make it inevitable that a Christian will sin, but it is a reminder that our innate sinfulness comes from the fact that we have been born into the kingdom of Satan and that sinfulness continues to expose us to the dangers inherent in the Devil's temptations. Even though we have been set free from the power of sin, our natural inclinations continue to make it appear attractive to us and serve as a reminder that we cannot do without the saving power of Christ.

What exactly is sinfulness, as opposed to the sinful acts we commit? Following the pagan Greek tendency to equate sinfulness with finitude, many of the church fathers thought of it as a weakness inherent in our human constitution. To their minds evil was a lack, an absence, or a deprivation of goodness that is the natural consequence of our separation from God. They reasoned that because God is the supreme good, to be cut off from him is to forfeit that goodness. The result is sin, or more precisely, a condition of sinfulness. Evil thoughts and deeds, or what we would call actual sins, are the inevitable consequence of this separation from God and feed our natural inclination to get as far away from him and his goodness as we can. Those who refuse to submit to God's will are bent on self-destruction and will be destroyed because of it. Whether this destruction is total annihilation or eternal punishment was less clear to the fathers, but the few who discussed the matter seemed to prefer eternal punishment because it was more consistent with the nature of God. The reason for this was that God hates nothing that he has made, and therefore will preserve even the most rebellious creature in being because he loves it as one of his creatures. But keeping such souls in being is also preventing them from achieving their desire for self-destruction and is therefore felt by those souls as a torment. God is always kind and loving toward his creation, but those who have been blinded by their disobedience to him do not appreciate that and experience his love as punishment for their sinfulness, if not for their particular sins. As the apostle Paul told the Corinthians: "The natural person does not understand the things of the Spirit of God" (1 Cor. 2:14).[2]

The idea that sin was essentially a lack or deprivation of good was common in the early church and remained the dominant view in the East.[3] A key element of the Eastern Orthodox view is that Adam's sin brought death into the world, and it is because of their mortality that all his descendants have sinned. They base this on their interpretation of Romans 5:12, which they read as: "Sin came into the world through one man, and death through sin, and so death spread to all men because all sinned." The correctness of this translation depends on the meaning of the ambiguous Greek phrase *eph' ho*, which is translated as "for which reason" by the Eastern churches but as "because" by most people in the West. Either meaning is theoretically possible, and therefore which of them is preferable needs to be determined by other criteria. For example, can we say that Adam was immortal before he fell and that sin brought mortality into the world? Everyone agrees that Adam died as a result of his sin, but that is not the same thing as saying that sin caused him to lose his original immortality. After all, Satan was immortal, but he did not lose that quality when he sinned. On the other hand, the man Jesus Christ was mortal, but that did not prevent him from being sinless as well. The relationship between sin and death therefore seems to be more complex than the Eastern Orthodox

---

[2] 1 Cor. 2:14. This verse has often been mistranslated and therefore misunderstood. We do not have a word precisely equivalent to the Greek *psychikos*, so it is frequently rendered as "natural," rather than as "unspiritual" or "unregenerate," which is what it really means. The result of this can lead to absurd translations, as when the English Standard Version describes the one who does not know God as a "natural person." It does not seem to have occurred to the translators that Jesus the Son of God is also a "natural person," as indeed are God the Father and the Holy Spirit!

[3] See John Meyendorff, *Byzantine Theology: Historical Trends and Doctrinal Themes* (New York: Fordham University Press, 1974), 143–46, for a discussion of this and a comparison with the position of the Western church.

churches (or at least their more representative theologians) have allowed. Adam was not created as an immortal being, but in the garden of Eden he was protected against death. When he fell, that protection was removed and he suffered the consequences as his nature was allowed to take its course. It is therefore preferable to say that sin is the cause of death and not the other way round, as most of the Eastern fathers apparently claimed.[4]

The main challenge to this viewpoint in ancient times came from the pen of Augustine of Hippo, who was forced to turn his attention to it because of the teaching of Pelagius, a British monk who was making a name for himself in Rome around the year 418. Pelagius seems to have been teaching something very similar to the Eastern doctrine of sin outlined above. Like his Eastern counterparts, Pelagius refused to accept the idea that there can be such a thing as inherited guilt, although he seems to have gone further than that by denying that there is any inherited sinfulness at all. He obviously could not deny the legacy of mortality, but he seems to have dissociated this from sinfulness to the point where it was possible for someone with good intentions to save himself by his own efforts. In reaction to this, Augustine wrote a number of trenchant treatises in which he exalted the necessity of the grace of God for salvation and denied that anyone could get to God without it. Pelagianism was duly condemned by the Western church, but its influence remained strong, and even the Protestant Reformers thought it was one of the chief obstacles they had to overcome in their preaching of the gospel. This can be seen from the Augsburg Confession, which was drawn up in 1530 as the first major statement of Protestant doctrine. It says: "We condemn the Pelagians and others who deny that the original flaw is sin, and in order to dissipate the glory of the merit and of the benefits of Christ, argue that man can be declared righteous before God by the strength of his own reason."[5] The struggle against Pelagius gave a new edge to questions of sin and grace in the Western church and forced it to reconsider what sin was and how it should be dealt with in the life of the Christian. In particular, it made subsequent Western theologians, almost all of whom saw themselves as latter-day exponents of Augustine, see that in some sense at least, sin was a thing in its own right and not merely an absence of good as the Eastern churches taught.

---

[4] The belief that mortality is the cause of sin is strangely similar to the pagan Greek idea that sin was the result of finitude. Christians could not say that because of their doctrine of creation, but the appearance of mortality within creation is a clever way of reintroducing the limitations imposed by finitude without actually saying so.
[5] *Augsburg Confession*, 2.2. See Gerald L. Bray, *Documents of the English Reformation*, 2nd ed. (Cambridge, UK: James Clarke, 2004), 606.

Sin as a Stain on the Soul

One of the consequences of the Augustinian doctrine of sin and grace was a deeper interest in the atoning work of Christ on the cross. This had always been understood primarily in terms of the two natures of Christ. As Gregory of Nazianzus put it: "What has not been assumed has not been healed."[6] But once sin came to be understood as a thing that had to be removed, the notion of sacrifice came to the fore. In what way and to what extent was Christ's death a sacrifice for sin? This was the question expounded by Anselm of Canterbury (1033–1109) in his great work *Cur Deus Homo?* Anselm explained that mankind's sinfulness was so great that only God could deal with it. His justice required sacrifice as payment for sin, and the Son of God became a man in order to pay that price. By taking our sins upon him, Jesus Christ satisfied the demands of God's justice and gained enough merit with God the Father to be able to pay for the sins of the entire human race. When he rose from the dead and ascended into heaven, he took that sacrifice with him, and there it remains as a kind of deposit and guarantee for the redemption of mankind.

In a parallel development, the Western church was coming to think of sin as a kind of congenital defect, inherited as a stain (*macula* in Latin) on the soul that was passed on from one generation to the next. The progress of this view can be measured by the development of the doctrine of the sinlessness of the Virgin Mary. Every Christian had always agreed that Christ was sinless, but as long as sin was understood primarily as the absence of God and his goodness, explaining this was not too difficult. A man who was also God obviously did not experience God's absence and was therefore without sin. On the cross, he became sin for us, which can be used to explain why he expressed a sense of God's abandonment for the first and only time in his life (Matt. 27:46 and Mark 15:34). However, if sin is thought of as a congenital defect, an entirely different problem presents itself, which may be expressed as follows: "If Jesus was a genuine human being and inherited his humanity from his mother, Mary, how was it that this humanity did not contain that defect?"

The only answer to this was to argue that at some point the defect had been removed from Mary. Most medieval theologians believed that this had occurred at the annunciation, when the archangel Gabriel declared that she was "full of grace," which they understood to mean that she had

---

[6] *Ep.* 101.

been cleansed from her sin before conceiving Jesus in her womb (Luke 1:28). Later on, under the pressure of popular piety as much as anything else, this idea was pushed to the point of saying that Mary herself was conceived and born without sin, presumably because her mother (and father?) had been cleansed before her conception. This is the doctrine of the so-called immaculate conception of the Blessed Virgin Mary, which since 1854 has been the official teaching of the Roman Catholic Church. It should be noted, however, that it has not been accepted by the Eastern churches, in spite of their high view of Mary and her perpetual virginity. Lacking any notion of sin as a congenital defect, the Eastern Orthodox churches have no room for the Roman doctrine, which makes no sense in the context of their theology.[7]

Another important difference between the East and the West concerns the question of guilt for sin, to which we have already referred. The Western church believes that because sin is inherited from Adam and Eve and because they were responsible for it, we have inherited that responsibility as well as the sin itself. As Augustine put it, the human race is a *massa damnata*, a condemned mass whose solidarity is nowhere more apparent than in its collective guilt for its congenital sinfulness.[8] The Eastern churches, on the other hand, do not accept the idea that one person can be held responsible for the sins of another. Because they believe that it is our mortality that causes us to sin and that we are not personally responsible for that, we cannot be held responsible for the sins of our ancestors but only for the sins we commit ourselves. Those who die without having sinned, like infants, therefore have no guilt before God and may be saved, whereas the medieval Western church taught that if they had not been baptized they would go to hell. It is here, perhaps more than anywhere else, that we see the serious consequences that can result from different understandings of the nature of sin.

The tendency to objectify sin and to regard it as a stain on the soul made it much easier to entertain the possibility of wiping it away, or of healing it as if it were a kind of disease. Thus we find that in the Western Middle Ages the concept of grace was developed with precisely that aim in view. Particular sins could be wiped away by applying the right amount of grace, which was understood as a cleanser or as a medicine. Baptism was the grace given to remedy original sin, which is one reason

---

[7] It is not the theology of any Protestant church either, though for other reasons (see below).
[8] Augustine uses the phrase in *Sermon* 293.8.

why it became so important to have babies baptized as soon as possible.[9] Postbaptismal sin had been a problem in the early church, especially in North Africa, where the Donatist movement insisted that anyone who sinned after having been baptized lost his salvation forever.[10] That view was rejected very early on, but the question of how to deal with post-baptismal sin remained. Augustine said that it was overcome by ongoing acts of divine grace, which were given to the regenerate soul in order to help it suppress sin and its effects. In the Middle Ages there developed an elaborate system of gradation according to which grace was dispensed in appropriate doses, mainly by means of the sacraments. This system was rooted in the primary distinction between moral sins and venial ones. Mortal sins were those which would send an impenitent person to hell, whereas venial sins were less serious and could be forgiven.[11] Sins were graded in much the same way as crimes against the law and were dealt with in a similar way. An appropriate penance was devised for each sin and was administered by the priest when the penitent sinner confessed to him. Upon performance of the penance, the sinner would be absolved by the priest and admitted to Holy Communion.

It is obvious that as views of this kind took hold, there would be a correspondingly greater concentration on the nature of particular sins. One of the most popular and well-known schemes of classification is the one that defines seven deadly sins, a cluster of vices that continues to attract a certain amount of attention even today. The idea that there were seven sins that were particularly serious is supposed to go back to Gregory the Great, who enumerated them in his *Moralia in Iob*.[12] In that great work Gregory mentioned seven vices that he thought should be particularly avoided, but he did not attempt to rank them in any particu-lar order, let alone suggest appropriate penances for them. That changed however in the later Middle Ages, when each of the sins was examined in great detail, and pride, which Gregory had mentioned last, was declared to be the most serious of them because it was regarded as the root cause of all the others.

The seven deadly sins are not particular acts but sinful attitudes of the heart and behavioral habits, all of which are condemned in one form or another in the Bible. No one is likely to dispute that greed (*avaritia*),

---

[9] The other reason was the extremely high infant mortality rate. Given the church's teaching that an unbap-tized baby would go to hell because of its inheritance of original sin, this concern is understandable.

[10] A view based on Heb. 6:4–6. The Donatists were named after Donatus, one of the early leaders of the sect.

[11] The Latin word *venia* means "forgiveness."

[12] *Moralia* 7, 28.34.

for example, or envy (*invidia*) is sinful, almost by definition, because they break the tenth commandment, which forbids coveting what belongs to others. Wrath (*ira*) is somewhat more complicated, partly because the Bible speaks of the wrath of God (who cannot sin) and partly because there is such a thing as righteous anger. The apostle Paul assumed that it was possible to be angry without sinning (Eph. 4:26), and although there has been a great deal of debate about what the nature of that anger might be, it does not detract from the fact that wrath is not always or necessarily sinful in itself. Gluttony (*gula*) is another one of the deadly sins that most people would surely disapprove of, though not everyone would treat it with the same degree of seriousness as the others. After all, gluttony is a sin against the self more than against anyone else, and this tends to lessen its significance in the eyes of most people.

The remaining deadly sins are sloth (*acedia*), lust (*luxuria*), and pride (*superbia*), all of which call for some comment since the modern meaning of these words is not always the same as what was meant by them in the Middle Ages. Sloth, as the Latin word for it indicates, is a spiritual sin that is not to be equated with mere laziness. It is rather an unwillingness to be diligent in pursuing the things of God, a fatigue in prayer and contemplation that becomes a tool the Devil uses to deflect us from those things. Anyone who has found it hard to concentrate in prayer, or to keep it up for any length of time, will know exactly what *acedia* is and will understand why it is such a deadly sin—it cuts us off from our communion with God by distracting us when we are engaged in it and trying to persuade us that it is not worth the effort. Lust (*luxuria*) is nowadays restricted to sexual sins in most people's minds, but as the Latin word for it shows, it really means a desire for anything beyond what we need for living our daily lives. There can be no doubt that the Bible teaches that this is wrong; we are told to be content with what we have and not to crave things that are unnecessary and potentially harmful to our spiritual well-being (Matt. 6:25–34).

The remaining sin is that of pride (*superbia*), listed last by Gregory but put first by his medieval interpreters, who believed that it was because Adam and Eve wanted a higher status than the one to which they were naturally entitled that they sinned and lost their original blessedness. Whether that was true or not, there is ample indication elsewhere in Scripture that pride is one of the most serious of sins and at least a hint that it was the cause of Satan's fall as well as Adam's (Ezek. 28:2–10). All the other sins are in some measure a reflection of pride and stem from it one way or another. As the Latin *superbia* indicates, pride is the attitude of a person who thinks more highly of himself than he ought to think (Rom. 12:3); it is not meant to refer to legitimate loyalty to and satisfaction with institutions and causes to which we are personally committed and of which we are rightly "proud." We are not talking here about taking pride in one's work, for example, but about an attitude that distorts our perception of ourselves and therefore harms our relationship to God and to other people.

The main thing to stress about the seven deadly sins is that they are attitudes, not actions, though of course what we think will influence what we do. In medieval theology, this distinction is especially important because the seven deadly sins serve as a reminder that human sinfulness is more than a series of acts, something that the medieval system of penance was in danger of forgetting. Particular sins might be traced back to one or more of these attitudes, but they could not be equated with any one of them, and in the end the deadly sins could not be compensated for or eradicated merely by doing penance.

It is important to remember this because, although in theory it might have been possible to confess every sin, perform adequate penance, and be restored to the communion of the church as a sin-free person, in practice that was very rare. Many sins went undetected, even by the sinner himself, and so were unconfessed and never entered the penitential system at all. Others might be too serious or too embarrassing for people to be willing to admit, and so they too escaped immediate detection. Then again, it might turn out that the penance imposed was inadequate or not performed to the right degree. But above all, the lingering sinfulness of heart and mind, as represented by the seven deadly sins, could not be dealt with in this way and so remained as a barrier to entry into the presence of God. Whatever the cause, most people died with an outstanding debt of sin that made it impossible for them to go straight to heaven.[13] However, the thought that most people would end up in hell, regardless of their good intentions, was too awful to contemplate, so the church came up with the notion of purgatory as a way of dealing with this problem.[14] Unlike hell, purgatory is a place of cleansing after death, where the souls of those who are still imperfect could work off their outstanding debt of sin by a life of constant penance. How long this might take is unknown, of course, but there is at least the assurance that eventually those souls

---

[13] The tiny minority who did were the "saints," who were then expected to intercede for those less fortunate than they.

[14] For the origins of this, see Jacques Le Goff, *The Birth of Purgatory* (Chicago: University of Chicago Press, 1984).

would end up in heaven with God. As time went on and this conception became more prevalent, the church accepted that it was possible to do extra penances on earth in the hope of reducing the time one would spend in purgatory after death. This extra penance was certified by the church as an "indulgence," which could be obtained for relatives and others who had gone before, as well as for oneself. Eventually the embarrassment and pointlessness of doing particular acts of penance was such that it became common to commute such penance for the payment of a sum of money, which the church determined in relation to the gravity of the offence—a system analogous to the modern practice of being fined, rather than being imprisoned, for what are only minor infractions of the law. Once the commutation of penance by financial payment became an established practice, it was only logical that this facility should be extended to indulgences as well. Indulgences could therefore also be sold and sometimes were, largely in order to raise extra funds for the church. It was the sale of such indulgences that provoked Martin Luther to revolt against the system, a rebellion that ushered in the Protestant Reformation and a complete rethinking of the whole idea of sin and sinfulness.

Sin and Justification by Faith Alone

Martin Luther's great breakthrough came when he realized that it was possible to be a sinner and yet justified in the sight of God at the same time. In the medieval system, that had been a logical impossibility because a person could only stand in the presence of God as an innocent man if he had already been cleansed from his sin. In other words, the more sanctified he was (by penance and other infusions of the divine medicine of grace), the more justified he would be considered to be. By reading the New Testament, and in particular the writings of the apostle Paul, Luther came to see that this was not the right way to understand the gospel. Like the Pharisees of old, the church of his day had lost any deep understanding of the innate sinfulness of mankind, which no amount of effort on our part can do anything about, even though that idea remained embedded in its official theology. As a young man, Luther had a brush with death that made him genuinely contrite and determined to put things right with God, and to do that he embarked upon the penitential discipline of the church with an unusual degree of enthusiasm. Yet however hard he tried to improve himself, Luther discovered that, despite everything, he was just as much a sinner as he had been before. That realization drove him to the brink of despair until God opened his eyes, and he realized for the first time what the Bible was actually saying. The righteous live by faith, not by works—by trusting in the forgiveness and infinite mercy of God and not in their own efforts.

As he worked this out, Luther came to understand that Jesus had not died for sins (as things) but for sinners (as persons). Sanctification was not a progressive cleansing of the stains left by sinful actions but union with Christ, who took our place on the cross and paid the price for our reconciliation with God. The believer is justified by being united with his Savior and covered with the divine righteousness that he brought to earth and lived out in his humanity. Union with Christ is not earned by any human activity but is a gift of God. It is bestowed by his grace and made effective in us by faith, which is the gift of God to believe in Christ. Once that union was effected, sins committed by the believer were and would continue to be covered by Christ's forgiving righteousness. Critics of Luther were quick to seize on this assertion and accuse him of maintaining that a sinner could get to heaven merely by believing that Jesus had saved him; no change of life was necessary or even desirable. It is true that Luther's confidence in the saving power of Christ's righteousness was such that he could even tell his associate Melanchthon to "sin boldly."[15] What Luther meant by that was that Melanchthon did not have to fear that his ongoing sins would cut him off from the grace of God, but of course it was easy for others to misinterpret such statements and misrepresent Luther's true doctrine, which they happily did.

Luther did not think that a believer could go on living a sinful life without doing anything about it. The reason for this was that, for him, to be united with Christ is to be filled with Christ's Spirit and thus to have his mind, which guides believers in ways that help them to avoid sin and overcome the sinfulness inherited by virtue of their descent from Adam. In this life it will never be possible to attain sinless perfection, but believers should not worry unduly about this. Faith in Christ leads to a spirit of repentance and forgiveness and deepens the believer's sense of union with Christ by making him ever more aware of his total dependence on Christ for his justification. A believer who sins (or who commits a crime) may still have to make amends for it in this life, but those amends will not be the basis of his claim to go to heaven when he dies. Entrance into heaven is by the grace of God, freely given in Christ without regard to any human effort.

---

[15] Martin Luther, "Letter 91," in *Luther's Works*, vol. 48, ed. J. Pelikan et al. (St Louis, MO: Concordia, 1955), 276–77.

Once Luther understood that, he quickly dropped the concept of purgatory, and before long he abandoned the entire medieval penitential system. The good works demanded of Christians were not proof of their worthiness to enter the presence of God but evidence that God was present and active in their lives.

This shift of emphasis from actual sins to the innate sinfulness of each human being brought about a new and deeper reflection on the work of Christ as mediator of the covenant between God and man. It had always been clearly understood that Christ was sinless and that it was his sinlessness that made it possible for him to become our Savior. It was precisely because he was not guilty of the sins he bore on our behalf that he could take our place before the judgment seat of God. Far from being the cause of his condemnation, his willingness to bear sins for which he was not personally responsible was a meritorious act that God the Father recognized as the basis for absolving us of our guilt and admitting us into his presence as his adopted children. In principle, all that had been long understood, but by shifting the focus of attention from the sins we commit to the broken relationship that makes us sinners in the sight of God, Luther and those who followed him transformed our understanding of the mediatorial work of the risen, ascended, and glorified Christ.

Before the Reformation, it was thought that when he ascended into heaven, the Son of God had taken the price paid for our sins and deposited it in a kind of heavenly bank, where his sacrifice constituted a kind of lump sum of grace that believers could draw on by using the so-called means of grace that were administered by the church and its priests. Christ had satisfied the demands of the Father's justice, so there was enough grace to go around to wipe away every sin, but this store of merit kept in heaven had to be drawn on in order to be effective in wiping away the misdeeds of everyday sinners.[16] By shifting their attention from those sins to their underlying cause, the broken relationship that cuts us off from God, the Protestant Reformers put a new emphasis on Christ's present (and eternal) mediatorial work at the right hand of the Father, where he continues to plead for mercy and forgiveness to be shown to us. To put it another way, when the Father looks at us directly, he sees only sinfulness and rebellion against him, but when he looks at us through the prism of Christ,

---

[16] Medieval theologians were not universalists, in the sense that they did not believe that everyone would eventually be saved, but the logic of their atonement theory would seem to point in that direction. If Christ's blood was sufficient to atone for every sin ever committed, how could it not do so? It is hard to believe that it would have failed in its purpose or that there was some blood left over after the last judgment.

he sees that we are covered and protected by his righteousness and forgives us for that reason. Our actual sins no longer count (and are no longer counted) because they stem from our inherent sinfulness, which has been redeemed by the sacrifice of Christ, who has restored us to the right relationship with God the Father.

One consequence of this new understanding is that good works performed by unbelievers must be regarded as sinful. This naturally scandalized those who believed in the meritorious value of good works and who saw the performance of them by unbelievers as signs of God's grace at work in them, but to the Protestant mind, this makes no difference as far as their salvation is concerned. A person is not saved by his works, so the good works of an unbeliever do not count toward that. On the other hand, there was a considerable danger that unbelievers would rely on their works for their justification in the presence of God and that if they did so, they would find themselves cruelly disappointed on the day of judgment. Furthermore, as sinners cut off from the grace and mercy of God, whatever they did was the product of that condition. John Calvin made a great point in his *Institutes* of showing that sinful human beings have not lost the image and likeness of God and that they are still capable of exercising the dominion over the creatures that was given to Adam. He cheerfully admitted that many great and wonderful things have been done by human beings who are in rebellion against God, and Christians have benefited from them as much as anyone else. The goodness of their works could be (and in Calvin's case was) freely acknowledged, but this does not have the slightest effect on their innate sinfulness. For all the good that they are capable of doing, they continue to be cut off from the grace of God and eternal life.[17] The reason for this is that human beings are totally depraved, a concept to which Calvin gives considerable prominence in his exposition of the nature of sin.[18]

Total depravity does not mean that every aspect of human life is completely sinful but rather that there is nothing in us that can struggle against the power of sin in our lives, because every part of our being has been affected by it. Human beings have a constant desire to believe that we are all a mixture of good and bad elements (which is true) and that with the right training and dedication the good elements can be marshaled and directed toward controlling and overcoming the bad ones (which is false).

---

[17] John Calvin, *Institutes of the Christian Religion*, 2 vols, ed. John T. McNeill, trans. Ford Lewis Battles, Library of Christian Classics, 20–21 (Philadelphia: Westminster, 1960), 2.2.12–19.
[18] Ibid., 2.1.9.

As the canons of the Synod of Dort, called in 1618 to settle differences of opinion over this and other matters, put it:

> All men are conceived in sin and are by nature children of wrath, incapable of any saving good, prone to evil, dead in sin and in bondage thereto; and without the regenerating grace of the Holy Spirit, they are neither able nor willing to turn to God, to reform the depravity of their nature, nor to dispose themselves for reformation.[19]

The shift from sins as acts to sinfulness as a broken relationship between the sinner and God was and still is the biggest hurdle preventing people from understanding the true nature of the gospel of Christ and accepting it. The Roman Catholic Church has never been prepared to affirm this teaching even though it recognizes that we are justified only by the grace of God moving us to put our faith in Christ. Many people who would call themselves Protestant do not accept it either, preferring to believe that there is some correlation between our actions and the reward that God the righteous judge will give us in return for them. This contradicts official Protestant doctrine, but anyone who doubts this need only consider an extreme example to see how true it is. Would Adolf Hitler have been saved if he had repented and put his faith in Christ at the very end of his life? The answer to this must be yes, but few people, including those Protestants who claim most ardently to believe in justification by faith and not by works, are prepared to accept what to them seems like an outrageous injustice. But however scandalous it may appear to some, the truth is that all of us are sinners cut off from the righteousness of God. It is not the gravity of our sinful works but the hopelessness of our fallen state that is at issue in deciding the great questions of sin and redemption, but as the extreme example mentioned above reminds us, remarkably few people are able to grasp (or accept) what this really means.

Sin and Holiness

The consequences of this unwillingness to accept the total depravity of the human race and our utter dependence on Christ for salvation from sin became apparent in the centuries following the Reformation. One of the factors that contributed to this was the fact that the proclamation of justification by faith alone did not lead to moral regeneration to the extent that might originally have been hoped for. It is hard to see into the lives of par-

---

[19] Canon 3/4.3. See Gerald Bray, ed., *Documents of the English Reformation* (Minneapolis, MN: Fortress, 1994), 466.

ticular individuals, many of whom undoubtedly were transformed by the preaching of the gospel, but its impact was limited. Protestant churches and societies continued to harbor corruption and sinfulness that stubbornly refused to go away, and those who were truly regenerate became increasingly dissatisfied with this situation. Reliance on the grace of God alone might be official Protestant teaching, but many people came to think that a proactive approach to this was needed if the effects expected from a work of grace were ever to materialize. The English Puritans, for example, were convinced that a stricter church discipline ought to be applied in order to discourage sinful behavior even among those who had not made a personal profession of faith, and they felt increasingly frustrated by the unwillingness of either the official church or the state to accede to their requests. For example, by the end of the sixteenth century they had mostly become strict Sabbatarians and were incensed at what they saw as the profanation of the Lord's Day by people playing sports after church. Yet when they launched a campaign against this, the king issued *The Declaration of Sports*, forbidding them to prevent lawful recreation on Sundays. This proved to be the last straw for some of them, and they left for America, where they tried to establish societies that would repress what they thought of as sin to a degree that they deemed adequate.

Puritan New England boasted of its religious freedom, but in reality it was a repressive society that detected "sin" at every turn. Most of the Puritans stayed at home and led a rebellion that temporarily succeeded in overthrowing the old order. In 1649 they too established what they thought was a "godly commonwealth" and promptly abolished almost every kind of popular amusement. It was even possible for a minister to lose his post if it could be proved that he had read *The Declaration of Sports* more than thirty years earlier, because that was supposed to indicate that he had a frivolous attitude toward sin! But whether we think of Puritan New England or of the English Commonwealth, we find that the end result was the same. Sin could not be eradicated from society, and attempts to do so by imposing the "reign of the saints" led only to hypocrisy and created an atmosphere of repression that was the very opposite of what was intended. That the Puritan experiment should end in a series of witch hunts is tragic but scarcely surprising. To achieve their aims, the Puritans had been forced to follow the path already traveled by the Pharisees and the medieval church. Once again, sin was defined by a series of socially unacceptable actions (like playing games on the Sabbath) but with the difference that they could no longer be paid for by a system of penance. Instead, sin had to be beaten out of the sinner, which led to various forms of ostracism that sometimes culminated in death, imposed by the authorities as the only way of cleansing society of its corruption.

Puritanism failed, but the desire for a purer form of life here on earth was not so easily quashed. The latter years of the seventeenth century and the first decades of the eighteenth have come to be seen as an age of license and of libertinism, in which every vice condemned by the Puritans was openly practiced. This however was the behavior of the elite, and it went against the grain of much popular sentiment that continued to desire moral and spiritual purity even if it could not attain it. The outbreak of the evangelical revival, also known as the Great Awakening, in the years after John Wesley's famous conversion in 1738 provided the occasion for this underground feeling to resurface and eventually become the dominant influence in society. The revival contributed to this, perhaps unwittingly, by its strong emphasis on the need for sinners to be born again in Christ. For some people this was a spiritual experience that did little to change their outward lives, but for others it brought about a significant transformation of their behavior. People stopped drinking, gambling, cheating, swearing, and lying. They began to apply themselves not only to Bible study but also to other useful occupations, often prospering in business and the professions because of their newfound sense of purpose and responsibility.

All that was good in itself, of course, but it was not long before people started to think that such behavior was the necessary consequence of spiritual renewal. From there it was a short step to thinking that encouraging social transformation would be a means of defeating sin. Societies for the "reformation of manners" became increasingly common and were closely associated with revivalist tendencies. In many cases these societies concentrated on genuine social evils and did tremendous work in limiting, and even eradicating, them. Swearing, drunkenness, and sexual misconduct were not only censured but also reduced, partly by the effects of genuine conversion to Christ and partly by efforts to check them by legal means. Evangelicals continued to insist on the absolute necessity of personal conversion and refused to believe that social change could come about in any other way, but the expectations placed on converts were so obviously linked to more general social reform that a certain merging of the two was understandable and probably inevitable. In the nineteenth century it was by no means unusual to find people who did not believe the doctrine of the Christian faith but who nevertheless thought that Chris-

tianity provided an indispensable moral foundation for society and supported the churches for that reason. The energetic efforts of evangelicals
to abolish slavery, reduce criminal behavior by prison reform, improve
medical services and treatment, eliminate child drunkenness and prosti-
tution—all these and more were applauded far beyond the boundaries of
the evangelical church and came to be accepted as normal behavior for
anyone professing to be a Christian.

As a result, it was not long before evangelistic campaigns developed into social reform movements, of which the most notorious (and
ultimately the most spectacularly unsuccessful) was the campaign for
the prohibition of alcohol, known colloquially as teetotalism. Total abstinence from alcohol, as opposed to the condemnation of drunkenness,
had never been part of Christian teaching before, and in many ways it
went against biblical practice. To justify it, its supporters had to redefine
temperance, a biblical virtue which at that time became synonymous with
"abstinence from alcohol" even though that is not what the word means in
the New Testament. By the standards of the so-called temperance movement, Jesus himself would have been thrown out of the church, an irony
that was unfortunately lost on those who thought it was an integral part
of the gospel.

Once again, as so often before, sin was redefined as a series of actions
that a true Christian ought to avoid. The precise definition of what these
actions were varied from time to time but usually included such things as
working or playing games on Sunday, dancing, card playing, smoking, and
theatergoing, in addition to drinking alcohol. Sexual misconduct of any
kind was also forbidden, and cohabitation outside matrimony was popu-
larly known as "living in sin." The reduction of sin to the level of a moral
code drawn up by well-meaning social reformers proved to be extremely
popular, and in places where evangelical Christians were numerous, that
code was often translated into legislation. Hard as it is to believe now, the
United States even wrote the abolition of alcohol into its constitution, an
amendment that only had to be repealed (by another amendment) when
its disastrous effects became apparent.[20]

The chief effect of this era on the Christian church has been to trivial-
ize sin and make holiness virtually incomprehensible to the younger generation, which can see the weaknesses of moralism but does not know

---

[20] It is widely recognized today that the chief effect of prohibition, as this was called, was to give criminal
gangs such as the Sicilian Mafia a golden opportunity to break the law with the connivance of a broad segment
of society and give gangsters an aura of glamor, which remains, long after the repeal of the law they flouted.

what to put in its place. For many people today, sin is an old-fashioned concept that may still carry sexual connotations, although the exact status of such things as divorce, which would have been a major sin before 1950, is hard to determine now. The word *sin* is also used nowadays in relation to rich foods and dieting (e.g., "this chocolate cake contains a sinful number of calories"), although the only connection to the Christian idea of sin is that both threaten undesirable consequences. That we have descended to this level in popular culture is a warning to the church that the modern world no longer understands the concept of sin or sinfulness, and that in turn means that it no longer understands the true meaning of the gospel.

Toward the end of his life, John Wesley came to believe that it was possible to have a second blessing after conversion that would produce a sealing of the Holy Spirit and lead to practical sinlessness. Strictly speaking, this was not a doctrine of sinless perfection, because Wesley continued to believe that the underlying sinfulness of man remained present in every human being, but it did lead to the possibility, even to the assurance, that a believer could avoid committing actual sins. Of course, on the surface this belief appeared to magnify the grace of God even more than had been the case in earlier times because the achievement of practical holiness was entirely the work of his Holy Spirit in the hearts and minds of believers, but it was offering more than anything the gospel actually promised them. The Reformers had envisioned the Christian life as one of ongoing repentance based on a deepening sense of personal sinfulness in the presence of God and had never thought in terms of a second blessing that would raise believers to a higher plane of existence, but Wesley's views added an extra dimension to this that was to have a considerable impact on the Protestant world long after his death.

Holiness movements were on the fringe of the mainline churches during the nineteenth century, although they created a subculture in the evangelical world, characterized by Pentecostalism in the early 1900s and since. This emphasis broke out of its ghetto in the 1960s, and today the idea of a second blessing has transmuted into different types of "charismatic" experience that have gained a foothold in all the major denominations, including the Roman Catholic Church, and are often promoted as solutions to problems people have in their lives. There may be a certain reluctance to brand these problems as "sins," perhaps because some of them, such as bankruptcy or depression, cannot really be classified in that way, but anyone who reads the literature distributed by organizations like the Alpha Course will be struck by the similarities between it and the eighteenth-century evangelical revival. Now, as then, there is a steady flow of reports about how lives are being transformed as sins of various kinds are exposed, confessed, and dealt with. The benefit for the individuals concerned is doubtless considerable, but once again it must be asked whether a focus on particular sins has replaced the more fundamental problem of the underlying sinfulness that causes them. Little is said about that in charismatic circles, where the meaning of the cross and the atoning work of Christ is sometimes underemphasized. It is hard not to think that, for all the talk about new life in Christ that is heard in the churches today, there is little real grappling with the deeper issues of sin and little awareness of what that really is. In the Roman Catholic Church also, the steep decline in confession and in penitential practices shows that there is a similar underemphasis on sin, which would have surprised an earlier generation but which seems to be increasingly characteristic of our times.

Sin and Society

Not everyone who claims descent from the evangelical revival movement of the eighteenth century would subscribe to the pietistic concept of holiness, and there is a small but vocal current of thought that openly rejects it as too narrow and wrongly focused. What distinguishes them from the holiness tradition is that they do not concentrate on the bad habits of individuals but on systemic failures in the structures of modern society. In their view, dealing with sin requires extensive social reform along the lines practiced by the leading nineteenth-century evangelicals but one which does more than simply right wrongs or redistribute resources more equitably. In their view, sin is something more than the perverse desires of individual people or the abuse of laws and institutions that would be fine if they operated properly. To their way of thinking, sin has entered the very fabric of the created order and disturbed it in fundamental ways. Whether this is true or not, the main difficulty with this theory is that it is extremely difficult to see what can be done about what they call "structural sin." Destroying existing structures is possible, but it is neither easy nor very likely to produce anything better, as twentieth-century revolutionary movements have amply demonstrated. Even if a perfect system could be discovered, it would still be administered by imperfect people, something that would be bound to compromise its effectiveness. If observation is any guide, it seems that most people who adopt this approach end up supporting particular causes such as saving the rainforests or combating discrimination against a particular social group. Worthy as these things may be in themselves, from the point of view of Christian theology they do exactly the same thing as the classical holiness movements have done: they reduce sin to a series of actions that can be avoided or reversed, but they do not get to the root of the problem. Very often people engaged in such struggles blur or do not recognize any distinction between the sacred and the secular, with the result that while they claim to be more spiritual than those who distinguish clearly between these two, they end up avoiding any mention of God or his standards of righteousness in the message they proclaim. Instead they speak the language of secular politics, and those among them who are ministers of the church frequently use their positions and prestige to make pronouncements on matters of which they have little knowledge, giving the impression that this is the only way to preach the gospel in the modern world. In the end, sin becomes anything they disagree with, and to eradicate it their opponents have to be crushed if not eliminated altogether. The struggle for justice ends up as a new kind of tyranny, and as has so often happened in the past, one form of sin is replaced by another, with the underlying sinfulness of mankind remaining as present and as powerful as it has ever been. How all this will play out in the end, only time will tell, but honesty compels us to admit that just as the root problem of human sinfulness has not changed since the fall of Adam, so the attempts to deny or control it, so that it can be defeated by human means instead of divine ones, are still the greatest obstacles to the preaching of the gospel of Christ today and seem likely to remain so for the foreseeable future.

8

A THEOLOGY OF
SIN FOR TODAY

JOHN W. MAHONY

Elie Wiesel's account of his experiences as a teenager in German concentration camps at the end of World War II is appropriately titled
Night.[1] His suffering in the face of radical human evil is shocking. The
hate, bigotry, and personal abuse that he endured force us to confront our
present shared human condition. It reminds us of our fallen condition
and estrangement from God. Are we today above such inhumanity and
cruelty? What about the more recent genocides in Somalia and Rwanda
and Darfur (Sudan)? Night is a fitting metaphor for human evil. And it
raises the question: How dark is the human heart? Is it possible that the
horror of the Holocaust or other expressions of genocide actually reflect
the darkness within each of us?

Darkness is a familiar biblical metaphor for human sinfulness and estrangement from God. It reflects God's judgment (being cast into "outer
darkness," Matt. 8:12; see also 2 Pet. 2:4; Jude 13) but also God's absence
from us.[2] Beyond this, darkness describes the world system, which is an-
tagonistic to God (Eph. 6:12, "For our struggle is not against flesh and
blood, but against . . . world forces of this darkness, against the spiritual

---

[1] Elie Wiesel, *Night* (New York: Hill & Wang, 1958). He encapsulates his experience: "Never shall I forget that
night, the first night in the camp, that turned my life into one long night seven times sealed" (34).
[2] Robert H. Gundry, "New Wine in Old Wineskins: Bursting Traditional Interpretations in John's Gospel (Part
Two)," *BBR* 17/2 (2007): 285–96. Gundry notes: "Jesus compares sunlight with himself as the light of eternal
salvation (see 8:12, 'the light of life,' and 1:4: 'in him was life and the life was the light of human beings'; also Ps
27:1: 'Yahweh is my light and my salvation'). By contrast, then, stumbling in the darkness of night represents
falling into eternal damnation, inaugurated by 'the resurrection of judgment' as opposed to 'the resurrection
of life' (John 5:29; compare 3:36)."

forces of wickedness in the heavenly places"[3]), as well as the darkness within each of us (Matt. 6:23, "If then the light that is in you is darkness, how great is the darkness!").

In the writings of John, darkness and light are metaphysically and ethically contrasting metaphors. In 1 John 1:5, he describes sin as the absence of God: "This is the message we have heard from Him and announce to you, that God is Light, and in Him there is no darkness at all." Further, the incarnation is the coming of the Light, who "shines in the darkness, and the darkness did not comprehend it" (John 1:5). Our world is a place of perpetual night.

In the ethical sense, humans embrace the "darkness" because their lifestyles are "evil" (3:19). We find comfort in the dark; it protects us from confronting our sinfulness. Jesus claimed: "I am the Light of the world; he who follows Me will not walk in the darkness, but will have the Light of life" (8:12). Alternately, if we are not walking in the light, we are in the dark: "He who walks in the darkness does not know where he goes" (12:35). The good news is that the darkness has been overcome by the light: "He rescued us from the domain of darkness, and transferred us to the kingdom of His beloved Son" (Col. 1:13; cf. 1 Pet. 2:9).

The study of human sin is an examination of this darkness from which believers have been rescued. We are initially struck by the depth of this darkness (just how "dark" is it anyway?) and the need to reexamine the biblical perspective. To accomplish this, we will begin with how the subject of sin is related to other areas of biblical teaching. This will give us a sense of how crucial the study of sin really is, as so many of the critical areas of the Christian faith rest upon a clear understanding of sin. The next section explores the post-fall descriptions of sin. Sin has many facets (actions, words, attitudes, even our present condition as humans), but these are simply perpetuations of sin; its essential nature is hidden in an avalanche of our dark reality. Finally, to expose the essence of sin, that is, what sin is to God, we will implement a pre-fall grid. The strategy here is to look at human sin from the perspective of the one who endured the full impact of temptation and defeated it. Jesus' probation placed him in a position to undergo the severest challenges to his righteous character. From his vantage point, the essence of sin is simply a willful act of rebellion against God. As we shall see, the biblical metaphor of darkness is an apt description of sin's consequences but is not sin in itself.

---

[3] Scripture quotations in this chapter are from *The New American Standard Bible*®. Copyright © The Lockman Foundation 1960, 1962, 1963, 1968, 1971, 1972, 1973, 1975, 1977, 1995. Used by permission.

Locating Sin on a Theological Map

The systematic nature of biblical teaching is a critical ingredient in biblical interpretation. Gabriel Fackre contended that systematic theology is comprehensive, that it encompasses all aspects of biblical teaching; it is coherent in that it shows how doctrines fit together without contradiction; it is contextual in that it interacts with contemporary challenges and questions; and it is conversational in that it allows voices from the past and the present to dialogue.[4]

Christian thought, then, is a seamless whole reflecting unity, diversity, and mutuality. It is one of the tasks of systematic theology to articulate and explain these biblical truths. A critical preparation for that task is the orderly arrangement of the separate doctrines. Strategically, we seek to maintain organic unity while representing diversity and mutuality in a balanced way. B. B. Warfield summarized the task of Christian theologians: "It is the business of systematic theology to take the knowledge of God supplied to it by apologetical, exegetical, and historical theology, scrutinize it with a view to discovering the inner relations of its several elements, and set it forth in a systematic presentation, that is to say, as an organic whole, so that it may be grasped and held in its entirety, in the due relation of its parts to one another and to the whole, and with a just distribution of emphasis among the several items of knowledge which combine to make up the totality of our knowledge of God."[5]

Historical Relationships

Interconnectedness, or mutuality of doctrines, and the impacts of individual doctrines are evident, first, historically. The doctrine of sin has been a major player among the different branches of Christendom. By the third century the Eastern and the Western churches differed in their understanding of original sin. The primary issue was guilt and the relationship between the human race and Adam (culminating in the Pelagian controversy).[6]

At the time of the Reformation, Protestantism reasserted a strong Augustinian understanding of sin against the more semi-Pelagian view of the Council of Trent. Centuries later, among the different Protestant groups

---

[4] Gabriel Fackre, "The Revival of Systematic Theology," *Int* 49/3 (1995): 230.
[5] B. B. Warfield, "The Task and Method of Systematic Theology," in *The Works of Benjamin B. Warfield*, vol. 9 (Grand Rapids, MI: Baker, 1981), 91–92.
[6] David L. Smith, *With Willful Intent: A Theology of Sin* (Wheaton, IL: Victor, 1994), 22. For more on the historical theology of sin, see in this volume Gerald Bray, "Sin in Historical Theology," 163–85.

sin became a key sticking point that identified the difference between liberals, who were openly Pelagian, and evangelicals.

Even into the present era, one of the clear distinctions between evangelicals, on one hand, and liberationists, process theologians, and most inclusivists, on the other, is the biblical teaching regarding sin. In the struggle between Calvinism and Arminianism, the central issue is soteriology. But even here a major difference is disparate interpretations of sin, specifically the issue of human ability versus human inability or the depth and nature of human depravity.

Theological Continua

Another way to calculate the importance of a biblical understanding of sin is through the use of a series of theological continua. For example, a high view of humanity (humans are basically good morally) and our capacity for good typically maintains a low view of sin's serious effects upon humanity. Alternately, a heightened view of sin (humans are radically depraved) will result in a reduced view of human capacity for spiritual good.

The theological understanding of Christ's work is also impacted by one's view of sin. A milder view of sin tends to parallel a nonpunitive view of the atonement. When the cross is viewed as an answer to the wrath of God, a clearly heightened view of sin (human helplessness before a holy God) is the presupposition.

God's grace is another area directly impacted by one's view of sin. The more sinful we appear to ourselves, the more we recognize the strategic nature of God's grace. In the matter of soteriology, a positive view of human ability coupled with an optimistic view of the human condition depreciates the need for salvation and opens the door for alternate interpretations of the nature of our deliverance from sin (e.g., liberationist definitions of salvation as deliverance from political, sexual, or racial exploitation). In terms of conversion, repentance and faith are directly related to the nature of sin. Thus, do we have the capacity to repent and believe, or are these capacities granted to us at conversion?

Finally, as became clear to Augustine, one's view of predestination is impacted by one's view of sin. A more severe view of sin prompts a more pronounced understanding of predestination and election. Alternately, modifications to God's free unconditional election (conditional election, for example) are supported by a less stringent view of human depravity.

Visual Approach

Another approach is the use of concentric circles, much like the ripple ef- fect on water when an object hits it. This visual technique can be applied to the entire scope of biblical teaching as well as to each individual area of thought. Functionally, each individual circle in the expanding set rep- resents a doctrinal truth that can be stated as a proposition. This permits the inclusion of every facet of the doctrine, every detail touched upon in Scripture. Also, in a concentric set of circles, we are moving from the cen- ter so that the smaller the circle, the greater the impact on the expanding whole. The smallest circle is the most important. In the case of biblical teaching, the innermost circle is a foundational truth upon which every- thing else depends, often called a core truth. The formal name for this is taxonomy, the prioritizing of doctrine. Choosing a core belief grants us an interpretive key, much like a key motif, by which the other beliefs are arranged and interpreted.

Diagram 8.1

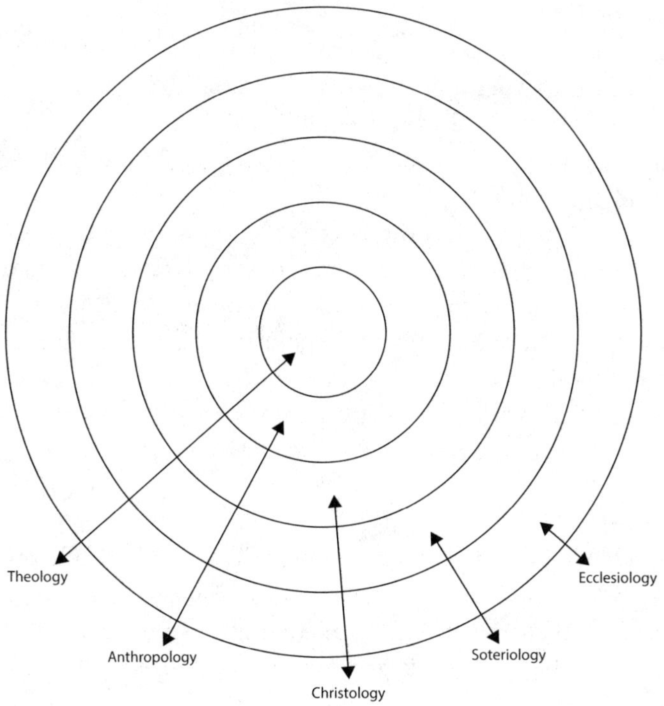

Theology

Ecclesiology

Anthropology

Soteriology

Christology

If we apply the visual of concentric circles to the entire system of Christian teaching, the innermost circle is theology, the biblical teaching about God (see diagram 8.1). In terms of theology, which is typically the most strategic concept of Christianity (at the center of all Christian thought), the first circle includes God's nature (his attributes and the Trinity). Here is also found big-picture concepts such as God's will and his works.

With the decision to create humankind in God's image, we encounter the second circle. Anthropology is the second circle because the creation of humanity is a work of God and therefore an aspect of theology. Further, both humanity and the problem of sin are defining characteristics of Christology, the third circle.[7]

The primary feature of anthropology is the creation of humankind, male and female, in God's image. Sin then follows humankind's creation, disrupting and corrupting the image as well as catastrophically impacting human existence. Human history, then, is the record of humankind's rebellion against its creator. It also reminds us that all of creation—and humankind in particular—was made to glorify God as well as to enjoy life without sin.

The remaining circles are directly impacted by sin. The biblical teaching about Christ structurally parallels the initial circle of theology in that the nature of Christ as God is preeminent. But the reality of human sin strategically impacts his incarnation and makes the cross the key to his display of God's glory.

Finally, when we reach the doctrine of salvation, the very nature of salvation is defined against human sin. Thus each facet of salvation (election, effectual calling, regeneration, conversion, justification, perseverance, and glorification) is a divine response to the lost human condition.

Sin is the ultimate anti-God and anti-human. In an expressive way, the concentric format is a dramatic commentary on the horrific nature of sin and the devastating results of its unwanted intrusion.

The Post-Fall Reality

The strategic importance of sin theologically and practically prompts us to ask about the nature of sin itself. Typically, post-fall definitions of sin (that is, those that reflect our fallen condition) come from either lexical analyses of the biblical words or from the various biblical images for sin

---

[7] The concentric circles also mirror the progress of biblical revelation, a format used in many systematic theologies.

(such as disease, defilement, or debt). Christian confessional statements, articles of faith, and systematic theologies contain definitions that have been coalesced from biblical usage and historical precedents. More recent efforts to define sin, however, reflect the existential and realist contexts of the last century: "[Sin] is universal, tragic estrangement, based on freedom and destiny in all human beings, and shall never be used in the plural. Sin is separation, estrangement from one's essential being."[8] Existentially, sin is a deep sense of dread or anxiety, the tension that arises from our finitude and the openness of the future.

The trend away from more objective statements about sin tends to cloud the issue of sin's essence. Compared to the existential, man-centered approach to sin, classic doctrinal statements such as the Westminster Larger Catechism defined sin with a clear reference to God and his law: "Sin is any want of conformity unto, or transgression of, any law of God, given as a rule to the reasonable creature." Within the Roman Catholic tradition, Thomas Aquinas defined sin as "a word, deed, or desire which is against the eternal law."[9] John Calvin defined sin as "unfaithfulness."[10] James Arminius claimed that sin is "something thought, spoken, or done against the law of God, or the omission of something which has been commanded by that law to be thought, spoken or done."[11]

Each of these definitions captures the essential meaning of sin as a violation of God's law, covenant, or will. They also reflect a traditional understanding of the historicity of Adam and interpret the account of the fall in Genesis 3 quite literally.[12] Consequently, sin is viewed more in relation to God. The perspective, however, is still post-fall.

A. H. Strong defined sin as the "lack of conformity to the moral law of God, either in act, disposition, or state."[13] In a subsequent clarification of the definition, he declared: "It therefore considers lack of conformity to the divine holiness in disposition or state as a violation of law, equally with the outward act of transgression."[14] "Lack of conformity," however, is only true of humankind after the fall of Adam; the expression cannot be applied either to Adam before the fall or to the incarnate Son of God. From a pre-fall perspective, the essential nature of sin is expressed in a single act

---

[8] Donald Capps, *The Depleted Self: Sin in a Narcissistic Age* (Minneapolis: Fortress, 1993), 45.
[9] *Systematic Theology*, 2.1, Q. 71.
[10] John Calvin, *Institutes of the Christian Religion*, 2 vols, ed. John T. McNeill, trans. Ford Lewis Battles, Library of Christian Classics, 20–21 (Philadelphia: Westminster, 1960), 2.1.4.
[11] H. Orton Wiley, *Christian Theology*, vol. 2 (Kansas City, MO: Beacon Hill, 1952), 86.
[12] See John W. Mahony, "Why an Historical Adam Matters for a Biblical Doctrine of Sin," *SBJT* 15/1 (2011): 60–79.
[13] A. H. Strong, *Systematic Theology*, 8th ed. (Old Tappan, NJ: Revell, 1907), 549.
[14] Ibid.

of rebellion; from a post-fall perspective, the violation of God's law is only one component among innumerable others.

In regard to the post-fall perspective, then, sin possesses many different facets and expressions. The Scripture also uses an array of terms for sin and describes it in many different ways. The following is a summary of the biblical usage and serves as an exposition of the post-fall reality.

Sin Is Both a Failure to Glorify the Lord and an Active Rebellion against His Established Standards

This twofold reality reflects both the absence of God's righteousness and the presence of human revolt. Every sin (thought, word, or action) possesses these dual components.

Lexical analysis of biblical terms clearly demonstrates this duality. Scripture uses many different words for sin, an indication of the richness and significance of the concept. The diversity of meaning among the Greek as well as the Hebrew terms, however, can be narrowed to two. The first are those expressions that view sin as a failure or a falling short. In this sense, sin is a failure to keep God's law (*anomia*, "lawlessness," 1 John 3:4), a lack of God's righteousness (*adikia*, Rom. 1:18), an absence of reverence for God (*asebeia*, Rom. 1:18; Jude 15), a refusal to know (*agnoia*, Eph. 4:18), and, most notably, a coming short of the glory of God (*hamartia*, "missing the mark," Rom. 3:23). Thus sin is the missing quality in any human action that causes it to fail to glorify the Lord fully. For example, can any of us affirm that we have wholly loved God as he requires? When the element of complete love for God, others, and even ourselves is missing from all our attitudes, motives, words, or actions, it makes them hideous before the Lord. Augustine called this negative aspect of sin a *privation*, an absence of the good quality that is inherent in creation. He also identified this privation as the essence of all sin.[15]

Another set of terms features the positive or active aspect of sin. Words such as *paraptoma* (trespass or deviation from a prescribed path), *parabasis* (to transgress), and *parakoe* (hearing that results in disobedience) emphasize dynamic resistance or disobedience in light of the commands of God. Adam's act in the garden is characterized by each of these terms (Rom. 5:14, *parabasis*; v. 19, *parakoe*; vv. 15–18, *paraptoma*). In

---

[15] Augustine, *City of God*, 9.13. Augustine was convinced that sin arose out of a corrupted will. He wrote: "Our first parents fell into open disobedience because already they were secretly corrupted; for the evil act had never been done had not an evil will preceded it." Thus, "the wicked deed, then—that is to say, the transgression of eating the forbidden fruit—was committed by persons who were already wicked."

each case a broken law is the focus. Post-fall sin is both a failure to reflect God's perfect standard as well as an active rebellion against his standards. The twofold aspect of sin was also referenced by Paul in Ephesians 2:1, in which he described spiritual death as expressed in "trespasses [*paraptoma*] and sins [*hamartia*]."

Sin Is Both Personal and Social

Sin by definition is a willful act. It began in the garden with an individual transgression. The different biblical terms apply primarily to personal sin. Even Paul's teaching on the universality of sin in Romans 1–3 has reference to the actions or words of individuals.

Sin, however, is more than simply personal transgression. The post-fall reality also features societal wrongs. Specifically, social sin has two dimensions. First, each individual act of sin disturbs the entire human network. My individual words and actions set in motion social consequences. All human choices are interrelated. Frederick Buechner compared the human context to a spiderweb in which every disturbance "set the whole thing a-tremble."[16] The sin of one man, Achan, resulted in the defeat of Israel at a little place called Ai (Joshua 7).[17] In the contemporary setting, it is not difficult to trace the repercussions of domestic violence, hate crimes, pornography, and divorce on families and the larger cultural context.

Social sin is also reflected in the societal structures that propagate the evils of prejudice, hate, and bigotry. What about the large publishing company that places undue pressure on editors and journalists to be the first with the story no matter how unethical their methods might be? Many situations come to mind in which a culture of deception is created to protect the organization. What about the institutions that are dominated by a culture of distrust, pitting employees against one another in a vicious circle of gossip and innuendo?

One major component of the prophetic ministry in Israel was the confrontation of societal sins, which violated the covenant and provoked the Lord's judgment. From the cycle of apostasy to judgment to repentance to restoration, the period of the judges reflects the continual societal drift toward idolatry. Israel was brought under God's judgment through the

---

[16] Quoted from Walter J. Burghardt, "All Sin Is Social," *The Living Pulpit* (October–December, 1999): 42.

[17] In Josh. 7:10–11 the corporate responsibility of the entire nation is unquestionable: "So the LORD said to Joshua, 'Rise up! Why is it that you have fallen on your face? Israel has sinned, and they have also transgressed My covenant which I commanded them. And they have even taken some of the things under the ban and have both stolen and deceived. Moreover, they have also put them among their own things.'" Achan was personally guilty, but the Lord held all the people responsible.

transgressions of Jeroboam: "He will give up Israel on account of the sins of Jeroboam, which he committed and with which he made Israel to sin" (1 Kings 14:16).

In the later prophets, Amos preached against injustice (5:12, "For I know your transgressions are many and your sins are great, you who distress the righteous and accept bribes and turn aside the poor in the gate"). Isaiah exposed the apostasy of the nation from God (Isa. 1:2–4), as well the corruption in the legal system (10:1–4). Jeremiah indicted the nation for its treatment of the fatherless (Jer. 5:28–29). The book of Jonah is an exposé of the downside of Jewish nationalism, a sectarianism that produced national distrust and hate.

Sin Is a Willful Act as Well as the Present State of Human Existence

The post-fall reality encompasses the entirety of our rebellious existence, what we do as well as who we are. Sin is a personal act. It arises from individual choice and is, therefore, a matter of personal responsibility (Ezek. 18:4). The student who cheats on an exam violates the code of conduct for the school but also violates the moral standards of God. The husband who betrays his marital vows by committing adultery is sinning willfully. In each case, a personal choice is made. Sin is a willful act.

Every act of sin, however, flows from a sinful condition or state of existence, which is also sin. Hardness of heart and unbelief are sin (Heb. 3:12, ". . . an evil, unbelieving heart that falls away from the living God"). Personal sins are not simply isolated events. All of our actions and words reflect who we are (Matt. 7:17, "The bad tree bears bad fruit"). We are fully responsible for our acts of sin as well as the state of sin in which we exist, even though we cannot change who we are ("Can the Ethiopian change his skin or the leopard his spots? Then you also can do good who are accustomed to doing evil," Jer. 13:23).

The Bible also uses the terms *sin* and *sins* in a carefully nuanced way (e.g., 1 John 1:8–10). One is the condition of sin and the other refers to the separate acts of sin. Robert Culver clarified this distinction:

> A careful reading of Scripture discovers a crucial distinction between sin and sins. This may be clearly perceived in connection with two similar sounding but subtly different passages, viz.: ". . . he will save his people from their *sins*" (Matt. 1:21); "Behold, the Lamb of God, who takes away the *sin* of the world!" (John 1:29). The former, "sins," has obvious reference to the many evil deeds of "people." The latter reference,

"the sin of the world," speaks of the world's guilt before God in which all men share.[18]

The theological explanation for this is called original sin. This doctrine includes the historic act of treason committed by Adam in the garden (Gen. 3:1ff.), the fact that all people enter human existence alienated from God (Ps. 51:5; Eph. 2:1) and are declared guilty because of Adam's sin, and the continuing state of rebellion against God in which we live and from which all sinful acts arise. We are "by nature children of wrath" (Eph. 2:3). "Original sin is not a sin which one commits. It resides in the very nature and being of man so that, even if not a single evil thought ever passed a person's mind, no idle word ever crossed his lips, and no evil deed issued from his hands, man's nature would still be corrupt because of this sin. It is born in us and is the source of all actual sins, whether they consist of evil thoughts, words, or deeds."[19] Phillip Hughes explains: "The doctrine of original sin postulates that the first sin of the first man, Adam, which was the occasion of the fall, is in a certain sense the sin of all mankind, and that accordingly human nature is infected by the corruption of that sin and the human race as a whole bears its guilt."[20]

Sin Reflects the Deep Corruption of the Human Heart

The Bible uses a number of graphic metaphors to describe the human condition in sin, theologically called *depravity*. Physical maladies such as blindness (absence of sight), deafness (absence of hearing), and muteness (absence of the ability to speak) highlight a vital missing component in each case. These physical conditions are not sinful in themselves (Jesus clearly indicates this in John 9) but serve as depictions of the spiritual condition of sinners. Metaphors for sin abound and serve as a great source for understanding human depravity. Gary Anderson documents the shift in metaphors from the OT emphasis upon sin as a burden to the NT emphasis upon debt (Matt. 6:12, "And forgive us our debts . . .").[21]

Among these descriptions of the human condition, few are more graphic than the biblical analysis of the human heart. Jesus pictures the heart as a fountain pouring forth all forms of sin (Matt. 15:19–20; Mark 7:21–22). In Jeremiah 17:9 the heart is described as deceitful, desperately

---

[18] Robert Culver, *Systematic Theology* (Fearn, Ross-shire, UK: Christian Focus, 2005), 339; emphasis original.
[19] Walter Nagel, "Sin as the Cause of God's Wrath," *CTM* (October 1, 1952): 28.
[20] Phillip E. Hughes, *The True Image: The Origin and Destiny of Man in Christ* (Grand Rapids, MI: Eerdmans, 1989), 125.
[21] Gary Anderson, *Sin: A History* (New Haven, CT: Yale University Press, 2010).

sick, and completely opaque: "Who can understand it?" The great wickedness that preceded the flood came from the corruption of the heart (Gen. 6:5; 8:21). Proverbs 21:4 declares, "Haughty eyes and a proud heart, the lamp of the wicked, is sin." Evil practices begin in the heart (Ezek. 11:21, "But as for those whose hearts go after their detestable things and abominations, I will bring their conduct down on their heads," declares the Lord GOD"). In Hosea 10:2, people are accounted guilty because their hearts are "faithless."

Jesus taught that the one who wrongfully desires a woman in his heart commits the act of adultery with her from the "heart" (Matt. 5:28). Paul claimed that "because of your stubbornness and unrepentant heart you are storing up wrath for yourself in the day of wrath and revelation of the righteous judgment of God" (Rom. 2:5). The writer of Hebrews called the heart "unbelieving" (Heb. 3:12). Interpreted holistically, the heart is not a separate mechanism in humans but is the entire person viewed from the deepest aspect of his or her being. Thus the sinful activities of an individual's life mirror the condition of the individual's heart before God.

Sin Simultaneously Involves Commission, Omission, and Imperfection

Sin is easily categorized as a deed done, a deed left undone, or a deed done with the wrong motive. When thinking of sin as commission (the deed done), we are talking about doing or saying or thinking the wrong thing. For example, when I was younger, I broke a window, lied to my dad about it, and blamed my brother for it. That lying was sin: I broke a moral code, knowingly and freely.

Sin as omission, on the other hand, is not doing or saying or thinking the right thing. Blaming my brother and failing to tell the truth is also moral fault.

Further, imperfection is refraining from doing or saying or thinking the wrong thing but instead doing or saying or thinking the right thing with the wrong motive or attitude. Using the broken-window incident from my personal life, had I told my dad the truth because I wanted to avoid the consequences, I would have acted correctly but without the best motives and therefore imperfectly.

All moral acts are judged by the standard of God's holy character expressed in his moral precepts. The Scottish Puritan John Colquhoun defined the moral law as "the declared will of God, directing and obliging mankind to do that which pleases him, and to abstain from that which displeases him."[22] The Ten Commandments are typically seen as the published expression of God's moral law.[23] Lying, stealing, killing, committing adultery, and disrespecting the sovereign Lord are overt acts. Breaking them constitutes the commission of a crime against the highest moral standard. Eight of the ten foundational codes are stated negatively in order to mark specific moral boundaries. But perhaps the commandments were also intended to be moral guides. For example, the prohibition against murder also seems to include the principle of the sanctity of human life. Thus failing to do all that we can to enhance human life is also sin and falls into the categories of omission and imperfection. Each sin in varying degrees includes commission, omission, and imperfection simultaneously.

Two reasons for this application of the law are apparent. One actually comes from the way the fourth (Sabbath keeping) and fifth (honoring parental authority) commandments are stated. They are positive in nature (that is, they are broken by failing to comply). Disobeying these commands constitutes omission. Consequently, failure to keep the Sabbath is also expressed as an overt act. Not reverencing the Sabbath denotes certain actions, words, or thoughts. Further, any lack of compliance from the heart ("Love . . . with all your heart") is to keep the Sabbath imperfectly.

The other reason is the summary of the commandments given by Jesus (Matt. 22:36–40; Mark 12:29–31). Love is a positive command. The bar Jesus sets for obedience regarding the first four commandments is to love God "with all your heart, and with all your soul, and with all your mind." Thus, have we ever *fully* complied with God's moral requirements? Jesus brings motives and attitudes into the mix. As a result, in the matter of the ninth commandment (no lying), are we always truthful to others and to ourselves? Have we reverenced God to the fullest of our ability (commandments 1–4)? When "OMG" is common even in our Christian culture, are we respecting his name and person completely?

Sin Includes Our Dispositions and Our Acts of Disobedience

Within each sinful action or nonaction is a set of attitudes and motives that are sinful as well. Greed is at the heart of stealing. Elisha's servant Gehazi followed the greed of his heart by lying to Naaman and receiving money and clothing that Elisha had previously refused. Upon his return, he faced the haunting question from Elisha: "Where have you been, Gehazi?"

---

[22] John Colquhoun, *A Treatise on the Law and the Gospel* (Orlando, FL: Soli Deo Gloria, 1999).

[23] W. T. Conner, *The Gospel of Redemption* (Nashville: Broadman, 1945), 13.

(2 Kings 5:25). Murder is an expression of hate. Joseph was almost killed and was sold into slavery because his brothers hated him (Gen. 37:4–5).

Jesus clearly links the attitude with the action (Matt. 5:21–22). The first epistle of John declares that the one who hates his brother walks about in darkness (2:11) and is a murderer (3:15) and a liar (4:20). Lust in the heart not only can lead to adultery and sexual immorality but is also treated with similar seriousness as the act of adultery itself (Matt. 5:28; note vv. 29–30, in which Jesus calls for radical steps in dealing with lust).

Sin Includes Guilt

Normally evil is classified into two types. One is natural evil (disasters and disease that are not tied to personal choice). Catastrophic events are called evil because of their often devastating effects. Natural evil is not directly produced by human sinfulness but is a result of it in a more general sense (Rom. 8:19–22). Yet, through the restraint of common grace, God's purposes are still served by it (Isa. 45:7, "The One forming light and creating darkness, causing well-being and creating calamity [rendered "evil" in the KJV]; I am the LORD who does all these").

The other form of evil is moral evil. Sin is moral evil. We use the terms *bad* (focus on the natural consequences) and *wrong* (focus on a broken moral law) to distinguish the two forms of evil.[24] Moral evil is a violation of a specific moral law by one who acts willfully.[25] The act makes us guilty before God. Guilt is the companion of broken law. Herein is the reason guilt is universal: Adam's act in the garden constitutes all guilty before God.

Guilt has two aspects. One is personal responsibility. Traditionally, theologians refer to this blameworthiness as *potential guilt*.[26] It is the guilt that follows an actual sinful act, reflected in guilty feelings. The other aspect of guilt is liability to punishment (called *actual guilt*). "All sin makes us guilty before God: it is not as if we can rebel or disbelieve or be prideful and self-centered 'just a little,' too little actually to incur guilt; for guilt

---

[24] Henry Clarence Thiessen, *Lectures in Systematic Theology*, rev. Vernon D. Doerksen (Grand Rapids, MI: Eerdmans, 1979), 171–72. Cf. Millard Erickson, *Christian Theology*, vol. 1 (Grand Rapids, MI: Baker, 1984), 412; William Dembski, *The End of Christianity* (Nashville: Broadman, 2009), 27–46.

[25] The Old Testament distinguishes between intentional and unintentional sins, but both incur guilt. Leviticus 4–5 affirms that unintentional sins constitute the person guilty and require atonement (4:3, 22, 27). In Ps. 19:12 David used a progression of sins beginning with "errors" (unintentional wrongs), then deliberate sin ("presumptuous sins"), and finally "great transgression." Stuart Perowne notes: "This completes the climax, which begins with involuntary, and advances to hidden, presumptuous, and at length ruling sins, which leave a man their hopeless slave." J. J. Stewart Perowne, *The Book of Psalms* (Grand Rapids, MI: Zondervan, 1966), 227. Morally, ignorance is no excuse for sin. All sin is against God and is morally wrong.

[26] Louis Berkhof, *Systematic Theology* (Grand Rapids, MI: Eerdmans, 1947), 232. He defined it as the "inherent quality of the sinner's demerit, ill-desert, which renders him worthy of punishment."

comes from turning in the wrong direction, however small the following step (Matt. 5:19; James 2:10)."[27]

Sin Is a Personal Affront to the God of the Bible and His Righteous Character

Isaiah's sinfulness became apparent when he encountered God's holiness (Isaiah 6). The same was true for Peter in the presence of Christ (Luke 5:8). Sin is not measurable except in light of God's character and law. James Orr writes:

> Sin, in other words, is not simply a moral, but is peculiarly, a religious conception. Sin is transgression against God; the substitution of the creature will for the will of the Creator; revolt of the creature will from God. It is this relation to God which gives the wrong act its distinctive character as sin (Ps. 51:4). It is, therefore, only in the light of God's character as holy—perfected, in Christ's teaching in the aspect of Fatherly love—and of God's end for man, that the evil quality and full enormity of sinful acts can be clearly seen.[28]

Sin therefore is egregious and beyond human depiction. We can judge wrongs (pedophilia, substance abuse, senseless and wanton acts of violence and sexuality) only from our limited context (how wrong they appear to us and how devastating the consequences might be). God's estimation of the wrongness of our sin is made in regard to the splendor of his own holiness. Righteousness is the standard of moral uprightness that God expects of all people (Ps. 96:10, 13; Jer. 9:24). It is God's holiness as applied to his relationship with his moral creatures. Righteousness is therefore the moral measure he uses to evaluate all our acts, words, and thoughts.

Ralph Venning, in his classic work on sin, *The Plague of Plagues*, notes the relationship of sin to God's holiness: "On the contrary, as God is holy, all holy, only holy, altogether holy, and always holy, so sin is sinful, all sinful, only sinful, altogether sinful, and always sinful (Gen. 6:5)."[29]

Essentially, because it is against God, sin is a "radical evil."[30] The extremity of sin's wickedness is exposed when seen in the light of the entire biblical revelation. A series of measurements will help us see sin's perversity. First, as we have seen, sin can be measured by the holiness of the

---

[27] Marguerite Shuster, *The Fall and Sin: What We Have Become as Sinners* (Grand Rapids, MI: Eerdmans, 2004), 135.
[28] James Orr, *Sin as a Problem of Today* (London: Hodder & Stoughton, 1910), 7–8.
[29] Ralph Venning, *The Plague of Plagues* (London: Banner of Truth, 1965), 31.
[30] Ted Peters, *Sin: Radical Evil in Soul and Society* (Grand Rapids, MI: Eerdmans, 1994).

one from whom we have revolted; it violates the Creator. Sin is the very antithesis of God's moral character. Next, it is measured by the height from which we have fallen—the perfect righteousness and complete enjoyment of God that Christ possessed, as well as the depths to which we have come as a race; it violates God's intent for us. Third, sin is measured by the length to which the Father went to redeem us; it violates the Son on the cross. His grace is most amazing when seen from the perspective of our demerit. Along with this, fourth, sin can be measured by the end for which we were created; it violates God's image in us. Christ is the bearer of the image, but so are we. How are we doing in relation to that task? How far short of that have we come? Fifth, we can measure the darkness of sin by the destination to which fallen humanity is rightfully headed (Rev. 20:11–15). Finally, the measure of sin from a missional perspective is the unfinished task to which he calls his representatives. Our mission is to be light bearers in a dark world, a world of over seven billion individuals, most of whom live each day in complete spiritual darkness because of sin. How close are we to getting the gospel to the more than seven billion people who now share the planet?

Sin Is a Rogue Element in God's Creation

Augustine understood sin as a *privatio boni*, the "privation of good." Accordingly, "good" characterizes God's creation (Gen. 1:4, 10, 12, 18, 21, 25, 31). For Augustine sin is the negation of that good. Sin does not actually exist but appears in the absence of the good. Consequently, sin is not a feature of the created world. In his work *The City of God*, he illustrates his meaning with silence and darkness. He writes: "Silence and darkness may be perceptible to us, and it may be true that silence is perceived through the ears, and darkness through the eyes. Yet silence and darkness are not percepts [*species*], but the absence [*privatio*] of any percept."[31]

Thus sin is not a substance created by God but is an absence within the good which he did create.[32] Further, sin arose through willful choices made by creatures whom God had created. The only avenue through which sin appears in creation is the open door of free choice. Consequently, sin is parasitic, a negative quality that has no actual existence in the created world but usurps the moral structures that God has instituted. In the simi-

---

[31] Augustine, *City of God*, in *Writings of Saint Augustine*, trans. Gerald G. Walsh and Grace Monahan (New York: Fathers of the Church, 1952), 12.7.
[32] Albert M. Wolters, *Creation Regained: Biblical Basics for a Reformational Worldview* (Grand Rapids, MI: Eerdmans, 1985), 44–56.

lar case of viruses, the parasite requires a host to live. In the same way, sin is a moral virus and exists only in the context of the good purposes of God.

Sin Is a Failure to Image the Creator to the World

Heaven and earth are perpetually demonstrating God's glory (Ps. 19:1–6). Humankind is the highest of God's earthly creation and shares the responsibility of spreading the fame of the triune God. We join with all nature in declaring the wonders of our great God. We bear the image of the one who created us. Because of the shared image we have been given dominion over the created order. Gerhard von Rad observes about this noble function: "Just as powerful earthly kings, to indicate their claim to dominion, erect an image of themselves in the provinces of their empire where they do not personally appear, so man is placed upon earth in God's image as God's sovereign emblem. He is really only God's representative, summoned to maintain and enforce God's claim to dominion over the earth."[33]

Humankind's role of imaging God before the creation was horribly disrupted by the fall of Adam. First, the fall placed the entire creation out of sync with God's basic moral design (Rom. 8:20, "For the creation was subjected to futility"). The original intent for God's image bearers was to be benevolent rulers, not malicious tyrants. The effect on creation ecologically is striking. Leon Morris notes: "Lacking the purpose for which it was designed, it has no purpose."[34] Instead of being a source of perpetual delight, creation is at odds with us. Paul goes on to describe the expectancy that grips creation in anticipation of "the revealing of the sons of God" (v. 19). C. S. Lewis pictures this beautifully in his series The Chronicles of Narnia, in which the return of human monarchs along with Aslan restores Narnia.

The corrupting of the image by Adam's fall also brought social collapse. The three cycles of emerging human cultures in Genesis 4–11 expose the violence and injustice of the fallen world. Advances in toolmaking and the domestication of animals are turned to selfish pursuits. Paul Jewett observes that "not only does increased killing follow immediately upon the use of metals, but also the city that was a sign of a newly settled life (4:17) soon becomes the city with a tower that symbolizes human ambition overreaching itself (11:4)."[35]

The task of believers as restored image bearers is still the exercise of

---

[33] Gerhard von Rad, *Genesis: A Commentary*, trans. John H. Marks (Philadelphia: Westminster, 1961), 57.

[34] Leon Morris, *The Epistle to the Romans* (Grand Rapids, MI: Eerdmans, 1988), 321.

[35] Paul K. Jewett and Marguerite Shuster, *Who We Are: Our Dignity as Human* (Grand Rapids, MI: Eerdmans, 1996), 357.

dominion in two strategic arenas. First, we are under a cultural mandate based upon Genesis 1:28. Family, church, human government, business, agriculture, and education are avenues through which the glory of Christ is expressed. It is our task to pursue his glory in all of these areas. Paul writes in 2 Corinthians 10:5, "We are destroying speculations and every lofty thing raised up against the knowledge of God, and we are taking every thought captive to the obedience of Christ." Kenneth Myers writes:

> Man was fit for the cultural mandate. As the bearer of his Creator-God's image, he could not be satisfied apart from cultural activity. Here is the origin of human culture in untainted glory and possibility. It is no wonder that those who see God's redemption as a transformation of human culture speak of it in terms of re-creation.[36]

The cultural mandate is an empty appeal without the other critical task we have as image bearers. Transforming culture begins with transforming the hearts of sinners. The gospel of Christ has that renovating power. Although the priority rests with the Great Commission, our responsibility to all creation is clear.

Sin Invites the Wrath of God

Romans 1:18 openly declares: "For the wrath of God is revealed from heaven against all ungodliness and unrighteousness of men who suppress the truth in unrighteousness." God's wrath is an expression of his holiness or moral purity. Therefore, his wrath "is simply his instinctive holy indignation and settled opposition of his holiness to sin, which, because he is righteous, expresses itself in judicial punishment."[37] Martin Luther writes:

> The source of God's wrath is the fact that men are altogether godless and ungodly in their life and behavior; and that is what brings down God's wrath. Man does not know God and despises him. This is the wellspring of all evil, the ferment that produces sin, the bottomless pit of iniquity, we might even say. What evils are bound to exist where God is not known and despised![38]

Just as all sin possesses negative/passive and positive/active aspects, it invites a negative and positive response from God. In Matthew 25:41,

---

[36] Kenneth A. Myers, *All God's Children and Blue Suede Shoes* (Westchester, IL: Crossway, 1989), 38.
[37] Robert L. Reymond, *A New Systematic Theology of the Christian Faith* (Nashville: Thomas Nelson, 1998), 639.
[38] Nagel, "Sin as the Cause of God's Wrath," 28.

Jesus describes the final judgment of the lost: "Then He will also say to those on His left, 'Depart from Me, accursed ones, into the eternal fire which has been prepared for the devil and his angels.'" The negative element is the removal from the sinner of all of God's favor and presence forever: "Depart from Me." This is the ultimate privation. Sinners have lived with a desire to have God's absence, and now they have it. Millard Erickson paraphrases the exchange between God and the sinner: "Sin is man's saying to God throughout life, 'Go away and leave me alone.' Hell is God's finally saying to man, 'You may have your wish.' It is God's leaving man to himself, as man has chosen."[39]

The second response is the positive imposition of punishment: ". . . into the eternal fire." Humankind openly rebels and transgresses God's moral will. Consequently, the sovereign Lord institutes punishment. The scene of the final judgment of humankind in Revelation 20:11–15 pictures the same scene: the judge on a throne, the judged standing before him, and the judgment in the lake of fire. They are cast away from his presence and punished forever in the lake of fire.

The cross of Christ grants certainty of God's withdrawal of his presence and the infliction of punishment upon sinners. If he did not spare his own Son, will he spare those who hate him? The only response of a holy God to sin is judgment. Venning observes: "What a hell of wickedness that must be which none but God can expiate and purge!"[40]

Sin Had a Definite Beginning in Human History and Will Finally Be Defeated

The biblical story arises out of three historical events: the creation of the universe, the intrusion of sin, and the redemption accomplished by Christ. It is a drama in three parts: the happy beginning, the tragic rebellion, and the spectacular finish. The story begins with a plan to create a world that reflects the wonder and majesty of the Creator (Rev. 4:11). Everything he creates is "good." The crown of that creation bears his exclusive image and is declared "very good" (Gen. 1:31). In this idyllic world God communes with his creation in perfect harmony.

With the appearance of sin, first among spirit beings who have been created to serve God, then among his personal image bearers, it seems

---

[39] Millard Erickson, "Is Hell Forever?" *Bibliotheca Sacra* 152/607 (1995): 259–72. See also Christopher W. Morgan and Robert A. Peterson, eds., *Hell under Fire: Modern Scholarship Reinvents Eternal Punishment* (Grand Rapids, MI: Zondervan, 2004).

[40] Venning, *The Plague of Plagues*, 110.

that the Creator has lost control of his creation. With the sin of the first couple in Eden, however, he immediately begins a retrieval project. Instead of destroying all that he has created, he begins the slow, tedious process of recovering the world and the people he created. Each new step toward final reclamation reflects his personal involvement. In an amazing act of personal sacrifice and love he sends his Son into the fallen world of sinners. Through his death and resurrection, the Creator triumphs over all his enemies. His glory is brilliantly displayed and his people freed from terrible enslavement to the flesh, the world, and the Devil. Finally, the victorious Lord returns as the triumphant king and, in a final display of awe-provoking power, puts an end to all sin from his creation.

What an incredible story it is! The entire sweep of human history is his-story. John writes:

> Then I saw a new heaven and a new earth; for the first heaven and the first earth passed away, and there is no longer any sea. And I saw the holy city, new Jerusalem, coming down out of heaven from God, made ready as a bride adorned for her husband. And I heard a loud voice from the throne, saying, "Behold, the tabernacle of God is among men, and He will dwell among them, and they shall be His people, and God Himself will be among them, and He will wipe away every tear from their eyes; and there will no longer be any death; there will no longer be any mourning, or crying, or pain; the first things have passed away." (Rev. 21:1–4)

The Pre-Fall Paradigm

Traditionally, the strategy to uncover the essence of sin involves projecting what we know about sin from the Scriptures as well as our own post-fall experience upon pre-fall Adam. For us, all sin originates in an unbelieving, proud heart (other options adopted by theologians beyond pride and unbelief include anxiety, selfishness, sensuality, sloth, and falsehood). But is unbelief or pride the root of Adam's sin? We are certainly not disputing that unbelief and pride played a role in the temptation. But to raise questions (reflecting human doubt) and lean toward going one's own way (human pride) were not sin for Adam until he acted upon them by taking the fruit. Adam's sin was coterminous with the intrusion of death as God's judgment (Gen. 2:17). During the temptation in Eden it is supposed (by Augustine, for example) that Adam became proud and yielded to his unbelief, which resulted in taking the forbidden fruit. The implication is that Adam entered the post-fall state of unbelief, which is sinful, and was corrupted before he actually ate the fruit. But for Adam unbelief was a choice;

he chose not to continue believing by disobeying a direct command of the Creator. Adam's rebellious act is the root of all sin, not his pride.

Adam's context is clarified when viewed from the perspective of Christ's sinless human character. In this regard Jesus is the clearest expression of pre-fall humanity and grants us insight into the moral uprightness of pre-fall Adam. Jesus' motives and attitudes throughout his earthly life lined up with his sinless nature. The same is true of Adam. It is clear that Adam remained sinless even as he contemplated eating the fruit. He became a sinner only when he chose to defy the command of the covenant Lord. The temptation he encountered sought to lead him to act independently of the sovereign Creator, but not because he was already corrupted by pride and unbelief. If so, he would have been a sinner before he actually sinned. The issue raised is the goodness of the original creation, as well as Adam's original righteousness. If Adam were created immature (as Irenaeus held) or were morally neutral (as Arminians contend), his original righteousness is challenged. It appears to make God the real author of sin because Adam lacked the ability to pursue righteousness within the context of a righteous, sinless nature. Strategically, a pre-fall grid or christological perspective clarifies for us Adam's perspective regarding temptation and sin.

Understandably, Satan appealed to the first pair's areas of sinless human limitation such as their desire to learn and experience new things (moral uprightness does not require omniscience), perhaps even their sense of entitlement given their image-bearing position in creation and the exclusive capacity of choice between all options. Adam had a unique position in relation to the rest of creation. Satan's scheme then was to provoke them to question the Creator, especially in the light of a "forbidden" fruit. The Creator had drawn a line. Thus, Satan's intent was to cause the pair to feel that the Creator was withholding something good from them. The prospect was that this fruit contained the key to all knowledge, which they certainly were created to pursue, as well as the portal to their own divinity. Adam faced a choice: to obey the Creator or to disregard God's prohibition and act upon his own initiative.

Perhaps, as C. S. Lewis explains it, Adam and Eve "wanted some corner in the universe of which they could say to God, 'This is our business, not yours.' But there is no such corner. They wanted to be nouns, but they were, and eternally must be, mere adjectives."[41] All we can affirm with

---

[41] C. S. Lewis, *The Problem of Pain* (New York: Macmillan, 1962), 80.

certainty is that sin for Adam was an act of rebellion, eating the fruit that God had commanded him not to eat. He chose a path not ordained by God, and that deviation in act produced total deviation in his nature. He may have "wanted some corner of the universe" independently of God, but we have no certainty of that. We are still left to question why a sinless being chose sin.

Measuring Adam's pre-fall state by Christ's sinless life may make this approach appear odd, initially. The implementation of Christ as a grid does not substantially change what we already know about sin, but it certainly clarifies the inward state of Adam during the temptation. In this way, the essence of sin is given a needed objectivity. Here is the overview: Adam's sin was an act of rebellion against a stated command of God, committed in a specific context in which an ultimate choice had to be made, a choice with devastating consequences. This choice was made by a righteous and therefore qualified representative for whom disobedience was an act of his entire person and a total contradiction of his moral direction.

Several critical features of this proposal need some comment. First, all sinning began with an act of rebellion. Basic to this disobedience is the presence of a positive and a negative component. The positive component is the assertion of personal rights, and the negative component is the rejection or overthrow of the rights of the one who gave the command. All disobedience carries these twin features.

Another aspect of our proposed definition is the existence of a stated command. Obviously, the command has an authority figure who issued it. Further, the one who was given the command understood it and had a clear choice to obey or disobey. The direction of his nature was toward righteousness.

Third, the essence of sin can only be viewed in the move from righteousness to unrighteousness. This requires a specific context for testing and an appointed representative who is entirely righteous. Finally, such disobedience has devastating effects, intensively (total depravity), extensively (universal), and eternally (nonstop, endless punishment in hell).

Covenantal Context

One of the most prominent features of the divine-human relationship is its covenantal context. God relates to all people through the instrument of a covenant. Biblical covenants were inaugurated through appointed mediators or representatives (Noah, Abraham, Moses). In the instance of moral probation, the Lord appointed two representatives. "Theologically speaking, the two Adams constitute the beginning and the end of the human society."[42] Actually, representation is clearly indicated by Paul in Romans 5:12ff.

Reminders of Jesus' role as our representative occur throughout his ministry. At his baptism Jesus identified with the people he had come to redeem (Matt. 3:15). Jesus' moral test was to learn "obedience" (Heb. 5:8) in order to become an understanding high priest (2:17–18). His complete obedience, called "active obedience," fulfilled all the moral law's demands.[43] Christ's substitutionary work on the cross, called "passive obedience," is identified by Paul as representational (Rom. 5:18–19). Even his victorious resurrection is realized in believers because he represents us (1 Cor. 15:22).

These two representatives were uniquely positioned and parallel each other in many ways. They were image bearers in the highest sense of the expression. Both were perfect reflections of God's design for humanity. They also were righteous in character, with no propensity to sin. Second, Adam and Christ experienced humanness in total dependence upon the Creator. They were alive spiritually and lived solely to serve the purposes of God. According to Paul, God's original design was the production of "good works" (Eph. 2:10). Next, the covenant representatives were both *posse non peccare* (able not to sin) and *posse peccare* (able to sin). They are the only humans who stood in that unique position with regard to sin. Finally, both representatives experienced testing, called "probation." The agent, goal, and substance of the tests were the same.

The outcomes of the tests were very different, however. In this regard, Adam failed the test by disobeying God's command; he made a single wrong choice. Christ, on the other hand, maintained obedience throughout his life; he perpetually chose righteousness. There are other differences. For example, Adam's physical context was pristine; Christ came into a very fallen world. Adam had no religious traditions and history to influence his decisions; Christ came during a time of severe religious scrutiny. Adam possessed an untested righteous character; Christ also possessed an untested righteous character as a human but had the righteous character of God (*non posse peccare*, not able to sin) as well. Jesus was, after all, God in the flesh. He was holy and as God was even beyond temptation. But he was tempted because he was completely human.

---

[42] Marguerite Schuster, *The Fall and Sin: What We Have Become as Sinners* (Grand Rapids, MI: Eerdmans, 2004), 8.
[43] John Gill, *Body of Divinity* (Atlanta: Turner Lassetter, 1965), 400. Gill writes: "It [Christ's active obedience] was wrought out in the room and stead of his people; he obeyed the law, and satisfied it in all its demands, that the righteousness of it might be fulfilled in them, or for them, in him, as their head and representative; hence he, being the end of the law for righteousness unto them, it is unto them and comes upon them."

The two natures of Christ granted him the capacity to face real temptation as well as an infinite capacity to experience it. Here is our primary reason for exploring the essence of sin through the lens of Christ.

Application of the Lens

Three matters are clear from Scripture: Christ was fully human, he was completely sinless, and he was God incarnate. These three features of the "lens" qualify him for testing and permit him to experience the full measure of testing. He encountered sin just as Adam did, yet with a great deal more at stake and with a great deal more intensity. Failure would have jeopardized his mission to glorify the Father and redeem sinners, thus unleashing the wrath of God upon all humans with no hope of redemption for them. Christ was completely human by choice; he was also sinless by nature and by choice. The perpetual submission of his will in the sacrifice of his human life is the basis of our redemption (Heb. 10:10).

First of all, Christ's humanity granted him the capacity to be tested. Through the incarnation, Christ experienced all the limitations of human existence. He was limited physically by time and space, by the simple process of maturation (Luke 2:40), by human dependence upon the physical world around him (hunger, thirst, weariness, anxiety, fear, weeping), and the threat of disease or injury (from the common cold to tooth decay to blisters from working with his hands). Jesus was limited mentally. He had to learn (vv. 40, 52) and often asked for information (John 11:34). Although he had great clarity about end-time events, he admitted that he did not know the time of his return (Matt. 24:36). Jesus was also limited psychologically. He endured emotions generated by his enemies' hatred and rejection as well as the unbelief and the helpless condition of the people he came to save. Finally, he was limited within his human spirituality. He spent many nights in prayer and worship (Mark 1:35; Matt. 14:23) and lamented that he was unable to share some deep spiritual truths with the disciples (John 16:12). Each of these areas came into play during his many tests.

Christ was also the fullest and clearest expression of the image of God. When viewed dimensionally, the original image has three components. First, the structural aspect is composed of rationality, morality, volition, emotion, creativity, and spirituality.[44] Jesus reflected each of these components and kept them in perfect balance. In structure we parallel Christ, even though we are fallen.

---

[44] Hughes, *The True Image*, 51–64.

Next is the functional capacity of the image. This is the operational hub. Sinners are spiritually "dead," which is reflected in our "trespasses and sins" (Eph. 2:1). The original capacity to desire God and pursue him in righteousness was lost in the fall. We have no contingent righteousness through which the image of God in us is directed. Jesus, however, was righteous, and the operation of the image in him was motivated and even compelled by a hatred of sin and a love for holiness. Dimensionally, then, this was the God-orientation of the image.

Third, the image granted humankind dominion over the created order. Jesus exercised this dominion in stopping a raging storm, walking on water, and multiplying bread and fish. Eugene Merrill also notes the interesting account of Jesus' temple tax in the mouth of a fish (Matt. 17:27). He observes: "Though again one might plead miracle here, it could equally as well be explained as the natural consequence of the sinless Man invoking the privilege of the original creation covenant in which he was to have dominion over 'the fish of the sea.'"[45]

Jesus was not only fully human but was also sinless and, therefore, completely unique. In all of his thoughts, attitudes, motives, words, and actions, he was without fault before a holy God ("And He who sent Me is with Me; He has not left Me alone, for I always do the things that are pleasing to Him," John 8:29). He challenged the religious elite of his day, "Which one of you convicts Me of sin?" (v. 46). Even in the context of human limitations and challenges he lived fully to honor and magnify the Father.

His followers clearly asserted his righteous character. Peter, who knew him best, declared that Jesus "committed no sin, nor was any deceit found in His mouth" (1 Pet. 2:22). As sinless (as incredible as that sounds for a human), Jesus is called an example (*hupogrammatos*—a tracing model used in writing or drawing): "For you have been called for this purpose, since Christ also suffered for you, leaving you an example for you to follow in His steps . . . [because there was not] . . . any deceit found in His mouth; and while being reviled, He did not revile in return; while suffering, He uttered no threats, but kept entrusting Himself to Him who judges righteously," vv. 21–23). Jesus' sinless life then became a paradigm for all humans, defining what it is to be fully human. Paul and John also affirmed his sinless character: "He made Him who knew no sin to be sin

---

[45] Eugene Merrill, "A Theology of the Pentateuch," in *A Biblical Theology of the Old Testament* (Chicago: Moody, 1991), 18.

on our behalf, so that we might become the righteousness of God in Him" (2 Cor. 5:21), and "in Him there is no sin" (1 John 3:5).

The third feature of the christological lens was Christ's divine nature. Jesus was a human with two distinct natures. Every act or thought of the person of Christ involved a human nature and a divine nature. Both were apparent throughout his human existence and remain intact in eternity. Possessing both natures uniquely qualified him as our high priest, who offered himself as a propitiation for sins. The human nature granted him the capacity to die for us, and the divine nature made the sacrifice effective on our behalf. Other facets of his earthly ministry required the two natures. His teaching ministry as a unique and final revelation of the Father was contingent on the human context and the divine authorization. His assertions of authority and kingship in relation to the kingdom of God as the "Son of Man" hinge upon both natures.

In the context of his temptation, we are hesitant to introduce the deity of Christ. On the one hand, there are the scriptural declarations that God is not tempted by sin (James 1:13). On the other hand, we know that the temptations that Jesus faced throughout his life were real. So did he simply experience these challenges as a human? It seems more comfortable to limit the temptation to the human nature.

But the reality is that through the incarnation God united himself to our humanity, even in its fallen nature. The incarnation granted the divine nature the vehicle through which he experienced certain things, such as suffering, death, and even temptation. The human nature matures morally and in every other way. Moral maturity for a human is contingent upon moral testing. Christ's divine and human natures cooperated at each step in that progression. In fact, throughout his entire life Jesus faced the intensification of this testing, culminating at the cross. Thus, he was perpetually being confronted with choices that fueled growth. But as God, these choices took on a much deeper meaning. Ultimacy became a feature of every choice he made. Obedience to the Father's will was his option, and the Father's honor was the goal.

Facing the Moral Chasm

I have vivid memories of my first trip to the Grand Canyon. My biggest concern on those trips was whether the motel had a swimming pool! So stopping to look at a huge hole in the ground did not have much appeal. While I certainly did not appreciate all that I was seeing, the sheer expanse left a real impression. The distance to the other side registered with me when I threw a rock out over the canyon (which you are not supposed to do). My rock dropped harmlessly about fifty feet away. I missed the other side by about ten miles! The chasm was so much wider than I thought. But what about our sin and the chasm that it creates between God and us? What is it about the nature of sin that creates such distance? Is it the infinite moral perfection of the one offended? Or is it in the contradiction that sin is before him?

Perhaps a new perspective will help. We will approach the issue using Christ's sinless humanity as our grid. Since Jesus possessed a sinless human nature that was united to an absolutely holy divine nature, what would have constituted sin to him? I realize that the immediate reaction to this approach may be skepticism. Clearly, Jesus did not sin, but he was confronted with it on a regular basis. What if he had caved in to the Devil? It appears that the chasm is best seen as the Son of God in the flesh facing the lure and possibility of disobeying his Father's will and choosing to do it anyway. His failure to obey at any point would have been incomprehensible and catastrophic. But so is sin. We are confronted with the ultimacy of sin.

From the wilderness to the long days of ministry with no place to lay his head, from Gethsemane to the cross, his human will, desires, and purposes were brought into perpetual conformity with the Father's. Jesus as the divine Son "learned obedience from the things which suffered" and was made "perfect" in the process (Heb. 5:8). John Brown asserts that this process was not reforming, as if Christ needed the discipline. Further, it was not primarily educational in the sense that he needed to learn how painful human suffering is, especially in regard to obedience. Rather, the expression "learned obedience" refers to his gaining experiential knowledge of suffering and the consequent fullness of obedience that he offered to the Father on the cross.[46]

What can we learn from Christ's continual probation that will help us in our search for the essence of sin? The first factor is the covenant in which he operated. The covenant of grace or redemption is a helpful format for interpreting the eternal arrangement between the Father and the Son through which God's people are redeemed. The Son embraced this covenant completely and lived to fulfill every stipulation that the Father imposed. The cross is at the heart of it. But his perpetual obedience that led to the cross qualified him to enter the office of our Great High Priest and present himself as the sacrifice for sin.

---

[46] John Brown, *An Exposition of the Epistle of the Apostle Paul to the Hebrews*, vol. 1 (Edinburgh: Oliphant, 1862), 249–50.

An analogy might be helpful. In virtually all human endeavors, rules define the activity. This is especially true in relationships. Marriage, for example, the highest human relationship, is built upon love, trust, and loyalty (also true in all wholesome relationships). But rules are required to provide structure and definition. Love is a motive for action and requires more than mere feeling to give it direction and purpose. For a husband to declare his love for his wife while he physically abuses her is not love at all. Jesus tied love to rules: "He who has My commandments and keeps them is the one who loves Me" (John 14:21), and, "If anyone loves Me, he will keep My word" (v. 23). Many other areas can be listed where relational rules apply: one's job, ministry, school, citizenship, even sports.

Rules define relationships. In sports, for example, some rules are basic. For example, respect for the other players, officials, coaches, and the game itself is a basic criterion. The fairness rule also applies: no performance-enhancing drugs! Then within each sport there are rules that apply only to that contest. When a participant violates a rule, a penalty is imposed.

But Jesus was obviously doing more than playing a game; he was conforming himself to a specific covenantal relationship. Thus, in this ultimate context in which the majesty of God and the future state of sinners were in view, the stakes were high and the consequences eternal. From this perspective, any violation of the covenant nullified it; sin then is any covenant-voiding act.

The second factor in Jesus' probation is the temptation itself. According to Mark's Gospel, immediately after Jesus was baptized by John he heard the Father's affirmation and was compelled by the Spirit to go away into the wilderness (1:9–12). Matthew and Luke fill in the details for us. Through the three tests the Devil apparently questioned Jesus' identity, played upon a confusion of his desires, and challenged his future.[47] Certainly Jesus was prompted to exercise his prerogative to choose a different path than the one laid out for him by the Father. But in each case (bread-pinnacle-nations) an alternate choice was a violation of the covenant of grace and a violation of his relationship with the Father.

At the heart of each challenge was the prospect of violating God's will and breaking covenant with him. In the case of the bread, he was challenged to yield to his human hunger, thereby placing himself under its control instead of trusting the provision of the Father. In the second test, he

---

[47] Russell D. Moore, *Tempted and Tried: Temptation and the Triumph of Christ* (Wheaton, IL: Crossway, 2011), 25–59.

was taken to the pinnacle of the temple and challenged to jump in order to demonstrate his true identity to the crowd below. The lure was the basic human need for personal affirmation or self-worth. Satan even quoted a biblical promise. But had Jesus given in, he would have been placing his personal vindication above his Father's designed path of humiliation. Finally, Satan gave him a glimpse of all the nations and offered them to Jesus for a simple act of worship. In this case, the Devil played to Jesus' desire to be the deliverer. In a not so subtle way Satan was seeking to receive honor from the Son of God and to defeat the purpose of redemption that Jesus was sent to accomplish. In each case, sin for Christ would have been the free exercise of his will against the Father's will expressed through an act.

A third factor is Jesus' special freedom to act. Jesus possessed actual freedom of alternate choice. Consequently, Jesus had the capacity to act in accord with his sinless human nature or to act in contradiction of it. Only two individuals possessed this exclusive capacity: Christ and Adam. Both are unique in human history, both acted within the context of a specific divine covenant, and both acted as representatives. This is the reason that the element of human will is crucial in the redemption of sinners. Hebrews 10:10 asserts that it is "by this will [Christ's willing obedience within the covenant that] we have been sanctified through the offering of the body of Jesus Christ once for all."

Heart of the Matter

Several matters become clear about the nature of sin from an incarnational perspective. First, the perspective supports our initial contention that the essence of sin is the violation of a specific command of God. Sin's essential features appear in the choice to disobey God. The movement by Adam or Christ from obedience to disobedience possessed two separate and distinct dimensions. First is the rejection of the command and the one who issued it. In this regard sin is a perpetual declaration of human freedom from God. The other dimension is the assertion of personal rights in setting an independent moral course. Any act of disobedience by Jesus would have possessed these two features. Sin then is both disregard and defiance. It disregards the rights and position of the Creator and defies the Creator by crossing a boundary he has set. The scene is much like the clay rising up against the potter and usurping the potter's rights over it (Rom. 9:21). In the case of Jesus, sin would only have occurred had he acted upon his own authority in defiance of the Father's purpose. In the context of temptation it was not sin for him to desire to satisfy his hunger when Satan proposed turning the stones to bread (or any of the other invitations for that matter). Would he be truly human and not desire the bread, or the sense of self-worth, or the deliverance of those he came to save? It was only in the act that sin is found and defined for us.

Second, from a post-fall perspective sin has many expressions. Attitudes, motives, thoughts, words, and deeds done and undone are all called sin in the Bible. But from the perspective of Jesus and the fall of Adam, the root from which all sins emerge is an historical act of rebellion against God. Thus, Adam's covenant violation makes all expressions of sin covenant violations. My son works at a local college as the intramural director. Among his responsibilities is overseeing the students' use of the facilities for basketball and other activities. Recently, he closed down the sports facility because of another activity on campus. A few students decided to play basketball and, because the facilities were locked, broke in. When my son arrived, the students were well-behaved, treating the facility respectfully as if he had been there the entire time. One problem remained. They violated the rules by breaking in. Thus, everything they did after that was a violation. They were on the wrong side of the rules. So are we in Adam. We are on the wrong side of a broken covenant and therefore everything we do, think, or feel is a continuing violation of that covenant. And every covenant violation is sin.

Finally, sin is essentially a contradiction. Viewed within a pre-fall grid, Jesus faced the ultimate incongruity. He had no desire to disobey his Father; rather, he loved him and desired only to honor him. Imagine facing the person you love the most and holding in your hand a loaded pistol. Then someone tells you to shoot him. The very thought of that is repulsive to you, but you still have the choice. Sin is choosing to follow the contradiction. Further, there was no rational basis to sin for Jesus. With nothing to gain from it and everything to lose, it was still an option. Jesus had no weak point in his will or his moral direction that created a propensity toward sin. Yet he possessed the prerogative to choose. That wrong choice is sin. Thankfully, the apostle Paul offers us good news: "Even so through one act of righteousness there resulted justification of life to all men . . . [and] through the obedience of the One the many will be made righteous" (Rom. 5:18–19).

Conclusion

"Past the point of no return, the final threshold / The bridge is crossed, so stand and watch it burn / We've passed the point of no return." These lines from *The Phantom of the Opera* express what we have all felt at times. Life is filled with those moments, like stepping across a line with no chance of turning back. It is that feeling of finality just as one skis or bungee jumps for the first time: the point of no return. Wedding vows or signatures on a mortgage have a similar finality.

Moral failures also have a point of no return. The word that haunts me at times is *don't*. With every bad decision I can hear that word ringing in my mind: "Just *don't* do it." Sin is like that. A word is spoken in haste, impossible to retrieve. One click of the mouse and one enters the world of porn, or online gambling, or illegal prescription drugs: "Just *don't* do it." Some decisions have more devastating consequences: pulling the trigger, leaving your spouse, giving away your virginity, or perhaps pushing the button to launch a nuclear weapon. There is a point of no return.

In the matter of sin, Christ makes this perfectly clear. Christ left heaven and entered the "before/after" historical context of humankind. Every decision he made on earth had a before and after. Christ is the image of God. He was righteous. Righteousness was a constituent feature of his nature, not because he was the incarnate God but because he was fully human, as God intended us to be. His righteousness granted him a special relationship with God. It also offered him a freedom to act morally that we as sinners do not have. Christ had the capacity to change his basic disposition toward God. All he needed to do was assert his personal right to act independently of God and refuse to submit to his will.

We are proposing that Adam possessed the same freedom to act. He was righteous and enjoyed a transparent relationship with the Creator. Yet he had the capacity to turn from that relationship by an act of rebellion. And he did. We also know by studying the life of Christ that Adam was no moral wimp. He was not deceived as Eve was (1 Tim. 2:9–15). He acted deliberately and maliciously. He did not cave to a weakness in his nature or his motives. We may never fully understand the reason for his action, but the fact of it is beyond dispute. He crossed the line. Crossing God's moral barrier is sin.

Adam passed the ultimate point of no return. His treacherous act is subsequently replicated in every sinful attitude and treasonous motive we possess and every godless thought, word, and action we commit. The root of all sin and the essence of sin itself is the act of turning from God in rebellion, an uprising that continues to the present moment. Thanks be to God that the uprising will be defeated and the rebellious will be judged and appropriately punished.

9

SATAN, SIN, AND EVIL

SYDNEY H. T. PAGE

How should the presence of evil in our world be understood? Can it be explained simply on the basis of immanent factors, or does it have a transcendent dimension? In addition to the evil wrought by people and what is sometimes called "natural" evil, the Bible speaks of supernatural perpetrators of evil. Chief among these is Satan, who is referred to as "the Evil One" a dozen times in the New Testament.[1] He appears as the epitome of evil in the pages of Scripture, but he does not stand alone. Allied with him are many other evil spirits who share his nature and do his bidding.[2] In this essay, we will look at the biblical teaching concerning Satan's relationship to sin and evil.

Satan: A Created Being

Evil has not always existed, nor has the Evil One. Scripture clearly represents Satan as being on the creature side of the Creator/creature distinction. The most explicit biblical teaching on this is found in Colossians 1:15–20. In verses 15–16 we read: "He [Christ] is the image of the invisible God, the firstborn over all creation. For by him all things were created: things in heaven and on earth, visible and invisible, whether thrones or powers or rulers or authorities; all things were created by him and for him."

---

[1] Matt. 5:37; 6:13; 13:19, 38; John 17:15; Eph. 6:16; 2 Thess. 3:3; 1 John 2:13, 14; 3:12; 5:18, 19. Unless otherwise indicated, biblical quotations in this chapter are from The Holy Bible, New International Version®, NIV®. Copyright © 1973, 1978, 1984 by Biblica, Inc.™ Used by permission. All rights reserved worldwide.

[2] The expression "evil spirit" occurs thirty-six times in the 1984 edition of the NIV. It is found in Judges 9:23; 1 Sam. 16:14, 15, 16, 23; 18:10; 19:9; Matt. 10:1; 12:43; Mark 1:23, 26, 27; 3:11, 30; 5:2, 8, 13; 6:7; 7:25; 9:25; Luke 4:33, 36; 6:18; 7:21; 8:2, 29; 9:42; 11:24; Acts 5:16; 8:7; 19:12, 13, 15, 16; Rev. 16:13; 18:2. Most of the NT texts in this list use an adjective that means "unclean" or "impure" (*akathartos*) rather than the normal adjective for "evil" (*ponēros*), and the 2011 edition of the NIV has "impure spirit" in these cases. The 2011 edition of the NIV uses "evil spirit" only in 1 Sam. 16:14, 15, 16, 23; 18:10; 19:9; Luke 7:21; 8:2; Acts 19:12, 13, 15, 16. Of course, many other terms are used of evil spirits, most notably "demons" (*daimōn* and *daimonion*).

This text affirms that Jesus was the agent through whom God created all things, including things that are "in heaven and on earth," both "visible and invisible." Clearly both of these expressions were intended to be all-inclusive. Moreover, the things "in heaven" in the first phrase correspond to the "invisible" things in the second, and the things "on earth" correspond to the "visible" things. The invisible things in heaven are those that are not subject to examination by our five senses but are nonetheless real. Good and evil spirits fall into this category.[3]

Paul demonstrates that he has spirits specifically in view when he adds that the created things include "thrones," "powers," "rulers," and "authorities." These terms refer to supernatural forces, at least some of which are evil. Ephesians 3:10 and 6:12 inform us that these powers inhabit the heavenly realms. Although Satan is not specifically mentioned in any of these texts, there can be little doubt that Paul believed that Satan was one of the heavenly beings that God created.[4]

Satan: A Fallen Being

Not only does Scripture present Satan as a created being, but also it presents him as a fallen being. Some think that we have references to the fall of Satan in Isaiah 14:12–15 and Ezekiel 28:12–19.[5] This is unlikely; however, that Satan fell is a good and necessary inference from the fact that Satan is a created being. The first chapter of Genesis makes clear that God's original creation was good, but Satan is undeniably evil. The natural inference is that, like human beings, Satan was created good but fell from that original state. But the fall of Satan is not just a matter of logical inference. We have a probable reference to it in 1 Timothy 3:1–7. Verse 6 warns against appointing a new convert to leadership, lest he "become conceited and fall under the same judgment as the devil." This text indicates that the Devil has done something deserving of punishment. It also suggests that his sin was the sin of pride, for that was the danger confronting the recent converts.[6]

---

[3] The creation of angels is also alluded to in Ps. 148:1–6 and Rom. 8:38–39, and Job 38:4–7 refers to angels' being present when God created the earth.

[4] A close connection between the Devil and these powers is evident in Eph. 6:11–12. Verse 11 says that Christians do combat with the Devil, but verse 12 refers to their adversaries as "rulers," "authorities," "powers of this dark world," and "spiritual forces of evil in the heavenly realms."

[5] I have discussed this issue briefly in *Powers of Evil: A Biblical Study of Satan and Demons* (Grand Rapids, MI: Baker, 1995), 37–42. For a more thorough treatment of Isa. 14:12–15, including some discussion of Ezek. 28:12–19, see John Day, *Yahweh and the Gods and Goddesses of Canaan*, JSOTSup 265 (Sheffield, UK: Sheffield Academic Press, 2000), 166–84.

[6] 2 Pet. 2:4 and Jude 6 (cf. 1 Pet. 3:19) refer explicitly to a fall of angels, but Satan is not mentioned in these texts, and there is good reason to think that they refer to a fall subsequent to the fall of Satan. Cf. Thomas Wolthuis, "Jude and Jewish Traditions," *CTJ* 22 (1987): 21–45, especially 24–27.

The activity of the Serpent in the garden of Eden has implications for our understanding of Satan's fall as well. Although Eve's tempter is consistently referred to as a serpent, and there is no direct reference to Satan in Genesis 3, it is commonly believed that the Serpent was an instrument through which the Devil worked. Indeed, this understanding is reflected in John 8:44, Romans 16:20, and Revelation 12:9 and 20:2. If it is legitimate to detect the influence of the Devil behind the Serpent, then Satan's fall must have preceded the fall of humankind. There is compelling evidence that Satan is a fallen being, but it is unlikely that the Bible describes his fall, and it would be wise to avoid speculation about it.[7]

Satan's Roles

Satan's involvement in sin and evil is depicted in three related but distinct ways in Scripture. He is portrayed as (1) a tempter, who seeks to entice people into sin, (2) a deceiver, who promotes error, and (3) an afflicter, who torments people in a variety of ways.

Satan as Tempter

When we think about the relationship between the Devil and evil, it is probably his role in temptation that comes immediately to mind. One of the works of the Devil is that he seeks to entice people into moral evil.[8]

Sex. Although Satan is portrayed as a tempter in Scripture, it is surprising how rarely he is mentioned in connection with the ethical teaching addressed to God's people. In only a handful of cases are believers warned that the Devil is behind the temptations they encounter. The earliest example of this is probably in 1 Corinthians 7:5, where Paul was dealing with self-control in the sexual realm. In the context, he was responding to a tendency to extreme asceticism in the Corinthian congregation. It appears that some had a very low view of sex and were even promoting sexual abstinence for married couples. Paul saw this as a dangerous practice and set out guidelines to control it. Once an agreed-upon period of sexual abstinence had come to an end, he advised couples: "Then come together again so that Satan will not tempt you because of your lack of

---

[7] John Calvin helpfully reminds us not to be too inquisitive about matters concerning which Scripture is silent, in *Institutes of the Christian Religion*, 2 vols, ed. John T. McNeill, trans. Ford Lewis Battles, Library of Christian Classics, 20–21 (Philadelphia: Westminster, 1960), 1.14.16.

[8] The first explicit reference to Satan as a tempter is probably in 1 Chron. 21:1, "Satan rose up against Israel and incited David to take a census of Israel." However, the interpretation of this text is problematic. See, e.g., Ryan E. Stokes, "The Devil Made David Do It . . . Or *Did* He? The Nature, Identity, and Literary Origins of the *Satan* in 1 Chronicles 21:1," *JBL* 128 (2009): 91–106.

self-control." His concern was that by abstaining from normal sexual relations with their spouses, the Corinthian ascetics were giving Satan an opportunity to tempt them to illicit sexual activity, perhaps with prostitutes (see 1 Cor. 6:15–16).

In 1 Timothy 5:14–15, we find a passage similar in character to 1 Corinthians 7:1–7 addressed specifically to widows. There Paul writes, "So I counsel younger widows to marry, to have children, to manage their homes and to give the enemy no opportunity for slander. Some have in fact already turned away to follow Satan." Like 1 Corinthians 7, this passage deals with a situation in which the Devil could take advantage of vulnerability in the sexual sphere.

Since the preceding context refers to young widows whose sensual desires overcome their dedication to Christ (1 Tim. 5:11), it is likely that Paul was concerned that young widows who attempted to lead a celibate life were putting themselves at risk. Though it might appear noble to refrain from contracting a second marriage, it would be better for them to remarry. Because they had neglected to do so, Paul says, some had already turned away to follow Satan. Paul does not say explicitly what these women had done to merit such strong criticism, but it may be that their desire for sexual intimacy had become so intense that they had formed relationships with unbelievers and had abandoned the faith.[9]

Note that in both 1 Corinthians and 1 Timothy, Satan is presented as one who is ready to exploit human weakness in the sexual realm, but in neither is he seen as one who forces people into sexual misbehavior. Indeed, in both instances, Paul suggests that Satan's efforts could be stymied by taking appropriate preventative measures.

Unwillingness to forgive. In addition to being mentioned in connection with sexual temptation, Satan is mentioned in connection with the temptation to withhold forgiveness. This issue is addressed in 2 Corinthians 2:5–11, where Paul encourages the Corinthians to forgive a repentant sinner. In verses 10–11 he writes, "And what I have forgiven—if there was anything to forgive—I have forgiven in the sight of Christ for your sake, in order that Satan might not outwit us. For we are not unaware of his schemes." Paul appears to be dealing with a situation in which a Christian had done something so seriously wrong that the church had found it necessary to discipline him.[10] The individual had, however, repented of

---

[9] See William D. Mounce, *Pastoral Epistles*, WBC 46 (Nashville: Thomas Nelson, 2000), 290–92, 297, 299.

[10] Older commentators generally assumed that Paul was referring to the man who, according to 1 Cor. 5:1–5, was involved in an incestuous relationship with his stepmother. More recent commentators have tended to

his sin, and now the question was whether the congregation would accept him back into their fellowship. Paul indicates that he has forgiven the individual, and he implores the Corinthians to do so as well. He reinforces his appeal with the warning that failure to forgive the brother would give Satan a victory, perhaps by plunging the offender into a state of despair from which he would not recover.

Anger. There is one more situation in which Paul attributes a specific temptation to Satan, and it relates to uncontrolled anger. In Ephesians 4:26–27, Paul writes: "'In your anger do not sin': Do not let the sun go down while you are still angry, and do not give the devil a foothold." Paul suggests that if believers fail to handle anger properly, then the Devil will exploit that failure to their harm and to the harm of the community of which they are part. Note that there are over thirty exhortations in chapters 4 to 6 of Ephesians, but this is the only one that specifically mentions the role played by the Devil in temptation. It is unclear why the Devil is mentioned in Ephesians 4:26–27 and not in connection with the other exhortations in Ephesians, but this certainly suggests that the biblical writers did not think it necessary to attribute all moral evil to the Devil. In fact, James reminds us that the source of temptation can come from within, when he writes, "each one is tempted when by his own evil desire, he is dragged away and enticed. Then, after desire has conceived, it gives birth to sin; and sin, when it is full-grown, gives birth to death" (James 1:14–15). Whatever role Satan plays in temptation does not diminish the responsibility of the individual for his behavior.

Satan as Deceiver

One of the activities attributed to Satan in Scripture is temptation, but this is only one of the works of the Devil. The Bible also portrays him as a deceiver. In John 8:44, Jesus describes him as "a liar and the father of lies." One of his strategies is to delude people and thus lead them astray.

The father of lies. Jesus' description of the Devil as "a liar and the father of lies" appears in a dispute between Jesus and some of the religious leaders in Jerusalem. The controversy centered on the extravagant claims that Jesus made about himself, beginning with his statement, "I am the light of the world. Whoever follows me will never walk in darkness, but

reject the connection with 1 Corinthians 5 in favor of the view that 2 Cor. 2:5–11 alludes to someone who had attacked Paul personally. For a presentation of the case for the modern consensus, see V. P. Furnish, *II Corinthians*, AB 32A (Garden City, NY: Doubleday, 1984), 164–68. For a defense of the traditional view, see David R. Hall, *The Unity of the Corinthian Correspondence*, JSNTSup 251 (London: T & T Clark, 2003), 223–35.

will have the light of life" (John 8:12). The leaders rejected Jesus' claims about himself and were hostile toward him. They professed to belong to God, but Jesus saw in their opposition to him evidence that their profession was false. Because they would not believe him, he pronounced this searing judgment upon them: "You belong to your father, the devil, and you want to carry out your father's desire. He was a murderer from the beginning, not holding to the truth, for there is no truth in him. When he lies, he speaks his native language, for he is a liar and the father of lies" (v. 44).

The notion that Satan was a murderer and a liar from the beginning goes back to the story of Eve and the Serpent in Genesis 3. The account of the fall implies that Satan is a murderer, that it was through the Serpent that death came into the world. It was at the Serpent's instigation that Eve ate the forbidden fruit, and thus death was introduced into the human experience.

The Genesis account also implies that Satan is a liar, since it was through misrepresenting the consequences of eating the forbidden fruit that the Serpent convinced Eve to eat it.[11] The Serpent denied what God had said and assured Eve that she would not die if she ate the fruit. The Serpent's *modus operandi* was to make what was detrimental appear harmless and even beneficial. Later, when trying to excuse her sin, Eve said, "The serpent deceived me, and I ate" (Gen. 3:13).

In John 8, Satan's deceptiveness is seen in the way that he keeps the religious leaders from recognizing who Jesus really is. Jesus says that the consequence of such unbelief is that they will die in their sins (v. 24). This shows us that one of the works of the Devil is to hinder people from placing their faith in Jesus and thus enjoying eternal life. Jesus also made this point in the well-known parable of the sower (Matt. 13:1–23; Mark 4:1–20; Luke 8:4–15).

The parable of the sower. In this parable, Jesus offers an explanation for the diverse responses to him and his message. In the story, some of the seed that is sown falls on the path and is eaten by birds. In his interpretation of the parable Jesus says, "Those along the path are the ones who hear, and then the devil comes and takes away the word from their hearts, so that they may not believe and be saved" (Luke 8:12). Though he does not attribute all human unbelief to the Devil, Jesus suggests that the Devil plays a role in keeping people from faith.

---

[11] Chapter 16 of the Greek recension of the pseudepigraphal work "The Life of Adam and Eve" records a conversation between the Devil and the Serpent. In verse 5 the Devil says to the Serpent, "Do not fear; only become my vessel, and I will speak a word through your mouth by which you will be able to deceive him [Adam]." M. D. Johnson, "Life of Adam and Eve," in *The Old Testament Pseudepigrapha*, ed. James H. Charlesworth (Garden City, NY: Doubleday, 1985), 2:277.

Blinding the minds of unbelievers. Paul makes a similar point in 2 Corinthians 4:3–4 when he writes, "And even if our gospel is veiled, it is veiled to those who are perishing. The god of this age has blinded the minds of unbelievers, so that they cannot see the light of the gospel of the glory of Christ, who is the image of God." Like Jesus, Paul found that some did not respond positively to his preaching. He traced this not to some defect in the message or in how it had been presented but to a defect in the hearers. They had been blinded by the master deceiver, whom he here calls "the god of this age."[12] They were being kept from seeing the truth and therefore were among those who were perishing rather than those who were being saved (2 Cor. 1:15).[13] No doubt there are a number of factors that account for why many who hear the gospel do not become Christ followers, but Scripture identifies the Devil as one of them.

In describing the world as being under the sway of the Devil, the biblical writers did not, of course, intend to suggest that all unbelievers have deliberately chosen to give their allegiance to him. On the contrary, those Jesus saw as victims of satanic deception typically saw themselves as people who already belonged to God and were not in need of salvation. It was precisely their sense of contentment with the status quo that was the problem. Note that it was the religious leaders in Jerusalem, not the prostitutes or tax collectors, whom Jesus described as children of the Devil. Spiritual blindness is often manifest in the delusion of self-sufficiency, and it is those who do not acknowledge their need of divine grace who thereby reveal that they are the children of the Devil.

False apostles. The Bible teaches that Satan plays a role in keeping unbelievers in darkness, but he is also represented as being behind the distortions of the truth that lead believers astray. In 2 Corinthians 11 the apostle Paul warns his readers about their vulnerability to false teaching, saying, "I am afraid that just as Eve was deceived by the serpent's cunning, your minds may somehow be led astray from your sincere and pure devotion to Christ" (v. 3). Later in the chapter, he describes the people who were promoting the deceptive teaching when he writes, "For such men are false apostles, deceitful workmen, masquerading as apostles of Christ. And no wonder, for Satan himself masquerades as an angel of light. It is

---

[12] It is striking that Paul calls the Devil "the god of this age," since in 1 Cor. 8:4, he writes, "We know that an idol is nothing at all in the world and there is no God but one." Obviously he does not think that Satan has the right to be called "God," but people have made him their god.

[13] Paul also refers to the Devil's influence over unbelievers in Eph. 2:2, where he describes the Devil as "the ruler of the realm of the air, of the spirit that is now at work in those who are disobedient." For a defense of this translation, see Andrew T. Lincoln, *Ephesians*, WBC 42 (Dallas: Word, 1990), 95–97.

not surprising, then, if his servants masquerade as servants of righteousness. Their end will be what their actions deserve" (vv. 13–15). Here the
errant are identified as servants of Satan who, like him, robe themselves
in a cloak of goodness in order to dupe the unwary.

It is vital to observe that Paul is here referring to professing Christians
who presented themselves as representatives of Christ. They claimed to
be "apostles of Christ," but in Paul's view they were "false apostles" (v. 13).
There has been a great deal of debate about the identity of the false apostles in 2 Corinthians.[14] It is clear, however, that they were highly critical
of Paul and that what they taught was at variance with his teaching. Paul
claims that, although they preached about Christ, they preached "a Jesus
other than the Jesus we preached" (11:4). They apparently boasted of the
visions they received (v. 1) and the miracles they performed (v. 12), promoting a form of triumphalism that emphasized their credentials and accomplishments to the neglect of self-denial and sacrificial service.

The connection that Paul draws between the false apostles and Satan
is a sobering reminder that the followers of Christ need to practice discernment and, as 1 John 4:1 says, "test the spirits to see whether they are
from God, because many false prophets have gone out into the world."[15]

Extreme asceticism. Paul detected the influence of the Devil on his
Corinthian opponents, who appear to have preached a gospel that had
no room for suffering and self-discipline, but he also believed that Satan
played a role in the error of those who promoted extreme asceticism. In
1 Timothy 4:1–2 we read, "The Spirit clearly says that in later times some
will abandon the faith and follow deceiving spirits and things taught by demons. Such teachings come through hypocritical liars, whose consciences
have been seared as with a hot iron." Here we see another instance of satanic deceptiveness. There is, of course, no reason to think that the teachers would have agreed that their teaching had a demonic source, but it
was Paul's judgment that they were misled and were misleading others.[16]

Of particular interest here is the substance of the teaching concerning

---

[14] For an overview of the various views concerning Paul's opponents in 2 Corinthians, see Murray J. Harris, *The Second Epistle to the Corinthians: A Commentary on the Greek Text*, NIGTC (Grand Rapids, MI: Eerdmans, 2005), 67–87.

[15] Other passages that encourage critical evaluation of what purports to be a message from God include Deut. 13:1–5; 18:20–22; Jer. 23:16–22; 27:9–10; 29:8–9; Matt. 7:15–20; 24:23–24; Mark 13:21–23; Luke 17:23; 21:8; and 1 Cor. 14:29.

[16] Cf. 2 Tim. 2:25–26, where Paul refers to some who had fallen prey to Satan's deceptions. He writes, "Those who oppose him [the Lord's servant] he must gently instruct, in the hope that God will grant them repentance leading them to a knowledge of the truth, and that they will come to their senses and escape from the trap of the devil, who has taken them captive to do his will." James 3:15; 1 John 4:1–3; and Rev. 2:24 also refer to satani-cally inspired teaching designed to lead believers astray.

which Paul was warning Timothy. In 1 Timothy 4:3 Paul says, "They forbid people to marry and order them to abstain from certain foods." Since both of these prohibitions relate to the body, it is likely that the teachers had embraced a form of dualism that denigrated what was material as unspiritual. This led to an extreme asceticism that included abstinence from sexual relationships and observation of strict dietary regulations.[17]

In response to this error, Paul appeals to the doctrine of creation. These false teachers, who prided themselves in their knowledge of the Old Testament, had overlooked one of its most basic claims, namely, that "everything God created is good" (1 Tim. 4:4). The doctrine of creation strikes at the heart of dualistic thinking. It affirms that the material creation must be inherently good, since it was made by a good God, who, according to the opening chapter of Genesis, pronounced it good.

In addition to appealing to creation, Paul states that "nothing is to be rejected if it is received with thanksgiving, because it is consecrated by the word and prayer" (1 Tim. 4:4–5). Here the apostle appears to be appealing to the common practice of giving thanks at meals. When people ask God's blessing on the food they eat, they acknowledge that it is a gift of God. How can anyone condemn people for eating that for which they quite properly have given thanks?

The accuser of our brothers. One of Satan's ploys as a deceiver is to bring unwarranted accusations against the people of God. In Revelation 12:10 he is referred to as "the accuser of our brothers, who accuses them before our God day and night." He adopts the role of a prosecuting attorney who stands before the divine judge to argue that believers are unworthy of God's grace and deserve nothing but punishment. Note that it is "our brothers," members of the Christian community, who are the objects of his accusations.

The accuser in Job. The concept of Satan as an accuser goes back to what is probably the earliest reference to him in Scripture. The first explicit mention of Satan is in the prologue of the book of Job. Here Satan appears with other angelic beings before God in heaven. God calls his attention to his faithful servant Job, saying, "There is no one on earth like him; he is blameless and upright, a man who fears God and shuns evil" (1:8). Satan, however, does not share God's favorable impression of Job and suggests that his piety is motivated by self-interest. He apparently

---

[17] This has notable similarities to the asceticism Paul contends against in 1 Corinthians 7 and Col. 2:16–23. Cf. P. H. Towner, "Gnosis and Realized Eschatology in Ephesus (of the Pastoral Epistles) and the Corinthian Enthusiasm," *JSNT* 31 (1987): 95–124.

can find nothing objectionable in Job's behavior, so he questions his motives. He then proposes a test to determine whether his assessment of Job is correct. "But stretch out your hand and strike everything he has," says Satan, "and he will surely curse you to your face" (v. 11).

God agrees to permit the testing of Job, with the proviso that Job is not to be harmed physically. As a result, Job suffers a series of devastating losses. Within a day he loses his wealth and his family, but Satan's cynicism concerning him proves to be unfounded. Rather than turn his back on God, Job declares:

> The LORD gave and the LORD has taken away;
> may the name of the LORD be praised. (v. 21)

Even though Job passed his test, Satan refuses to acknowledge defeat, and in the second chapter of Job he proposes a second test, saying, "A man will give all he has for his own life. But stretch out your hand and strike his flesh and bones, and he will surely curse you to your face" (vv. 4–5). God agrees to permit Job to be tested yet again, and again Job persists in remaining loyal to God.

The interactions between God and Satan in the prologue of Job clearly represent Satan as an accuser. In the case of Job, Satan's accusations have no basis, but Satan refuses to acknowledge this. Even when Job passes the initial test that he proposes, Satan continues to charge him with impure motives.

The accuser in Zechariah 3:1–2. Satan is also seen in the role of accuser in Zechariah 3:1–2. The third chapter of Zechariah consists of a description of a vision the prophet had around 520 BC, shortly after the return of the Jews to Judah following the Babylonian exile. The prophet writes, "Then he showed me Joshua the high priest standing before the angel of the LORD, and Satan standing at his right side to accuse him. The LORD said to Satan, 'The LORD rebuke you, Satan! The LORD, who has chosen Jerusalem, rebuke you! Is not this man a burning stick snatched from the fire?'"

Zechariah 3:1 specifically indicates that the reason Satan was present was so that he might accuse Joshua. Curiously, the accusations he intended to bring against Joshua are not stated. He is silenced before he has an opportunity to voice them, so we never hear what they are. Presumably, he wanted to expose the complicity of the priesthood in the apostasy of Judah that led to the exile. He could well have charged that the priests had become so corrupt that they did not deserve to officiate at the rebuilt temple. Whereas in Job the accusations of Satan are groundless, in this situation there was good reason to think the priests should be disqualified from serving in the temple. Nevertheless, God was favorably disposed towards Joshua and Jerusalem. Although Satan wanted to see the priests and their people punished, God was determined to be gracious toward them.

Satan as Afflicter

As we have seen, Satan appears as an accuser who brings unfounded charges against Job in the prologue of the book of that bears his name. But he is much more than an accuser; he is also a tormentor who afflicts Job with a variety of misfortunes. It is to that aspect of his work that we turn now.

Job the righteous sufferer. The first test of Job's integrity that Satan proposes involves taking what he has from him. He loses his oxen, donkeys, sheep, camels, servants, and children. In the second test, God allows Satan the freedom to attack Job's person but forbids him to take Job's life. In consequence, Job is afflicted with painful sores from head to toe, and he ends up sitting among the ashes, scraping himself with a piece of broken pottery. Having already lost his possessions and his children, he now loses his health.

The first two chapters of Job make it abundantly clear that Job's sufferings were not punishment for any religious or ethical failing on his part. On the contrary, he was a person of unusual piety and moral integrity; in fact, it was precisely for that reason that God called Satan's attention to him. One of the primary lessons that the book of Job teaches is that there is not a direct correlation between one's behavior and one's fortunes.[18] The bulk of the book consists of a running dialogue between Job and four friends who have come to comfort him in his distress. Job's friends all operate with the assumption that people get what they deserve in this life, but they are woefully mistaken. Their simplistic theology of divine retribution, in which suffering is invariably understood to be a sign of God's displeasure, is horribly wrong.

Job is an outstanding example of someone whose sufferings are not due to disobedience on his part, but he is not alone. The biblical narratives are filled with accounts of individuals who experienced undeserved suffering, most notably Jesus.

---

[18] Robert Alden says, "One purpose of the book, like the lament psalms and Ecclesiastes, was to address this matter of exceptions to the general principle of just rewards." *Job*, NAC 11 (Nashville: Broadman, 2001), 40.

Although suffering need not be punishment for a particular sin, there is a sense in which all suffering is due to sin. The Bible begins and ends with pictures of a world without suffering. The early chapters of Genesis describe the world before the entrance of sin. God declares that his creation is good, and the first humans are portrayed as enjoying an idyllic existence in the garden of Eden. The closing chapters of the book of Revelation describe the new heaven and the new earth that God has prepared for his people. There we read, "There will be no more death or mourning or crying or pain, for the old order of things has passed away" (21:4). The way the Bible portrays our original state and our final destiny shows that suffering is not an essential aspect of human life.

The book of Job is clear in its insistence that Job's sufferings were not a divine punishment for sins that he had committed. It is, however, more ambiguous about who was responsible for his tribulations. Satan suggests that if Job is to suffer loss, then God will have to strike him. In Job 1:11 Satan says to God, "But stretch out your hand and strike everything he has, and he will surely curse you to your face." On the other hand, the account of the second test portrays Satan as the one who afflicts Job. Job 2:7 says that after receiving God's permission, "Satan went out from the presence of the LORD and afflicted Job with painful sores from the soles of his feet to the top of his head." Who then is responsible for Job's afflictions—God or Satan?[19]

The prologue of Job certainly attributes Job's afflictions to Satan and also suggests that his purposes in afflicting Job are malicious. It does not, however, demand that one choose between God and Satan. The entire narrative presupposes that God is sovereign and that Satan is under his control. The narrator of the prologue of Job obviously understands Job's troubles as being, in some sense, due to God's will. God is, after all, the one who decides to allow Satan to torment Job. However, when we seek to explore how God is involved in human suffering, we enter an area that is both difficult and dangerous. It is difficult because it has to do with the mysterious ways of God, and it is dangerous because one must be careful not to compromise the biblical teaching concerning either God's sovereignty or his goodness.[20]

---

[19] Job's afflictions are, of course, also attributed to human adversaries and natural phenomena. The Sabeans and Chaldeans carried off his children and camels, and a mighty wind brought down the house in which his children were feasting and killed them.

[20] On this issue, see John M. Frame, "The Problem of Evil," in *Suffering and the Goodness of God*, ed. Christopher W. Morgan and Robert A. Peterson, Theology in Community 1 (Wheaton, IL: Crossway, 2008), 141–64, especially 157–64.

The book of Job teaches that God is ultimately in control of all that happens, evil as well as good, but this is not to say that he has the same relationship to both.[21] God may be seen as the giver of good, in that good comes directly from him and expresses his loving nature. He is behind the evil that humans experience as well, but here his loving character is obscured. The author of Job expresses this distinction by portraying God as one who gives permission that Job suffer, rather than afflicting him directly, and by portraying Satan as one who acts out of malice, whereas God mercifully sets limits on the harm he can inflict.

This does not, of course, help us to understand why a good God allows bad things to happen, especially to those who are undeserving of punishment. In fact, neither the book of Job nor any other book in the Bible attempts to do so. As far as Job is concerned, when he finally has the confrontation with God that he desires, he learns nothing new about the reasons for his suffering. Rather, God reminds Job of the great gulf between the Creator and the creature. He shows Job his wisdom and might as displayed in creation and reminds Job of his own weakness and limitations. Essentially, he reveals to Job that only one who is his equal can judge whether he is governing the world properly, and Job is far from being his equal. Job's response is to acknowledge that God does not owe him an explanation for his actions, but he owes God his reverent obedience nonetheless.[22]

One of the ways Satan afflicts Job is through physical illness, probably a severe case of boils. Job 2:7 says that Satan "afflicted Job with painful sores from the soles of his feet to the top of his head." Job is not the only person to become the object of such a satanic attack in the Bible. In Luke 13:10–17, we find the story of Jesus' healing a woman whose condition is attributed to Satan.

The woman Satan had bound. Luke tells us that Jesus was teaching in a synagogue one Sabbath when he noticed a woman who was severely crippled. He informs us that she had suffered from this condition for eighteen years and "was bent over and could not straighten up at all" (13:11).

---

[21] The clearest statement that God is responsible for both good and evil is in Isa. 45:7, where God says,

> I form the light and create darkness,
> I bring prosperity and create disaster;
> I, the LORD, do all these things.

See also Deut. 32:39; 1 Sam. 2:6–7; Lam. 3:38; and Amos 3:6.

[22] Cf. Martin A. Shields, "Malevolent or Mysterious? God's Character in the Book of Job," *TynBul* 61 (2010): 255–70. On the mysterious nature of God's will, see also Deut. 29:29; Ps. 36:6; and Rom. 11:33–34.

This description suggests that the woman was suffering from ankylosing spondylitis, a form of arthritis that affects the joints of the spine. This is a chronic disease in which the sacroiliac and vertebral bones can fuse or grow together so that the spine becomes rigid and inflexible.

Jesus called the woman to him and told her that she was set free from her infirmity. Immediately after he laid his hands on her, she was able to straighten up. The synagogue ruler objected because Jesus had performed this miracle on the Sabbath. In reply Jesus said, "You hypocrites! Doesn't each of you on the Sabbath untie his ox or donkey from the stall and lead it out to give it water? Then should not this woman, a daughter of Abraham, whom Satan has kept bound for eighteen long years, be set free on the Sabbath day from what bound her?" (vv. 15–16). Our interest here is in how Jesus describes the woman's condition, namely, as being bound by Satan. Like the ox or donkey in his illustration, she had been tied up until he set her free, and the one who had tied her up was the Devil.

This is the only place in the Gospels where Jesus specifically attributes an illness to Satan, and Luke is the only evangelist who records it. It appears that Luke saw the woman's malady as an example of the havoc Satan has wrought in God's good creation. Did Luke think that the Devil had singled this woman out for this attack, as he had singled out Job? Probably not. It is more likely that he believed that the Devil was behind this and all illness in a more general way. This finds support in the only other text in his writings that draws a connection between disease and the Devil. In Acts 10:38, he records a fascinating statement made by the apostle Peter. Peter summarizes the earthly ministry of Jesus by reminding his hearers of "how God anointed Jesus of Nazareth with the Holy Spirit and power, and how he went around doing good and healing all who were under the power of the devil, because God was with him." Note that Peter describes those who benefited from Jesus' healing ministry as being "under the power of the devil."

Since this statement is found in a summary of Jesus' healing ministry, Peter cannot have been thinking only of special cases in which individuals were the personal objects of satanic attack. Nor can he have had in view only those who were demon possessed. He was referring to all whom Jesus had healed. Regardless of the nature of their affliction or its etiology in the natural realm, they were victims of the malice of the Devil. Peter seems to have believed that all illness had a satanic dimension.

Scripture suggests that one way Satan afflicts people is through taking away their health. Satan also appears in Scripture as one who stands behind the persecution of the faithful. In fact, the Gospels indicate that this was one of the ways in which the Devil attacked Jesus himself.

Opposition to Jesus. All the evangelists speak of how Jesus was hated and mistreated when he was on the earth. In the fourth Gospel, the hostility that was directed against Jesus is traced back to the Devil.

In John 8:37 and 40, Jesus says that some of the religious leaders in Jerusalem were out to kill him, and in verse 44 he tells them, "You belong to your father, the devil, and you want to carry out your father's desire. He was a murderer from the beginning, not holding to the truth, for there is no truth in him." Jesus saw the hostility of his human enemies as an expression of the same cruel intent that motivated the Serpent in the garden of Eden.

The betrayal of Jesus by Judas plays a vital role in Jesus' passion, and both Luke and John portray Judas as an instrument of the Devil. Luke tells us that prior to the celebration of the Last Supper, Satan entered Judas, and as a result, he contacted the chief priests to discuss how he might betray Jesus (22:3–4). In his account of the supper, John mentions that Satan had prompted Judas to betray Jesus (13:2) and says that Satan entered Judas when he took a piece of bread from Jesus (v. 27). Given the heinous nature of the betrayal of Jesus, it is hardly surprising that Luke and John believed that the Devil was directly involved in it.

John is unique among the Gospels in the way it portrays the involvement of Satan in Jesus' death. In addition to indicating that it was Satan who incited Judas to betray Jesus, it informs us that in his Farewell Discourses on the eve of his arrest, Jesus told his disciples that he was about to confront Satan. In John 14:30–31 Jesus says, "I will not speak with you much longer, for the prince of this world is coming. He has no hold on me, but the world must learn that I love the Father and that I do exactly what my Father has commanded me."[23] The fourth evangelist makes it clear that the crucifixion of Jesus was not due solely to the betrayal of Judas, the plotting of the religious authorities, and the miscarriage of Roman justice. Behind all of these was the sinister work of Satan.

Opposition to the followers of Jesus. Jesus warned his disciples that they, like he, would be the objects of satanic attack. In Luke's account of the Last Supper, he records that Jesus said to Peter, "Simon, Simon, Satan has asked to sift you as wheat. But I have prayed for you, Simon, that your faith may not fail. And when you have turned back, strengthen your brothers" (22:31–32). Note that even though Jesus is addressing Simon

---

[23] See also John 12:31 and 16:11.

personally, he tells him that both he and his fellow disciples will be sifted by Satan. The "you" in verse 31 is plural in the original, indicating that Peter is not the only one that Satan intends to sift. Note also that, as in the prologue of Job, he has to ask God's permission to attack the disciples.

There is also a reference to satanic attack on the disciples in the High Priestly Prayer of Jesus in John's Gospel. In John 17:15 Jesus prays for his followers, saying, "My prayer is not that you take them out of the world but that you protect them from the evil one." Like Jesus, they would face satanically inspired hostility and would need divine protection.

Opposition to the early Christian movement. Satan was behind not only the persecution faced by Jesus and his original disciples but also the persecution that the early church encountered. In 1 Thessalonians 3:5 Paul writes, "For this reason, when I could stand it no longer, I sent to find out about your faith. I was afraid that in some way the tempter might have tempted you and our efforts might have been useless." What sort of temptation did Paul have in mind here? The preceding context shows that Paul was thinking of the temptation to abandon the faith because of persecution.[24]

Peter, as well as Paul, represents the Devil as the instigator of the persecution faced by the early Christian communities. In 1 Peter 5:8–9 he tells the beleaguered Christians in northern Asia Minor, "Be self-controlled and alert. Your enemy the devil prowls around like a roaring lion looking for someone to devour. Resist him, standing firm in the faith, because you know that your brothers throughout the world are undergoing the same kind of sufferings." No doubt Peter believed that it was the Devil's goal to destroy the faith of believers by prompting unbelievers to malign and mistreat them.

Although both Paul and Peter allude to Satan's role in the persecution of the church, it is John, the author of Revelation, who develops this theme most fully. In the letters to the seven churches in Revelation 2–3, he identifies the Devil as the source of persecution in Smyrna and Pergamum. In the letter to Smyrna he writes, "Do not be afraid of what you are about to suffer. I tell you, the devil will put some of you in prison to test you, and you will suffer persecution for ten days. Be faithful, even to the point of death, and I will give you the crown of life" (2:10). Some of the believers in Smyrna were going to be imprisoned for their faith, and John suggests that those who would imprison them would be acting on the orders of the Devil.

---

[24] Cf. Gene L. Green, *The Letters to the Thessalonians*, PNTC (Grand Rapids, MI: Eerdmans, 2002), 164–65.

John implies that the Devil was behind the persecution of Christians in Pergamum as well. John describes this city as the place "where Satan has his throne." He then adds, "Yet you remain true to my name. You did not renounce your faith in me, even in the days of Antipas, my faithful witness, who was put to death in your city—where Satan lives" (v. 13). Here we see that Pergamum already had one martyr, a believer named Antipas, and that there could well be more.

In Revelation 12–13 John returns to the idea that Satan is the instigator of persecution. Chapter 12 begins by describing a vision of a woman who is about to give birth and a fearsome red dragon who stands ready to devour her child. The woman bears a male child who is destined to rule all the nations on earth. The child is caught up to God, where the dragon cannot reach him, and the woman flees to the desert for protection from him. Then the scene shifts to a war in heaven, in which Michael and his angels contend against the dragon and his angels. The dragon is defeated and thrown down to earth, where he pursues the woman and her offspring. When his initial attempt to kill the woman fails, he goes off to attack the rest of her offspring, who are identified as "those who obey God's commandments and hold to the testimony of Jesus" (v. 17).

The language in Revelation 12 is obviously symbolic, and scholars differ over the interpretation of some of the details. Nevertheless, the main ideas John is trying to convey are quite clear. There can be no doubt that the child is Christ and the dragon is the Devil. The vision describes Christ's coming to earth and the Devil's hostility toward him. Christ's entrance into the world precipitates a great battle in heaven, the result of which is Satan's defeat. Having been conquered in the heavenly realm, Satan directs his venom against God's people on earth. Here John is showing his readers that, even though Christ's coming has resulted in the Devil's being vanquished, he is still active, and his rage is now directed at "those who obey God's commandments and hold to the testimony of Jesus." Christians must expect to come under satanic attack and to be persecuted.[25]

Chapter 13 continues to deal with the theme of the persecution of the church. It describes a fierce beast that emerges from the sea. The beast is empowered by the dragon and, among other things, is "given power to make war against the saints and to conquer them" (v. 7). A second beast emerges from the land. The primary function of this beast, which is later identified as "the false prophet," is to incite people to worship the first beast.

---

[25] Cf. Jerry L. Sumney, "The Dragon Has Been Defeated—Revelation 12," *RevExp* 98 (2001): 98–113.

It is most probable that the original readers of Revelation would have thought of the Roman Empire when they read of the beast from the sea, and of the worship of the emperor when they read of the beast from the land. John's visions reminded them that the Devil was at work in the opposition they faced from a hostile Roman state and from anti-Christian religion in the form of the imperial cult.[26]

In Revelation 16 we have a vision in which God sends seven angels to pour out seven bowls of his wrath on the earth. When the sixth bowl is poured out, three evil spirits emerge from the mouths of the dragon, the beast from the sea, and the beast from the land, now called the false prophet. These spirits go out to gather the rulers of the various nations for one final onslaught against the church, the battle of Armageddon (vv. 12–16). John returns to the battle of Armageddon in 19:19–21 and 20:7–10. The outcome of the battle is that the dragon, the beast, and the false prophet suffer a crushing defeat and are thrown into the lake of burning sulfur. However, before they are conquered, they gather the rulers of earth and induce them to attack God's people. With his description of how history will end, John shows his readers that persecution will continue and, in fact, intensify before Christ returns.

The Defeat of Evil

We have seen that the Bible affirms that there is a transcendent dimension to evil. There is an Evil One who wreaks havoc in our world, and he does so by seeking to entice people into disobedience, by blinding them to the truth and leading them into error, and by afflicting them with all kinds of hardships and adversity. Nevertheless, the Bible does not promote a spirit of defeatism. Though it takes evil with full seriousness, it also claims that evil shall not prevail because the forces behind it have been, are being, and will be defeated.

Satan's Past Defeat

Scripture speaks of the conquest of Satan in a variety of ways. It has past, present, and future aspects, but it is the first of these that is most prominent in the New Testament. Repeatedly the New Testament writers express their confidence that Christ has conquered Satan and his minions so that he is now a defeated foe from whom believers have nothing to dread.

---

[26] Cf. Richard Bauckham, *The Theology of the Book of Revelation*, New Testament Theology (Cambridge, UK: Cambridge University Press, 1993), 35–39.

Hebrews 2:14–15. No text gives clearer expression to the idea that Jesus defeated Satan through his incarnation and death than Hebrews 2:14–15. Here we read, "Since the children have flesh and blood, he too shared in their humanity so that by his death he might destroy him who holds the power of death—that is, the devil—and free those who all their lives were held in slavery by their fear of death."[27] The notion that Jesus came to earth and died on the cross for the salvation of sinful human beings is a familiar one and is clearly taught in Scripture. Less familiar is the idea expressed in this text, namely, that Jesus became man and gave his life in order to defeat Satan; yet this is an equally important truth. These two understandings of the significance of the incarnation and atonement are not contradictory but complementary. In fact, we might say that the salvation of human beings and the defeat of Satan are inextricably tied together.[28] Because of Christ's death on the cross, the Devil has lost his power over believers, and he is no longer able to keep them captive to the fear of death.

John 12:31–33. There is a text that is very similar to Hebrews 2:14–15 in the Fourth Gospel. John 12:31–32 records that Jesus said, "Now is the time for judgment on this world; now the prince of this world will be driven out. But I, when I am lifted up from the earth, will draw all men to myself."[29] These words were spoken shortly after Jesus made his triumphal entry into Jerusalem and have reference to his upcoming death. The prince of this world is obviously the Devil (cf. 14:30 and 16:11), and Jesus is declaring that he is about to suffer a crushing defeat and be "driven out." He connects the reversal that the Devil will suffer with his own being lifted up and drawing people to himself. Interestingly, the verb used here frequently refers to the expulsion of demons from those who were demon possessed.[30] Jesus appears to be saying that the Devil is about to suffer the same fate as his underlings. Jesus will expel him, just as he had expelled them, and Satan will lose his power over those who had been his subjects.[31]

---

[27] This is the translation in the 2011 edition of the NIV. The 1984 edition translated the verb in verse 14 (*katargeō*) as "destroy," but "break the power of" is a more accurate rendering.

[28] On the biblical teaching concerning the cross as the means through which Satan was defeated, see John R. W. Stott, *The Cross of Christ* (Downers Grove, IL: InterVarsity, 1986), 227–51.

[29] On this text, see Judith L. Kovacs, "'Now Shall the Ruler of This World Be Driven Out': Jesus' Death as Cosmic Battle in John 12:20–36," *JBL* 114 (1995): 227–47.

[30] This verb (*ekballō*) is so used in Matt. 7:22; 8:16, 31; 9:33, 34; 10:1, 8; 12:24, 26, 27, 28; 17:19; Mark 1:34, 39; 3:15, 22, 23; 6:13; 7:26; 9:18, 28, 38; and Luke 9:40, 49; 11:14, 15, 18, 19, 20; 13:32.

[31] Although the imagery is different in Rev. 12:8–9, the vision of Satan's being thrown out of heaven after being defeated by Michael and his angels probably refers to the same victory over Satan as John 12:31. The picture of Satan's being chained and thrown into the Abyss in Rev. 20:1–3 may refer to this as well, though this is much more controversial. For a defense of the view that the visions in Revelation 12 and 20 refer to the same events, see G. K. Beale, *The Book of Revelation: A Commentary on the Greek Text*, NIGTC (Grand Rapids, MI: Eerdmans, 1999), 992–95.

John alludes to Satan's fate again in 16:22, but there he says that the Devil "stands condemned," using a different figure of speech from that in 12:31. The language of condemnation suggests that the Devil has been tried and found guilty. The trial is over, and the judge's decision is in. The only thing that remains is the execution of the sentence.[32]

Colossians 2:15. Oddly enough, the apostle Paul nowhere refers explicitly to the death of Jesus as a victory over Satan. He uses the imagery of conflict and victory when reflecting on the meaning of the death and resurrection of Jesus, but he speaks of conflict with and victory over evil powers (in the plural). The key text in this connection is Colossians 2:15, where he writes, "And having disarmed the powers and authorities, he [Christ] made a public spectacle of them, triumphing over them by the cross."[33] Paul maintains that through the cross, Christ won such a great victory over the powers of darkness that they were disarmed. In other words, they lost their power over believers. He further states that Christ has triumphed over them, using a verb that described the victory parade that would be held when a victorious Roman general returned to Rome. Paul alludes to this practice to create an unforgettable picture of how complete Christ's victory on the cross was. Already his enemies, including the Devil, have suffered the humiliation of being paraded as trophies of war.

Immediately before this reference to cosmic conquest, Paul says that God "forgave us all our sins, having canceled the written code, with its regulations, that was against us and that stood opposed to us; he took it away, nailing it to the cross" (vv. 13–14). Paul obviously saw a close connection between the defeat of the evil powers, mentioned in verse 15, and the fact that the guilty verdict we deserve and its accompanying punishment have been annulled through the cross, mentioned in verse 14.

In a memorable analogy, biblical theologian Oscar Cullmann compared the victory Jesus won over Satan on the cross to D-Day in the Second World War.[34] D-Day was the decisive battle in the war. Victory Day was still almost a year away, but the landing at Normandy marked the critical turning point in the war. In a similar way, the pivotal battle with the Devil took place in the life, death, and resurrection of Jesus. There,

---

[32] Whereas John suggests that the crucial battle between Jesus and the Devil took place at Calvary, the other evangelists focus on an earlier confrontation between the two, namely, the temptation in the desert that followed Jesus' baptism. Cf. Matt. 4:1–11; Mark 1:12–13; and Luke 4:1–13.

[33] Other texts that refer to Christ's defeat of the evil powers or their submission to him include 1 Cor. 15:24; Eph. 1:20–21; Phil. 2:9–10; Col. 2:10; and 1 Pet. 3:19, 22.

[34] Oscar Cullmann, *Christ and Time: A Primitive Christian Conception of Time and History*, trans. F. V. Filson, rev. ed. (London: SCM, 1951), 84.

Satan was decisively defeated. He continues to fight, but he is fighting in a losing cause, and the final outcome is not in doubt.

Satan's Present Defeat

The Bible not only claims that Christ vanquished Satan on the cross; it also claims that the Devil repeatedly experiences defeat in the period between the advents. Scripture contends that the followers of Christ have the ability to rout the Evil One and that they will, in fact, do so.

Romans 16:20. Of particular interest in this connection is a brief text near the end of the book of Romans. As he brings his letter to a close, Paul writes, "The God of peace will soon crush Satan under your feet" (16:20). Writing decades after the crucifixion, Paul says that Satan is about to be overcome. Obviously, he is not referring to the victory Jesus won over Satan on the cross. Furthermore, he does not say that the Devil will be subdued by Christ but by Christians. The feet that will crush Satan belong to the Roman believers.

The picture of Satan's being crushed under someone's feet is undoubtedly drawn from Genesis 3:15, where we read in the curse pronounced on the Serpent that the offspring of the woman would crush the head of the offspring of the Serpent. Paul suggests that this promise would be fulfilled in the victories that the Roman Christians would achieve in their battles with Satan. Presumably, he believed that such victories were possible only because of the prior victory of Christ, but his emphasis in Romans 16 is not on that victory in the past but on the victories his brothers and sisters in Rome would enjoy in the present.[35]

James 4:7 and 1 Peter 5:9. Two texts in the New Testament urge Christians to resist the Devil. In James 4:7, we read, "Submit yourselves, then, to God. Resist the devil, and he will flee from you." This has a close parallel in 1 Peter 5:9. After describing the Devil as a roaring lion, Peter says, "Resist him, standing firm in the faith, because you know that your brothers throughout the world are undergoing the same kind of sufferings."

James and Peter take it for granted that Satan will assault believers. Resistance would not be necessary if one never came under attack. The type of attack Peter had in mind consisted primarily of persecution, with the accompanying temptation to apostasy. The context in James suggests

---

[35] A similar promise of victory over the Devil is found in 2 Thess. 3:3, where we read, "But the Lord is faithful, and he will strengthen and protect you from the evil one." Compare Jesus' words to the seventy-two disciples in Luke 10:19, "I have given you authority to trample on snakes and scorpions and to overcome all the power of the enemy; nothing will harm you."

that he was thinking of temptation more broadly, but especially temptations associated with selfishness and pride.

The command to resist the Devil implies that believers will be able to stand their ground. In fact, James attaches a promise to the command, assuring his readers that if they do resist the Devil, the Devil will flee from them. The idea that believers can put the Devil to flight encourages besieged Christians to face their adversary with confidence, knowing that they can and will prevail.

Paul encourages the same attitude in his discussion of the armor of God. He even uses the very word that James and Peter use to refer to resistance, though this is not obvious in our English translations. The verb translated "resist" in James and 1 Peter also appears in Ephesians 6:13, but there it is translated "stand your ground" in the sentence, "Therefore put on the full armor of God, so that when the day of evil comes, you may be able to stand your ground."

Overcoming the Evil One in 1 John. The idea that Satan is being defeated in the lives of Christians in the present age is especially prominent in 1 John. John teaches that when people become believers, they win a victory over the Devil. In 1 John 1:14 he refers to young men who "have overcome the evil one." Presumably he believed that this victory had been achieved when they came to faith and turned "from darkness to light, and from the power of Satan to God" (Acts 26:18).[36]

It is because of that initial victory that Christians have reason to believe that further victories are possible. In 1 John 5:18 we read, "We know that anyone born of God does not continue to sin; the one who was born of God keeps him safe, and the evil one cannot harm him." John is not claiming here that Jesus will keep believers from committing acts of sin; in fact, 1 John 1:10 says that those who claim to have no sin make God out to be a liar. However, he does contend that believers are not held in bondage to sin by Satan. It is normal for unbelievers to sin, for "the whole world is under the control of the evil one" (5:19), but the Devil does not control the followers of Jesus.

Satan's Future Defeat

Although Jesus won a decisive victory over the Devil at Calvary, the Devil continues to wage war against the saints. There is coming a time, however,

---

[36] Christians are frequently portrayed as overcomers in the book of Revelation. See Rev. 2:7, 11, 17, 26; 3:5, 12, 21; 15:2; and 21:7. The verb translated "overcome" (*nikaō*) appears twenty-eight times in the New Testament. Six of these occurrences are in 1 John, and seventeen are in the book of Revelation.

when the full impact of Christ's victory will be realized, and the Evil One will meet his final doom.

Matthew 25:41. Jesus makes a brief allusion to the ultimate fate of the Devil in his parable about the sheep and the goats. In this parable he says that the Son of Man will divide people into two groups when he comes in his glory. Some will be welcomed into the Father's kingdom, but to others he will say, "Depart from me, you who are cursed into the eternal fire prepared for the devil and his angels" (Matt. 25:41). Here we learn that God has prepared a place of punishment for Satan and his allies, and it is just a matter of time before they are consigned to it.

Revelation 20:7–10. The most familiar biblical passage referring to the ultimate fate of the Devil is unquestionably Revelation 20:7–10, and it paints a similar picture to Matthew 25:41. This passage describes a final, climactic battle at the end of human history. Satan is temporarily given freedom to deceive the nations and marshals a huge army to attack the people of God. The satanically inspired hordes march upon Jerusalem and surround it. Then we read, "But fire came down from heaven and devoured them. And the devil, who deceived them, was thrown into the lake of burning sulfur, where the beast and the false prophet had been thrown. They will be tormented day and night for ever and ever" (Rev. 20:9–10).

There are differences of interpretation about the events that lead up to Satan's final defeat, but Revelation clearly states that the defeat itself will be sudden and complete.[37] Moreover, the Devil's final condemnation is absolutely certain. The Devil will in the end be punished, and his punishment will be severe and permanent. Note that the final victory over the Devil will be the result not of human resistance but of divine intervention. Though believers can expect to win victories over their great adversary in this life, only God can eradicate the influence of the Devil from the earth and mete out the punishment he deserves, and he will do so at the second coming. Revelation 20:7–10 contains the last reference to Satan in Scripture, and it is very appropriate that the last word concerning the Evil One is that his final and most ferocious attack will be unsuccessful and will result in his condemnation and punishment.

Knowing that the Devil's doom is certain, believers can face with perseverance and hopefulness the challenges of life in a world where his evil

---

[37] Compare 2 Thess. 2:8, which says that Christ will overthrow the man of lawlessness (generally understood to be the Antichrist) suddenly and completely when he returns. See also 1 Cor. 15:23–24.

influence is all too evident, looking forward with eager anticipation to that day when his influence will finally come to an end and evil will be no more.

Conclusion

Every time we open a newspaper and watch the nightly news on television, we are bombarded with evidence of the terrible presence of evil in our world. According to the Christian Scriptures, evil ought not to be attributed to factors within the natural realm alone. It also has a supernatural dimension. The Devil and his angels have a part to play in the evil we encounter, whether it takes the form of incitement to immorality, promulgation of error, or so-called natural evil.

Although Satan is the supremely Evil One, and his powers are great, Scripture is careful to maintain that he is a created being and is subordinate to the Creator and Sustainer of the universe.[38] Moreover, his work does not relieve human beings of responsibility for their decisions and actions, nor is it incompatible with the presence of immanent causes of evil. John, for instance, had no qualms about attributing in Revelation 2:10 the incarceration of believers by their human adversaries to their great adversary.

The followers of Christ have an enemy who is variously described as "the prince of this world," "the god of this age," and "the ruler of the kingdom of the air"; however, his power is circumscribed and temporary. As Martin Luther reminds us so well in his great hymn "A Mighty Fortress Is Our God,"

> And though this world, with devils filled, should threaten to undo us,
> We will not fear, for God hath willed His truth to triumph through us:
> The Prince of Darkness grim, we tremble not for him;
> His rage we can endure, for lo, his doom is sure,
> One little word shall fell him.

---

[38] I have explored this theme in "Satan: God's Servant," *JETS* 50 (2007): 449–65.

10

SIN AND TEMPTATION

DAVID B. CALHOUN

When temptation sorely presses,
In the day of Satan's pow'r,
In our times of deep distresses,
In each dark and trying hour,
By thy mercy, O deliver us,
Good Lord.[1]

Everyone experiences temptation every day and, perhaps, every hour. It is such a common experience that we get used to it and tell jokes about it, like the one about the man who said he could resist everything but temptation.

Our temptations tell us, or should tell us, a great deal about ourselves. We all are tempted and so should not be judgmental about the sins of each other. When a Christian woman heard the sad story of a person who had stumbled into sin, I heard her say, "I have those weeds in my garden." If we don't have the same weeds in our gardens, we have other weeds just as bad. We are not alike, and so we experience different temptations in different ways.

We are alike, however, in trying to explain, at least to ourselves if not to others, why we yield to a temptation. Like Adam and Eve in the garden, we blame everyone but ourselves for our sin. We think that what we did was not so bad, or that everyone is doing it, or that we were in a situation that made it almost inevitable that we do it. Some who are not Christians

---

[1] James J. Cummins, "Jesus, Lord of Life and Glory," 1839.

(and sometimes Christians) may not distinguish temptation from yielding to temptation. They see it as just doing what people do, what they want to do. Other non-Christians, perhaps most, may feel guilty because of things that they have done and regret the trouble that it has caused them and others. But they do not know what to do with that guilt. Temptation comes to us in many ways, Clarence Edward Macartney said in a sermon:

> In every circumstance of life, every lot, every association, every labor, every pleasure or hardship, there is a possible temptation. There are temptations for the body, for the mind, for the soul. There are the temptations to the appetite, to selfishness, dishonesty, to the evasion of duty, the disregard of others' rights, indifference to others' sorrows; pride, sloth, envy, suspicion, taking up an evil report against our neighbor, and the subtle, but even more dangerous, temptations to doubt, to unbelief.[2]

Some temptations may seem to us trivial or inconsequential, but all temptations are serious. The Puritan Thomas Manton wrote: "Lesser sticks set the great ones on fire."[3] Lutheran pastor and theologian Helmut Thielicke says that every temptation brings the possibility that we may be "torn away from God. . . . Through small and great events in our life, little fondnesses and great passions, we can be brought to the point where we lose contact with the Father."[4] In whatever shape it comes—the desire for illicit sex, the love of money, prideful ambition—temptation moves us to reject God's Word and deny his rule over our lives. Rather than seeking first the kingdom of God and his righteousness, we seek first our kingdom and our own way. Calvin described temptation as the desire to "seek out something of our own that reposes in ourselves rather than in God," the temptation that came to our first parents from Satan.[5] By the sin that comes when we yield to temptation, we remove God from the throne of our lives. Even a "small" sin, even a "quick" one, tears us away from God.

What Is Temptation?

The Greek noun *peirasmos* is used twenty-one times in the New Testament and translated in the English Standard Version as "temptation," "test," or "trial." "Tempt" in the King James Version means test in an unrestricted sense, in accord with older English usage. It is only since the

[2] Clarence Edward Macartney, *The Lord's Prayer* (New York: Revell, 1942), 69.
[3] Thomas Manton, *Temptation of Christ* (Fearn, Ross-shire, UK: Christian Focus, 1996), 164.
[4] Helmut Thielicke, *Our Heavenly Father: Sermons on the Lord's Prayer* (New York: Harper & Row, 1960), 119–20.
[5] John Calvin, *Institutes of the Christian Religion*, 2 vols, ed. John T. McNeill, trans. Ford Lewis Battles, Library of Christian Classics, 20–21 (Philadelphia: Westminster, 1960), 2.2.10.

seventeenth century that the word's connotation has been limited to test-ing with evil intent. We will combine test and trial as similar in English and think of the Greek word as having two distinct meanings—test-trial and temptation. The context often makes clear which of these words is to be used in English translation, but it is sometimes difficult to choose the correct one. The note of testing, however, rather than temptation in the sense of seducing, is uppermost in biblical teaching.

Furthermore, the two different meanings of the word *peirasmos* usu-ally seem to overlap. Temptation can be a test or a trial; in fact, it always is. Temptation is a test to which a person is subjected by God or by the Devil. Or we may say that temptation is a test that comes from both God and the Devil, because the Devil, who is the tempter, cannot act without God's permission. J. I. Packer explains: "Temptations are Satan's work; but Satan is God's tool as well as his foe, and it is ultimately God himself who leads his servants into temptation, permitting Satan to try to seduce them for beneficent purposes of his own."[6] In a sermon during the beginnings of the Nazi horror, Dietrich Bonhoeffer said the same thing: "Nothing can happen on earth without the will and permission of God. Satan also is in God's hands. He must—against his will—serve God."[7]

If temptation, then, is the work of the Devil and, in a sense, also the work of God, so are trials. Trials are testing situations in which the Chris-tian faces new possibilities of both good and evil. God does not tempt anyone, but he tests everyone, and Satan seeks to turn those tests into temptations. Satan tries to influence our response to his own advantage by manipulating circumstances, within the limits that God allows him. God's purpose in testing us is the strengthening of our spiritual life; but Satan's purpose is to change that test or trial into a temptation that will lead to spiritual defeat. Joseph said to his brothers, "You meant evil against me, but God meant it for good" (Gen. 50:20). In our trials and tests Satan means evil, but God means good. When viewed from the standpoint of Satan, our own fallen nature, and the appeal of the world, a difficult expe-rience may be a temptation, but when viewed in terms of God's intention for us, it is a test. By tempting us, the Devil tries to drive us away from God, but sometimes what he actually accomplishes is to drive us "directly into the very hands of God," as in the case of Job.[8]

---

[6] Cited in Derek Thomas, *Praying the Saviour's Way: Praying the Lord's Prayer* (Fearn, Ross-shire, UK: Chris-tian Focus, 2002), 114.
[7] Dietrich Bonhoeffer, *Creation and Fall and Temptation* (New York: Macmillan, n.d.), 112.
[8] Ibid., 113.

A test or trial becomes a temptation when a person is moved to disobey God or to doubt or blame God for his or her trouble, as Job's wife suggested that Job do: "Curse God and die" (Job 2:9). A trial is to be endured by God's grace, as Job did when he replied to his wife: "Shall we receive good from God, and shall we not receive evil [or disaster in the ESV alternate translation]?" (2:9–10). James wonderfully summed up the whole book of Job in a few words: "You have heard of the steadfastness of Job, and you have seen the purpose of the Lord, how the Lord is compassionate and merciful" (James 5:11). In our times of trial and temptation, God will be compassionate and merciful; we are to endure, to be steadfast, to refuse to be torn away from God.

In a letter of consolation, the Southern Presbyterian theologian James Henley Thornwell prayed for a friend who had lost a son, that God would "preserve her from all temptation to distrust His goodness, or murmur at His ways." He added: "Our times of trial are times of temptation; and precious is that faith which loses nothing but its dross in the heat of the furnace."[9]

What Does the Bible Say about Temptation?

There are many passages in the Bible that present what we might call "the theology of temptation," but more often the Bible tells "the story of temptation"—from the temptation of Adam and Eve in the first book of the Bible to the last book in the Bible, where we find the temptations that faced the seven churches of Asia and those that will face God's people in the end times.

In the Old Testament God tested the people of Israel to see (or actually to show, because God already knows) whether they would be true to him. "God left [Hezekiah] to himself, in order to test him and to know all that was in his heart" (2 Chron. 32:31). It was Israel and not the heathen nations whom God put on trial. Such tests of faith and obedience are part of the special relationship between God and his covenant people. "It is for discipline that you have to endure. God is treating you as sons" (Heb. 12:7).

God treated Abraham as a son when he commanded him to sacrifice Isaac. How easily that test could have become a temptation for Abraham to question God, to hate God, and to reject him. But Abraham resisted, and he obeyed God promptly and sincerely (Gen. 22:1–14). When the

---

[9] B. M. Palmer, *The Life and Letters of James Henley Thornwell* (Edinburgh: Banner of Truth, 1974), 217.

people of Israel transgressed the covenant, God allowed them to be troubled by the nations still in the land after the death of Joshua. He tested the people, "whether they will take care to walk in the way of the LORD as their fathers did, or not." The test became a temptation, and the temptation became sin, as the people murmured against God and doubted his covenant promise (Judges 2:20–23).

King David was tempted by the naked body of a beautiful woman, and his yielding led to adultery and complicity in the death of the woman's husband (2 Sam. 11:1–27). Tempted by lust, David was later tempted by pride. In 2 Samuel 24:1 we read that "the anger of the LORD was kindled against Israel, and he incited David against them, saying, 'Go, number Israel and Judah.'" By numbering the people for military purposes, David showed lack of trust in the Lord and pride in his great army (1 Sam. 24:3, 10). In 1 Chronicles 21:1 it is Satan who "incited David to number Israel." The Lord allowed Satan to tempt David to number Israel, thus carrying out God's will.

There are other temptation stories in the Old Testament, but the best known and the most important is the first one—the temptation of Adam and Eve (Gen. 3:1–7). The Westminster Confession of Faith sums up the biblical story and its meaning:

> Our first parents, being seduced by the subtlety and temptation of Satan, sinned in eating the forbidden fruit. . . . By this sin they fell from their original righteousness and communion with God, and so became dead in sin, and wholly defiled in all the parts and faculties of soul and body. They being the root of all mankind, the guilt of this sin was imputed; and the same death in sin, and corrupted nature, conveyed to all their posterity descending from them by ordinary generation.[10]

By their yielding to the temptation of Satan, Adam and Eve were torn away from God and brought themselves and all their descendants (except Jesus) into "an estate of sin and misery."[11]

Think of the many temptation stories in the New Testament. The disciples on the Sea of Galilee were tempted to doubt Jesus' protection and care for them (Matt. 14:22–33), as was John the Baptist in prison (11:1–6). The disciples questioned Jesus' provision for the great crowd that had gathered to hear him (14:13–16). Peter was tempted to reject

---

[10] Westminster Confession of Faith, 7:1–3.
[11] Westminster Shorter Catechism, Q. 17.

Jesus' words about his coming death (16:21–23). The rich young man was tempted by "the love of money" (19:16–22). Judas was tempted to betray Jesus (26:14–16), and Peter was tempted to deny him (vv. 69–75). The disciples were tempted to sleep in Gethsemane (vv. 36–46). Ananias and Sapphira were tempted to deceive the church (Acts 5:1–11). Peter was tempted to question God's plan for the Gentiles (10:1–16). John Mark was tempted to abandon his missionary work (13:13 and 15:36–38). There are other such stories, but by far the most important temptation story in the New Testament, and in the entire Bible, is the temptation of Jesus in the wilderness (Matt. 4:1–11).

There Christ, the second Adam, undid what the first Adam had done. There the true Israel, in contrast to the first Israel, remained faithful "in the wilderness." He refused to doubt God's care or to put God to the test or to fall into idolatry (vv. 7–10). Jesus quoted three biblical texts, all from Deuteronomy, in resisting the same temptations to which Israel had yielded.

In the language of John Milton, the temptation of Adam and Eve led to "Paradise lost"; the temptation of Jesus to "Paradise regained." The temptation of Adam and Eve brought about the fall of mankind; the temptation of Christ brought about Satan's fall. The promise of Genesis 3:15 was realized in the victory of "the Son of Man" over the "ruler of this world" (John 12:31–34).

All other temptations in the Bible and in human history have to do with these two stories. Either we fall like Adam, or we stand and Satan falls, as he did in the temptation of Christ. The fall of Satan is repeated again and again in temptations resisted and in the victories of God's people over the Devil. When the seventy-two disciples returned with good reports of their mission, Jesus said: "I saw Satan fall like lightning from heaven" (Luke 10:18). Paul wrote to the Christians at Rome: "The God of peace will soon crush Satan under your feet" (Rom. 16:20). Satan's final fall is described in Revelation 20:10, when he will be "thrown into the lake of fire" to suffer there "forever and ever."

How Could Jesus Be Tempted?

Was Jesus really tempted? Yes. He was tempted by Satan in three specific ways in the wilderness (Matt. 4:1–11). During his earthly life he was tempted "in every respect . . . as we are" (Heb. 4:15). He was tempted, and tempted repeatedly, but he did not sin. How could it be that Christ was really tempted when he could not sin? The Bible does not say that he could not sin but that he did not sin.

Christ did not defeat Satan in the wilderness by calling on his divine power as God (as God he could not sin) but by drawing on the Word of God and the power of the Holy Spirit (so that as man he did not sin). Jesus was tempted as a human being, and as a human being he felt the force and power of the temptations of Satan. But as a faithful and obedient child of God, he trusted in God and overcame the tempter. The Holy Spirit, who led Christ into the wilderness to be tempted by the Devil, stayed with him and provided help in his time of need. Toward the end of his earthly life, Jesus told the disciples that "the ruler of this world is coming. He has no claim on me, but I do as the Father has commanded me" (John 14:30–31). The reason that Satan had no claim on Christ was not that Christ was God but that, as a man, he did what the Father commanded.

The New Testament writers do not attempt to explain how Christ as God could be tempted. They simply state that he was tempted like us and that he did not sin. And they tell us how important it was for our salvation that he did not sin. Because he "knew no sin," he could take our place "so that in him we might become the righteousness of God" (2 Cor. 5:21). Our salvation hung in the balance in the wilderness when Jesus was tempted, as our fate as sinners was determined when Adam and Eve were tempted in the garden. Christ was tempted like us, and he was tempted for us. "For because he himself has suffered when tempted, he is able to help those who are being tempted" (Heb. 2:18). "For we do not have a high priest who is unable to sympathize with our weaknesses, but one who in every respect has been tempted as we are, yet without sin. Let us then with confidence draw near to the throne of grace, that we may receive mercy and find grace to help in time of need" (4:15–16). The exalted Christ carries with him the memory of his sufferings so that he can help those who are tempted. Because Jesus the Son of God was tempted like we are, we have a sympathetic high priest in heaven; because Jesus was tempted, yet without sin, we have a Savior who ransomed us with his precious blood "like that of a lamb without blemish or spot" (1 Pet. 1:19).

Does God Lead Us into Temptation?

"Let no one say when he is tempted, 'I am being tempted by God,' for God cannot be tempted with evil, and he himself tempts no one" (James 1:13). "While God may try us," wrote John Owen, "he never entices us."[12]

Why then was Jesus "led up by the Spirit into the wilderness to be

---

[12] John Owen, *Sin and Temptation* (Minneapolis: Bethany, 1996), 117.

tempted by the devil" (Matt. 4:1)? The Spirit led Jesus into the wilderness, as God leads us throughout our lives. But the Spirit did not tempt Jesus, as God does not tempt us. God is in control of all things, but he is not the author or the source of all things. He rules over all, even the temptation of Adam and Eve in the garden and the temptation of Jesus in the wilderness, but he did not tempt Adam and Eve. He did not tempt Jesus, and he does not tempt us.

Why then does the Lord's Prayer teach us to pray, "Lead us not into temptation, but deliver us from evil" (Matt. 6:13)? The petition seems to imply that God may lead us into temptation. If he leads us into temptation, like the Spirit led Jesus into the wilderness to be tempted by the Devil, it must be for a just and righteous cause, for his glory and our good. If God leads us into temptation, his purpose is not to tempt us to sin. What, then, does the petition mean that God "lead us not into temptation"? There have been a number of interpretations. Calvin, following Augustine, states that the two parts of the petition are not to be separated; they are bound together by the word "but" in the middle. So the prayer should read: "In order that we may not be led into temptation, deliver us from evil. . . . Being conscious of our own weakness, we ask to be defended by God's protection. . . . Our powers are not adequate to living well, except as far as God supplements them."[13] Very true, but why then do we ask God not to lead us into temptation?

N. T. Wright says that "Gethsemane suggests the deepest meanings of the prayer: 'Do not let us be led into the Testing, but deliver us from Evil.'"[14] The petition, therefore, is not for deliverance from temptation but from testing. But why pray that we not be led into testing when the Bible says that tests and trials are good and profitable for us? G. P. Hugenberger argues that the petition means "Lead us not into trial"—that is, the kind of punishments described in 2 Peter 2:4–8 (the fall of the angels, the flood, and the destruction of Sodom and Gomorrah). Peter assures us that "the Lord knows how to rescue the godly from [such] trials."[15] So we are to pray that we will not be called upon to face such trials, especially those punishments to come in the end times. This petition of the Lord's Prayer is preceded by two others that are immediate and ongoing—"Give us this day our daily bread" and "Forgive us our debts." "Lead us not into tempta-

---

[13] John Calvin, *A Harmony of the Gospels: Mattthew, Mark and Luke, Calvin's New Testament Commentaries*, vol. 1 (Grand Rapids, MI: Eerdmans, 1972), 212.

[14] N. T. Wright, *The Lord and His Prayer* (Grand Rapids, MI: Eerdmans, 1996), 67.

[15] G. P. Hugenberger, *The Lord's Prayer: A Guide for the Perplexed* (Boston: Park Street Church, 1999), 45.

tion" would seem to be a similar request for help here and now rather than deliverance from a future trial in the end times.

Clarence Edward Macartney believes that the prayer means, "Do not bring us to hard testing." It is a prayer to be kept "from the presence of dangerous temptations which may prove too strong for us."[16] We can pray that God not lead us into temptation or permit us to be tempted as God permitted Satan to tempt Job. God, however, does not promise that he will not lead us into hard testing or temptation. He promises that he will not let us be tempted beyond our ability but will, with the temptation, provide a way of escape that we may be able to endure it, as he did for Job (1 Cor. 10:13).

Leon Morris writes that "the worshiper knows his own weakness and in this prayer seeks to be kept far from anything that may bring him to sin."[17] Similarly, Helmut Thielicke reads the prayer as, "Let nothing become a temptation to me."[18] God has not promised, however, that we will not be tempted but that we will not be tempted beyond our ability to endure. D. A. Carson holds an unusual view that "Lead us not into temptation" is "a figure of speech that negates the contrary" (a "litotes," an understatement in which an affirmative is expressed by the negative of the contrary, as in "not a bad singer") and so is "just a forceful way of saying 'lead us into righteousness.'"[19]

John Stott combines some of the above suggestions when he writes: "The sinner whose evil in the past has been forgiven longs to be delivered from its tyranny in the future. The general sense of the prayer is plain. . . . Perhaps we could paraphrase the whole request as 'Do not allow us so to be led into temptation that it overwhelms us, but rescue us from the evil one.'"[20] Darrell Johnson suggests praying the prayer this way:

> Our Father, we cannot stand up under very much pressure. We are not wise enough to recognize and then counter the work of the evil one. When you lead us to the test, when life itself brings us to the test, do not let the test become a temptation, but rescue us. Rescue us from the subtle strategies of the evil one, and help us to trust you.[21]

---

[16] Macartney, *The Lord's Prayer*, 70.

[17] Leon Morris, *The Gospel according to Matthew* (Grand Rapids, MI: Eerdmans, 1992), 148.

[18] Helmut Thielicke, *Our Heavenly Father*, 121.

[19] D. A. Carson, *The Sermon on the Mount: An Evangelical Exposition of Matthew 5–7* (Grand Rapids, MI: Baker, 1987), 70–71.

[20] John R. W. Stott, *The Message of the Sermon on the Mount (Matthew 5–7)* (Leicester, UK: Inter-Varsity, 1978), 150.

[21] Darrell W. Johnson, *Fifty-Seven Words That Change the World: A Journey through the Lord's Prayer* (Vancouver: Regent College Press, 2005), 98.

The petition "lead us not into temptation" is a prayer that we would be kept in the hour of severe trial; it is an acknowledgment of our spiritual frailty and our need for God's constant help. It is an important prayer for all of us, and especially for "anyone who thinks that he stands . . . lest he fall" (1 Cor. 10:12). The prayer underscores the reality of evil, our weakness to resist, and the possibility of victory by God's help. It asks God to keep us from yielding to temptation and to deliver us from the power of Satan, the Evil One.

Martin Luther is reported to have said that he went to bed with the fifth petition of the Lord's Prayer—"Forgive us our debts, as we have forgiven our debtors"—and woke up with the sixth—"Lead us not into temptation, but deliver us from the evil one."[22] Looking back over the day, we pray for God's forgiveness; looking ahead to a new day, we pray for God's help.

What Are the Sources or Causes of Temptation?

On December 14, 1944, C. S. Lewis gave the annual commemoration address at King's College, University of London. Lewis told his young audience:

> Everyone knows what a middle-aged moralist . . . warns his juniors against. He warns them against the World, the Flesh, and the Devil. But one of this trio will be enough to deal with today. The Devil I shall leave strictly alone. The association between him and me in the public mind has gone quite as deep as I wish. . . . As for the Flesh, you must be very abnormal young people if you do not know quite as much about it as I do. But on the World I think I have something to say.[23]

The desire to do wrong that temptation arouses may come from our environment ("the world") or our sinful human nature ("the flesh") or from Satan ("the Devil")—or, most likely, from a combination of all three. In our temptations, writes John Owen, "we must deal not only with a cunning devil, but also with a cursed world and a corrupt heart."[24]

How Does the World Tempt Us?

"Do not love the world or the things in the world. If anyone loves the world, the love of the Father is not in him. For all that is in the world—the

---

[22] Johnson, *Fifty-Seven Words*, 91.
[23] C. S. Lewis, *The Weight of Glory: And Other Addresses* (San Francisco: HarperCollins, 2001), 143.
[24] Owen, *Sin and Temptation*, 110.

desires of the flesh and the desires of the eyes and pride of life—is not from the Father but is from the world" (1 John 2:15–17). Poet, playwright, and first president of the Czech Republic, Vaclav Havel, wrote that "the alien world into which we are thrown beckons to us and tempts us. . . . We are constantly being exposed to the temptation to . . . adapt ourselves to the world as it presents itself to us, to sink into it . . . and thus to simplify our existence-in-the-world."[25]

The aspect of the "world" that C. S. Lewis addressed in his sermon is the deep desire people have to belong to a select circle. We are tempted to surrender or compromise the welfare of other people, justice, compassion, our own sexual purity, and many other things just to be part of an "inner ring." "Of all passions," Lewis said, "the passion for the Inner Ring is most skillful in making a man who is not yet a very bad man do very bad things."[26] The world entices us to fit in with, to adjust to, to experiment with, its values—that is, "the desires of the flesh and the desires of the eyes and pride of life" (1 John 2:16). Magazines, television, the movies, books, the Internet, people we know, and those we don't know tempt us to become "worldly" in countless ways. The daily temptations of the world we face can tear us away from God because "if anyone loves the world, the love of the Father is not in him" (v. 15).

The world that tempts us is not the world that God made and that we can love even in its broken state but is the world that we made by the rebellion of our first parents and by our own daily reenactments of that scene of rebellion in the garden of Eden.

How Does the Flesh Tempt Us?

In his address at King's College, C. S. Lewis told the students that he would not speak about the temptations of the flesh. He said: "As for the Flesh, you must be very abnormal young people if you do not know quite as much about it as I do." Lewis was obviously referring to the matter of sex. Lewis's friend Dorothy Sayers wrote an essay with the title "The Six Other Deadly Sins" in which she told about a young man who said to her "with perfect simplicity: 'I did not know there were seven deadly sins: please tell me the names of the other six.'"[27] The other six are pride, covetousness, envy, gluttony, anger, and sloth. To these seven deadly sins in their almost infinite combinations we are tempted by our fallen flesh.

---

[25] Vaclav Havel, *Letters to Olga* (New York: Knopf, 1988), 320.
[26] Lewis, *The Weight of Glory*, 154.
[27] Dorothy L. Sayers, *Christian Letters to a Post-Christian World* (Grand Rapids, MI: Eerdmans, 1969), 138.

"Each person is tempted when he is lured and enticed by his own de-sire" (James 1:14). It is amazing what dazzling glory one's imagination can supply for breaking a commandment such as "You shall not steal" or "You shall not commit adultery." First Timothy 6:9 speaks of "many senseless and harmful desires that plunge people into ruin and destruction." Our desires transform what is really "senseless and harmful" into something that seems to us smart and fulfilling. John Owen wrote: "In theory we abhor lustful thoughts, but once temptation enters our heart, all contrary reasonings are overcome and silenced."[28] So we reach out again to take the forbidden fruit, not really believing, like Adam and Eve, at least for a time, that what we are doing is "senseless and harmful."

There are internal causes of sin and external causes. The external causes are as diverse as the world in which we live. The internal causes are as complicated as we are. "The heart is deceitful above all things, and des-perately sick; who can understand it?" (Jer. 17:9). Augustine wrote in his Confessions: "Man is a vast deep, whose hairs you, Lord, have numbered . . . yet it is easier to count his hairs than the passions and emotions of his heart."[29] In one of her books, George Eliot refers to "the deep human soul within us, full of unspoken evil and unacted good."[30]

The Devil found no opening in Christ's life through which he could enter. Satan "entered into Judas" (Luke 22:3–4), but he could not enter into Jesus. When Satan comes to us, he finds doors and windows through which he can enter. As Helmut Thielicke put it, "We ourselves are far too ramshackle not to provide the tempter with opportunities to slip through the back door of our heart."[31]

According to John Calvin, there still remains in the regenerate "a smoldering cinder of evil" or "a fountain of evil, continually producing desires which allure and stimulate" us to sin. By this Calvin did not mean "those inclinations which God so engraved upon the character of man at his first creation," but "only those bold and unbridled impulses which contend against God's control" in fallen but redeemed people.[32]

How Does the Devil Tempt Us?

In his talk to the King's College students, C. S. Lewis said that he would leave the Devil strictly alone because "the association between him and

---

[28] John Owen, The Works of John Owen (Edinburgh: Banner of Truth, 1967), 6:105.
[29] Augustine, Confessions, trans. Henry Chadwick (Oxford, UK: Oxford University Press), 4.14.
[30] George Eliot, Scenes of Clerical Life (Oxford, UK: Oxford University Press, 1988), 252.
[31] Thielicke, Between God and Satan (Edinburgh: Oliver and Boyd, 1958), 127.
[32] Calvin, Institutes, 3.3.10–12.

me in the public mind has gone quite as deep as I wish." Lewis was referring to his *Screwtape Letters,* in which he had given a humorous but true-
to-life description of the strategies of Satan.[33]

The world is all around us, our fallen human nature resides within
us, and the Devil and his agents are above and around and sometimes in
us. "For we do not wrestle against flesh and blood, but against the rulers,
against the authorities, against the cosmic powers over this present darkness, against the spiritual forces of evil in the heavenly places" (Eph. 6:12).
Thielicke wrote: "Behind all the dangers in our life and behind all the dark
menaces that overshadow it, there is a dark, mysterious, spellbinding figure at work. Behind the temptations stands the tempter, behind the lie
stands the liar, behind all the dead and the bloodshed stands the 'murderer from the beginning.'"[34]

Satan is a spiritual force of evil.[35] Thomas Manton said: "He was cast
out of heaven himself, and he is all for casting down."[36] And he is diaboli-
cally clever. He "disguises himself as an angel of light" (2 Cor. 11:14). The
"devout" Devil asks seemingly innocent but leading questions (as he did
in the garden with Eve) and freely quotes Scripture (as he did in the wilderness with Jesus). Bonhoeffer said, "The voice of the tempter does not
come out of an abyss" marked "Hell." "It completely conceals its origin. It
is suddenly near to me and speaks to me."[37] One of the old Puritans said,
"The devil is a master fisherman: he baits the hook according to the appetite of the fish."[38] Paul warned the Corinthians not to "be outwitted by
Satan" and not to be "ignorant of his designs" (2 Cor. 2:11). Calvin wrote:
"If it is the devil's word that exalts man in himself, let us give no place to it
unless we want to take advice from our enemy."[39]

Satan won a great victory over Adam and Eve in the garden. He then
won unnumbered little victories over the descendants of Adam and Eve,
but not always. The Devil suffered many defeats along the way when God's
people obeyed God rather than him. See the long list in Hebrews 11 of
those Old Testament saints who by faith overcame Satan. In the wilderness, the Devil came and tried to find a way into Jesus' mind and heart. He
stood at the door and knocked. He knocked three times, and he knocked

---

[33] C. S. Lewis, *The Screwtape Letters* (New York: Macmillan, 1976). In *Perelandra* Lewis uses his imagination and
biblical knowledge to describe the temptation of Eve by the Devil as it may have happened in the planet of Venus.
[34] Thielicke, *Between God and Satan,* 132.
[35] See the chapter by Sydney Page, 168–85.
[36] Manton, *Temptation of Christ,* 64.
[37] Bonhoeffer, *Creation and Fall and Temptation,* 102.
[38] "Reflections," August 2011, C. S. Lewis Institute.
[39] Calvin, *Institutes,* 2.2.10.

as loud as he could, but Jesus forced him to stand outside. And then Jesus said, "Be gone, Satan" (Matt. 4:10).

The Devil left him, but he did not stay away. The Devil's primary purpose was to offer Jesus a way to avoid his redemptive work on the cross. When Jesus did not yield to his direct temptations in the wilderness, Satan changed his strategy. He sometimes was able to work through Jesus' closest friends. When Jesus began "to show his disciples that he must go to Jerusalem and suffer many things . . . and be killed," Peter took him aside and began to rebuke him, saying, "Far be it from you, Lord! This shall never happen to you." Knowing where that advice was coming from, Jesus said to Peter, "Get behind me, Satan! You are a hindrance to me. For you are not setting your mind on the things of God, but on the things of man" (Matt. 16:21–23). Satan knew all too well that Christ's dying on the cross would not be Satan's victory but his ruin. He would indeed succeed in bruising the heel of Christ, but on that cross Christ would win the promised victory by bruising the head of the Serpent (Gen. 3:15).

Satan was defeated by the cross of Christ, but he was not finished. He failed to prevent God's salvation of sinful human beings, but he continues to work tirelessly to do all that he possibly can to create sin in our lives, conflict in the church, and chaos in the world. "There is nothing the tempter does not know how to use in order to tear nations and individuals from God's hand," said Thielicke.[40] Satan works, and he works feverishly because "he knows his time is short" (Rev. 12:12).

When Does Temptation Become Sin?

John Owen wrote: "Let no one fear sin without also fearing temptation. . . . Satan has put them so close together that it is very hard to separate them."[41] Sin is not only an outward act but also an inward disposition, as shown by the tenth commandment ("You shall not covet," Ex. 20:17) and by the Sermon on the Mount ("Everyone who looks at a woman with lustful intent has already committed adultery with her in his heart," Matt. 5:28). Jesus did not mean that lustful thoughts are the same as lustful acts but that the seventh commandment can be broken in thought as well as in deed. There is value, of course, in stopping with the lustful thought and not doing the sinful act. But embracing the thought breaks the commandment.

The church fathers attempted to distinguish the presence of corrupt-

---

[40] Thielicke, *Between God and Satan*, 124.
[41] Owen, *Sin and Temptation*, 122.

ing thoughts from the harboring of them. Thomas Aquinas, following Augustine and others, defined an evil thought as a "sin of lingering delight." The sin is not merely because of the length of time ("lingering") involved but also because of an acceptance ("delight") that is "not prompt in inhibiting, [but] deliberately holding and turning over what should have been cast aside as soon as it touched the mind, as St Augustine said."[42]

In *Paradise Lost* Milton follows his narration of Eve's dream of eating the forbidden fruit with Adam's reassuring comment—"Evil into the mind of god or man / May come and go, so unapproved, and leave / No spot or blame behind."[43] In *The Pilgrim's Progress* Christian and Faithful arrived in the town of Vanity, where the Vanity Fair was held all year long. Beelzebub was "the chief lord of the fair" through which pilgrims had to pass on their way to the Celestial City. Even "the Prince of princes" had to come this way, writes Bunyan. Beelzebub invited the Prince to buy of his vanities and promised to make him lord of the fair if he would buy. "But he had no mind to the merchandise, and therefore left the town without laying out so much as one farthing."[44] In Bunyan's story, Christ indeed faced temptation but did not succumb to it, not even in his mind. In Milton's poem, the temptation in Eve's dream left no "spot or blame behind," but, alas, that was not true when she actually met the Serpent in Genesis 3.

Luther said, "We are bound to suffer temptations, in fact, to be deeply involved in them. . . . There is . . . a great difference between feeling temptation and yielding to it, saying yes to it." Luther used this famous illustration to explain the difference between temptation and sin: "In the book on the old fathers of the church we read that a young brother wanted to be rid of his evil thoughts. The old father said: 'Dear brother, you cannot prevent the birds from flying in the air over your head, but you can certainly prevent them from building a nest in your hair.'"[45]

Jesus told the disciples, "Watch and pray that you may not enter into temptation" (Mark 14:38). This does not mean simply to be tempted; we may encounter temptation without entering into it. "As long as temptation merely knocks outside the door," John Owen wrote, "we remain free. But when it enters and parleys with the heart, reasons with the mind, and entices and allures the affections . . . then we enter into temptation."[46]

[42] Thomas Aquinas, *Summa Theologiae*, 1a–2ae. 74.6.
[43] John Milton, *Paradise Lost*, bk. 5, 117–19.
[44] John Bunyan, *Works of John Bunyan* (Edinburgh: Banner of Truth, 1991), 3:128.
[45] Martin Luther, *What Luther Says: An Anthology*, 3 vols, comp. Ewald M. Plass (St. Louis: Concordia, 1959), 3:1344.
[46] Owen, *Sin and Temptation*, 104.

Read and ponder Bunyan's tract *A Caution to Stir Up to Watch against Sin* (written "to be tacked to the wall of one's house"):

> Sin rather than 'twill out of action be,
> Will pray to stay, though but a while with thee;
> "One night, one hour, one moment" will it cry,
> "Embrace me in thy bosom, else I die:
> Time to repent, [saith it], I will allow,
> And help, if to repent thou know'st not how."
> But if you give it entrance at the door
> It will come in, and may go out no more.[47]

How Can We Overcome Temptation?

We endure trials by saying yes, as Job did—"The LORD gave, and the LORD has taken away; blessed be the name of the LORD" (Job 1:21). We overcome temptations by saying no, as Jesus did—"Be gone, Satan" (Matt. 4:10). The Devil tempts us, using the world and our own sinful flesh as his allies, and he is also clever enough to try to block our ways of escape. In a sermon, "God's Promise for Our Temptations," Gardner Calvin Taylor, for forty-two years pastor of the Concord Baptist Church of Christ in Brooklyn, said:

> With the temptation, there comes a way out. God hides the way out inside the temptation. God puts daybreak in the midnight. God puts peace in the confusion. God puts healing in the hurt. It is as if He says to whatever or whoever it is that stands against His child, "You strike and I will protect. You hurt and I will heal. You slander and I will glorify. You embarrass and I will honor. You pull down and I will lift up. You curse and I will bless. You block the path; I will open a highway. You close the door and I will open it. You muddy My child and I will clean him until he stands in the spotlessness of My own righteousness."[48]

Victory over temptation is not gained in the moment of temptation. It is won in the daily living of our redeemed lives. It is won as we "make every effort to supplement [our] faith with virtue, and virtue with knowledge, and knowledge with self-control, and self-control with steadfastness, and steadfastness with godliness, and godliness with brotherly affection, and brotherly affection with love" (2 Pet. 1:5–7). C. S. Lewis has Screwtape say to Wormwood: "It is funny how mortals always picture us [demons] as

---

[47] Bunyan, *Works*, 2:575.
[48] Gardner C. Taylor, *Chariots Aflame* (Nashville: Broadman, 1988), 168.

putting things into their minds: in reality our best work is done by keeping things out," such as Scripture, prayer, and contentment.[49] When we find ourselves neglecting Scripture and prayer and losing contentment in our Christian lives, we are opening ourselves up to great danger. The Devil will not miss an opportunity like this.

How can we then overcome temptation?

Trust God

"God is faithful, and he will not let you be tempted beyond your ability, but with the temptation he will also provide the way of escape, that you may be able to endure it" (1 Cor. 10:13).

"Though we rightly despair of our weakness," writes Philip Hughes, "we can never despair of his strength."[50] "The Lord knoweth how to deliver the godly out of temptations" (2 Pet. 2:9 KJV). John Owen wrote: "To believe that He will preserve us is, indeed, a means of preservation."[51]

In the *Confessions*, Augustine tells about his student and friend Alypius who, in "the whirlpool of Carthaginian morals," was sucked into "the folly of the circus games." Through Augustine's influence, Alypius was delivered from his enthusiasm for the violent games, holding them "in adversion and detestation." But one day some of his companions used "friendly violence" to take him to the amphitheater, despite his "energetic refusal and resistance." Alypius was confident of his power to resist temptation and said: "If you drag my body to that place and sit me down there, do not imagine that you can turn my mind and eyes to those spectacles. I shall be as one not there, and so I shall overcome both you and the games." At the place of the games he "kept his eyes shut and forbade his mind to think about such fearful evils" that were taking place. But hearing a great roar from the crowd, he was overcome by curiosity. "Supposing himself strong enough to despise whatever he saw and to conquer it, he opened his eyes. He was struck in the soul by a wound graver than the gladiator in his body, whose fall had caused the roar. . . . As soon as he saw the blood, he at once drank in savagery and did not turn away." He returned to the games, even taking others with him. Later God again delivered him and "taught him to put his confidence not in himself" but in God. "This experience," Augustine wrote, "rested in his memory to provide a remedy in the future."[52]

---

[49] Lewis, *The Screwtape Letters*, 25.
[50] Philip E. Hughes, *No Cross, No Crown: The Temptation of Jesus* (Wilton, CT: Morehouse-Barlow, 1988), 31.
[51] Owen, *Sin and Temptation*, 123.
[52] Augustine, *Confessions*, 6.7–9.

The memory of God's deliverance in the past does help us, but we cannot depend on that alone. We sometimes sing, "Yield not to temptation, for yielding is sin; each victory will help you some other to win."[53] Victory over temptation does not come solely from our record of past victories but from our moment-by-moment trust in God and his grace to deliver us. "Be strong in the Lord and in the strength of his might" (Eph. 6:10).

Obey God's Word

"I have stored up your word in my heart, that I might not sin against you" (Ps. 119:11).

Timothy Keller points out how Jane Eyre resists the temptation to become Mr. Rochester's mistress: "She does not look into her heart for strength—there's nothing there but clamorous conflict. She ignores what her heart says and looks to what God says. The moral laws of God at that very moment made no sense to her heart and mind at all. They did not appear reasonable, and they did not appear fair . . . [but] God's law is for times of temptation, when body and soul rise in mutiny against their rigour." It is on God's Word, then, not on her feelings and passions, that she plants her foot.[54]

Jesus resisted Satan's temptations by quoting the Word of God (which he had stored up in his heart). Adam and Eve fell to the Devil's strategy by misusing the words that God had spoken to them. In Lewis's Chronicles of Narnia, the White Witch, like the Devil, "is always attractive, almost irresistible; to resist her takes every ounce of moral fortitude, every device of memory that you can summon to help you recall what was true no matter what deception she now blinds you with."[55] Of one thing we can be sure in the moment of temptation is that God's Word is true, no matter what the world, the flesh, and the Devil say or imply to the contrary.

Take your stand upon the Word of God and refuse to be moved. Stand on the Ten Commandments. Stand on the Sermon on the Mount. Take your stand with Jesus in the wilderness when he answered Satan, "Man shall not live by bread alone, but by every word that comes from the mouth of God" (Matt. 4:4). Thomas Manton wrote: "Our Saviour fights for himself. Yet he also fights for us, and to teach us how we also must fight in this same warfare."[56]

---

[53] Horatio Palmer, "Yield Not to Temptation," 1868.
[54] Timothy Keller with Kathy Keller, *The Meaning of Marriage: Facing the Complexities of Commitment with the Wisdom of God* (New York: Dutton, 2011), 223.
[55] Thomas Howard, *Narnia and Beyond: A Guide to the Fiction of C. S. Lewis* (San Francisco: Ignatius, 2006), 55.
[56] Manton, *Temptation of Christ*, 13.

Watch and Pray

"Watch and pray that you may not enter into temptation. The spirit indeed is willing, but the flesh is weak" (Matt. 26:41). "Be sober-minded; be watchful. Your adversary the devil prowls around like a roaring lion, seeking someone to devour" (1 Pet. 5:8).

Temptation comes first, then sin. The roaring lion is heard before he devours his prey. Temptation is a warning, a red light, a sign of danger. The normal function of pain is to alert us to disease and injury. The spiritual function of temptation is to put us on guard against the danger of sin. Bonhoeffer wrote:

> The heart of man is revealed in temptation. Man knows his sin, which without temptation he could never have known; for in temptation man knows on what he has set his heart. The coming to light of sin is the work of the accuser, who thereby thinks to have won the victory. But it is sin which is become manifest, which can be known and therefore forgiven. Thus the manifestation of sin belongs to the salvation plan of God with man, and Satan must serve this plan.[57]

Watch for besetting temptations that lead to besetting sins. These temptations reveal to us that on which we are setting our hearts. And they also should teach us what radical discipline is called for in our lives.

> Woe to the world for temptations to sin! For it is necessary that temptations come, but woe to the one by whom the temptation comes! And if your hand or foot causes you to sin, cut it off and throw it away. It is better for you to enter life crippled or lame than with two hands or two feet to be thrown into the eternal fire. And if your eye causes you to sin, tear it out and throw it away. It is better for you to enter life with one eye than with two eyes to be thrown into the hell of fire. (Matt. 18:7–9)

Jesus uses hyperbole (intentional overstatement) to emphasize the necessity for rigorous self-discipline and radical removal of causes of besetting temptation before it leads to sin and finally to judgment.

Watch and pray. "While watching, also pray to the Lord unceasing. He will free thee, be thy stay, strength and faith increasing. O Lord, bless in distress and let nothing swerve me from thy will to serve thee."[58] Luther reminds us that "as [Satan] does not weary of assaulting us, we may not

---

[57] Bonhoeffer, *Creation and Fall and Temptation*, 112–13.
[58] Johann B. Freystein, "Rise, My Soul, to Watch and Pray," 1694.

weary of persevering in prayer and in hope until we gain the victory."[59] Bonhoeffer says that "we should never argue with the devil about our sins, but we should speak about our sins only with Jesus."[60] Charles Haddon Spurgeon prayed: "O my Saviour, let me not think myself able to bear the indulgence of any known sin because it seems so insignificant. Keep me from sinful beginnings, lest they lead me on to sorrowful endings."[61]

Flee and Fight

The Bible instructs us to flee from temptation. "Flee from sexual immorality" (1 Cor. 6:18). "Flee from idolatry" (10:14). "Flee youthful passions" (2 Tim. 2:22). But the Bible also teaches us to stand and fight. In fact, in one passage we are told both to flee and to fight (1 Tim. 6:11–12). How can this be?

Bonhoeffer wrote: "There is no resistance to Satan other than flight. Every struggle against lust in one's own strength is doomed to failure. Flee—that can indeed only mean, Flee to the place where you find protection and help, flee to the Crucified."[62] We flee to Christ; then we are ready to "fight the good fight of faith" (1 Tim. 6:12). We come to the Lord; and then we can "put on the whole armor of God, that [we] may be able to stand against the schemes of the devil" (Eph. 6:11). We submit to God— we flee to God—and then we can resist the Devil and he will flee from us (James 4:7). "From heaven the Lord gives to the defenceless the heavenly armour before which, though men's eyes do not see it, Satan flees."[63]

Use Your Time Wisely

"Look carefully then how you walk, not as unwise but as wise, making the best use of the time, because the days are evil" (Eph. 5:15–16). And the Evil One "prowls around like a roaring lion, seeking someone to devour" (1 Pet. 5:8). It is important for Christians to use their time wisely, to be about the Lord's business, lest they give Satan opportunity to lure them into sin. In *Nearing Home*, Billy Graham gives advice for the elderly that applies equally to the young: "The devil delights in someone who is idle or bored; he knows this leads to temptation or discouragement. But the person who is occupied with worthwhile activities is far less vulner-

---

[59] *What Luther Says*, 3:1347.
[60] Bonhoeffer, *Creation and Fall and Temptation*, 125.
[61] Mark Water, ed., *The Encyclopedia of Prayer and Praise* (Peabody, MA: Hendrickson, 2004), 140.
[62] Bonhoeffer, *Creation and Fall and Temptation*, 118.
[63] Ibid., 127.

able. Remember the Bible's admonition: 'Do not give the devil a foothold' (Eph. 4:27)."[64]

In Jesus' parable of the talents, a nobleman called ten of his servants, gave them each ten talents, and said, "Engage in business until I come" (Luke 19:13). The wise did what he said; the foolish wasted their time with other things and suffered the consequences. In Paul's letter to Timothy, he urges that younger widows not become "idlers" but copy the "good works" of the older women and so give Satan "no occasion for slander" (1 Tim. 5:9–14).

It was "the spring of the year, the time when kings go out to battle. . . . But David remained in Jerusalem." Something was wrong: the kings went out to battle, but this king did not. Then "late one afternoon, when David rose from his couch and was walking on the roof" of his house, he saw a woman bathing and soon found himself involved in adultery and worse (2 Sam. 11:1–5).

John Bunyan said that he wrote *The Pilgrim's Progress* in prison to divert himself "from worser thoughts, which make me do amiss."[65] Dorcas was "full of good works and acts of charity" (Acts 9:36). She was busy doing good things. Satan despairs of a woman like that, because he cannot find a foothold (Eph. 4:27).

What Happens When We Confess Our Sins?

"But with you there is forgiveness, that you may be feared"—that is, worshiped and served (Ps. 130:4). "If we confess our sins, he is faithful and just to forgive us our sins, and to cleanse us from all unrighteousness" (1 John 1:9). He is faithful because he has promised; he is just because Christ died in our place. All of us are tempted, and all of us sin. Irish writer Sean O'Faolain said that "and" was the most hopeful word in the English language.[66] And it is the most hopeful word to a sinner. Our sin is not the end of the story. Adam and Eve were tempted; they sinned; "and they heard the sound of the Lord God walking in the garden in the cool of the day" (Gen. 3:8). David was tempted; he sinned; "and the Lord sent Nathan to David" (2 Sam. 12:1). Peter was tempted; he sinned; "and Peter remembered the saying of Jesus" (Matt. 26:75).

Christ asked the Christians in Laodicea to "be zealous and repent." They had torn themselves away from God by their sin, but he came to them. He said: "Behold I stand at the door and knock. If anyone hears my

---

[64] Billy Graham, *Nearing Home: Life, Faith, and Finishing Well* (Nashville: Thomas Nelson, 2011), 47–48.
[65] John Bunyan, *The Pilgrim's Progress* (Edinburgh: Banner of Truth, 1977), vi.
[66] "The New York Times Book Review," January 8, 2012.

voice and opens the door I will come in to him and eat with him, and he with me" (Rev. 3:20). Not only does God invite us to come back to him when we have sinned; he comes to us.

What Are the Results of Temptation?

Temptation leads to sin, and, for the unrepentant, sin leads to spiritual death. "Each person is tempted when he is lured and enticed by his own desire. Then desire when it has conceived gives birth to sin, and sin when it is fully grown brings forth death" (James 1:14–15). James describes the deadly progression from evil desire, to being dragged away, to enticement, to conception, to birth, and finally to death. This sixfold progression proceeds from the mind, to the affections, to the will, to outward action, and to spiritual death.

But in the wisdom, the love, and the power of God, testing-trial-temptation has a positive result in the life of a Christian. Thomas Howard writes in *Narnia and Beyond*:

> It is often by ordeal that each of the characters is tested in Narnia. The test is twofold . . . first, to find out what a person is made of; and then to teach that person how to be something that he is not (brave or obedient or merciful or generous). . . . But then we discover that there is a third, even more important point to the test: it always seems to be for the sake of another. There is no question of mere pointless testing, temptation, or suffering.[67]

"To be tempted is to be tested," writes Philip Hughes. "Each temptation comes to us as a challenge to stand firm and be faithful, as a step to be climbed rather than an occasion for falling, as an opportunity for blessing rather than for surrender to the shame and guilt of defeat. . . . Temptation is an invitation to step downward and backward; but it is also an opportunity to step upward and forward."[68] Temptations present to us a challenge in which we may wither and die or grow and mature.

The psalmist wrote, "It is good for me that I was afflicted, that I might learn your statutes" (Ps. 119:71). Temptation and testing are the schoolrooms of God where he teaches us. Luther said, "I did not learn my theology all at once, but I had to search deeper for it where my temptations took me."[69] "If I live longer," Luther said, "I certainly want to write a book

---

[67] Howard, *Narnia and Beyond*, 63.
[68] Philip E. Hughes, *No Cross, No Crown: The Temptation of Jesus* (Wilton, CT: Morehouse-Barlow, 1988), *viii*, 26.
[69] Franklin H. Littell, ed., *Reformation Studies: Essays in Honor of Roland H. Bainton* (Richmond, VA: John Knox, 1962), 46.

on temptations, for without these a man cannot appreciate Holy Scripture, faith, or the fear and love of God; nay, he who has never been in temptations cannot know what it means to have hope."[70]

Testing makes us more like Christ. "Although he was a son, he learned obedience through what he suffered" (Heb. 5:8). John Owen wrote: "Someone has said, 'Christ was made like unto us, that He might be tempted; and we are tempted that we may be made like unto Christ.'"[71] Through testing and temptation Paul learned humility: "So to keep me from becoming conceited because of the surpassing greatness of the revelations, a thorn was given me in the flesh, a messenger of Satan to harass me, to keep me from being conceited" (2 Cor. 12:7).

Testing brings spiritual strength. James wrote: "Count it all joy, my brothers, when you meet trials of various kinds, for you know that the testing of your faith produces steadfastness. And let steadfastness have its full effect, that you may be perfect and complete, lacking in nothing" (James 1:2–4). Testing renews in our hearts and minds the blessings of the covenant. "I . . . will refine them as one refines silver, and test them as gold is tested. They will call upon my name, and I will answer them. I will say, 'They are my people'; and they will say, 'The LORD is my God'" (Zech. 13:9). Temptation and testing enable us to help others. "Simon, Simon, behold, Satan demanded to have you, that he might sift you like wheat, but I have prayed for you that your faith may not fail. And when you have turned again, strengthen your brothers" (Luke 22:31–32).

Trials endured bring praise and glory to God. "In this you rejoice, though now for a little while, if necessary, you have been grieved by various trials, so that the tested genuineness of your faith . . . may be found to result in praise and glory and honor at the revelation of Jesus Christ" (1 Pet. 1:6–7). And steadfastness in trials will be rewarded. "Blessed is the man who remains steadfast under trial, for when he has stood the test, he will receive the crown of life, which God has promised to those who love him" (James 1:12).

> Now to him who is able to keep you from stumbling and to present you blameless before the presence of his glory with great joy, to the only God, our Savior, through Jesus Christ our Lord, be glory, majesty, dominion, and authority, before all time and now and forever. Amen. (Jude 24)

---

[70] *What Luther Says*, 3:1351.
[71] Owen, *Sin and Temptation*, 103.

11

REPENTANCE THAT SINGS

BRYAN CHAPELL

Imagine a junior league coach instructing his young pitchers as they watch game films of some historic major leaguers: "Now, men, watch Luis Tiant closely. He's a very fine pitcher. When he starts his windup, he pivots on one foot, and then, to gather momentum, he actually turns his back on the batter before spinning around to deliver the pitch. See how he turns his back to the batter? Don't do that!"

"Now," says the coach during the next film clip, "I want you to see the windup of Fernando Valenzuela. He faces the batter as an all-star pitcher should. Watch him. Watch how, when he is right at the apex of his windup, he looks up in the air and rolls his eyes back in his head before delivering the ball. See how he takes his eyes off the plate? Don't do that!"

Finally, as the last clip rolls, the coach says, "The pitcher I really want you to watch is Dwight Gooden. This is a straight-ahead, eyes-on-the mitt, great pitcher. The mechanics are great. The form is great. His windup is picture perfect. See how he tries to be perfect with each pitch? Don't do that either. It will eat a hole in your soul, as Dwight Gooden learned through much heartache in his life."

This imaginary pitching coach speaks with real wisdom not only about the mechanics of pitching but also about the nature of the human spirit. His words echo what Jesus also teaches about how the pursuit of self-perfection can assault the soul. We are not accustomed to thinking this way. We understand how sin can become a harsh taskmaster and place us under bondage by its allurements and compulsions. However, we do not usually consider that vigorously striving after holiness apart from the provisions of our union with Christ can be just as enslaving.

If we fail to understand how we rely on God's grace alone to make us right with him, our Christian walk necessarily becomes a showy parade of pride in spiritual gifts and achievements, permeated with envy of others' accomplishments. Such pride and envy will also create an insatiable appetite for spiritual experiences that will prove we have met, or can gain, God's approval. Jesus wants to liberate us from the unappeasable demands of personal merit. Thus, he must turn us away from the mistaken belief that the perfection of our performance will gain his favor. To do so he introduces us to a rich young man who wants to use his "major league" religious performance to gain God's favor:

Mark 10:17–22

As Jesus started on his way, a man ran up to him and fell on his knees before him. "Good teacher," he asked, "what must I do to inherit eternal life?"

"Why do you call me good?" Jesus answered. "No one is good—except God alone. You know the commandments: 'Do not murder, do not commit adultery, do not steal, do not give false testimony, do not defraud, honor your father and mother.'"

"Teacher," he declared, "all these I have kept since I was a boy."

Jesus looked at him and loved him. "One thing you lack," he said. "Go, sell everything you have and give to the poor, and you will have treasure in heaven. Then come, follow me."

At this the man's face fell. He went away sad, because he had great wealth.[1]

This account of the rich young man may seem a strange place to learn the nature of repentance. We typically think of this young man as one who refuses to repent. Yet by this inverse image we are able to distinguish what true repentance must be and, perhaps, may see enough of ourselves mirrored to seek a new path toward God. Acting virtually as the "coach" of our repentance, Jesus uses this encounter to say to us, "See? See how this young man strives to make himself right before God? See how he uses his words and his actions to convince himself that he deserves what God grants? Don't do that! You need to repent of all confidence in your accomplishments—as well as all fault in your failures—to know God's grace."

Repentance that rests on grace alone is not easily reconciled with our instinctive patterns of thought, so Jesus arrests our attention with the surprising way that he responds to the young man's request. Jesus' words

---

[1] Scripture quotations in this chapter are from The Holy Bible, New International Version®, NIV®. Copyright © 1973, 1978, 1984 by Biblica, Inc.™ Used by permission. All rights reserved worldwide.

trouble us because they initially seem to affirm the young man's suspicion that we earn God's favor with our good deeds. However, Jesus uses the desires and claims of the young man to reveal to him—and to us—the anemia of human goodness even when it engages in religious exercise. Against the background of the cross, and with the example of the young man, Jesus tells us that though the outward form of our spiritual observances may be great, and the mechanics of our religious performance seemingly perfect, they still lack what is needed for spiritual health.

This lesson is particularly apt for those whose religious exercises are conscientious and disciplined. Especially in church settings where we consistently teach the importance of obedience to God, there can be a strong inclination to see what we do so meticulously, strenuously, seriously, and sacrificially as what secures our standing with God. It will not. While God requires and blesses our obedience, we do not secure our eternal relationship with him by our actions. Even words of repentance will not heal when they become only a religious ritual we repeat to make ourselves right with God. Why? What keeps well-intended religiosity from qualifying as biblical repentance? We learn the answer by identifying what is missing from this religious young man's heart even as he bows before Jesus and calls him "good teacher."

A Loathing of Sin's Evil

Jesus works in behalf of this rich man by causing a number of powerful spiritual truths to converge that should make the man perceive the depth of his spiritual poverty. Jesus points first to the uniqueness of God's holiness.

The Holiness of Our God

The young man runs up to Jesus and addresses him as "Good teacher" (v. 17). To this courteous greeting Christ offers a troubling but instructive rebuke: "Why do you call me good? . . . No one is good—except God" (v. 18). True repentance always begins by understanding the astonishing truth of this simple statement: only God is good. There is none like him. No one is comparable. No one measures up. Between his perfection and our performance there is a gulf unbridgeable by human means. As high as the heavens are above the earth, so far is God's goodness above our own.

Jesus' words echo the experience of the prophet Isaiah, who saw a vision of God on his throne above the earth (Isa. 6:1–8). Though Isaiah's world was falling apart due to the corruption of the people of Israel, God remained undiminished, even untouched by the deterioration of human affairs. The essence of our God's holiness is that he is wholly other. He is separate from anything that would sully his glory or diminish his perfection. He is majestic, elevated, high and lifted up. He is not entangled by his creatures' failures. He is not tainted by earth's stain. He is pure. The radiance from that purity is so brilliant that even the heavenly hosts cover their eyes and themselves in his presence. They want neither to see nor to be seen in the intensity of the blinding and burning illumination of God's holy glory. Nothing created, either in heaven or on earth, appears as virtuous in the presence of this glorious holiness. Only God is truly good.

Before the purity of God's nature, all human righteousness withers into inadequacy. Many sensed this anew at the national clergy conference hosted by the Promise Keepers movement in February 1996. Forty-five thousand church leaders gathered in the Georgia Dome in Atlanta. During one of their meetings a conference leader led the clergy in an antiphonal recitation of the angelic chant of Isaiah 6: "Holy, holy, holy is the LORD Almighty; the whole earth is full of his glory." As the forty-five thousand voices filled the stadium with the resounding proclamation of the holiness of God, some got out of their seats and knelt on the ground. Others fell face-downward in recognition and honor of the majesty of God's holiness.

These church leaders' worship demonstrated why true repentance starts with recognition of the holiness of our God. We cannot rightly perceive the greatness of his goodness without apprehending the puniness of our own. Such a realization causes us to fall down in humility before God as did psalmist and apostle when apprehension of God's unique goodness tore from their hearts this assessment of humanity: "There is no one who does good, not even one" (Rom. 3:12; cf. Ps. 14:3). Only God is good.

The Reality of Our Sin

Jesus knows that the young man will not apprehend the significance of God alone being good, so he engineers an exchange that should clarify the truth. To the young man's question, "What must I do to inherit eternal life?" Jesus replies, in essence, "Keep the commandments" (Mark 10:18–19).

Jesus' response startles us. It sounds as though he is telling the young man that good works really do forge the path of salvation. Before we go further, we have to ask, did Jesus really believe that our deeds would save us? The answer lies within the passage. The account begins with the words, "As Jesus started on his way . . ." (v. 17), and by its end we learn where he was going. "We are going up to Jerusalem," he [Jesus] said, "and the Son of Man will be betrayed to the chief priests and teachers of the law. They will condemn him to death and will hand him over to the Gentiles, who will mock him and spit on him, flog him and kill him. Three days later he will rise" (vv. 33–34). Christ's plan makes it clear that he did not believe that our works would save us. He knew that he had to die for that. Jesus' instructions to the rich young man do not reflect a plan of salvation but underscore the Lord's plan of revelation—to help the man see himself.

The young man asks, "What must I do to inherit eternal life?" The question itself reveals a certain amount of hubris. We cannot *do* anything to *inherit* something. What we inherit comes to us by virtue of our birth and what someone else has done (which is a vital spiritual truth for those who believe that we inherit heaven as a result of our rebirth and what Christ has done). But Jesus plays along with the pretentious question by offering a preposterous answer.

Jesus says, "If you want to get eternal life from a holy God on the basis of what *you* do, then keep all of his commandments." That is to say, "If you really think that it's all up to you, then the way that you gain eternal life is plain: be perfect!" Samuel Bolton explains the rationale of Christ's strategy:

> When men will be saviors of themselves, when they look for righteousness by the law, Christ bids them go and keep the commandments . . . and this He does to humble them and bring them to Himself. But if men are humble and broken by a sight of their sins, then, without mention of the law at all, He comforts them with the free promises of grace, saying: "Come unto Me, all ye that labor and are heavy laden, and I will ease you."[2]

The young man's proposal to justify himself before God is plain to Jesus and clarifies why Jesus must speak to him in such an abrupt manner.

Even more preposterous is what the young man says next. To Jesus' proposal that he should keep all the commandments, the young man replies, "Teacher, . . . all these I have kept since I was a boy" (v. 20). We must consider these words in the light of those preceding. Jesus has just said, "Only God is good." Now, what does the young man reply only seconds later? "I am, too"!

With his claim to have kept *all* the commandments, the man elevates himself to the stature of God. In doing so, he has committed the worst sin possible for a Jew: he has broken the first commandment against having other gods. Yet because he does not perceive how preposterous is his claim to have achieved the holiness that God requires and alone pos-

---

[2] Samuel Bolton, *The True Bounds of Christian Freedom* (1645; repr. Carlisle, PA: Banner of Truth, 1978), 107–8.

sesses, the man remains unaware of the horror of his wrong. The words of
the book of Revelation well apply to this man:

> You say, "I am rich; I have acquired wealth and do not need a thing." But
> you do not realize that you are wretched, pitiful, poor, blind and naked.
> (Rev. 3:17)

The rich young man's words and actions remind us that, without apprehension of God's holiness, we cannot see the reality of our sin. True
repentance must include awareness of the magnitude of our spiritual destitution; therefore, real repentance must begin with recognition of God's
incomparable and unachievable holiness.

When we do not apprehend the true nature of our wrongdoing, we do
not hate it sufficiently to seek its expulsion. True repentance requires grief
and remorse that cries out, "How could I have done such a thing? Please,
God, take the guilt and presence of this evil from my life!"

Without such a loathing of the sin that has been magnified by God's
holiness, not only will we fail to repent; we will not even see our wrong.
Steve Brown, the wonderful radio preacher of grace, recently reported the
reaction of a man to a sermon in which Steve confessed to being "a sinner
as much in need of God's pardoning grace as anyone else." Said the man
afterwards, "All my life, I've heard pastors and missionaries say what awful
sinners they are, but you are the first one I believe . . . because you seem to
believe it."[3] Confession of such need of grace will not come until we begin
viewing our lives from heaven's holy perspective.

Few of us will believe that we are in dire need of repentance if we base
our understanding of our own need on comparisons to the obvious failings of others. It is the comparison to God's holiness that makes what is
minor in the world's eyes wrenching to the Christian heart. That is why
Paul would say, late in his ministry, "Christ Jesus came into the world to
save sinners—of whom I am the worst" (1 Tim. 1:15). As Paul grew in
Christ, he became increasingly aware of his sinfulness before a holy God.[4]
The more our understanding of God matures, the more we recognize our
need of repentance.

I too must recognize that true repentance will not come until I believe
that I am the worst of sinners. This does not mean that I have committed

---

[3] Steve Brown, commencement address, Covenant Theological Seminary, St. Louis, MO, May 1989.

[4] Paul's self-assessment as he progressed through life was first that he was the "least of the apostles" (1 Cor.
15:9), then that he was "less than the least of all God's people" (Eph. 3:8), and finally that he was the "worst of
sinners" (1 Tim. 1:16).

the most heinous of crimes. Rather, I must acknowledge that with the privileges, position, background, and knowledge God has given me, my sin is a greater betrayal of my Savior than the actions of those who act in ignorance and disadvantage. None of us can truly repent or become spiritually mature until this realization and humility grips us.

The Evil of Our Righteousness

To make us realize how great is our need of repentance, Jesus gives us a special perspective in this passage. To expose this young ruler to the depth of his sin, Jesus, who knows that the young man will not face his sin, confronts him with "the evil of our righteousness." The early American evangelist George Whitefield first used this phrase to confront the self-righteous with the inadequacy of their own goodness to qualify them for heaven.

I rediscovered the arresting power of Whitefield's phrase when recently talking with another pastor in an airport restaurant about the nature of true repentance. When I said, "George Whitefield taught that we need to sense not only the evil of our sin but the evil of our righteousness," a woman listening nearby turned to us. "Oh no!" she said. "Do you mean that I have to feel guilty for good, too?" I smiled and said, "No, that is not really the point, but God wants us to know that our good works are not good enough to make him love us. That is why we need Jesus no matter how good we think we are." The goodness in our good works can be truly good and a blessing to others. There is a danger in making people think that there is nothing they can do that will please God or help others. Still, there is never sufficient goodness in our best works to make them truly holy by God's ultimate standard.[5] That is why our best works still fall short of qualifying us for heaven.

A problem of wealth? Jesus must make plain to the rich young man the inadequacy of our best works for building a ladder to heaven. When the man says that he has kept all the commandments, Jesus probably at least raises a mental eyebrow and observes the situation. Here is a man who has just blasphemed God by claiming to be as holy as he; yet this blasphemer thinks he is good enough for God! So if he really thinks that he has fulfilled all of God's law, what can Jesus require that will make the man realize that our goodness, even remarkable goodness, falls short of all the holiness God requires?

---

[5] B. B. Warfield, "Miserable Sinners Christianity," *The Works of Benjamin B. Warfield*, vol. 7 (Grand Rapids, MI: Baker, 1931), 126–32.

Jesus indicates that the man lacks only "one thing" to gain what he desires. Then Jesus indicates the magnitude of that one thing. Jesus says that the young man must "go, sell everything you have and give to the poor. . . . Then come, follow me" (Mark 10:21). By his appearance and responses the young man has made it plain that he is living for himself. When Jesus identifies this "one thing" lacking, the man readily recognizes what Jesus requires. He requires everything.

We should not interpret Jesus' words as meaning that all wealthy people must give away all their money in order to gain heaven. While Jesus makes clear that wealth can be a stumbling block to our trusting in him (v. 25), God also grants wealth for his purposes (e.g., 1 Chron. 29:12–14; Prov. 22:4; Luke 8:3; Acts 16:14–15). Before we give all our wealth away (for in comparison to most of the world, virtually everyone in North America is "wealthy"), we should recognize the danger of inverting the message of this account. Were we to teach that any great act of human effort or charity qualifies us for heaven, then we would fall into the error of the rich young man's perspective.

Christ's message to this young man is that nothing we can do will give us standing before God; nothing we can do is enough. Even if the man were to sell all he has and give to the poor, he still must continue to "follow" Jesus. And if the rich young man were to follow Jesus, where would that road lead? It would lead to a cross in Jerusalem where Jesus will show that his resources alone can pay what God requires.

A rite of passage! Even marvelous obedience does not contain sufficient goodness to merit God's acceptance. This understanding matures our repentance as we realize that if even our best works fall short of God's holy requirements, then our faults are all the more despicable.

One of the things my father taught all his sons was how to use a cross-cut saw. His daddy and his daddy's daddy had taught their sons, and my father was not going to let this rite of passage for rural Southern manhood end with him. One brisk fall morning we began sawing on a log that we did not know had a rotten core. When we had just sawed partially through the log, it split and fell off the sawing frame. The timber hit the ground so hard that a large piece was sheared off the rotten log. In my childhood imagination the unusual shape of the sheared piece looked like a horse head. It so captured my interest that I took it home with me after that day of sawing.

For my father's next birthday, I attached a length of two-by-four board to that log head, attached a rope tail, and stuck on some sticks to act as legs. Then I halfway hammered in a dozen or so nails down the two-by-four body of that "horse," wrapped the whole thing in butcher block paper, put a bow on it, and presented it to my father. When he took off the wrapping, he smiled and said, "Thank you, it's wonderful . . . what is it?"

"It's a tie rack, Dad," I said. "See, you can put your ties on those nails going down the side of the horse's body." My father smiled again and thanked me. Then he leaned the horse against his closet wall (because the stick legs could not keep it standing upright), and for years he used it as a tie rack.

Now, when I first gave my father that rotten-log-horse-head tie rack, I really thought it was "good." In my childish mind this creation was a work of art ready for the Metropolitan Museum. But as I matured, I realized that my work was not nearly as good as I had once thought. In fact, I understood ultimately that my father had received and used my gift not because of its goodness but out of *his* goodness. In a similar way our heavenly Father receives our gifts not so much because they deserve his love, but because he *is* love.

A new measure. The "great disproportion" between our good works and God's holiness never goes away in this life. Our works will never earn God's affection, just as they will never merit his pardon. Our best deeds will never be sufficiently free of the contamination of human motive and imperfection that they are acceptable to God on their own merit.[6] As the authors of the Westminster Confession wrote,

> As they are wrought by us, they [our good works] are defiled, and mixed with so much weakness and imperfection, that they cannot endure the severity of God's judgment. . . .
>
> Believers being accepted through Christ, their good works also are accepted in Him; not as though they were in this life wholly unblameable and unreprovable in God's sight; but that He, looking upon them in His Son, is pleased to accept and reward that which is sincere, although accompanied with many weaknesses and imperfections.[7]

Not only do our good works not pardon our sin; they are, in fact, so mixed with our sinfulness that, if God did not act in love, they would actually be subject to his judgment. This understanding of the "evil of our righteousness" gives us a new measuring rod for our sin, which we would not dare to use were we not certain of God's grace.

---

[6] John Calvin, *Institutes of the Christian Religion*, ed. John T. McNeil, trans. Ford Lewis Battles (Philadelphia: Westminster, 1960), 3.15.3.
[7] Westminster Confession of Faith, 16.5.6.

If even our good works are blameworthy, then what is the true character of our sin? The answer can only be that it is utterly abhorrent to God—and should be to us. We cannot repent until this reality has hit us. John Colquhoun, in his classic description of the means of spiritual growth, wrote that true repentance is characterized by "a sense not only of our evil doings, but of the evil of our doings; not only of our sin but of the exceeding sinfulness of our sin."[8]

The repentance that enables our progressive sanctification does not come without our learning to loathe the evil of our wrongdoing. This loathing becomes the true attitude of our hearts as we meditate on the holiness of our God, the reality of our sin, and even the evil of our righteousness. These are the graces of perception that God supplies in his Word to break us from our affection for the sin that so easily entangles us (Heb. 12:1).

God wants us to understand the true malignancy of our sin—the problem is too severe to be remedied by our goodness. Even if the extent of the disease is not readily apparent to human eyes, the Bible's analysis of the seriousness of our condition should cause us to examine all the arteries, vessels, and capillaries of the way we live. As we test all our relationships, patterns of speech, entertainments, habits, and even religious practices, we progressively discover the cancerous cells that threaten our spiritual health. These discoveries will create healthy dissatisfaction with our level of personal goodness even as they turn us toward the true means of our ultimate healing.

A new discernment. A friend told me recently of his pastor's response to a sharp criticism. The pastor's response to his critic was, "I will listen to every word that you have to say and take it to the Lord for examination. I want to be corrected if I am wrong." Remarkable to the man who reported this to me was his pastor's greater desire to discern the possible evil in his own heart rather than to dodge blame or reproof. This is the mark of a repentant heart: it recognizes the awfulness of sin (even hidden sin) and listens to the prompting of the Spirit and the counsel of others to see "if there is any offensive way in me" (Ps. 139:24). The unrepentant person cannot face sin, and therefore seeks to blame others, minimize the sin, or deny its presence. The repentant person sees sin as it truly is—an assault on the peace and purity of the soul—and thus is thankful for correction.

The benefits of repentance for the relationships of our lives were re-

---

[8] John Colquhoun, *Repentance* (1826; repr. Carlisle, PA: Banner of Truth, 1965), 17.

flected in a recent letter from Ugandan missionary Rick Gray. He wrote of an event in his life that demonstrated the necessity of discerning the contaminating evil even in a work as noble as translating catechism lessons:

> I need to be aware of my subtle tendency to make ministry an end in itself: whereby I do things so that I can feel good about myself. . . . Another peril of ministry becoming too activity-focused is that it causes me to lose sight of Jesus, and to lose the sense of His Spirit's leading. While checking the 1st draft of the "Katekisimo" [catechism] I became intent on finishing a certain amount of pages per day. One afternoon as time was ticking away, and my dear Mubwisi co-translator struggled to come up with just the right Lubwisi word to express the English meaning, I grew impatient with him. I became harsh and unsympathetic to his inability to go faster. My penchant to get the job done blinded me to Christ's presence with us, and deafened me to the Spirit's conviction of my sin.
>
> Unless I maintain a Jesus-centeredness in the midst of ministry, I will be unable to love people well and bring glory to God. Only as I realize my self-worth is determined by how awesome is the Savior's love for me, and not by how productive is my work for Him, will I be free from my drivenness and need to accomplish tasks. When I gaze upon his nail-pierced hands and believe they are actually reaching out to embrace me, then I am empowered to reach out with similar compassion and care to those around me.[9]

The understanding that we should desire repentance because it removes contaminants from our relationship with God and with others helps distinguish false from true repentance. False repentance is less concerned with the spiritual contamination of sin than it is with the personal consequences of sin. True repentance is chiefly concerned with the wrong we have done to our Savior and to others. Repentance of the first kind is self-preoccupied; true repentance is a selfless seeking of spiritual fellowship and renewal. False repentance flees correction; true repentance seeks it.

A Longing for Sin's Cure
Because true repentance makes us sense the depth and awfulness of sin, it naturally leads to the next element of repentance that is missing in the rich young ruler's responses. If our sin is truly abhorrent to us, then we want to be rid of it. We long for a cure to the disease of sin. At least two at-

---

[9] Rick Gray, World Harvest Mission and Mission to the World prayer letter, summer 1999.

titudes characterize this longing: a desire to offer confession and a desire
to receive grace.

A Desire to Offer Confession

Again Jesus indicates what true repentance requires by making clear what
the rich young man will not offer. In his professing that he has kept all
the laws, the rich man displays not only his ignorance of the real requirements of the Law but also his lack of desire to open his heart to God.
When the Spirit has truly touched our hearts regarding the presence and
awfulness of our sin, confession leaps to our lips. We see our sin for the
spiritual poison that it is, and we long to spit it out. This young man indicates no such longing. He desires to receive reward rather than to offer
confession (Mark 10:17). True repentance is not so much asking, "What
honor do I get from my faith?" but rather, "How may I give myself in humility to God?" The heart that is most spiritually sensitive and committed
is simultaneously most aware of its need of grace.[10]

During the Great Awakening, when the Spirit of God revived much
of our nation's early faith, Jonathan Edwards was presiding over a massive
prayer meeting. Eight hundred men prayed with him. Into that meeting
a woman sent a message asking the men to pray for her husband. The
note described a man who in spiritual pride had become unloving, proud,
and difficult. Edwards read the message in private and then, thinking that
perhaps the man described was present, the great preacher made a bold
request. Edwards first read the note to the eight hundred men. Then he
asked if the man who had been described would raise his hand so that the
whole assembly could pray for him.

Three hundred men raised their hands. Each had been convicted by
the Spirit of their sin, and now they longed to confess. A repentant life
is so characterized. Rather than hiding sin, or minimizing it, or blaming
others, the repentant heart longs to confess.

Humble acknowledgment of our wrong characterizes the prayer times
of the repentant life. We do not hide from God matters large or small, obvious or obscure. We not only want to confess to God the sin we are aware
of; we pray for his Holy Spirit to reveal the things hidden from our own
consciences so that we might confess them as well (Ps. 19:12–14). True
repentance is evident when we are as much concerned about deep and
hidden sins as we are about the faults that others can observe. The repen-

---

[10] G. C. Berkouwer, *Faith and Sanctification*, trans. John Vriend (Grand Rapids, MI: Eerdmans, 1957), 117.

tant heart desires full confession. It is more concerned about relationship with God than about reputation among men (Ps. 51:4–6).

A Desire to Receive Grace

If we know that our best works will not merit pardon for sin, and we long to confess wrong so that we may be rid of it, then what ultimately must we seek? We ultimately seek grace. Unlike the rich young man, who wants to "do" something so that he can broker his good works into spiritual blessing (Mark 10:17), the repentant heart senses its unworthiness and yearns for God to fix the damage to our souls that we cannot fix.

A Christian friend told me recently that he and his wife had discovered that their daughter had disobeyed them and handled the family car in a way that caused an accident. The daughter could not afford to pay for the repairs or the traffic ticket. So the parents paid for the repairs and the fine with the agreement that their daughter would pay them back over time. The parents did not need her money but hoped that making her responsible would help teach her lessons needed for her own safety and maturity.

The payback system required some discipline and diligence from the daughter, and she struggled to keep the arrangements. The parents had to keep reminding her of her obligations, which frustrated the daughter as well as the parents. Finally, after one of the reminding sessions, the daughter exploded: "Daddy, don't you and Mom know that I realize what I did was wrong? I know I was irresponsible. I know it is my problem. I wish you all would just get off my case so that I could figure out a way to fix this." Replied her father, "Honey, what I really want you to figure out is that by yourself you can't fix this."

Our heavenly Father's words are quite similar. Because we too easily echo the words of the rich young man—"What must I do . . . ?"—God replies, "What I really want you to know is that what you 'do' will never be enough to fix your situation. Your sin is too great and your abilities are too limited for you to fix the mess of your life. You need my grace. You must turn away from all of your own resources and trust that only what I provide will fix your situation."

A willingness to rest. We can mentally assent to these truths about grace without applying them to the ways we actually deal with guilt. The failure of grace to affect our hearts may be evident in our very words of confession. What we consider "our repentance" may simply be a good work that we are trying to offer God as a way of brokering our pardon. We can find ourselves saying, in effect, "See, God, I feel real guilty. I got down on my knees, prayed the prayer for pardon, and tried to make things right. I said and did what you wanted. Now are you happy?"

There is nothing intrinsically wrong with any single component of such repentance, unless we are trusting that offering such a plea to God will make him forgive us. If we view repentance in this way, we make repentance itself a work. In effect, we offer God the bribe of our contrition for his forgiveness. While contrition is necessary, the degree and duration of our remorse is not what earns our pardon. We have already seen that no human activity is without stain before God's holiness. This means that even the "work" of repentance cannot merit forgiveness.

Repentance is not so much a doing as a depending. It is not so much a striving for pardon as a posture of humility. In true repentance we confess our total reliance on God's mercy. We acknowledge the inadequacy of anything we would offer God to gain his pardon. In true repentance we rest upon God's grace rather than trying to do anything to deserve it. We lean heavily on the words of Isaiah: "In repentance and rest is your salvation, in quietness and trust is your strength" (Isa. 30:15).[11]

Reliance on God alone for mercy is the essence of repentance. We can make a grave mistake by overemphasizing the human-action implications of "repentance" supposedly derived from the biblical term's historical origins. The Hebrew word we translate as repentance means "to turn."[12] If we are not careful, we may press this vocabulary insight to imply that repentance is primarily a turning from doing bad things to doing good things or, at least, saying the right things to God. Repentance is not a work of turning to new behaviors or to any conjured phrases or emotions in us. The songwriter reminds us, "Not what I feel or do can give me peace with God; not all my prayers and sighs and tears can bear my awful load."[13] Such human efforts cannot be our basis for being made right with God.

Repentance is not a turning from one category of works to another; rather, it is a turning from human works entirely to God. The Westminster Shorter Catechism says this beautifully in answering the question: "What is repentance unto life?" The answer:

---

[11] Even the faith through which God saves us is itself not a work. Rather, it also is a resting in Christ. The Westminster Shorter Catechism describes it thus: "Faith in Jesus Christ is a saving grace, whereby we receive and rest upon him alone for salvation, as he is offered to us in the gospel" (Q. 86).

[12] The New Testament term is *metanoia*, which means to change one's mind. However, the biblical context for the term implies more than simply thinking new and right thoughts that God will honor because we are now doing (or even thinking) good stuff to make up for the previous bad stuff. *Metanoia* is a total change of personal orientation, a grieving for what formerly brought us gratification and a looking away from anything in us to merit God's forgiveness as we depend instead on his mercy alone.

[13] Horatius Bonar, "Not What My Hands Have Done," *The Trinity Hymnal* (Philadelphia: Great Commission Publications, 1998), no. 461.

> Repentance unto life is a saving grace, whereby a sinner, out of a true sense of his sin, and apprehension of the mercy of God in Christ, doth, with grief and hatred of his sin, turn from it unto God, with full purpose of, and endeavor after, new obedience.[14]

New obedience follows true repentance, but we put no hope for pardon in what we do. Repentance is not real if we have no intention of correcting our ways, but the correction is not a condition of our forgiveness.

In biblical repentance we turn to God alone—relying on his mercy and grace—not to anything in us or done by us in order to secure his mercy. These truths also indicate that, while Scripture commands us to identify our sin and sorrow for it, neither the accuracy of our identification of the sin nor the degree of our sorrow for it compels God to forgive us. There is great comfort in this for the conscientious believer who recognizes that we are always inaccurate (or incomplete) in our perception of sin and never adequate in our remorse for it.

We can confess whatever our heart knows to be our sin, with the confidence that God's heart is large enough to cover what we are unable fully to expose (Ps. 19:12–13). In so doing we even confess the inadequacy of our repentance, with the confidence that we can rest under the broad mantle of his grace. Like the man who cried to Jesus, "I do believe; help me overcome my unbelief" (Mark 9:24), we should be able to say to God, "I repent even of the inadequacy of my repentance, in order that I may rely solely on your mercy."

Remorse precedes true repentance. Changed behavior follows true repentance. But this necessary prelude and postlude of true repentance are *not* themselves the essence of repentance. True repentance is a denial that anything in us ever would or ever could satisfy God's holiness or compel his pardon. We humbly concede that we can offer him nothing for what he alone can give. Then we rest in his promise to forgive those who humbly seek him. Remorse for our sin makes us repentant; but it should also make us so aware of the inability of our hearts adequately to register what God requires that we do not trust our sorrow to make us right with God. Similarly, while our gratitude for God's pardon should make us "endeavor after new obedience," the very source of our gratitude—awareness of the awful shortcoming of all our actions—keeps us from trusting in our obedience to make us deserving of God's forgiveness.

---

[14] Westminster Shorter Catechism, Q. 87.

A desire for renewal. Repentance, therefore, is fundamentally a humble expression of a desire for a renewed relationship with God—a relationship that we confess can be secured only by his grace. We long for his pardon, presence, and Spirit to repair the damage our sin has caused to our relationship with him. Through this we learn another mark of false repentance: a primary concern with bartering away the consequences of sin. True repentance, though certainly not desiring to face those consequences, willingly accepts them if they move us closer to fellowship with and understanding of our God. This is so because biblical repentance is primarily concerned with the renewal of our fellowship with him.

True repentance that springs from a desire for renewed intimacy with God is never the fruit of fleeing the punitive God of our imaginations. Mindful of God's love, we approach him with humility but also with deep longing. Repentant hearts cry out to him as for a distant loved one, "Let me draw near to you, my Lord. My heart and my flesh cry out for the living God. How I yearn for the reality of your love afresh in my life. Please do not persist in anger for my sin, but let me know your unfailing love" (see Psalms 84 and 85). Only awareness of unfailing divine love can produce what the repentant heart seeks when it prays, "Create in me a pure heart, O God, and renew a steadfast spirit within me. Do not cast me from your presence or take your Holy Spirit from me. Restore to me the joy of your salvation and grant me a willing spirit, to sustain me" (Ps. 51:10–12).

Repentance confesses to God, "God, forgive me. The allure of this temptation was more real to me than the beauties of your promises and presence." Repentance implores God, "Please graciously restore the reality of your care into my heart and life so that your love will be so precious that I cannot further exist with my betrayal of you. Help me to meditate more upon the character of your love revealed by Christ's sacrifice than upon the circumstances of my life that make me doubt you." Repentance petitions, "God, I want to seek you the way simple people do when they say that they know you are near by the way that your Word has become alive in their souls." None but the biblically repentant heart seeks after God with such unashamed love.

A Loving of the Savior

To love God as fervently as biblical repentance requires, we must know his character. So we are also led, in this account of the unrepentant rich man, to see deeply into the heart of our Savior. This revelation only makes more sad the preoccupation with self that keeps the rich young man from giving himself to the one who is love.

True repentance (which the rich young man lacks) demands apprehension of the ugliness of sin, but it also requires seeing the beauty of the Savior. Even if our wrongdoing is abhorrent to us, we still will not turn to the one who can deal with it if he is no more attractive to us than our sin. This is why Paul reminds us that "God's kindness leads you toward repentance" (Rom. 2:4). If we perceive God to be only an ogre in the sky waiting to pounce on those who do not properly bow and scrape, then biblical repentance—requiring a love response to God—is impossible. Thus, to make true repentance not only possible but desirable, the Gospel of Mark lets us peek behind the curtain of the Savior's thoughts so that we will know his character and desire his fellowship.

Delight in His Vision

In view of the young man's blasphemous boasts, few verses are more precious in Scripture than the one that describes Jesus' attitude toward him. How does Jesus react to the rich man who has just refused to acknowledge his sin and has portrayed himself as being the equal of God? Allowing us to see behind the Savior's eyes, the Bible says, "Jesus looked at him and loved him" (Mark 10:21). This revelation of the undeterred heart of our Lord should serve as a magnet to our souls when we have wandered from his ways.

I remember the night in high school when I stayed out too late, well beyond my curfew. I had been having fun with my friends, and the time got away from me. I was wrong, and no excuse would make my actions right. I did not want to go home because I thought that I knew what was waiting for me there. An arms-crossed, toe-tapping, voice-raised, punishment-dispensing set of parents would be at the door. Knowing that each minute of further delay was digging me deeper into trouble, I still didn't rush to go home. I simply could not motivate myself to go and confront the anger that I was sure was waiting for me.

There was no incentive to turn from my wrong when I believed that my return home would only commence my punishment. When I finally did go home, an upset mother and father met me as I expected, but their reactions were a surprise. Though they told me that we would have to deal with the wrong the next morning, they hugged me and told me how happy they were that I was safe. Though I had sinned against them, they said and showed that they loved me. I may have missed a curfew a few times after that, but never by so much. And never again did I fear going home.

Because I knew my parents' love even in their correction, I matured under their care. This is our heavenly Father's intention also. He encourages us to turn to him in repentance, not by promising that there will be no correction for our sin but by showing us his heart through the ministry of Jesus. This account paints the rich young man's sin darkly so that the love of Jesus will shine more brightly. He is able to love even those who arrogantly resist his will. He can know the worst of our sin and still look at us and love us. Because God's character never changes, he looks at us in our sin and still loves us. His arms remain open, and his ears are still attentive to our cry. He may be angry at our rebellion, but he is never angry at our return (2 Chron. 30:9; Isa. 44:22; Jer. 3:14, 22; 4:1; Joel 2:12–13; Zech. 1:3). His kindness draws us back to him and away from our sin.

Delight in His Path
The quality of the love in Christ's arms is revealed not only by the look in his eyes at this stage of his journey but also in his sacrifice at the journey's end. The beauty of our Savior shines in both the love he showed and in the life he shared. For our blasphemies and pride, for our rebellion and arrogance, he would surrender himself to die (Mark 10:33). The beauty of love displayed in our Lord's willingness to walk this path encourages us to walk with him just as he encouraged the rich young man to do.

My first date with my wife came when I was on an outing with her family. As the new, single minister of their little country church, I was invited to the family's picnic. We went to a restored Victorian-era village known as Elsah, Illinois, snuggled into the bluffs along the Mississippi River.

Though the October air was cool, the day was bright, and after our lunch the young woman I had just met offered to show me the village, which she had already visited many times. Against the brilliant hues of the fall leaves in the sunlight, this beautiful blonde with green eyes in a red sweater asked me, "Would you like to take a walk with me?" It was not a difficult question to answer. I said, "You bet!" Her beauty made me delight to follow her.

Jesus reveals a different kind of beauty about himself, of course, in this passage as he shows his love for the unlovable. Still, seeing our Lord's loveliness of heart, we know what the young man's response should be when Jesus says, "Follow me" (v. 21). The natural response of one who has seen the beauty of the Savior is to follow him.

We delight to walk with our Lord down the path of life because through our repentance we have understood how altogether lovely he is (Song 5:16). Our obedience is not the foundation or condition of God's receiving our repentance; it is the natural outflow of a heart that has experienced his grace. Our new willingness to follow Christ helps reassure us that we have experienced the transforming power of grace. Our delight in walking with him validates love for him in our hearts even amid remorse for sin against him. Thus, though there may be many stumbles and setbacks along the path, true repentance leads naturally to new obedience.

Though the Bible does not teach that obedience is a condition of God's pardon, it cautions against thinking that God will forgive where there is no real change of heart. God is not waiting for us to fix our lives before he forgives us, for then none would be forgiven; but he does not promise forgiveness where repentance is not sincere. While we should not delay repentance until we have corrected our sin, we also should not think that God will accept repentance from a heart still in rebellion against him. If repentance is only a tool to manipulate God into averting the consequences of our wrongdoing, without any real intention of changing our ways, then we should remember that God will not hear those who cherish sin in their heart (see Ps. 66:18; James 4:6).

Still, God is pleased to receive sincere confession "although accompanied by many weaknesses and imperfections."[15] He will forgive even though we remain susceptible to temptation and may repeatedly fail to do what he—and we ourselves—desire (see Gal. 5:17; Rom. 7:19–25). Through repentance God provides the spiritual nourishment we need to walk his path, even though we may need to partake of that sustenance many times. What will keep us returning to the table of repentance is delight in the fare that our Lord spreads for us there—his pardon, his grace, his tutelage, his love, and our joy.

Delight in Him

The reason we should keep on the Savior's path despite the stumbles that distress us is evident in the mental state of the rich young man as the story ends. As he leaves without repentance, there is something else missing from his life: he has no joy. "He went away sad, because he had great wealth" (Mark 10:22).

We ought to ask, "Why did he go away sad? He still had all his money."

---

[15] Westminster Confession of Faith, 16.6.

The simple answer is that he did not have Jesus. By not being willing to leave his other god, wealth, the young man kept himself from fellowship with the Lord. He denied himself the blessings of walking with his Savior.

In terms that we wish the rich young man would understand, songwriter Lynn DeShazo describes the repentant heart's perception of Christ:

> Lord, you are more precious than silver,
> Lord, you are more costly than gold,
> Lord, you are more beautiful than diamonds,
> And nothing I desire compares with you.[16]

Repentance that renews precious fellowship with our incomparably wonderful God ultimately furthers our joy. Just as we cannot enter into true repentance without *sorrow* for our guilt, we cannot emerge from true repentance without *joy* for our release from shame.

Neither of these emotions merits forgiveness or makes repentance work, but repentance operates effectively only within the environment of a conscience filled with *both* of these natural responses to grace. This is why, after his sin with Bathsheba, David confesses to God, "Against you, you only have I sinned and done what is evil in your sight," and prays also, "Let me hear joy and gladness; let the bones you have crushed rejoice. . . . Restore to me the joy of your salvation. . . . O Lord, open my lips, and my mouth will declare your praise" (Ps. 51:4, 8, 12, 15). Thus, the repentant life is characterized by each of the following: an apprehension of the destitution of all our works; a confession of wrong with a willingness to turn from it; *and,* an appreciation for the pardoning grace of God, which results in joy.

Repentance That Sings

If we could see the dimensions of spiritual illness as plainly as we can the effects of physical disease, then perhaps the nature and effects of repentance would be more obvious to us. On November 8, 1995, Dan and Carol Walker welcomed to the world a newborn son, Joel Daniel. Just ten or fifteen minutes after the newborn had finished his first feeding, he turned completely blue and went limp in his mother's hands. Carol screamed, "What's wrong with my baby?"

A nurse took Joel Daniel from his mother's arms and ran with the newborn to the nursery to try to restore his breathing. Carol later wrote,

---

[16] Lynn DeShazo, "More Precious Than Silver" (Mobile, AL: Integrity Music, 1979).

"Dan, myself, and others in the room began praying earnestly that our boy would live. Each passing moment seemed like an eternity. We wanted the miracle of life for our son! The next minutes and hours we continued to cry out to God on behalf of our firstborn child. Finally, the nurse came in with the words, 'Your son is alive.'"

Due to a rare disorder that kept a valve at the base of the child's esophagus from operating properly, his life had been in greater danger than anyone had known. This one episode did not end the danger. After repeated crises, the parents desperately wanted the surgery that would provide a cure. Despite the difficulty such early surgery would be for them and their baby, Carol and Dan longed for it. When the day of the surgery came, friends gathered with the parents in the baby's hospital room to await the outcome. Again, prayers were earnestly offered for the health of the child. Finally, the doctor came to report that the surgery was over, and that Joel Daniel would be fine. The small crowd in the room cheered, and burst into spontaneous singing of the Doxology:

> Praise God from whom all blessings flow;
> praise him all creatures here below,
> praise him above, ye heavenly host:
> praise Father, Son, and Holy Ghost.[17]

When they perceived how great was the physical danger, these parents longed for a cure. Then, in recognition of their personal helplessness, they called for the one who could help. They put themselves entirely in the healing hands of another, and, when help mercifully came, they were filled with joy.

When the attack of sin on our soul is as real to us as such a physical attack on our bodies, then how we are to seek God's help and respond to it will be clear. In the light of God's holiness, we will perceive how awful is the disease of our sin and how helpless we are against it. Then we will cry out to God for the help that he alone can give. And when his mercy has made us whole, recognizing how great is our rescue we will experience overwhelming joy.

Viewing the spiritual dynamics of repentance through the analogy of a physical healing corrects some common misconceptions of what God expects of us. No one doubts that God expects repentance, but what characterizes a repentant life? As most would expect, a repentant heart ex-

---

[17] Thomas Ken, "Doxology," *Trinity Hymnal*, no. 731.

presses an honest loathing of our spiritual disease and a longing for God to heal our relationship with him. But surprising as it may seem, a life characterized by repentance also exhibits joy. When we have seen the malignancy of the sin in our soul and have perceived how freely God's mercy flows to remove it from our lives, we naturally exhibit joy.

The evidence of complete repentance is not the stereotypical gritted teeth and grinding resolve or even groaning and groveling. The reverberations of repentance sound more like singing. Yes, God can lead us through a dark night of the soul to enable us to see and to grieve for sin. And as we wrestle against our pride and rebellion to find rest in the mercy of God, we may know great pain. But when we have understood, trusted, and received the freeing grace of repentance, rejoicing fills our hearts. Without this joy that is our strength, the new obedience that should be the fruit of true repentance is impossible. Like the rich young man we, too, go away sad and unwilling to follow Jesus. By contrast, biblical repentance renews in us thanksgiving and gratitude for God's mercy. Knowing his pardon, we delight to serve him with a childlike love and a willing mind. Repentance renews our joy.

SELECTED BIBLIOGRAPHY

Anderson, Gary A. *Sin: A History*. New Haven, CT: Yale University Press, 2009.

Andrews, Reddit, III. *Sin and the Fall*. Gospel Coalition Booklets. Wheaton, IL: Crossway, 2011.

Augustine of Hippo. *Two Books on Genesis: Against the Manichees; and, On the Literal Interpretation of Genesis, an Unfinished Book*. Translated by Roland J. Teske. Washington, DC: Catholic University of America Press, 1990.

———. "City of God," in *Writings of Saint Augustine*. Translated by Gerald G. Walsh and Grace Monahan. New York: FC, 1952.

Bavinck, Herman. *Reformed Dogmatics*, Vol. 3, *Sin and Salvation in Christ*. Grand Rapids, MI: Baker, 2006.

Beale, G. K. *We Become What We Worship: A Biblical Theology of Idolatry*. Downers Grove, IL: InterVarsity Academic, 2008.

Berkouwer, G. C. *Sin*. Studies in Dogmatics. Grand Rapids, MI: Eerdmans, 1971.

Biddle, Mark. *Missing the Mark: Sin and Its Consequences in Biblical Theology*. Nashville, TN: Abingdon, 2005.

Blocher, Henri. *Original Sin: Illuminating the Riddle*. NSBT. Grand Rapids, MI: Eerdmans, 1997.

Boda, Mark. *A Severe Mercy: Sin and Its Remedy in the Old Testament*. Winona Lake, IN: Eisenbrauns, 2009.

Bonhoeffer, Dietrich. *Creation and Fall and Temptation*. New York: Macmillan, n.d.

Burnside, Jonathan. *Signs of Sin: Seriousness of Offence in Biblical Law*. Sheffield: Continuum International/Sheffield Academic Press, 2003.

Calvin, John. *Institutes of the Christian Religion*. 2 vols. Edited by John T. McNeill. Translated by Ford Lewis Battles. Library of Christian Classics, 20–21. Philadelphia: Westminster Press, 1960.

Campbell, Iain D. *The Doctrine of Sin in Reformed and Neo-Orthodox Thought*. Fearn, Ross-shire, UK: Mentor, 1999.

Capps, Donald. *The Depleted Self: Sin in a Narcissistic Age*. Minneapolis: Fortress, 1993.

Carter, C. W. "Hamartiology: Evil, the Marrer of God's Creative Purpose and Work." In vol. 1 of *A Contemporary Wesleyan Theology*. Edited by C. W. Carter, 237–82. Grand Rapids, MI: Zondervan, 1983.

Edwards, Jonathan. *Freedom of the Will*. New Haven, CT: Yale University Press, 1957.

———. *Original Sin*. Edited by Clyde A. Holbrook. New Haven, CT: Yale University Press, 1970.

Goldingay, John. *Old Testament Theology*. Downers Grove, IL: IVP Academic, 2003.

Griffiths, Steven M. *Redeem the Time: Sin in the Writings of John Owen*. Fearn, Ross-shire, UK: Mentor, 2001.

Guthrie, Donald. *New Testament Theology*. Leicester, UK: Inter-Varsity Press, 1981.

Hoekema, Anthony A. *Created in God's Image*. Grand Rapids, MI: Eerdmans, 1986.

House, Paul R. *Old Testament Theology*. Downers Grove, IL: InterVarsity, 1998.

Hughes, Philip Edgcumbe. *No Cross, No Crown: The Temptation of Jesus*. Wilton, CT: Morehouse-Barlow, 1988.

———. *The True Image: The Origin and Destiny of Man in Christ*. Grand Rapids, MI: Eerdmans, 1989.

Jacobs, Alan. *Original Sin: A Cultural History*. New York: HarperCollins, 2008.

Johnson, S. Lewis. "Romans 5:12: An Exercise in Exegesis and Theology." In *New Dimensions in New Testament Study*. Edited by Richard N. Longenecker and Merrill C. Tenne, 298–316. Grand Rapids, MI: Zondervan, 1974.

Lewis, C. S. *The Screwtape Letters*. New York: Macmillan, 1976.

———. *The Weight of Glory: And Other Addresses*. San Francisco: HarperCollins, 2001.

Lundgaard, Kris. *The Enemy Within: Straight Talk about the Power and Defeat of Sin*. Phillipsburg, NJ: P&R, 1998.

Luther, Martin. *The Bondage of the Will*. Translated by J. I. Packer and O. R. Johnston. Old Tappan, NJ: Revell, 1957.

Mahony, John W. "Why an Historical Adam Matters for a Biblical Doctrine of Sin." *SBJT* 15, no. 1 (2011): 60–79.

Manton, Thomas. *The Temptation of Christ*. Fearn, Ross-shire, UK: Christian Focus, 1996.

McFarland, Ian A. *In Adam's Fall: A Meditation on the Christian Doctrine of Original Sin*. Chichester, West Sussex, UK: Wiley-Blackwell, 2011.

McMinn, Mark R. *Sin and Grace in Christian Counseling: An Integrative Paradigm*. Downers Grove, IL: InterVarsity, 2008.

Menninger, Karl. *Whatever Became of Sin?* New York: Bantam, 1988.

Milne, Bruce A. "The Idea of Sin in Twentieth-Century Theology." *TynBul* 26 (1975): 3–33.

Moore, Russell D. *Tempted and Tried: Temptation and the Triumph of Christ*. Wheaton, IL: Crossway, 2011.

Morgan, Christopher W., and Robert A. Peterson, eds. *Suffering and the Goodness of God*. Theology in Community 1. Wheaton, IL: Crossway, 2008.

———. *Hell under Fire: Modern Scholarship Reinvents Eternal Punishment*. Grand Rapids, MI: Zondervan, 2004.

Morris, Leon. *The Wages of Sin*. London: Tyndale, 1954.

Murray, John. *The Imputation of Adam's Sin*. Grand Rapids, MI: Eerdmans, 1959.

Orr, James. *Sin as a Problem of Today*. London: Hodder & Stoughton, 1910.

Owen, John. *The Mortification of Sin*. Fearn, Roth-shire, UK: Christian Focus, 1996.

———. *Sin and Temptation*. Minneapolis: Bethany, 1996.

Page, Sydney H. T. *Powers of Evil: A Biblical Study of Satan and Demons*. Grand Rapids, MI: Baker, 1995.

———. "Satan: God's Servant." *JETS* 50 (2007): 449–65.

Parker, David. "Original Sin: A Study in Evangelical Theory." *EvQ* 61, no. 1 (1989): 51–69.

Peters, Ted. *Sin: Radical Evil in Soul and Society*. Grand Rapids, MI: Eerdmans, 1994.

Peterson, Robert A., and Michael D. Williams. *Why I Am Not an Arminian*. Downers Grove, IL: InterVarsity, 2004.

Plantinga, Cornelius, Jr. *Not the Way It's Supposed to Be: A Breviary of Sin*. Grand Rapids, MI: Eerdmans, 1995.

Poe, Harry Lee. *See No Evil: The Existence of Sin in an Age of Relativism*. Grand Rapids, MI: Kregel, 2004.

Pyne, Robert A. *Humanity and Sin*. Dallas: Word, 1999.

Ramm, Bernard. *Offense to Reason: The Theology of Sin*. San Francisco: Harper & Row, 1985.

Reymond, Robert L. *A New Systematic Theology of the Christian Faith.* 2nd rev. ed. Nashville, TN: Thomas Nelson, 1998.

Rosner, Brian S. *Greed as Idolatry: The Origin and Meaning of a Pauline Metaphor.* Grand Rapids, MI: Eerdmans, 2007.

Schreiner, Thomas R. *New Testament Theology: Magnifying God in Christ.* Grand Rapids, MI: Baker Academic, 2008.

Shuster, Marguerite. *The Fall and Sin: What We Have Become as Sinners.* Grand Rapids, MI: Eerdmans, 2004.

Smith, David L. *With Willful Intent: A Theology of Sin.* Wheaton, IL: Victor/Bridgepoint, 1994.

Sproul, R. C. *Willing to Believe.* Grand Rapids, MI: Baker, 1997.

Thielicke, Helmut. *Between God and Satan.* Edinburgh: Oliver and Boyd, 1958.

Thomas, Derek. *Praying the Saviour's Way: Praying the Lord's Prayer.* Fearn, Ross-shire, UK: Christian Focus, 2002.

Venning, Ralph. *The Sinfulness of Sin.* Edinburgh: Banner of Truth, 1993.

Vlachos, Chris. *The Law and the Knowledge of Good and Evil: The Edenic Background of the Catalytic Operation of the Law in Paul.* Eugene, OR: Wipf & Stock, 2009.

Wenham, Gordon J. "Original Sin in Genesis 1–11." *Chm* 104 (1990): 30–21.

NAME INDEX

SUBJECT INDEX

SCRIPTURE INDEX

THEOLOGY IN COMMUNITY

FIRST-RATE EVANGELICAL SCHOLARS
TAKE A MULTIDISCIPLINARY APPROACH
TO KEY CHRISTIAN DOCTRINES

Edited by CHRISTOPHER W. MORGAN
and ROBERT A. PETERSON

OTHER BOOKS IN THE SERIES:
Suffering and the Goodness of God
The Glory of God
The Deity of Christ
The Kingdom of God

For more information visit www.crossway.org.